SOME DESCENDANTS OF ORLANDO BAGLEY OF AMESBURY, MASSACHUSETTS

VOLUME 1 – 4TH EDITION

By
Timothy W. Bagley

Original Research and Manuscript by
Dr. Norton Russell Bagley and Martha (Bagley) Anderson

SOME DESCENDANTS OF ORLANDO BAGLEY OF AMESBURY, MASSACHUSETTS

SOME DESCENDANTS OF ORLANDO BAGLEY OF AMESBURY, MASSACHUSETTS

VOLUME 1 – 4TH EDITION

By
Timothy W. Bagley

Original Research and Manuscript by
Dr. Norton Russell Bagley and Martha (Bagley) Anderson

IN MEMORIAM AND DEDICATION

A few years after I first began to research my family history and genealogy in 1988, I was contacted by Dr. Norton Russell Bagley of New Hampshire who was eager to see my research on the Bagleys in Maine and to share his encouragement, insight, wisdom, humor, and guidance. In 1998, when I first printed and shared with him *The Bagleys and Related Families of Washington County, Maine, and Beyond: A Genealogical Profile of Our Ancestral Families Volume 1 – In America, Volume 2 – In Europe, and Volume 3 – Ancestral Charts*, Norton was extremely supportive and eagerly discussed the new and expanded Bagley lines I had found or updated.

Norton passed away in 2014 at 94, and while many years and generations removed may have separated us as cousins, he was a dear friend, confidant, mentor, and was always anxious to hear about my latest world travels. He asked me to share and distribute my work, as well as his own, with other researchers to try to ensure that our efforts may be of some use to anyone interested in the Bagley family.

In 2017, Plymouth State University, where Norton was a professor for many years, posted a loving tribute along with some photos at https://library.plymouth.edu/bagley. They note in part that:

> *"Dr. Norton Bagley's philosophy was always "The most important part of teaching is what happens between the teacher and the pupil. That is what makes the child want to learn." Several years ago Dr. Bagley donated property to Plymouth State; the proceeds from its sale established a scholarship endowment. A Plymouth alumnus, Dr. Bagley received his M.Ed. from Boston University and his Ph.D. from the University of Connecticut. In 1972, Dr. Bagley received the Granite State Award for outstanding service to education in the state. "I'll never forget him," noted one alumnus, among the many who remember him fondly. "He is the reason I went to college at all." He retired in 1982.*

The work that Norton and his sister did was an inspiration for many of us and laid the foundation for most of the research done on the Bagleys in America.

- Timothy W. Bagley

TABLE OF CONTENTS

INTRODUCTION BY
DR. NORTON RUSSELL BAGLEY

We first began this work in an effort to create our own connection to Orlando Bagley of Amesbury, MA. The work just grew as we obtained more information and as kind Bagleys and others supplied us with much data. A genealogy is never finished; not only does it need constant up-dating but one discovers more and more branches. One also finds that one has to research other Bagley families to separate them from one's own as, for example, the Samuel Bagley line of Boston. Sometimes branches connect, sometimes they don't – at least not that we can discover in this country.

In 1973 we compiled what material we had on the Orlando line, the Edward Bagley line of New Brunswick and Salt Lake City, and assorted other lines. We sent these to various libraries and historical societies and sold some to others who were interested and who helped us, at cost. We were fortunate in getting a great deal of feed-back. The present edition, the third*, represents the corrections and additions to date. The Samuel Bagley and Edward C. lines have been greatly enlarged and several odds and ends of lines have now been correctly connected.

*__Note:__ *No usable, digital files of the original, 4ᵗʰ edition documents still exist. This printing is based on scanned copies of the final manuscripts from Dr. Norton Russell Bagley, which he asked that I continue to add to, work on, and distribute as able. I have made only small, minor corrections to his original text in some of the opening sections for formatting purposes and the rest remains his last manuscript.*

We now have three volumes, the first two are on the Orlando Bagley line; the third is on various other Bagley lines: the Samuel line, the Edward line, Luther of Providence, RI, Samuel of Orange, John of Waterboro, ME, the Stanstead, QUE lines, the Haverhill, MA line, etc. We have not been able to connect these to Orlando or to themselves, although we are reasonably certain of some connections, e.g., the John of Waterboro, ME, probably goes with the Orlando line.

Each Bagley is numbered under parents, together with the dates of his or her birth and death, if known. The same number is carried over into the body of the work in its appropriate place. Each Bagley about whom something is known or who lived to maturity thus appears twice. Once under his or her parents, and again when a more complete description of that Bagley's life is given. Using the number found at the completion of the work, for example, one can find the same number again under that Bagley's parents, and then using the Bagley's parent's number go back to Orlando. There is a complete index of Bagleys by name and by the Bagley number, and a complete index of names other than Bagley together with the number of the Bagley where the name will be found. In some instances, numbers are carried over from volume one to volume two.

No material has been included that we cannot prove from some kind of record, and we cite the record. Where record is lacking, but circumstantial evidence is great, the word probably is used. We have not included material based on mere hunch or wishful thinking. In addition to the material found in these volumes, we have hundreds of file cards on Bagleys whom we cannot prove as to where they go. Wherever evidence is conflicting, we try to cite both sides of the argument.

We thank various people who have supplied information under their numbers in the text or close to the lines they supplied material about. We wish especially to thank our mother, Estella (Floyd) Bagley Maloney for long hours spent on work in vital records and town reports, to Michael Vacca for long hours spent in cemeteries and in searching and filing index cards, to Isabelle Bartholmew of Salt Lake for many hours spent in copy deeds and other records from Salt Lake City archives, to Elizabeth Nichols, a descendant of Orlando through the Mack and Joseph Smith lines; and Paul Anderson, who became an expert in ferreting out information from deeds and wills.

Unfortunately, Mrs. Anderson died in 1987, so that she did not live to see this latest revision. Her work on other families and especially in proving the descent of Anthony Colby, marks her memorial as does this work.

INTRODUCTION TO USING THIS BOOK AND RELATED VOLUMES

Some Descendants of Orlando Bagley of Amesbury, Massachusetts, Volumes 1 and 2, are provided as written and annotated by Dr. Norton Russell Bagley and his sister. Norton was unable to provide me with the digital files of his work, so the work is saved from scans of his original prints. While the original prints may not provide the highest quality, they have allowed me to continue to share his work as he requested and at some point, in the future, I hope to be able to complete retyping all of his research to allow for a newer reprint.

Volumes 1 and 2 include:
- An updated introduction and forward from Norton
- Bagley Index for Volume 1
- Index of Names Other Than Bagley for Volume 1
- Bagley Index for Volume 2
- Index of Names Other Than Bagley for Volume 2

Especially for the Bagley lines in Waldo County and Washington County, Maine, and for the ancestral lines of families related to the Bagleys, please see my work in *The Bagleys and Related Families of Washington County, Maine, and Beyond: A Genealogical Profile of Our Ancestral Families, Volume 1 – In America, Volume 2 – In Europe, and Volume 3 – Ancestral Charts*.

Companion works and research done by Norton and/or his sister for *Some Descendants of Orlando Bagley* may be found in:
- *Families Related to the Bagley and Floyd Families, 2nd Edition*
- *Notes on Bagley Lines, Volumes 1 and 2, 3rd Edition*

FORWARD BY DR. NORTON RUSSELL BAGLEY

In 1066, the Sieur de Macei[1] came with William the Conqueror to the conquest of England. Apparently, he was granted lands near the Welsh border, near Chester. One of his younger sons received the manor of Bagley (for low lying). His name is uncertain, but his descendants are all the known Bagleys, whatever the spelling of their names (there are 10 variations). Officials spelled the name according to the way it sounded to them, which depended upon the local dialect. Some of the descendants went to Ireland, apparently with Richard Strongbow[2], and spelled the name 'Begley'. The Bagley book *Notes on Bagley Lines* contains a history of the Bagleys in England.

The tradition is that three Bagley brothers came to Boston; Orlando, Samuel, and Thomas. We have traced the descendants of Orlando and Samuel, but have not been able to find Thomas. For years, the relationship of Orlando to Samuel was uncertain, but recently English records tend to confirm that they were brothers. The Samuel line is found in the *Notes on Bagley Lines* book.

The members of the Orlando line settled in Amesbury, Massachusetts where they were selectmen, sheriffs, and town clerks. Some of Orlando's descendants spread to Kingston and Candia, New Hampshire and then to the Eastern Townships of Canada. Some refused to take allegiance to the King of England and came back into upper New York and ended up in Haverhill, Massachusetts. Another branch went to Maine and settled in Durham, Liberty, and Montville and then on Downeast to Jonesport, and Machias. Another branch from New Hampshire went to Vermont, to Hartland, and hence to Durham and Cairo, New York and then to Pennsylvania, Ohio, and to other states of the old Northwest, and from there to the West Coast. A few were found in the South. Like most New England families, the Bagleys scattered widely in their quest for better land and a better life.

The Bagleys were a typical Yankee family, serving in the Revolutionary war, War of 1812, a few in the Mexican War, and a host in the Civil War. They served as officials in their communities and churches, worked to clear the land, went to sea, and did their stint in the mills and factories. A few gained wider fame. Colonel Jonathan Bagley

---

[1] Sieur is French for 'Sir' as was used as a title of respect. Sieur de Macei. There are several theories of the origin of the name, including:

English (Norman) and French. Habitation name from any of various places in Northern France which get their names from Gallo-Roman personal name of Maccius plus the local suffix- acum.
(Dictionary of Surnames, P. Hanks & F. Hodges, OUP)

A great Cheshire family of whom from their numerousness the proverb, however uncomplimentary, runs "As many Masseys as asses." The founder of the family in England was Harmon Massie, a Norman, who accompanied the Conqueror and acquired Dunham in Cheshire, which has from that circumstance ever since borne the suffix of Massey. From what part of Normandy that personage came is not known, but there are several places in the province from which, with equal claims to probability the name might reasonably be deduced: viz Mace-sur-Orme near Alencon: Macei in the arrondissement of Avranches: Marcei, in that part of Argantan, and Marcei on the Broise near the town of Avranches, the seat of an ancient Barony. (A Dictionary of Family Names of the United Kingdom, ed M.A. Lower, pub John Russell Smith, London, 1860.

[2] Richard Strongbow was Richard de Clare, Earl of Pembroke, from Wales. He was sent to Ireland in 1168 by King Henry II to restore Dermod MacMorough as King of Leinster.

was paymaster of the Massachusetts troops in the French and Indian War. He was a great landholder and died intestate, land poor. The second Orlando's daughter Sarah, married John Mack and they were the maternal ancestors of Joseph Smith, the Prophet of the Church of Latter-day Saints (Mormons). Mary Baker Eddy, a faith healer, stayed at Sarah Bagley's house who took Mary to meet John Greenleaf Whittier, the poet. There was Captain Valentine Bagley who was shipwrecked off the Arabian coast and returned home to dig the Captain's Well in Amesbury. Whittier wrote a poem about that episode. Dr. William Chandler Bagley was developer of the educational philosophy of Essentialism, which has reappeared in the "No Child Left Behind" policy of modern days. John Bagley was governor of Michigan. Further thought will produce others.

My sister, Martha (Bagley) Anderson and her husband Paul, set out o trace the Derry, New Hampshire line of Bagleys. As with all genealogies, the venture grew and grew. I become involved, as did Michael Vacca. All of us became acquainted with multiple graveyards, vital records, probate records, and church records. Too, we heard from Bagleys all over the country and some became good friends. We found we had to research the Samuel Bagley line and other lines to distinguish like-named individuals. We came across the Edward Bagley line of New Brunswick and Salt Lake City from whom many Mormon Bagleys descend. Unfortunately, we have never been able to connect this line to the other lines. We amassed a great file of Bagleys whose place in the known Bagley lines is unknown. We have saved these for other researchers.

More recently, Timothy Bagley, world traveler and currently in government service in Washington, DC, has undertaken to make the Bagley material which he has found, and our material, more available.

Family searching is fun and frustrating. Bagley, wherever and whoever you are, help to enlarge our knowledge of this family.

Good hunting,

Dr. Norton R. Bagley

Sometime teacher, professor, college dean, and author

Note: This was the last forward provided by Dr. Norton Russell Bagley in 2008.

BAGLEY FAMILY ORIGINS

Bagley is from the Saxon, meaning a rising or swelling ground that lies untilled; from boelge, a rising or swelling, and Leagh or ley, plain or pasture ground.

The original spelling appears to have been Baggiley, but it has been, and is, spelled in a variety of ways including Baggley, Bagly, Baggulley, and Bagley.

It appears to have been adopted in England by a man named Macey or Macei, who was seated at Baggiley in the time of William, the Conqueror. William made numerous trips to England, accompanied by small parties of kinsmen and others. There is an account of one of these trips, when he was accompanied by two nephews and eight lesser kinsman, among the latter, Hama de Macei. Macie is a well-known placed name in Normandy near Avranch.

From Plea Rolls, it appears that John, Lord of Baggiley, in 1170 had sons: Hamon, Howekin, William, Peter, and John. It is not clear if Hamon Massey or John was the first ancestor of the Baggileys in England who came with William and became owners of the Manor of Baggiley from whence the name comes. King in his History of England, dated 1650, states that Baggiley was located in Bulkley Hundred in the Kingdom of March, known as the Vale Royal in England, which reaches from London to the river Mersey which divided Cheshire from Lancashire. When Thomas Bagley of Virginia died in 1672, he mentions his brothers who lived at Macclesfield, Cheshire, England. (See British Bagleys in Notes on Bagley Lines)

About the reign of King John (1213-1216, Hamon of the house of Baggiley was Baron of Dunham-Massey, and during the time "Hamon Massey, and descended from the other Hamon, before named, gave unto Matthew de Bromhal, Duckenfield and two other parts of Baggiley which the father of the said Matthew held of said Hamon, as his inheritance in knight's service to him and his heirs." This Hamon was involved in the rising of the Northern Barons against King John.

In the 15th century, the Baggileys of Cheshire had much interest in Lancashire, the next county, moved over there and changed the name to Baguley. From Cheshire through the several counties going west, the name Bagguley or nearly so is prevalent. But going south the name Bagley is present even in London and other counties; for instance, Ipswich from where the Bagleys first came to America, who were shipwrights and sea captains. Thomas Baggaley of Salt Lake City who had done research on the Bagleys in England here cites the Bagleys who settled in Boston.

Some books say there is one coat of arms for the Bagley family and that it is the same regardless of how the name is spelled or the family's immediate origins. This statement does not seem to be correct for Orlando Bagley. In Worcester, MA Genealogical Society, there is a book containing the coats of arms of early MA families including one for Orlando Bagley, and it is not the one commonly accepted for the Bagleys.

SOME DESCENDANTS OF ORLANDO BAGLEY, VOLUME 1

1. **Orlando Bagley** 1, b about 1624, living 1662, but supposedly dead soon thereafter; m Mar 6, 1653, Sarah Colby, who d May 18, 1663, Boston, MA, supposedly after the birth of a child. (Boston MA R)

Orlando came from England, probably from Ipswich, but just at what date is not known, He lived in Boston from 1658 to 1663 (Essex Antiquarian) and was subsequently of Salisbury, MA, probably of that part now called Amesbury as his name is on the official "Macey-Book" of that town, but not on the official records nor any lot of land grants in the town of Salisbury, now Amesbury, MA. (Salis. MA R) No Bagley is named on any deeds or probate records prior to 1677. However, Orlando Bagley's name is on a paper dated Mar 19, 1654, on a list of inhabitants and commoners here in the new town (Salis, MA R). His name is not listed on a similar petition. Indeed it is difficult to prove that the first Orlando ever lived in Amesbury at all, but it is known that he lived in Boston where he probably died in 1663. When the new town, Amesbury, was incorporated in 1666, Orlando was probably dead and reference after that date refers to his son, Orlando. When Merrill in his History of Amesbury, Massachusetts, mentions Orlando Bagley's name under the list of thirty-six voters at the incorporation of Amesbury, he evidently included all who had been voters from 1654 to 1666.

Evidently Orlando was a man of some standing since he m Sarah Colby, dau Anthony Colby and Susanna (Haddon). Anthony, the first Colby to come to New England, was in Boston as early as 1630, as he is listed as a member of the church at that time. He was the son of Thomas and Beatrice (Felton) Colby of Playford, Eng., and was probably of Roos Hall, Beccles, Suffolk Co., and hence, through the female line, a descendant of six signers of the Magna Carta. He came to MA, probably in the company of Governor Winthrop, since he is called "Planter" and was of Boston, thence of Cambridge, where he built the first house, then was one of the founders of Amesbury, where his house was built in 1647. He d Feb 11, 1660 (Salis MA R). His wife, Susanna, d July 8, 1689, under the name of Whitridge, having m William Whitridge, in 1663/64 (Salis MA R). Some sources believe Anthony Colby's wife was Susanna Sargent, dau William, but we think the above is correct.

The division of the estate of Anthony Colby of Salisbury, late deceased, made by Tho. Bradbury and Robert Pike, Apr 9, 1661, by order of the county court held at Salisbury "To ye widow for hir part & the two youngest children: to ye Sarah, ye wife of Orlando Bagley: one cowe & one 3 yeere old steere, 8 pounds; a young hourse, 10 pounds, another cowe, 4 pounds, 10 shillings: ore payed by Isaac Colby to Orlando Bagley for ye which the estate was debtor 5 pounds 19 shillings, 8 ds."

Petition of Thomas Challis, Orlando Bagley, Ephraim Weed and Ebenezer Blasidell for some part of the estate of their grandfather Anthony Colby formerly of Salisbury left in the hands of their grandmother Susanna widow of Anthony, administratrix of his estate, after Susanna Whitreg, deceased; the Court ordered the division of the estate Apr 9, 1661, and it was allowed 14:2m (Essex Co, MA Probate R).

Children:
2. John 2, b 1656; d Aug 31, 1658 (Boston, MA R)
3. Orlando 2, b Feb 18, 1658; d 1728 (Boston & Essex Co, MA R)
4. Sarah 2, b Jan 14, 1660; d Sept 30, 1661 (Boston, MA R)
5. Mary 2, b Jan 5, 1661/62; d before 1700; may have m William Colby (Boston & Essex Antiquarian R)
6. Sarah 2, b Mar 2, 1662/63 (Boston, MA R); d Feb 24, 1721, Lyme, CT (CT R)

3. Orlando Bagley 2, Orlando 1, b Feb 18, 1658; d 1728; m (1) Sarah Sargent, Dec 22, 1681 (Ames MA R), b Feb 29, 1651/52 (Salis MA R), dau William Sargent & Elizabeth (Perkins); William Sargent being one of the first settlers of Ipswich, MA. She d Oct 3, 1701/02 (Ames MA R). He m (2) Sarah Annis, published Mar 25, 1703/04 (Ames MA R), dau Charles & Sarah (Chase), who Coffin says came from Enneshelen, Ire., where he was b 1658. Sarah Annis Bagley d 1729 (Essex Co MA Probate R) Pillsbury and Bagley Ancestry says she was b 1675.
     Orlando was a yeoman, an ensign in Lt Caleb Moody's Company in 1708, signed the oath of allegiance, Dec 20, 1677, signed a training band petition in 1680, was a freeman in 1690, was constable in Amesbury, and occupied the third row in the meetinghouse, where, it was voted "only important men could sit", and settled in the Sargent homestead near Academy lot in Amesbury (Ames MA R). As constable, on May 2, 1692, he brought Susanna Martin, widow, of Amesbury, to Salem Village, where she was executed for witchcraft. She was said to have been a friend of long standing.
     After the death of his first wife, Orlando came into possession of her estate, her children releasing to the father all their "Right, Title and Interest to all ye Housing, Lands, Meadows, Orchards, and other Estate Bequeathed by William Sargent to his daughter Sarah Sargent, now deceased, formerly ye wife of Sd Orlando Bagley" (Essex Co MA R).
     In 1712, he conveyed to his sons, Orlando Bagley, Junior, and John Bagley, "Partly of natural affection which I do bear unto them, and partly of ye sume of seventy pounds" his farm at Pond Hills, the eastern part to go to Orlando and the western half to John (Ames MA R).
     His will was made Feb 12, 1723/24, proved Jan 6, 1728/29; inventory dated Feb 21, 1728/29, in sum of 939 pounds, 10 shillings. Mentioned in will are wife Sarah, who was sole executor, sons: Benjamin, Orlando, John, Jacob & Joseph; daus Sarah Weed, Judith Carter, Anne Bagley and Hannah Bagley (Essex Co MA Probate R).

Children:
7. Orlando 3, b Dec 14, 1682 (Certified copy in his own handwriting; Ames MA R say b 1687; d May 3, 1756 (Ames MA R)
8. Sarah 3, b Feb 27, 1683/84 (Ames MA R); living 1733 (Essex Co MA R)
9. John 3, b Jan 21, 1685; d Mar 9, 1727/28 (Ames MA R). His tombstone says he d Mar 11, 1728, Merrimac, MA.
10. Jacob 3, b Dec 13, 1687 (Ames MA R); d Dec 25, 1767 (Essex Co MA R)

11. Judith 3, b Nov 13, 1690 (Ames MA R)
12. Joseph 3, b Jan 26, 1704/05 (Ames MA R); d Feb 9, 1772 (Salis MA R)
13. Benjamin 3, b Nov 10, 1707 (Ames MA R)
14. Anne 3, b Aug 14, 1709 (Ames MA R)
15. Hannah 3, b Mar 29, 1712 (Essex Antiquarian: birth not recorded Ames MA R)

6. **Sarah Bagley 2, Orlando 1,** b Mar 2, 1662/63; d Feb 24, 1721, Lyme, CT; m John Mack, Apr 5, 1681 (Salis MA R), b Mar 3, 1653, Inverness, Scotland, came to New England about 1669, arriving at Boston, but later settling at Salisbury, MA. There is a tradition among his descendants that he was one of those early Scot immigrants who dropped part of their names retaining the prefix only, "thereby being better able to escape persecution for their religious beliefs."

After the birth of their first child, they moved to Concord, MA, where the births of six children are recorded. They moved to Lyme, CT, in 1696. He d Feb 24, 1721. They are the maternal great great grandparents of Joseph Smith, founder of the Church of Jesus Christ of Latter Day Saints.

Children:
16. John 3, b Apr 29, 1682 (Salis MA R); d before Feb 15, 1725, when his will was probated
17. Sarah 3, b Aug 28, 1684 (Concord, MA R); d Jan 18, 1755; m Matthew Smith, Nov 28, 1706, son Matthew & Mary (Cutler), who d Dec 6, 1751
18. Elizabeth 3, b Oct 28, 1686 (Concord, MA R); d Mar 15, 1750
19. Lydia 3, b May 28, 1689 (Concord, MA R); d Feb, 1716
20. Josiah 3, b Dec 16, 1691 (Concord, MA R); d Nov 21, 1769
21. Orlando 3, b Dec 16, 1691 (Concord, MA R); d Jan 28, 1768
22. Jonathan 3, b Feb 28, 1695/96 (Concord, MA R)
23. Ebenezer 3, Lyme, CT, Dec 8, 1697; d 1777
24. Mary 3, b Nov 10, 1699
25. Rebecca 3, b Oct 4, 1701
26. Johanna 3, b Sept 17, 1703
27. Deborah 3, b Oct 11, 1706; d Feb 4, 1776

7. **Orlando Bagley 3, Orlando 2, Orlando 1,** b Dec 14, 1682; d May 3, 1756; m Dorothy Harvey, Feb 13, 1705/06 (Ames MA R), dau John & Sarah (Barnes); she d Jan 2, 1757 (Ames MA R).

This Orlando had in his possession a certified copy of his birth in his own handwriting, dated 1749. It also contained his father's marriage to Sarah Sargent on Dec 22, 1681. On Oct 13, 1712, he was chosen town clerk, which office he held for forty-two years from 1712 to 1754; also the right to keep a public school, "to teach to wright and sipher such as shall come to him, they paying as he and they agree"; in 1716, he gave land for a school (Ames MA R). His land was near the town pound. He possessed fine business talents and grew in popularity as age came on. He served several years as selectman and held courts, officiating as trial justice on many occasions. Wills and deeds in his handwriting are numerous, and his marriages for several years far exceeded those of the minister, numbering one hundred in all. He helped tunnel The Ridge in Amesbury, and in 1753, when another effort was made to recovery the ferry, called Amesbury Ferry, he was one of those chosen to search the records in order to ascertain the condition of the claim in regard to it. On Apr 16, 1736, at a meeting of the First Church in Amesbury, it was proposed that their brother, Orlando Bagley and their brother John Tuxbury be appointed to the service to discuss with their brother Thomas Hoyt his frequent neglect of the public worship and the Sacraments of the Lord's Supper and report the reason thereof (First Church, Ames MA R).

Administration on his estate was granted to his widow, May 31, 1756 (Essex Co MA Probate R). Second administration on his estate Apr 6, 1757 to Orlando Bagley of Kingston, NH, Gentleman (NH Probate R). The inventory of his estate amounted to 5,086 pounds. Because he died intestate, a committee was appointed Aug 3, 1757 by the court to divide the estate among his children (NH Probate R).

Children:
28. Orlando 4, b Feb 21, 1706/07 (Ames MA R); d 1770 (NH Probate R)
29. Sarah 4, b Oct 22, 1708; d Mar 16, 1801 (Ames MA R)
30. Henry 4, b Aug 25, 1711 (Ames MA R); d Aug 24, 1776 (Rockingham Co NH Probate R)
31. David 4, b May 25, 1714 (Ames MA R); d before Jan 26, 1799 (Rockingham Co NH Probate R)
32. Merah 4, b Mar 22, 1717
33. Jonathan 4, b Mar 23, 1717; d Dec 18 or 28, 1780 (Ames MA R)
34. Dorothy 4, b June 16, 1719 (Ames MA R)
35. Judith 4, b Dec 2, 1721 (Ames MA R); probably d before Aug 3, 1757 (Rockingham Co NH Probate R)
36. Thomas 4, b Jan 18, 1722/23; d Sept 17, 1771 (Ames MA R) (Another source gives a son Jacob, b Mar 31, 1723/24; and a son John, b June 20, 1724/25 who m Martha Currier. Omits Anna who m Jeremiah Currier).

8. Sarah Bagley 3, Orlando 2, Orlando 1, b Feb 27, 1683/84; living 1733; m (1) Henry Lancaster, July 15, 1703 (Ames MA R), son Joseph & Hannah, b 1682, Amesbury, d 1709, and Sarah was granted adm on his estate May 2, 1709 (Essex Co MA Probate R); she m (2) Apr 11, 1713, Elisha Weed, son Ephraim & Elizabeth (Colby), b Sept 15, 1689 (Ames MA R), d before June 25, 1733, when as widow, Sarah was granted adm on his estate (Essex Co MA Probate R).

At a meeting of the town in 1702, it was granted to Sarah Bagley and others "that they should have the two hundermost seats of ye short seats of ye women's gallery in our meetinghouse towards ye south-east corner of it in to a pew and of improving of it for their own use" (Amesbury, MA R). There were seven young ladies all unmarried at the time, and their selection of a place to build a pew showed a very commendable modesty. Whether their course was the means of procuring husbands or not, certain it is that this fine-looking pewful soon disappeared till the pew was finally empty.

Children:
37.   Judith 4, b July 29, 1704; d Mar 20, 1751/52 (Ames MA R)
38.   Mary 4, b July 5 or 29, 1706 (Ames MA R)
39.   Sarah 4, b Jan 10 or 18, 1707/08 (Ames MA R)
40.   Hannah 4, b Oct 20, 1709 (Ames MA R)
41.   Elizabeth 4, b Aug 17, 1713 (Ames MA R); d young
42.   Orlando 4, b Mar 23, 1715 (Ames, MA R)
43.   David 4, b Feb 2, 1716/17 (Ames, MA R)
44.   Henry 4, b June 2, 1719 (Ames MA R); d July 12, 1738 (Salis MA R)
45.   Elisha 4, b Sept 5, 1721 (Ames MA R)
46.   Dorothy 4, b Sept 30, 1723 (Ames MA R)
47.   Anne 4, b Mar 21, 1725/26 (Family R); Ames MA R give month and day but no year
48.   Bagley 4, b Apr 20, 1728 (Ames MA R)

9.   John Bagley 3, Orlando 2, Orlando 1, b Jan 21, 1685; d Mar 9, 1728/29; m Hannah Fowler, Apr 7, 1708 (Ames MA R), dau William & Hannah (Dow), b Apr 4, 1692, d Mar 16, 1759 (Ames MA R).
       He was a snowshoe man in 1708 in the Indian War. He held office as selectman in Amesbury several times and town meetings were often adjourned to his house. His wife, Hannah, was made adm of his estate, Apr 15, 1728; he died intestate (Essex Co MA Probate R).
       Oct 18, 1735, Hannah was left 10 pounds by her father's will, and her brother Thomas left her 25 pounds, old tenor, by his will, dated May 4, 1750 (NH Probate R).

Children:
49.   Anna 4, b May 18, 1709 (Ames MA R); living 1770 (NH Probate R)
50.   John 4, b Dec 22, 1710 (Ames MA R); d Oct, 1782 (Essex Antiquarian)
51.   Moses 4, b Sept 17, 1715; d May 6, 1806 (Ames MA R)
52.   Hannah 4, b about 1717 (birth not recorded Amesbury)
53.   Timothy 4, b Oct 12, 1719; d Apr 22, 1759 (Ames MA R)
54.   Rhoda 4, b May 10, 1723 (Ames MA R); living 1745 (Essex Antiquarian)
55.   Sarah 4, b Apr 10, 1725 (Ames MA R); living 1745 (Essex Antiquarian)
56.   Merriam 4, b Aug 19, 1727 (Ames MA R); living 1730 (Essex Antiquarian)

10. Jacob Bagley 3, Orlando 2, Orlando 1, b Dec 13, 1687; d Dec 25, 1767; m (1) Hannah Stanwood, Jan 21, 1712/13 (Ames MA R) by Rev Thomas Wells, dau Samuel and Hannah (Pressey) of Gloucester and Amesbury, MA, b Sept 20, 1687. Her brother John Stanwood of Pemaquid, ME, left her 10 pounds in his will, dated Oct 27, 1748 (Me Wills). He m (2) Kezia Colby, June 2, 1748 (Ames MA R), widow of David Currier & dau Samuel Colby & Dorothy (Ambrose), who d Nov 3, 1754; he m (3) Hannah Jameson, Mar 13, 1755, widow of Timothy Currier and widow of Jonathan Blaisdell, and dau John Jameson & Esther (Martin) of Amesbury

(Ames MA R). On Aug 22, 1755, Hannah Bagley was dismissed from the Second Church at Salisbury to the First Church of Amesbury (Ames MA Church R).

He was a blacksmith. In 1747 he was rated for a vessel that was taken and received an abatement of 1 pound 13 shillings 9 pence (Ames MA R). He owned a negro servant called Cato and on May 9, 1742 the First Church of Amesbury records show "that Cato, Negro servant to Jacob Bagly own'd the Coven't & was baptized. Also on May 22, 1748, "Cato, Negro servant to Jacob Bagley, received full communion." In 1746, it was voted that Jacob Bagley take care of all idle persons in the town according to the law (Ames MA R).

His will, dated Dec 25, 1767, the same day he died, and proved Feb 23, 1773 (Essex Co MA Probate R), mentions wife Hannah; son William, deceased; dau Hannah Currier, wife of Richard Currier; granddaughter Jerusha, wife of Ezra Worthen. Richard Currier and Enoch Bagley were executors.

Children: (All Amesbury, MA R)
57. William 4, b Oct 9, 1713; d Nov 29, 1746
58. Elizabeth 4, b Jan 18, 1715/16; d Nov 1, 1795 (Salis MA R)
59. Jerusha 4, b Jan 1, 1717; d Apr 13, 1718
60. Jerusha 4, b Nov 29, 1719; probably d before 1767 as not in father's will
61. Jacob 4, b Nov 30, 1721; d Feb 4, 1724
62. Hannah 4, b June 6, 1723; living 1767
63. Jacob 4, b June 30, 1724; d Jan 15, 1747
64. Samuel 4, b Dec 21, 1728; d Feb 4, 1729

11. Judith Bagley 3, Orlando 2, Orlando 1 , b Nov 13, 1690; m Apr 25, John Carter, Jr. (Ames MA R), son John & Martha (Brown) (Ames MA R). They lived in Kingston later in life.

Children: (Salisbury, MA R except last)
65. Abigail 4, b May 21, 1712
66. Thomas 4, b Oct 29, 1713
67. John 4, b Sept 14, 1715
68. Samuel 4, b Jan 14, 1717/18
69. Ephraim 4, b Mar 30, 1719
70. Benjamin 4, b Feb 5, 1722/23
71. Orlando 4, b Aug 30, 1724
72. Moses 4, b Apr 14, 1734 (Ames MA R)

12. Joseph Bagley 3, Orlando 2, Orlando 1 , b Jan 26, 1704/05; d Feb 9, 1772; m Lydia Kendrick, published Nov 5, 1727 (Ames MA R). She survived him and remained his widow, adm being granted to son Joseph, Dec 25, 1786 (Essex Co MA Probate R). He was probably the Col Joseph Bagley who served at Fort William Henry during the French and Indian War. He was a husbandman and then a yeoman and lived in Amesbury until 1760 when he moved to Salisbury, MA. In 1736 he bought land in Hampton, NH. On Jan 18, 1735/36, he renewed his Baptismal Covenant at First Church, Amesbury, MA.

He is buried at Salisbury Plains Cemetery, MA. No stone there in 1957, altho the Essex Antiquarian lists a stone in the early 1900's. He made his will Dec 21, 1763, proved June 29, 1772; his wife being executrix (Essex Co MA Probate R).

Children: (Ames MA R except as noted)
73. Lydia 4, d Oct 28, 1729
74. Sarah 4, b Dec 18, 1730; d Nov 19, 1735
75. Lydia 4, b July 13, 1733; d Sept 12, 1735; baptized July 15, 1733, First Church, Amesbury, MA
76. Joseph 4, b Jan 7, 1735/36; d Sept 25, 1791 (Salis MA R); baptized Jan 18, 1735/36, First Church, Amesbury, MA
77. Benjamin 4, b Feb 26, 1738
78. Abel 4, b July 4, 1740; d Oct 17, 1815 (Salis MA R)
79. Sarah 4, b Apr 12, 1743; mentioned in father's will in 1763; Essex Antiquarian says she was living in 1774
80. Mary 4, b Sept 12, 1749; mentioned in father's will in 1763
81. Lydia 4, b May 7, 1754; d July 26, 1843 (NH Pension Rolls)

13. Benjamin Bagley 3 Orlando 2 Orlando 1 , b Nov 10, 1707; lived in Amesbury and was a yeoman in 1735 and a trader in 1739. His brother Joseph sold land to him Nov 15, 1743 (Essex Co MA Deeds). Mr. Clarence Bagley's records say he m Elizabeth Colby of Amesbury, who d Mar 9, 1786.

14. Anne Bagley 3, Orlando 2, Orlando 1 , b Aug 14, 1709; m Abel Merrill, Feb 5, 1729/30 (Ames MA R), son Thomas & Judith (Kent), b Aug 28, 1709 (Salis MA R), d Apr, 1789 (Newbury, MA R). He was a ship carpenter and lived in Amesbury, MA until 1738 when he moved to that part of Newbury which, in 1764, was incorporated as Newburyport, MA.
    Anne was dismissed from First Church, Amesbury, to Third Church of Christ, Newbury, MA, July 22, 1743 (Ames MA Church R).

Chiildren:
82. Sarah 4, b Jan 15, 1731/32 (Ames MA R)
83. Thomas 4, b June 21, 1736 (Ames MA R; Newbury, MA R say June 20, 1736)
84. Anne 4, b June 10, 1740 (Newbury, MA R)
85. Mary 4, baptized Apr 17, 1743 (Newbury, MA R); d young
86. Ruth 4, baptized Mar 23, 1745. 46; d May 23, 1746 (Newbury, MA R)
87. Mary 4, b Apr 8, 1751 (Newbury, MA R)
88. Christopher 4, b Oct 30, 1755 (Newbury, MA R)

15. Hannah Bagley 3, Orlando 2 Orlando 1 , b Mar 29, 1712; m Oct 21, 1731, Thomas Merrill (Salis MA R), son Thomas & Judith (Kent), b Jan 5, 1710/11 (Salis MA R), d Jan 11, 1801, in South Hampton, NH. Both were dismissed from Second Church, Amesbury, MA, to church in Bradford, MA in 1734 (Second Church R).

Children:
89. Abel 4, b Nov 14, 1732 (Salis MA R); baptized Jan 19, 1734/35 (Second Church, Ames MA R)

90.   Orlando 4, b Dec 4, 1734; d Jan 24, 1736/37 (Salis MA R)
91.   Nathan 4, b Dec 17, 1736 (Salis MA R); d Jan 10, 1801
92.   Judith 4, b Nov 9, 1738 (Salis MA R); m William Sampson
They had dau Hannah who m Ezra Mead II.   Their   son   Hilon   m
Lydia Barnes. Hilon's son William m (2) Susan Cowgill and   had
Harlan who m Asenath Fowler. Their son Elmo   Mead   m   Mildred
Mildred Hamilton. Their dau was Alice Meade   Cope   who   lived
Winfield, KS. (Family R)
93.   Lydia 4, b Nov 12, 1740; d Dec 9, 1816
94.   Abel 4, b Jan 18, 1742/43
95.   Hannah 4, d young
96.   Thomas 4, b Jan 4, 1745/46; d Nov 15, 1790
97.   Sarah 4
98.   Hannah 4, b Feb 2, 1750

28.   Orlando Bagley 4, Orlando 3, Orlando 2 Orlando 1 , b   Feb
21, 1706/07; d 1770; m Mary Kendrick, July 23, 1728 (Ames   MA
R), dau John & Frances (Burnham), b Oct 11, 1704, Ipswich,   MA
(Ipswich, MA R).

      He was the eldest son and when his father's estate   was
divided by the committee appointed by the court,   he   received
the first and second shares, situated partly in Kingston   and
partly in Newton, NH. he received a mill-pond right   situated
in Kingston, NH; forty-five acres and three-quarters,   more   or
less (NH Probate R). He lived in Amesbury for   a   time   and
later moved to Kingston. He   was   a   yeoman,   then   styled
Gentleman and called Lieutenant.
      On Feb 18, 1741/42, he signed a petition for a new parish
at Newton, NH (Newton, NH R). May, 1738, he signed a petition
to set off the east parish at Kingston. He   is   mentioned   in
the will of John Currier of Kingston in 1757 and went bond for
Ruth Hoyt in the sum of 500 pounds in Aug, 1745, and surety on
estate of Jacob Morse of Kingston, May 31,   1758,   in   sum   of
1000 pounds; at one time he was worth   over   5000   pounds   (NH
Provincial R).
      He d   intestate   and   adm   was   granted   to   Jacob   Gale,
Gentleman, Feb 23, 1770. Account of adm: receipts 121   pounds
11 shillings, 4 pence; expenditure 34 pounds   5   shillings   11
pence. Allowed Dec 30, 1772 (NH Probate R).

Children:
99.   John 5, b July 16, 1729   (Ames   MA   R);   baptized   Second
Church, Amesbury, by Mr March, Aug 17, 1727; d young
100.   Ann 5, baptized Jan 24, 1730/31, Second Church, Amesbury
101.   Orlando 5, b June 27, 1732 (Ames MA R)
102.   John 5, baptized Feb, 1733/34, Second Church,   Amesbury;
d Nov 14, 1738
103.   Seth 5, b June 18, 1735 (Ames MA R);   baptized   Aug   17,
1735, Amesbury; d Sept 26, 1738
104.   Phineas 5, b Mar 31, 1737 (Ames MA R); baptized May   29,
1739, Second Church, Amesbury
105.   Merah or Mary 5, baptized Oct 8, 1738, Kingston,   NH;
Nov 14, 1738 (Kingston, NH Church R)
106.   Seth 5, b Oct 27, 1739 (Kingston, NH   R);   baptized
18, 1739, at Kingston; d Sept 24, 1804 (Salis MA R).   Ames
R say he was born in Amesbury, Nov 28, 1739.

107. Mary 5, b Sept 11, 1740 (Kingston NH R); baptized Kingston, Sept 13, 1741
108. Dorothy 5, b July 6, 1743 (Kingston, NH R); baptized Kingston, July 10 1743, Kingston
109. Sarah 5, baptized Kingston, NH, Sept 2, 1744 (Kingston Church R)
110. John 5, baptized Kingston, NH, Mar 30, 1746 (Kingston, NH Church R). *This is the John who m Hannah French & went t Watibous me as shown by Edward - French French genealogy)*

29. **Sarah Bagley 4, Orlando 3, Orlando 2, Orlando 1** b Oct 22, 1708; d Mar 16, 1801; m (1) Moses Sargent of Amesbury at Amesbury, Nov 9, 1729 (Ames MA R), son Thomas and Mary (Stevens), b Aug 21, 1707, d July 24, 1756, ae 49 (Ames MA R). He was a farmer. She m (2) Nov 14, 1757, Rev William Johnson of Amesbury (Ames MA R). She m (3) Dr. Roger Merrill, Oct 3, 1774 (Ames MA R), the Rev Johnson having d Feb 22, 1772 (Newbury, MA R). Dr Merrill was b Mar 10, 1713 (Newbury, MA R), probably son Nathaniel & Hannah (Stevens), d May 12, 1791 (Newbury, MA R).

        She received as her share of her father's estate, the eighth share, nine acres of land, more or less.

Children: (Ames MA R; all by Moses Sargent)
111. Orlando 5, b Apr 21, 1728; d Apr 3, 1803
112. Mary 5, b Mar 5, 1730
113. Sarah 5, b Nov 25, 1733; m May 2, 1754, Josiah Sargent
114. Dorothy 5, b Nov 8, 1736
115. Christopher 5, b May 18, 1740; d Nov 10, 1830; m Anne Sargent
116. Moses 5, b Jan 14, 1742; d Jan 31, 1743/44

30. **Henry Bagley 4, Orlando 3, Orlando 2 Orlando 1** , b Aug 25, 1711; d Apr, 1776. Received the seventh share of his father's estate, nine acres of land, more or less. Lived Amesbury, MA, then in Newton, NH, and, in his old age moved to Candia, NH. Mrs. Brown of Houston, TX, a descendant says he m Anne Winthrop.

        Oct 26, 1739, he was set off to pay his minister's school rate in the East Parish of Kingston, NH. He was annexed to the East Parish, Kingston, in 1739, and was in Newton, NH, by 1755 (Kingston & Newton, NH R).

        Apparently because of his illegitimate child, he was not a member of the church. On Apr 14, 1751, Anne, wife of Henry Bagley, was taken into full communion at Second Church, Amesbury. On Apr 12, 1752, Henry was taken into full comunion at Second Church. On Dec 3, 1758, he and his wife were gathered into the church at Newton (Second Church, Ames MA R). The fact of his being admitted into formal full communion meant that his children, heretofore not baptized, were all baptized at the same time (See below).

        Apr 1, 1766, Henry Bagley of Newton sold to William Bailey land in Newton, house and barn and pew in the meetinghouse. Anne Bagley is given as his wife on this deed. Jacob Bagley of Candia, NH was made adm of his estate, Apr 24, 1776, and the inventory was 35 pounds, 8 shillings, 10 pence (Rockingham Co NH Probate R). On Sept 29, 1794, Jacob Bagley sold 70 acres of land left by his father Henry; heirs, Jonathan, David, Samuel, Hannah, Winthrop, Jacob, and Anna. The deed is signed by Jacob and Mary or Molly (Rockingham Co NH Deeds).

Children:
117. Henry 5, b Apr 24, 1730 (Ames MA R). This child evidently was illegitimate, the birth being recorded under Currier, the mother Mary Currier, probably dau Benjamin & Abigail (Brown), b June 13, 1714. Her name was Currier in 1748. In those days illegitimate children took the father's name and Henry, Jr., was brought up by his father; Henry, Jr. d before Feb 1803
118. Winthrop 5, b Apr 25, 1734 (Ames MA R)
119. Jonathan 5, b Aug 5, 1736 (Ames MA R); baptized Oct, 1753, Newton, NH; d Mar 1, 1819, Candia, NH (NH R)
120. Dorothy 5, b Mar 12/13, 1738 (Ames MA R)
121. David 5, b May 4 or 6, 1740 (Ames MA R); baptized Oct, 1753, Newton, NH; d before 1786
122. Samuel 5, b Aug 29, 1742, (Ames MA R); baptized Oct, 1753, Newton, NH; d Apr 25, 1805 (Candia, NH R)
123. Jacob 5, baptized Newton, NH, Oct 2, 1753 (Ames MA R)
124. Hannah 5, baptized Newton, NH, Oct 2, 1753 (Ames MA R)
125. Anna 5, baptized Second Church, Amesbury, Nov 9, 1755

31. David Bagley 4, Orlando 3, Orlando 2, Orlando 1, b May 25, 1714; d before Jan 21, 1799; m (1) Mary Huntington, Mar 20, 1734/35 (Ames MA R), dau William C. & Mary (Goodwin), b Jan 13, 1712/13 (Ames MA R); m (2) Rachel (Currier) Wells, Feb 8, 1773 (Newton, NH R). he and his first wife renewed their baptismal covenant at First Church, Amesbury, MA, Apr 14, 1742.

Lived in Amesbury, and then moved to Newton, NH, where he signed a petition Feb 18, 1741/42 for a new parish. He was called yeoman, then captain, then Gentleman, Moderator of a town meeting at Newton to decide the question of dividing the town, Aug 15, 1768, and on a committee appointed to petition ther legislature about acts relative to the selectmen, Mar 30, 1769 (Provincial Papers). Feb, 1759 went bond in amount of 1000 pounds for adm estate of Enoch Challis. His land mentioned in estate of Abraham Merrill, Sept 14, 1762; signed bond with Thomas Elliott in amount of 500 pounds, Sept 26, 1760, for guardianship of Timothy Elliott, son of John (NH Provincial Papers). Received from his father's estate, the third share, nine acres of land, more or less. It appears that his father had given him land previously as the record says "David's other land in sd farm which he had of his father in his lifetime." He owned land in Kingston, Newton and Warner, NH (Rockingham Co, NH Deeds). It is either he or his son who is on the Proprietor's list of Warner, NH, in 1767; also in grant of Masonian Proprietors, dated Dec 24, 1767 (NH Provincial Papers). In 1796, he gave to his son Elijah land in Newton and Warner; a witness to this deed was David Bagley, Jr. (Rockingham Co, NH Deeds).

His will, made Nov 20, 1792; proved Jan 21, 1799; inventory $2446,32; mentions wife Rachel: sons: David, Joshua, Elijah;

daus: Mary Gould, Judith Favor, wife of Cutting Favor; Sarah Collins, late wife of Joseph Collins, deceased; Dorothy Currier, wife of Thomas Currier, deceased. His dau Elizabeth is not mentioned and probably d young (Rockingham Co NH Probate R).

Children: (All Amesbury, MA R except as noted)
126.   David 5, b Jan 1, 1735/36; d young
127.   Mary 5, b 1738; living 1792
128.   Judith 5, b July 20, 1740; d Apr 17, 1828 (History of Bristol, NH)
129.   Sarah 5, b May 15 or 17, 1743
130.   David 5, b July 20, 1745; baptized Oct 13, 1745; living 1792
131.   Dorothy 5, b Jan 11, 1748; baptized June 5, 1748; deceased by 1792
132.   Elizabeth 5, b Apr 16, 1750; baptized July 21, 1751; not mentioned in father's will in 1792 probably died young
133. Joshua 5, b Apr 17, 1752; baptized Oct, 1753, Newton, NH; d Apr 9, 1809 (Tombstone, Newton, NH, and Warner, NH R)
134.   Elijah 5, baptized Aug 23, 1756; d Feb 2, 1814

32.   Merah Bagley 4, Orlando 3, Orlando 2, Orlando 1 , b Mar 23, 1717; m David Webster, Oct 8, 1738.

33.   Jonathan Bagley 4, Orlando 3, Orlando 2, Orlando 1 , b Mar 23, 1717; d Dec 18 or 28, 1780; m Dorothea Wells, Dec 9, 1736 (Ames MA R), dau John, son of Rev Thomas Wells, of Amesbury & Dorothy (Hoyt). She d his widow, Aug, 1781 (Ames MA R). Both he and his wife renewed their baptismal covenants at First Church, Amesbury (Church R).
    He began as a husbandman and lived at the Ferry in Amesbury in a house built by Timothy Currier in 1736, and which he purchased in 1750; burned 1893. He received from his father's estate the sixth share, nine acres of land, more or less. He became an esquire in Dec, 1766. In a letter from Gov Barnard of MA, to the Governor of NH, Jonathan is mentioned as a member of a committee of the MA General Court which surveyed the branches of the Salmon Falls, in NH. Apparently he was chairman of a committee to settle Maine and NH boundaries (NH Provincial Papers). He was a member of the General Court in 1776 and of great service in the Revolution in obtaining men for the army. From the time of his first appearance in public life in 1740, he held many public offices, being first elected representative in 1743 and being chosen eleven times thereafter. In 1780, he was on a committee chosen to consider a new form of state government. At the time of his death, he owned nearly one thousand acres of land including the farm at Pond Hills where his father had lived and which he gave to his son Orlando. He was a member of the General Court when the new state government was formed and was again elected as the first representative from Amesbury under the new government.
    His war record was impressive. In 1740, he was clerk in a military company. In Feb, 1746, he was captain of the 5th company, 5th MA Regt, Col Robert Hale. This regt was on the

first expedition to Louisburg. He was colonel as early as 1755 as Ipswich in the Massachusetts Colony says "that Capt John Whipple of the hamlet commanded a company in Colonel Bagley's regt in service from Apr, 1755, to December and January following". He was present at the council of war held at a camp at "Grate Crossing Place", Aug 22, 1755, at which the Honorable Major General Johnson presented his plan for campaign against Crown Point (NH Provincial Papers). On Nov 13, 1755, his regt met with a thousand troops at Fort William Henry, where they held a council of war and agreed on a garrison, Col Bagley to be chief. He was at Lake George in Apr, 1757, where a great army was stationed for the conquest of Fort Ticonderoga. On June 15, 1758, about four o'clock, Col Bagley's regt began to come into Flatbush, and on June 23, he received orders to march toward Ft Edward on arrival of Col William's regt at Schenectady. The regt arrived at Ft Edward on June 29th. On July 5th, their tents were struck and the men embarked in boats and, after a brief camp during the day, they rowed all night, landing at daybreak at the Narrows. As all the bridges had been burned, they had to make a long detour through the thick woods. After marching about two miles, they were attacked in front by 3000 Frenchman and Indians; Col Bagley's regt being ordered to charge the enemy on the right. Lord Howe was killed in this battle. After the reduction off Montreal, Col Bagley's regt was stationed in the West Indies. He was again commissioned colonel in the Essex Co, MA regt in 1767, 1768, 1773, and 1774 (Mass Rev War Rolls).

He built a wharf with his father, midway between Mr Lowell's wharf and Timothy Currier's from the bank to the channel of Powow River. On Sept 28, 1761, he purchased from Stephen Emery a grist and sawmill, and was required to give a bond in the sum of 1000 dollars sterling to faithfully perform the conditions with respect to grinding corn for the inhabitants of the town of Newbury, MA, agreeable to the conditions in which the said stream was granted to John Emery. He extended the business and served the town as miller for 25 years. The executors of his will, under a license at Newburyport, sold the two grist mills with land adjoining, deed dated June 2, 1786. In 1750, he purchased the house and wharf at the Ferry of Timothy Currier and asked the town to exchange the fifty feet of land granted him in 1741 for fifty feet next to his wharf, and his request was granted. On July 2, 1756, the East Parish bought one and a half acres of land from Jonathan Bagley for a meetinghouse. In 1772, the new town pound was built on a lot given by him as well as the money for building it.

Jonathan was a great holder of land. He was one of the grantees of the town of Bath, NH; owned 5/49th of half a grant in Alexandria, NH, altho the latter grant was never legal; it being revoked in July, 1773, but he did get some land in Alexandria, Lot No 35, first division and Lot 37, second division. His name is not mentioned on a list of grantees later in 1780; however, the land in Alexandria was sold by Orlando Bagley, his executor (NH Provincial Papers & Grafton Co NH Deeds).

He also owned land in Royalsborough, ME, now Durham. On June 26, 1766, he was chosen by the proprietors to lay out a road and build a log house there for accommodation of the settlement. Everett Stackpole in his _History of Durham, ME_ says: "He was the most active agent of the proprietors in the settlement of Royalsborough and spent much time there between 1770 and 1780, his farm consisting of Lots 82, 83, and 84. Bagley's barn is mentioned in 1791. Tradition says that a house built by him stood close to the northern line of Lot 83 and near the River Road. The part of Royalsborough known as Bagley's Gore was granted to him by the General Court of MA. Here three of his sons owned farms. He was owner of what was long known as Chandler's Mill in the western part of town.

So much of his wealth was tied up in long-term land speculation that he died insolvent. His will was dated Mar 23, 1779; proved Feb 15, 1781. Commissioners were appointed July 8, 1783, and the estate was finally settled Sept 5, 1796. Witnesses were Enoch, Daniel and James Bagley. His widow Dorothy made her will in 1779 and adm on her estate was granted Sept 20, 1781 (Essex Co MA Probate R). His will does not mention all his children known to be living at that time, probably because he had already given them land before the will was made.

Children: (Amesbury, MA R)
135. John 5, b Oct 18, 1737; d Jan 14, 1830; but not in father's will
136. William 5, b Jan 14/15, 1738/39; not mentioned in father's will
137. Jonathan 5, b May 10, 1741; d Apr 1, 1742
138. Valentine 5, b Jan 1, 1742/43; d Apr, 1780
139. Dorothy 5, b Feb 12/13, 1744/45; living 1816 (_History of Durham, ME_)
140. Orlando 5, b Nov 5, 1747; d May 23, 1807
141. Jonathan 5, b July 29, 1750; d Sept 26. 1791; not mentioned in father's will
142. Sarah 5, b Dec 25, 1751; d Mar 4, 1752
143. David Wells 5, b Oct 5, 1753; not mentioned in father's will
144. Sarah 5, b Feb 10, 1756; d 1776

34. Dorothy Bagley 4, Orlando 3, Orlando 2, Orlando 1, b June 16, 1719; d Sept 1770; m (1) Nathaniel Brown, Feb or Mar 23, 1737/38 (Ames MA R), son Nathaniel & Elizabeth (Wentworth), b Jan 19, 1714/15 (Salis MA R), d Dec 14, 1752; estate appraised at 529 pounds 11 shillings and one pence (Essex Co MA Probate R). She m (2) Jacob Morrill of Salisbury, MA, Nov 12, 1754 (Salis MA R), son Jacob & Elizabeth (Stevens), b Sept 3, 1711, called, Jr., until 1754, d Mar 23, 1788 (Salis MA R). After Dorothy's death, he m Abigail Burbank, Apr 9, 1771. who d Nov 1, 1806 (Salis MA R). His will was made Feb 24, 1784; proved June 30, 1788 (Essex Co MA Probate R).

Children: (Salisbury MA R; first 7 by Brown; others by Morrill)
145. Elizabeth 5, b Jan 31, 1738/39; m Oliver Morrill of

South Hampton, NH, Dec 5, 1755
146.   Abram 5, b Aug 31, 1741
147.   Dorothy 5, b Jan 12, 1743/44; baptized Salisbury First Church, Jan 22, 1744; m Aug 17, 1779, Michael Worthen of Chester, NH
148.   Sarah 5, b Nov 14, 1745; m Oct 10, 1763, John Knapp
149.   Judith 5, b Feb 14, 1747; m Feb 12, 1779, Jonathan Morse
150.   Nathaniel 5, b June 19, 1750
151.   Orlando 5, b Apr 2, 1753; m May 24, 1779, Mary Hotchkiss
152.   Lois 5, b Sept 1, 1755; d about 1778
153.   Moses Sargent 5, b Mar 2, 1757
154.   John 5, b Apr 6, 1759; m about 1781 Dolly Bagley
155.   Jonathan 5, b Apr 6, 1761
156.   Dolly 5, b Aug 10, 1762; d unm May 9, 1781

36.   Thomas Bagley 4, Orlando 3, Orlando 2, Orlando 1 , b Jan 18, 1722/23; d Sept 17, 1771; m Ruth Webster of Salisbury, MA; intentions, Jan 22, 1746/47, at Second Church, Salisbury (Salis MA & Church R), dau Israel & Susanna (Morrill), b Apr 8, 1727 (Salis MA R). On Mar 6, 1748/49, both renewed their baptismal covenants at First Church, Amesbury.

   He was a yeoman and lived in Amesbury until 1759, when he moved to Salisbury, MA. He received of his father's estate, the 4th share, nine acres of land, more or less.

   His wife was granted adm of his estate, Oct 29, 1771; inventory 441 pounds, 187 shillings. His wife was made guardian of Sarah and Enoch, minors over 14, and Susanna, Dorothy and Ruth, minors under 14, Sept 29, 1772 (Essex Co MA Probate R). She m (2) David Osgood, Oct 1, 1772, and was his wife in 1790 (N. E Genealogical Register).

   Thomas is buried Salisbury Plains Cemetery; headstone in very poor condition in 1957.

Children:
157.   Israel 5, b Oct 25, 1747; d Aug 22, 1797 (Ames MA R)
158.   Thomas 5, b May 2, 1750 (Ames MA R)
159.   Philip 5, b May 22, 1752 (Ames MA R)
160.   Sarah 5, b June 15, 1755 (Ames MA R)
161.   Enoch 5, b Feb 4, 1758 (Ames MA R); d Nov 30, 1842 (Tombstone, Troy, ME)
162.   Ruth 5, b June 30, 1760 (Salis MA R)
163.   Dorothy 5, baptized July 22, 1764 (Salis MA R); d Jan 15, 1827 (Salis MA R)
164.   Susanna 5, baptized July 22, 1764 (Salis MA R); d unm 1778 (Essex Antiquarian)

49.   Anna Bagley 4, Orlando 3, Orlando 2, Orlando 1 , b May 18, 1709; living 1770; m Jeremiah Currier of Amesbury, MA, and Kingston, NH, May 1, 1729, son John & Judith (Stevens), b Aug 8, 1706 (Ames MA R). he probably d by 1761. A Jeremiah Currier of Kingston, NH, d before 1761 as adm on his estate was granted to Jeremiah Currier with Jonathan Blaisdell, blacksmith, and Daniel Rowell, husbandman, as sureties, all of Kingston, in the sum of 1000 pounds, Aug 26, 1761. Warrant dated Aug 27, 1761, authorizing Ebenezer Batchelder, yeoman of Kingston to appraise the estate. Inventory, Sept 16, 1761,

amount 7265 pounds and 10 shillings, signed by Jeremy Webster and Ebenezer Batchelder. Account of adm: receipts 75 pounds, 12 shillings, 6 1/4 pence, allowed June 9, 1768 (NH Probate R). This is undoubtedly the Jeremiah Currier who m Anna Bagley as he would have had a son Jeremiah old enough to adm his estate. Certainly he d before 1770 as he is not mentioned in his son's Eliphalet's will, but his will is.

Eliphalet Currier's will, dated Mar 22, 1770, mentions his mother and leaves her 5 pounds, lawfull money," to be paid to her by his executor when demanded by her but if it should not be demanded in her lifetime by her, my will is that he not be obliged to pay it to any of her heirs-in-law" (NH Probate R).

Children:
165.   John 5, b Jan 31, 1729/30 (Ames MA R); probably d Oct or Nov 1735. Kingston NH Church records give one child as dying Oct 30, 1735, and another Nov 18, 1735, but gives them only as the Currier children. They died of Quinsey throat canker which caused the deaths of many children. There could be a child b in 1733/34 but who d in 1775, instead of John, but if John or his children were living in 1770, Eliphalet's will would probably have mentioned them.
166.   Hannah 5, b Dec 3, 1731 (Ames MA R); d Oct or Nov 1735
167.   Hannah 5, b Aug 25, 1736; living 1770
168.   Jeremiah 5, b Dec 19, 1738; living 1770
169.   Judith 5, b Oct 14, 1741; not mentioned in brother's will in 1770
170.   Moses 5, b June 30, 1740; living 1770
171.   Eliphalet 5, b Apr 10, 1747; d before June 27, 1770 (NH Probate R). His will dated Mar 22, 1770, mentions only mother, brother and sisters but no wife or children
172.   Ann 5, b May 28, 1750; living 1770

50.   John Bagley 4, John 3, Orlando 2, Orlando 1 . b Dec 22, 1710; d Oct, 1782 (Ames MA R); m Judith Sargent, Oct 9, 1734, dau Joseph & Elizabeth (Carr), b Oct 1, 1716, d his widow, Oct 9, 1813 (Ames MA R). She was 97 and d Pond Hills, blind in later years, but retained memory & hearing. She could recall when the road over Pond Hills was nothing but a cart path. Feb, 1735/36. He & his wife renewed their Baptismal covenants at First Church, Amesbury.

Was town clerk of Amesbury from 1760 to 1775, but his handwriting was inferior to that of Orlando and Thomas who preceded him. He d intestate and his son Aaron was appt adm, Mar 26, 1787; inventory 128 pounds, 16 shillings 4 pence. May 28, 1787, declared insolvent.

Children: (Ames MA R except as noted)
173.   Elizabeth 5, b Oct 4, 1735
174.   Merriam 5, b Jan 5 or 6, 1737
175.   John 5, b Aug 28, 1739
176.   Joseph 5, b Aug 23, 1741; d at Lake George as soldier in French & Indian War, Aug 21, 1760
177.   Judith 5, b Aug 15 or 23, 1743
178.   Daniel 5, b Feb 3, 1745; d 1781

179.   Jacob 5, b Jan 8, 1747; probably s before Sept 27, 1798 (Essex Co MA Probate R)
180.   Moses 5, b May 2, 1750; d before Nov 30, 1776 (Rockingham Co NH Probate R)
181.   Sarah 5, b Mar 30, 1752; d Nov 11, 1752
182.   Aaron 5, b Oct 5, 1753; d July 18, 1833 (tombstone, W Topsham VT)
183.   Philip 5, b Dec 9 or 19, 1755; d Apr 24, 1844 (Newburyport MA R)
184.   Sarah 5, b Nov 6, 1757; d Mar 12, 1850, unm (Family R)
185.   Hannah 5, b Jan 10, 1761; d unm, Feb 7, 1848 (Newburyport MA R)

51. Moses Bagley 4, John 3, Orlando 2, Orlando 1 , b Sept 17, 1715. He was a yeoman and lived in Amesbury; no record of marriage has been found; adjudicated non compos mentis in 1760; d in Amesbury. His brother John was made his guardian, Mar 27, 1760 (Essex Co MA R).

52. Hannah Bagley 4, John 3, Orlando 2 Orlando 1 , b about 1717; m John Colby, Nov 1, 1750 (Ames MA R). He may have been son of Jacob & Mary (Frame), and Hannah was his second wife. Jacob Colby & Mary (Frame) had a son, John, b June 19, 1707 (Ames MA R), who m Jan 12, 1737/38, Alice Davis, b June 1, 1713, dau John & Ruth Jewell, widow of Thomas Jewell. However, it may have been some other John, not known. Mrs. Stormont of Miami, FL, says she m John Colby, son of John & Mary (Frame), Dec 12, 1737 /38.

Children: (Ames MA R)
186.   John 5, b Jan 8, 1751/52
187.   Thomas 5, b June 1, 1753
188.   Hannah 5, b Sept 11, 1755
189.   Molly 5, b Mar 28, 1761; d Jan 5, 1780; m Rev Joseph Quimby, minister of Baptist Church in Center Sandwich, NH

53. Timothy Bagley 4, John 3, Orlando 2, Orlando 1 , b Oct 12, 1719; d Apr 22, 1759; m Mary Thompson, Jan 2, 1745 (Ames MA R), dau Peter & Hannah, b May 26, 1724 (Ames MA R).
    She was adm of his estate, July 23, 1759. Guardianship of Timothy, son of Timothy, aged over 14 to Mary Bagley, Oct. 1765 (Essex Co MA Probate R). Mary Bagley of Amesbury, widow and adm of Timothy Bagley, deceased, sold land to Jonathan Kimball of South Hampton, yeoman, five acres in South Hampton, Dec 30, 1762 (Rockingham Co NH Deeds).

Children: (Birth dates, Ames MA R)
190.   Timothy 5, b Oct 26, 1749; d Aug 23, 1825 (Candia, NH R)
191.   Peter 5, b Jan 21, 1753; living 1840 (Vermont Historical Gazeteer by Hemenway
192.   Isaac 5, b Nov 6, 1757; d Feb 1, 1839

54. Rhoda Bagley 4, John 3, Orlando 2, Orlando 1 , b May 10, 1723. Acording to the Essex Antiquarian, she was living in Amesbury in 1745, unm, but she apparently m Thomas Challis, Nov 22, 1744 (Ames MA R), son John & Sarah (Frame), b Oct 15,

1720, probably d Mar 12, 1752 (Ames MA R)

Children: (Ames MA R)
193.   Eunice 5, b Jan 5, 1745/46
194.   John 5, b Apr 21, 1750

55.   Sarah Bagley 4, John 3, Orlando 2, Orlando 1, b   Apr   10,
1725.   According to the Essex Antiquarian, she was living,
unm, in Amesbury in 1746, but it appears she m Jacob Tuxbury
in 1746 (Ames MA R), son Isaac & Sarah (Sargent), b Dec 15,
1723, probably d June 13, 1754, ae 31 (Ames MA S R).   Sarah is
not listed in the heirs of her father's estate in 1730.

Children: (Ames MA R)
195.   Isaac 5, b Aug 17, 1747
196.   Jacob 5, b Nov 10, 1748
197.   Hannah 5, b Aug 27, 1750
198.   Jonathan 5, b Mar 22, 1753

57.   William Bagley 4, Jacob 3, Orlando 2, Orlando 1 ,   b Oct
9, 1713; d Nov 29, 1746.   A mariner, lived in Amesbury, in
colonial wars in the first expedition to Louisburg.   He was
taken prisoner and died on board a prison ship.   He and his
brother Jacob went on the expedition together.   He was captain
of the sloop Susannah bound for Cape Breton which was captured
by L'Aurne.
      He m Susannah Webster of Salisbury, Aug 18, 1740 (Ames MA
R), dau Israel & Susanna (Morrill), b Feb 18, 1719/20 (Salis
MA R), d Sept 30, 1808.   She m (2) David Currier, Mar 13, 1749
(Ames MA R), son David & Keziah (Colby), b Mar 6, 1734/35
(Ames MA R).   His will was made June 18, 1770; proved   Dec 5,
1778, wife Susannah mentioned (Essex Co MA Probate R).
      William and his wife Susannah renewed their baptismal
covenants at First Church Amesbury, Nov 23, 1740.
      After William's death, David Currier was appointed
guardian of Jerusha and Merriam Bagley, Sept 28, 1758, and
John Bagley was appointed guardian of Enoch and William, Jan
5, 1758 (Essex Co MA Probate R).

Children: (Ames MA R)
199   Enoch, b Apr 27, 1740; d Sept 13, 1814
200.   William 5, b Dec 26, 1741; d Sept 30, 1808 (Family R)
201.   Jerusha 5, b Sept 9, 1743; d Feb 4, 1819
202.   Anne 5, b Dec 2, 1745; d Jan 23, 1748
203.   Merriam 5, b about 1744/45; birth not recorded Ames   or
Salis MA R

58.   Elizabeth Bagley 4, Jacob 3, Orlando 2, Orlando 1 , b Jan
18, 1715/16; d Nov 1, 1795; m June 27, 1734, Samuel Adams
(Ames MA R), son Archelus & Sarah (March), intentions dated
Oct 21, 1731 (Salis MA R), b Newbury, MA, Apr 29, 1710
(Newbury MA R); lived in Salisbury and was a joiner until
about 1750 when he became a shipwright.   He d Salisbury, MA,
May 16, 1747, ae 57 (Salis MA R).   She is mentioned in her
father's will, Dec 25, 1767.

Children: (Salis MA R)
204. Jacob 5, b Mar 28, 1735; d Aug 29, 1753
205. Archelus 5, b Oct 23, 1736 (?)
206. Hannah 5, b Oct 20, 1738; d Aug 13, 1796 (Ames MA R)
207. Samuel 5, b Sept 29, 1740; d Sept 9, 1741 (Ames MA R)
208. Elizabeth 5, b Aug 13, 1742; living 1798
209. Mary 5, b June 3, 1747
210. Anna 5, b May 25, 1750; d Sept 28, 1785
211. Sarah 5, b Dec 24, 1754; living 1798

62. Hannah Bagley 4, Jacob 3, Orlando 2, Orlando 1 , b June 6, 1723; living 1780; m Richard Currier, Feb 19, 1750 (Ames MA R), son David & Keziah (Colby), b Nov 27, 1730 (Ames MA R).

Children: (Ames MA R)
212. Jerusha 5, b Apr 20, 1751
213. Jacob Bagley 5, b Apr 10, 1753; d Aug 17, 1831
214. Richard 5, b May 30, 1755; d young
215. Sarah 5, b June 9, 1756; d young
216. Hannah 5, b Feb 9, 1758; d young
217. Richard 5, b July 20, 1762
218. David 5, b Nov 23, 1766
219. Elizabeth 5, b May 25, 1768; living 1780

63. Jacob Bagley 4, Jacob 3, Orlando 2, Orlando 1 , b June 30, 1724; d Jan 15, 1747, of pleurisy. He and his brother William were in the first expedition to Louisburg. Records ordered to Jacob Bagley, Jr., being in "ye service at Cape Brittain in captivity, 2 pounds 60 shillings."

76. Joseph Bagley 4, Joseph 3, Orlando 2, Orlando 1 , b Jan 7, 1735/36; d Sept 25, 1791; m Rhoda True, Jan or Feb 6, 1763 (Salis MA R), dau Henry & Mary (Allen), b Feb 2, 1742/43, d Nov 28, 1770 (Salis MA R). Both were admitted to the Second Church, Salisbury, MA, Sept 1, 1765. He was a blacksmith. Family checks with Census of 1790.
     Probably the Joseph of Salisbury, private, Capt Henry Morrill's Co, Col Caleb Cushing: Mar - Apr 20, 1775 in respect to Apr 19, 1775, Lexington Alarm, 4 days service.
     On Aug 8, 1778, he was appointed guardian of his children: Anna, Miriam and True since they had inherited from their grandfather. Adm on his estate granted to his son True, Dec 26, 1791 (Essex Co MA Probate R).

Children: (Salis MA R)
220. Anna 5, b Mar 9, 1765; d single in Boston, Feb 8, 1850, ae 85 (Mass R)
221. Miriam 5, b Oct 23, 1767; d Nov 24, 1849
222. True 5, b Aug 19, 1770; d June or July 26, 1833

77. Benjamin Bagley 4, Joseph 3, Orlando 2, Orlando 1 , b Feb 26, 1738; m (1) Judith Wells, Nov 15, 1757 (Ames MA R); probably m (2) Sarah Swett, Sept 21, 1762, at Salisbury Second Church (Salis MA R). Probably a soldier under Amherst and believed to be the Benjamin Bagley of Falmouth, ME, taxed for

two polls in 1766.

Probably the Benjamin Bagley who served in the Revolution from Falmouth, ME: Served in Continental Army for Col Peter Noyes (1st Cumberland Co) regt, dated Nov 20, 1778; joined Capt George White's Co, Col Benjamin Tupper's 10 regt. Continental army pay accounts for service from Jan 18, 1777 to July 7, 1777. Reported taken prisoner July 7, 1777; also Capt White's Co, Col Francis' regt; roll made up for 62 days rations from date of enlistment, Jan 18, 1777, to time of arrival at Bennington (Mass Rev War Rolls).

It is possible that he had children born in ME for whom we have no record.

Child:
223.   Sarah 5, b Dec 2, 1758 (Ames MA R)

78. Abel Bagley 4, Joseph 3, Orlando 2, Orlando 1 ,b July 4, 1740; d Oct 17, 1815; m Sarah Dow about 1762, dau Josiah & Mary (Wadleigh), b Dec 15, 1745 (Salis MA R), d Aug 12, 1790. He lived in Rowley and Salisbury, MA and died by drowning.

He was probably a soldier under Amherst in 1759 and was a Revolutionary soldier in Capt Joseph Page's Co; he marched to the Lexington Alarm, Apr 19, 1775, 19 1/2 days service. Also in Capt Moses Nowell's Co, Col Titcomb's regt; roll made up time of arrival at Providence, RI, May 4, 1777; discharged July 4, 1777; service 2 months 9 days (MA Rev War R).

Children:
224.   Stephen Hunt 5, b Dec 12, 1763 (Rowley, MA R); d Jan 26, 1849 (Tombstone, Salisbury Plains, MA Cem.)
225.   Elias 5, b Apr 8, 1765 (Rowley, MA R); d 1816 or soon after (Rockingham Co NH Probate R)
226.   Dorcas 5, b 1769; d Apr 28, 1854 (Salis MA R)
227.   Joseph 5, b Sept 27, 1766 (Rowley, MA R); d Jan 2, 1849, ae about 82 (Salis MA R)

79.   Sarah Bagley 4, Joseph 3 Orlando 2, Orlando 1 , b Apr 12, 1743; living 1774; m Jonathan Bayley of Amesbury, June 6, 1763 (Salis MA R). It appears that the children recorded on Amesbury records under Jonathan and Sarah Bagley should belong here, as their child Jonathan is recorded under both Bagley and Bayley.

Children:
228.   Jonathan 5, b Oct 16, 1763 (Ames MA R)
229.   Benjamin 5, b Apr 7, 1763 (Ames MA R)
230.   Deborah 5, b Jan 3, 1770, Salem, NH
231.   Sarah 5, b Apr 16, 1772, Salem, NH
232.   Rachel 5, b June 30, 1775, Salem, NH
233.   Thomas 5, b Jan 1780, Salem, NH

80. Mary Bagley 4, Joseph 3, Orlando 2, Orlando 1 ,b Sept 12 1749; living 1763; probably m Ebenezer Runnels, Jr., May 8, 1771, at Haverhill, MA (MA R).

81. Lydia Bagley 4, Joseph 3, Orlando 2, Orlando 1 , b May 7,

1745; d Warren, NH, July 26, 1843; m Moses Brown, June 18, 1778, son Lt. William & Elizabeth (Shortridge), b Sept 23, 1753 (Salis MA R). They moved to Greenland, NH, then to Wentworth, NH, and finally to Warren, NH (NH Rev War Rolls).

He was a Revolutionary soldier and pensioner, a blacksmith and farmer. She also received a pension after his death on July 13, 1836. Pension records say "two children settled abroad" but give only one child by name.

Child:
234.   Sally 5, b 1787 (NH Pension Rolls)

100.   Ann Bagley 5, Orlando 4, Orlando 3, Orlando 2, Orlando 1 baptized Second Church, Amesbury, MA, Jan 24, 1730/31; m at Kingston, NH, Aug 24, 1749, Jonathan French (Kingston, NH Church R).

Children:
235.   Jonathan 6, baptized May 1, 1757 (Kingston, NH Church R)
236.   Moley 6, b Feb 9, 1750 (Danville, NH R)
237.   Nancy 6, b Sept 30, 1754 (Danville, NH R)
238.   Samuel 6, b July 28, 1755 (Danville, NH R)
239.   Jonathan 6, b Aug 7, 1760 (Danville, NH R)

101.   Orlando Bagley 5, Orlando 4, Orlando 3, Orlando 2, Orlando 1 , b June 27, 1732; m Rebecca (Fitts) French, dau Nathaniel Fitts & Abigail (Heases), probably wife of Eliphalet French whom she m Apr 1, 1747. She b Dec 28, 1728, d Salisbury, MA, Apr 11, 1764 (Salis MA R). He was called captain and lived at Kingston, NH. Probably the Orlando Bagley who served on expedition against Crown Point in 1757, under Col. Nathaniel Merserve, company of Elisha Winslow, from May 12 to Nov 21.

Child:
240.   Molly 6, b Aug 17, 1761 (Salis MA R)

104.   Phineas Bagley 5, Orlando 4, Orlando 3, Orlando 2, Orlando 1 , b Mar 31, 1737; m Dec 27, 1757, Mary Hobbs at Kingston, NH (Church R). Probably the Phineas in expedition against Crown Point, regt of Col Nathaniel Meserve of Portsmouth, company Edward Winslow, May 16 - Nov 1, 1757; also Lt Col John Goffe's special force to defend the western frontier, Apr 11 - Nov 10, 1758. Also Crown Point expedition of 1760, Mar 31 - Nov 27. No children on Kingston, NH church records.

Child:
241.   Phineas, Jr. 6 There is a Phineas, Jr., who was in Dunbarton, NH in 1809. Since there is no other Phineas in the Orlando line nor in any other Bagley lines traced to this point, it appears this is probably right.

106.   Seth Bagley 5, Orlando 4, Orlando 3, Orlando 2, Orlando 1 , b Oct 27 or Nov 28, 1739; d Sept 24, 1804; m Abigail Greeley, intentions Dec 25, 1775 (not on Salis MA R but in

Greeley Genealogy. New England Genealogical Register says m Feb 17, 1767. She was b June 10, 1749, dau Illsley & Sarah (Morrill).

He was a soldier in the Rev War, Col Caleb Cushing's regt on Lexington Alarm, Apr 20, 1775, service 6 days (MA Rev War Rolls). Census of 1810 gives an Abigail as 30-40 with 1M under 10 and 2M 15-20 as of Amesbury, MA. If this is the right Abigail, there may have been more children.

Children:
242.   Sally 6, b Sept 6, 1775 (Salis MA R)
243.   Benjamin 6, b June 16, 1782; d Nov 25, 1825 (Salis MA R & tombstone, Amesbury which gives ae 47 at death)

110.   John Bagley 5, Orlando 4, Orlando 3, Orlando 2 Orlando 1 baptized at Kingston, NH, Mar 30, 1746; m Hannah French, Apr or June 24, 1769, at Kingston (Church R). No other information has been found - could go with Waterboro, ME line or Stanstead, QUE line. There is a John on Census of Candia, NH, who is unaccounted for. *This is the Waterboro ME line*

117.   Henry 5, Henry 4, Orlando 3, Orlando 2, Orlando 1 , b Apr 24, 1730 (recorded under Currier as his mother was Mary Currier; father given as Henry Bagley, but no marriage). He d Hartland, VT, Feb 22, 1796 (Hartland, VT R); m Lydia or Abigail Weed, May 11, 1747 (Ames MA R). The marriage record gives Lydia but children on records are given under Henry & Abigail.

Henry lived in Weare, NH, for a time but moved to Hartland, VT, probably about the time his sons Orlando and Thomas did in 1788.

Following from Probate Court records of Windsor Co, VT: " On the 1st Tuesday of February, 1803, Ebenezer Kelly and Thomas Bagley, both of Hartland, VT, were appt administrators of Henry Bagley, late of Hartland." There was no will and the estate was never settled. Census of 1790 gives four in his household.

Children: (Ames MA R except as noted)
244.   Dorothy 6, b Oct, 1747
245.   Sargent 6, b Jan 8, 1749/50
246.   Molly 6, b July 25, 1752
247.   Orlando 6, b May 30, 1755; d in Ohio about 1824
248.   Thomas Jefferson 6, b Feb 26, 1761; d June 19, 1838 (Tombstone Hartland, VT & Pension R)
249.   Henry 6, b Nov 9, 1763; d Sept 20, 1847 (Tombstone, Windsor, VT
250.   Winthrop 6, b Jan 8, 1768

118.   Winthrop Bagley 5, Henry 4, Orlando 3, Orlando 2, Orlando 1 , b Apr 25, 1734. Probably one of the detachment of foot soldiers, Aug 16, 1757, in Haverhill, MA, commanded by Joseph Badger, ensign of said company, out of Lt Col John Osgood's regt that marched on the last alarm for the relief of Fort William Henry as far as Worcester, MA (History of

119. Jonathan Bagley 5, Henry 4, Orlando 3, Orlando 2, Orlando , b Aug 5, 1736; d Mar 1, 1819 (Candia, NH R); m Anne Favour of Newton, NH, Dec 16, 1757, b 1738, d Apr 27, 1836 (Candia, NH R).

He lived in Amesbury, MA, and Newton, NH, until 1767, when he moved to Candia, NH. He was styled lieutenant and gentleman, is on the Candia Tax list in 1778, 1800 and 1810; was tax collector for Candia in 1784 and selectman in 1788; signed the Association Test in Candia, Apr, 1776 . In 1776 his parish tax was abated because he was a Baptist. On June 15, 1773, it was voted in Candia that there should be a pulpit built in the meetinghouse within 6 months and Jonathan Bagley entered his dissent (Candia, NH R). In 1810 he conveyed his rights in a mill and millyard to Nathan Bagley (Rockingham Co, NH Deeds).

He was a Rev War soldier and served as ensign in 1777 in Capt Moses Baker's Co, took part in the Stillwater and Saratoga battles in Lt Col Willard's regt, Gen Whipple's brigade (NH War Rolls). Later he guarded prisoners from Burgoyne's army at Winter Hill, Boston.

He made his will Mar 17, 1809; proved May 19, 1819. Moses Bagley was executor by request of Jonathan's widow, May 19, 1819. His will mentions wife, Anne; sons: John, Winthrop, Cutting, Jonathan, Moses, William and Nathan; daus: Dolly Thornton, wife of William Thornton; Polly Ward, wife of Simon Ward; Sally Duncan (mentions her children); Elizabeth; and Christina. On Nov 19, 1812, he made a codicil to his will and gave his dau Elizabeth, now Elizabeth Bennett, wife of Jeremiah Bennett, one dollar and to her two daus, Elizabeth and Ruth Bennett, twenty-five dollars to be equally divided between them (Rockingham Co NH Probate R).

Children:
251.   John 6, b Feb 11, 1759 (Newton & Candia, NH R).   His deposition for a pension says he was b in Newton, MA.   This later became Newton, NH.   He d Aug 29, 1833 (Tombstone, East Durham, NY)
252.   Dolly 6, b Oct 20, 1760 (Newton & Candia, NH R); probably d young
253.   Dorothea 6, b Nov 19, 1761 (Candia, NH R); d Dec 25, 1849 (Tombstone, Thornton, NH)
254.   Winthrop 6, b Aug 19, 1762 (Ames MA R). Deposition for pension says b Amesbury. He d July 21, 1853 (Tombstone, Thornton, NH)
255.   Cutting 6, b Jan 5, 1764 (Ames MA & Candia, NH R); d 1818 (DAR records, which must be in error since adm on his estate was granted June 19, 1817 (Catskill, NY Probate Records)
256.   Barnard 6, b Aug 25, 1766 (Ames MA R); probably d before his father as not mentioned in will in 1809
257.   Henry 6, b Jan 5, 1767 (Candia, NH R); d at New Orleans, 1792 (Candia, NH R)
258.   Jonathan 6, b Nov 11, 1769 (Candia, NH R); d Feb 2, 1853 (Tombstone, Searsmont, ME)

259. William, 6, b Nov 11, 1769 (Candia, NH R); d 1815
260. Molly 6, b Nov 11, 1773 (Candia, NH R); not in father's
will in 1809
261. Nathan 6, b Nov 29, 1775 (Candia, NH R); d Sept 27,
1848, ae 75 (NH R)
262. Elizabeth 6, b Jan 26, 1776 (Candia, NH R)
263. Moses 6, b Nov 6, 1778; d July 1, 1823 (Candia, NH R)
264. Sarah (Sally) 6, b July 29, 1781 (Candia, NH R);
probably d before 1809 as not mentioned in father's will but
her children are.
265. Joshua 6, b May 5, 1783 (Candia, NH R); not mentioned in
father's will
266. Christiana 6, b Aug 15, 1786 (Candia, NH R)

121. David Bagley 5, Henry 4, Orlando 3, Orlando 2, Orlando 1
b May 4, or 6, 1740, baptized Oct, 1753, Newton, NH; d before
1786 (Southbury, CT R). While we have no documentary proof,
strong evidence suggests that this David is the same David of
Southbury, CT. His son, Barnard, in his pension deposition
says he was brought up in Candia, NH, a few rods from John
Bagley's. Barnard, David and Winthrop, from time to time,
refer to their "Honored father, David Bagley" and it is known
that David of Southbury, CT had sons by these names.
     David Bagley of Woodbury, CT m Hannah or Sarah Bronson,
Mar 4, 1769 (Southbury, CT R). He probably m (2) Oct 1, 1775,
Agnes Hickok of NY state (Southbury, CT R). On Sept 15, 1790,
Annis (Agnes and Annis were interchangeable) Bagley of
Southbury, CT, widow of David, deceased, m Meridan Stetson of
Southbury CT. Barnard, David and Winthrop Bagley, all sold
land left to them by "their honored father, David Bagley." In
his deed, Barnard mentions Annis, widow of David. It would
appear that Barnard, David and Winthrop were David's children
by an unknown woman since their ages would make them born
before David's marriage in 1769. Ebenezer's mother was called
Jemima (last name unknown) and she lived with Ebenezer in
Warner, NH. Her connection with David or with Barnard, David
or Winthrop is unknown.

Children:
267. Ebenezer 6, b about 1763, tombstone says d Nov 29, 1841,
ae 77 (Warner, NH R). His mother was Jemima, d Sept 30, 1831,
ae 102, making her b about 1729 (Tombstone, Warner, NH). A
check of all vital records in places where Bagleys are known
to have lived reveals no marriage of a Jemima and David, nor
births of the elder sons. However, Candia, NH records are
scanty. Barnard Bagley says in his pension deposition that he
was born in Newton, but there is no record of his birth there.
The tradition of the Bagleys of Warner is that they came from
Amesbury (Warner was once granted as New Amsbury), and it
known that other Bagleys from Amesbury settled there. The
Newton, NH, Bagleys all came from Amesbury. Ebenezer is known
to have lived in Durham, NY, where Barnard settled and one of
his children died there. Barnard's brothers, David and
Winthrop, can be traced to the same locality. When Barnard
Bagley died in 1838, he left part of his estate to his son
Henry and parts to David and Barnard Bagley of Warner, NH

"sons of my deceased brother Ebenezer." A difficulty here is that according to his tombstone, Ebenezer died after Barnard. Warner was one of the cemeteries in which the old stones were recarved during WPA days and many mistakes were made by the carvers. We conclude that Ebenezer was brother to Barnard and a son of David; that David had children by Jemima or others. We have never been able to find any other Ebenezer Bagleys than the one who lived for a time in Durham, NY, and then moved to Warner, NH.

268. Barnard 6, b Aug, 1764, Newton, NH (Pension Rolls); d Dec 16, 1838, ae 75, East Durham, NY (Tombstone)

269. Winthrop 6, in 1792 sold left him by "his honored father" David Bagley of Southbury, CT (CT Deeds)

270. David 6 in 1792 sold land left him by "his honored father" David Bagley of Southbury, CT (CT Deeds)

271. Dolly 6 on list of family of David Bagley of Southbury & Woodbury, CT

272. Anne 6 b June 28, 1781 (Southbury, CT R); d 1852/57

273. Hulda 6, b Nov 10, 1783 (Southbury, CT R)

274. Harry 6 (Harvey or Henry) on list of family of David Bagley

122. Samuel Bagley 5, Henry 4, Orlando 3, Orlando 2, Orlando 1, b Aug 29, 1742; d Apr 25, 1805; m Nov, 1762, Mehitable at Candia, NH, who d Apr 27, 1834, at her daughter's C. H. Robinson (Candia, NH R).

He is on Candia, NH tax lists in 1778 and 1800. Rev War soldier serving as private in Capt Moses Baker's Co, from Candia, NH, which marched to Saratoga to join the Continental Army in 1777, in Col Willard's regt (NH War Rolls).

His will was made Nov 13, 1804; proved June 17, 1805; his wife was made executrix, June 17, 1805 (Rockingham Co NH Probate R). Mehitable conveyed land to her son Samuel, July 22, 1807 (Rockingham Co, NH Deeds). The Census of 1790 gives 2-2-5; that of 1810 gives 1F5-10, 1F 40-50.

Children:
275. David 6, b Mar 3, 1763 (Ames MA & Candia, NH R); d 1841, at West Topsham, VT (VT R)

276. Sarah 6, b Sept 1, 1765 (Ames MA & Candia, NH R); d before 1804 as her father's will states she is dead · and mentions heirs of his dau Sarah

277. Elijah 6, b Dec 7, 1766 (Ames MA & Candia, NH R); probably d before 1804 as not mentioned in father's will. There is an Elijah Bagley who d Feb 19, 1801, at Craftsbury, VT, but we cannot prove connection

278. Molly (Mary) 6, b Oct 29, 1768, Candia, NH R); living 1804

279. Jacob 6, b Dec 5, 1770 (Candia, NH R); living 1804

280. Samuel 6, b Jan 30, 1773 (Candia, NH R); living 1851 (Grafton Co, NH Deeds)

281. Mehitable 6, b Oct 10, 1774 (Candia, NH R); d Sept 1, 1812 (Belfast, ME R) m Christopher ?? of ??

282. Lydia 6, b May 5, 1777 (Candia, NH R); living 1804

283. Dolly 5, b Oct 9, 1780 (Candia, NH R); living 1804

284. Anna 6, b May 7, 1786 (Candia, NH R); living 1804

Connection between Bagley line & William John Walker, Box 292, Strafford, NH

Lydia Bagley dau of ~~Jonathan~~ *Samuel & Mehetable* of Candia, NH, b May 5, 1777; d Dec 6, 1816, Raymond, NH; m Capt Elisha Towle, June 14, 1801. They had a dau Hannah P., b July 22, 1811, Raymond, who m at Candia, George Larkin Dodge, b 1810, Salem, MA. They had a dau Sarah Jane Dodge, b Oct 6, 1834, Raymond, NH who m Mar 13, 1853, Raymond, NH, Samuel Plummer Ladd, b Feb 19, 1829 at Epping, NH. Their dau Laura Jane Ladd, m John Walker, These were the grandparents of William John Walker.

285.   Ruth 6, b June 28, 1789 (Candia, NH R); living 1804

123.   Jacob Bagley 5, Henry 4, Orlando 3, Orlando 2, Orlando 1
baptized Newton, NH, Oct 2, 1753 (probably born before that
date because Henry's children were not baptized at birth but
when he was readmitted to the church), m Mary or Molly.
        He moved to Candia, NH and was probably the Jacob Bagley
who signed the Association Test there in Apr, 1776.   Probably
the Rev War soldier in Col Isaac Wyman's regt, Capt Joseph
Dearborn's Co, July, 1776, in continental service against
Canda.   Advanced wages and bounty (NH War Rolls).   No record
of his war service in Washington, DC Archives.
        He moved to Montville, ME, about 1780. However, a Jacob
is still listed on Candia, NH Census for 1790 with 2-4-7.

Children:
286.   James 6, b 1769; d Aug 1825, ae 56 (Montville, ME R)
287.   Rhoda 6, b 1787; d Dec 9, 1870, ae 83 (Family R)
288.   David 6, b Apr 12, 1793 (Lee, ME R); d Sept 28, 1871, ae
78 (Tombstone, Lee, ME)
289.   Mary 6, b 1783; d Sept 16, 1805 (Family R)
290.   Levi 6, b 1775; d May 3, 18--, ae 65 (Tombstone,
Montville, ME cannot be read)
291.   Henry 6, b 1798; d Mar 13, 1871, ae 73 (Tombstone,
Montville, ME)
292.   Hannah 6, b 1779, Montville, ME (Family R)
293.   Eliza 6, b 1781, Montville, ME (Family R)
294.   Nancy 6, b 1796, Montville, ME (Family R)
295.   Jacob 6, b 1800, Montville, ME (Family R)
296.   William 6, b 1772, Montville, ME (Family R)

127.   Mary Bagley 5, David 4, Orlando 3, Orlando 2, Orlando 1
b 1738 (?); living 1792; m Nathan Gould of Newton, NH, Dec 25,
1757 (Ames MA R).

Child:
297.   Nathan 6

128.   Judith Bagley 5, David 4, Orlando 3, Orlando 2, Orlando
1, b July 20, 1740; d Apr 17, 1828; m Capt Cutting Favour, son
Cutting & Mary (Wells), b Mar 11, 1736/37, d Hill, NH, Mar 8,
1822, ae 85 (Ames MA R & tombstone, Hill Center, NH).   There
is no remaining tombstone for Judith.
        Capt Favour was the first permanent settler in New
Chester, now Hill, NH, having made a settlement in the early
months of 1766. Mrs Favour was probably the first white women
in the new town. The site of his log cabin was about a mile
south of Smith's River. He owned large tracts of land in New
Chester and New Hampton, NH; was a member of the Committee of
Safety in New Chester in 1776 and served as lieutenant in the
Bennington campaign in 1777 and later at Saratoga (History of
Bristol, NH by Musgrove.)

Children : (History of Bristol, NH)
298.   Sarah 6, b Newton, NH, Dec 24 or 28, 1759; d Hill, NH,
May 28, 1843

299. John 6, b Newton, NH, Jan 15 or 17, 1762; d in snow storm, Jan 15, 1782
300. Mary 6, b Newton, Jan 21, 1764; d Apr 15, 1844
301. Jacob 6, b Newton, May 21, 1766
302. Isaac 6, b Hill, Aug 24, 1768, the first white child b in New Chester; d Mar 28, 1859
303. Judith 6, b Hill; d New Hampton, June 15, 1850
304. Elizabeth 6, b Hill, Feb 10, 1772
305. Dorothy 6, b Hill, Oct 6, 1774
306. Hannah 6, b Hill, Aug 6, 1775
307. Moses 6, b Hill, July 11, 1778; d Oct 7, 1825 (Tombstone, Hill Center)
308. Aaron 6, b Hill, Aug 13, 1780; d Sept 4, 1835 . (Tombstone, Hill Center)

129. Sarah Bagley 5, David 4, Orlando 3, Orlando 2, Orlando 1, b May 15 or 17, 1743; d before 1779; m Joseph Collins, Jan 17, 1760, at Kingston, NH (Kingston, NH R). Her father's will, dated Nov 20, 1792, mentions her as Sarah Collins, late wife of Joseph Collins, deceased.

Children: (Kingston, NH R)
309. Moses 6, b Aug 6, 1761
310. Joseph 6, b Mar 17, 1763
311. Sarah 6, b Sept 29, 1767
312. Mary 6, b Sept 9, 1770

130. David Bagley 5, David 4, Orlando 3, Orlando 2, Orlando 1 b July 20, 1745; baptized Oct 13, 1745; living 1820; m (1) Hannah Ferrin, dau Jonathan & Sarah (Wells), b Dec 17, 1746 (Ames MA R), d May 20, 1789 (Warner, NH R); m (2) Hannah Colby of Warner, NH, Jan 17, 1792 (Warner, NH R).

He went to Warner, NH, and it is a question whether it is he or his father listed on the Proprietors' Records in 1767. A David Bagley is listed on Proprietors of Warner in 1767 and on Masonian Proprietors, Dec 24, 1767 (NH Provincial Papers). The History of Warner, NH says that Joshua Bagley was the father of David, but this is a mistake, and Harriman confused Joshua Bayley with Bagley. There was a Joshua Bagley in Warner before 1773, but it was David's brother and not his father. Their father was David Bagley of Newton, NH. This Joshua Bagley could not have been town clerk in 1766 as Harriman says as he would have been only thirteen years old, and he could not have signed a petition to settle in Warner with his family at the age of eleven. The Bagley, Harriman has listed as one promising to settle in Warner in 1763 should read Joshua Bayley.

One June 28, 1769, David and two others were chosen as a committee to prosecute trespassers. In 1767, he was given a grant of land in New Rye, NH. At Amesbury, MA, Oct 24, 1771, David and one other were chosen a committee to get the town incorporated. At a meeting held in 1772 at Warner, David and one other were chosen a committee to repair the road to Perrystown and probably some provision was made at that meeting to build a bridge over Amesbury River, for the next year, 1773, the bridge was built. At an annual meeting, Mar,

1784, the Proprietors took steps for having ample grounds set off for a meetinghouse lot, for a cemetery, and for a permanent training field: David Bagley and one other were appointed a committee to carry forward this project. They attended to their duties and reported that they had set off from the meetinghouse lot, thirteen acres for a burying ground, a training field and highways. He was selectman in 1779 and town clerk 1781-82, and in that year the town voted to provide a record birth book. In 1783 and 1784, he was elected selectman and town clerk. He was town clerk from 1787 to 1795; then again from 1797 through 1820, except for the year 1812. He built the first framed house in Warner in 1774 (Harriman).

By his father's will, David was left land in Warner. In 1768 Jonathan Ferrin of Newton, NH willed to his dau Hannah Bagley the sum of 7 pounds, 10 shillings, lawful money (NH Probate R).

David was a Rev War soldier in Daniel Flood's Co, in 1776.

Children:
313. Nathan 6, b Mar 13, 1768, Warner, NH; d Nov 1, 1843 (Tombstone, West Topsham, VT)
314. Jonathan 6, b Aug 13, 1772 (Warner, NH R); d Nov 1, 1860 (Bradford, NH R & tombstone
315. Elizabeth 6, b Sept 16, 1774 (Warner, NH R)
316. Philip 6, b July 16, 1777 (Warner, NH R)
317. Sarah 6, b Dec 2, 1779 (Warner, NH R)
318. Molly 6, b Feb 10, 1783 (Warner, NH R)
319. Hannah 6, b Nov 13, 1788 (Warner, NH R)
320. David 6, b Oct 17, 1794 (Warner, NH R)
321. Joshua 6, b Dec 29, 1796 (Warner, NH R); d Aug 21, 1866, unm (Tombstone, Warner, NH)

131. Dorothy Bagley 5, David 4, Orlando 3, Orlando 2, Orlando 1, b Jan 11, 1748; baptized June 5, 1748; d before 1792 as her father's will made Nov 20, 1792, says "Dorothy Currier wife of Thomas Currier, deceased." He was probably son of Ebenezer and Ann (Jones), b Dec 1, 1745 (Ames MA R). Merrimac, MA cemetery gives the following children for Thomas & Dorothy Currier: Rebecca Bagley Currier, d Feb 3, 1843, ae ae 37; Dorothy, d Dec 16, 1808, ae 21; Leonard, d Nov 11, 1849, ae 42. If these are the children of Dorothy Bagley and Thomas Currier only Dorothy would have been born before 1792 when Dorothy Bagley is known to have been dead. Thomas' second wife was also named Dorothy. There is no definite proof that this is the right Thomas Currier, altho the name Bagley is certainly suggestive.

133. Joshua Bagley 5, David 4, Orlando 3 Orlando 2, Orlando 1 b Apr 17, 1752; baptized Oct, 1753; d Apr 9, 1809. His death is entered on Warner, NH vital records, but both he and his wife have tombstones in Newton even though his wife, Judith d Apr 28, 1821, ae 70, at Warner.

He was a Rev War soldier in Col David Gilman's regt; enlisted Dec 1776, Daniel Gordon's Co. Regt raised by State of New Hampshire and sent to re-inforce the army in New York from Dec 1776 to Jan 5 and Mar 15, 1777 (Grave regional records of NH American Legion).

He conveyed land to his brother Elijah in Newton, Sept 9, 1799 (Rockingham Co NH Deeds).

His will, proved Apr 29, 1809, mentions wife but not by name; daus: Dorothy and Judy; also Isaac Morrill who was my daughter Lydia's executor. Will witnessed by Charles, Enoch and Moses Bagley. Inventory of his estate was $2123.50, May 29, 1809. Inventory showed 42 acres of land in Kingston, NH (Rockingham Co, NH Probate R).

Children: (Newton, NH R except as noted)
322. Mary 6, b Aug 17, 1774; probably d young
323. Molly 6, b Aug 17, 1774; probably d young. These two children could have been twins or one and the same. On Newton, NH records we found Mary's mother given as Lydia, and Molly's as Molly. NH Historical Society Records under Newton give Judith as mother of both Mary and Molly. Molly was a nickname for Mary.
324. Ruth 6, b Mar 7, 1778; d May 13, 1806 (Tombstone, Newton)
325. Lydia 6, b Oct 2, 1780; d May 31, 1804 (Tombstone, Newton)
326. Dolly 6, b Sept 20, 1782; d Apr 11, 1847 (Tombstone, Newton)
327. Judith 6, b Jan 17, 1787; mentioned in father's will in 1809

134. Elijah Bagley 5, David 4, Orlando 3, Orlando 2, Orlando 1 baptized Aug 22, 1756; d Feb 2, 1814; m Theodate Sanborn, dau Worcester & Hannah (Fowler), b Sept 15, 1751 (Sanborn) Genealogy); probably m (2) Hannah Sanborn of Kingston, NH, Aug 23, 1795 (Kingston, NH R), d Newton, July, 1842.

Elijah lived in Newton and bought land there from one Peake. Jonathan Sanborn and Hannah Bagley, wife to Elijah Bagley of Newton, NH, are given as guardians of John Sanborn, her son, and sold land in Kingston, Jan, 1801, and bought land in Newton in the same year (Rockingham Co, NH Probate R).

Hannah Bagley and David Bagley were adm of Elijah's estate and an account was given Mar 20, 1816 (Rockingham Co, NH Probate R).

Children: (Newton, NH R)
328. David 6, b Feb 22, 1777; d Oct 5, 1854 (West Topsham, VT R & Tombstone)
329. William 6, b July 22, 1779; d before Sept 7, 1809 (Essex Co MA Probate R)
330. Enoch 6, b Jan 13, 1782; d May 19, 1823, Newton
331. Hannah 6, b Sept 13, 1785; living 1842
332. Elizabeth 6, b Aug 29, 1787; d Apr 15, 1847 (Tombstone, Newton)
333. Sarah (Sally) 6, b Jan 13, 1790; d Dec 24, 1848 (Tombstone, Newton)
334. Molly (Polly) 6, b July 10, 1792; d Dec 12, 1840

(Tombstone, Newton)

135. John Bagley 5, Jonathan 4, Orlando 3, Orlando 2, Orlando
1, b Oct 18, 1737; d Jan 14, 1830. In 1805, he sold a portion
of the Bagley farm at Royalsborough, ME to Elijah Macomber.
History of Durham, ME says he inherited the old Bagley farm in
Durham from his father, but is more probable that his father
gave it to him before his death as John Bagley is not
mentioned in Jonathan's will in 1779. He m 1764, Mary Lowell.

136. William Bagley 5, Jonathan 4, Orlando 3, Orlando 2,
Orlando 1 , b Jan 14/15, 1738/39; not mentioned in father's
will in 1779; probably m Rebecca Hildreth at Dracut, MA, Nov
28, 1771; dau Josiah & Rebecca (Wright), b Jan 22, 1741/42
(Dracut, MA R).

138. Valentine Bagley 5, Jonathan 4, Orlando 3, Orlando 2,
Orlando 1 , b Jan 1, 1742/43; d Apr, 1780; m Sarah Currier,
Dec 21, 1763 (Ames MA R), b July 5, 1743, dau Daniel & Electa,
d Dec 7, 1821 (Ames MA R). She m (2) published Nov 13, 1790,
David Blaisdell (Ames MA R)
    He was a miller and yeoman and lived in Amesbury, MA;
owned land on the County Road in Durham, ME, in 1770, and
received part of his father's farm on River Road in Durham,
Feb 7, 1779.
    In an account of Moses Cooper of those who sent
provisions to Cambridge, MA for the use of the army in Rev
War, we find Valentine Bagley who received 3 pounds, 16
shillings and 8 pence for 23 pounds of pork.
    Sarah was Granted adm of Valentine's estate, Oct 12,
1781, and on the same day was granted guardianship of William,
2 yrs old, son of Valentine Bagley (Essex Co, MA Probate R).

Children: (Newbury, MA Records except as noted)
335. John 6, b Jan 31, 1765; d Apr 19, 1826 (Salis MA R)
336. Dorothy 6, b Jan 20, 1767; d Aug, 1788 (Ames MA R)
337. William 6, b 1769; d 1773, ae 2 (Ames MA R)
338. Sally 6, b 1771; d 1773, ae 2 (Ames MA R)
339. Valentine 6, b Jan 1, 1773; d Jan 19, 1839 (Ames MA R)
340. William 6, b May 27, 1780; d July 12, 1812, ae 33
(Tombstone, Ames MA)

139. Dorothy Bagley 5, Jonathan 4, Orlando 3 Orlando 2
Orlando 1 , b Feb 12, or 13, 1744/45; living 1816; m John
Cushing, Esquire, of Boxford, MA, Dec 1, 1763, son Rev John &
Elizabeth (Martyn), b at Boxford, May 1, 1741; d Freeport, ME,
1813, graduate of Harvard in 1761.
    They moved to Salisbury, MA, until the death of his
father in 1722, when they moved to Boxford, MA, where his
father had been pastor for 30 years. In 1782, they moved to
Durham, ME, bringing his widowed mother after having resided
for a time in North Yarmouth, ME. Dorothy was living in
Freeport, ME, in 1816, but is said to have died shortly
thereafter. He was a capt in a Co in Col Samuel Johnson's
regt of militia which marched on the Lexington Alarm in 1775.
    They lived on the northern part of lot 80 in Durham.

Traces of the old house, which decayed over fifty years ago (1899) may still be seen, on a hillock near the bank of the river just south of the gully. John Cushing was a prominent man in Durham, serving as moderator of the town meeting in 1783 and as selectman, town treasurer, and on various committees. In 1790, he moved to Freeport, ME, where he was justice of the peace, selectman, treasurer, a judge, and member of the General Court of MA. He was on the Board of Overseers of Bowdoin College from 1796 to 1813 (History of Durham, ME).

Children:
341. Elizabeth 6, b Sept 1, 1767 (Boxford, MA R); d Freeport, ME, June, 1858
342. Dorothy 6, b May 2, 1769 (Boxford, MA R); d Dec 28, 1863 (History Durham, ME)
343. John 6, b June 23, 1771 (Boxford, MA R) d Pownal, ME
344. Jonathan 6, b Sept 14, 1773; d Freeport, ME
345. Edward 6, b Jan 17, 1778; d Jan 16, 1797 (History Durham, ME)
346. Sarah 6, b Mar 12, 1785; d same day (History Durham, ME)

140. Orlando Bagley 5, Jonathan 4, Orlando 3, Orlando 2, Orlando 1, b Nov 5, 1747; d Nov 23, 1807 (Ames MA R); m Hannah Pearson, Apr 27, 1770, d Oct 4, 1825 (Ames MA R), dau Mary Currier & widow of Thomas Pearson.
     Lived in Amesbury and in 1788 was styled "Gentleman". He received the homestead in Amesbury, MA, from his father and deed for 400 acres of land on the county road in Durham, ME, where he did not remain because he lived at the homestead in Amesbury. Probably marched to the Lexington Alarm in 1775.
     Both he and his wife renewed their baptismal covenants on Aug 18, 1800, at First Church, Amesbury. He made his will May 12, 1807; proved June 3, 1807. He mentioned wife Hannah; son, Jonathan; dau Dorothy (Essex Co MA Probate R).

Children:
347. Dorothy 6, b July 5, 1771; d 1818 (Ames MA R); family records say d Apr 6, 1815
348. David Wells 6, b Oct 25, 1774 (Ames MA R); not mentioned in father's will in 1807
349. Molly (Mary), b Dec 3, 1776 (Ames MA R); not mentioned in father's will in 1807
350. Hannah 6, b Jan 4, 1782 (Ames MA R); not mentioned in father's will in 1807
351. Jonathan 6, b Jan 8, 1785 (Ames MA R); d June 23, 1861 (Tombstone, Londonderry, NH)

141. Jonathan Bagley 5, Jonathan 4, Orlando 3, Orlando 2, Orlando 1, b July 29, 1750; d Sept 26, 1791; m Sarah Currier, Jan 17, 1773 (Ames MA R), dau Barnard & Mary (Emery), b Feb 22, 1757; left destitute, and m (2) Ephraim Morrill of Warner, NH, Nov 6, 1785 (Ames MA R). Amesbury records say that "the sd Sarah declared before me and several other witnesses that she had no estate of her own or any that was her late husband's and the clothes that she was married in was borrowed

clothes, Nov 6, 1785." This was a device used to prevent
creditors of a first husband from collecting from the second.
Adm on estate Sept 26, 1791.

Children:
352.   Mary 6, b Mar 27, 1773 (Ames MA R)
353.   Sarah 6, b Sept 16, 1778 (Ames MA R)

142. Sarah Bagley 5, Jonathan 4, Orlando 3, Orlando 2,
Orlando 1 ,b Feb 10, 1756; d 1776; m Nathan Bartlett. He
probably m (2) Mrs. Hannah Blaisdell, Nov 15, 1779 (Ames MA
R).

Child:
354.   Dorothy 6, b Oct 25, 1773 (Ames MA R); mentioned in
grandfather's will May 23, 1779

157. Orlando Israel Bagley 5, Thomas 4, Orlando 3, Orlando 2,
Orlando 1, b Oct 25, 1747; d Aug 22, 1797; m Mary Snow, Apr
21, 1768 (Salis MA R), b Kingston, NH, May 19, 1747, probably
moved to Durham, ME, between 1770 and 1773, as their third
child was born there.
     Israel died at Savannah, GA, of yellow fever.   Col
Jonathan Bagley deeded him land in Durham, Oct 2, 1782.   In
1784, he deeded his son Enoch land.
     The following sketch is from History of Durham, ME, by
Stackpole: " Captain O. Israel Bagley settled in Royalsborough
early in the year 1770, on lot 37, and built a large two-story
square house which is still standing (1899), and was the
oldest house in Durham. Just north of his house was his
store, and a little further on, in the alder swamp was a
potash manufactory. His house was also a public inn, as his
account book shows; he was a shoemaker, withal. He built the
first grist mill, run by wind. He built the River Road from
S. W. bend to Lewiston Falls. The first school in
Royalsborough was kept at his house. He frequently was
moderator and one of the officials of the town. He was
captain of the earliest militia company known in
Royalsborough. About 1790 he abandoned storekeeping and
became master of a vessel, the Mary Ann. He kept the first
store in Royalsborough and his account book in 1899 was in
possession of William D. Roak. It is a book twelve inches
long by four wide and contains 263 pages, bound in sheep skin,
well-sewed. It was evidently used as an account book by his
father, Thomas Bagley, before it came into his possession.
Entries are found in it as early as Apr 17, 1745."

Children:
355.   Mary 6, b Nov 22, 1768 (History of Durham, ME)
356.   Elizabeth 6, b Apr 26, 1770; baptized Apr 7, 1771
(Second Church, Salis MA)
357.   Hannah 6, b Durham, ME, June 14, 1773; d Oct, 1843
(History of Durham, ME)
358.   Susannah 6, b Mar 9, 1777; d June 5, 1798 (History of
Durham, ME)
359.   Thomas 6, b 1779, Ripley, ME; d Apr 26, 1842 (ME R)

360. Enoch 6, probably, if Israel deeded land to his son Enoch, he must have existed but we have not been able to pick him up later

158. Thomas Bagley 5, Thomas 4, Orlando 3, Orlando 2, Orlando 1, b May 2, 1750; m (1) Molly Weir or Wier, May 31, 1773 (Salis MA R), d his consort in Salisbury, MA, Jan 23, 1818 (Salis MA R); probably m (2) Belinda Knowles of Seabrook, intentions Aug 12, 1818 (Salis MA R), as he is the only Thomas who could have styled "Jr" at that date. Census of 1790 gives five in his household over 16 years old.
     He was a Rev War soldier, private in Capt Henry Morrill's Co, Apr 20, 1775, Service 6 dys. Also, private Capt Oliver Titcomb's Co, Col Jacob Gerrish's regt of guards service from Feb 3, 1778 to Apr 2, 1778, guarding prisoners of Burgoyne's army after his surrender. Roll dated Winter Hill (MA War Rolls). He enlisted July 8, 1778 in Capt Jonathan Evan's Co, and served six months at North Kingston, RI. Enlisted Oct 14, 1779 in Capt Stephen Perkin's Co, Col Gerrish's regt. This regt detached from the militia of Suffolk and Essex Counties to reinforce the army of General Washington. Discharged Nov 22, 1779 (MA Rev War Rolls).

Children: (Salis MA R)
361. Rhoda 6, b May 18, 1774
362. Polly 6, b May 2, 1776; d Sept 26, 1804 (History of Sanbornton, NH)
363. Sukey 6, b Jan 20, 1779
364. Ruth 6, b Aug 10, 1783; probably d Jan 13, 1829
365. Amos 6, b June 18, 1792; d Aug 8, 1811
366. Joseph 6, b June 18, 1792

160. Sarah Bagley 5, Thomas 4, Orlando 3, Orlando 2, Orlando 1, b June 15, 1755; m Elliott Frost of Royalsborough, ME, July 28, 1774 (Salis MA R). He d Jan 3, 1840, ae 92.

Children: From History of Old Kittery, ME
367. Ruth 6, b Brunswick, ME, Mar 6, 1777; d Aug 30, 1798
368. Thomas 6, b Berwick, ME, Jan 13, 1776; d Aug 21, 1779
369. Ruth 6, b Mar 1778, at Berwick, ME (may be same as Ruth above)
370. Sarah 6, b 1780, Berwick, ME
371. Eliott 6, b Jan 28, 1782, Sanford, ME
372. Thomas 6, b May 14, 1784
373. Elizabeth 6, b May 15, 1786
374. William 6, b Sept 23, 1788
375. Levi 6, b Oct 29, 1791
376. Enoch 6, b July 22, 1794
377. James 6, b Oct 28, 1796
378. Dolly 6, b Oct 30, 1799
379. Love 6

161. Enoch Bagley 5, Thomas 4, Orlando 3, Orlando 2, Orlando 1, b Feb 4, 1758; d Nov 30, 1842; m Merriam Hoyt, Apr 5, 1781, b 1762, d July 19, 1844 (History of Durham, ME and tombstones, Troy, ME). He was a shipwright and lived first in

Amesbury and later in Durham and Troy, ME. He signed a petition in May 1777 for a separate militia from East Kingston, NH. He was a joiner in 1789 and moved to Troy, ME, between 1797 and 1802. He sold his pew in the Congregational Church in Durham, ME, and was one of the committe to see the meetinghouse finished.

He was a Rev War soldier, and the NH Rev War Rolls give the following: " Abstract form Capt Henry Butler's Pay Roll for his company in Col Thomas Bartlett's regt raised for the State of NH for the defense of West Point, 1780, Enoch Bagley. Entered July 4, 1780; discharged Oct 25, 1780. Service 3 months and 22 dys."

The following from NH Pension Rolls: "Aug 5, 1832, Jan 14, 1833, and June 3, 1824, Enoch Bagley of Troy, Kenebec Co, ME, deposed that in Apr 1775, he enlisted as a sergeant under Capt Butler from Loudon, NH, and marched to West Point; service 4 months, that he was born in Salisbury, MA, Feb 4, 1757; lived in Kingston, NH, at the time of entrance and about 30 years ago moved to Troy, that part of the time he was at Kittery Point where he was employed in manufacturing Cartridge boxes and Stocking guns, that Col Salts officiated at Kittery Point as an enginner in laying out the fortifications, thas he Enoch Bagley labored on the fort there built and wheeled away the first barrelful of earth that was excavated on the ground."

"Andrew Mace of Readfield, ME, a Revolutionary pensioner testified to acquaintance with Enoch Bagley since they were boys together in Kingston, NH, and also to serving with him at Kittery Point."

"Service for 3 months and 22 days in Henry Butler's Co, beginning from July 4, 1780, was all that could be found."

"June 10, 1854, Reuben Bagley of Bangor for himself and Jonathan Bagley, Israel Bagley, Thomas H. Bagley and Sarah Smith, Children and heirs-at-law of Enoch Bagley, who d in 1842, applied. Rejected because six months service not proven."

Children: (From History of Durham, ME, or from tombstones, Troy, ME)
380. Jonathan 6, b June 8, 1782; d Mar 8, 1881, tombstone says d Feb 28, 1881
381. Enoch 6, b Jan 8, 1788; d Feb 16, 1864
382. Ruth 6, b 1790; d Dec 19, 1831
383. Israel 6, b July 1, 1793; d Mar 28, 1868
384. Thomas H. 6, b 1797; d Oct 18, 1877
385. Moses 6, b 1798; d Sept 12, 1869
386. Reuben 6, b Sept or Oct 21, 1802; d May 11, 1892
387. Sarah (Sally) 6, b Feb 23, 1805; d Oct 24, 1882

163. Dorothy Bagley 5, Thomas 4, Orlando 3, Orlando 2, Orlando 1, baptized July 22, 1764; probably m John Morrill, son Jacob & Dorothy (Brown). Dorothy (Brown) Morrill was the widow of Nathaniel Brown and Jacob Morrill's second wife. Intentions of m between Dorothy Bagley and John Morrill, Apr 21, 1781 (Salis MA R); he b Apr 6, 1759, d Nov 16, 1811 (Salis MA R). He made his will Oct 12, 1811; proved Dec 5, 1811; mentions wife Dorothy (Essex Co MA Probate R). He was of the

West Parish, Salisbury, MA, and was a blacksmith. She d his
widow Jan 15, 1827, ae 63 (Salis MA R).

Children:
388. Susannah 6, living in 1811; probably oldest child
389. Dorothy 6, living 1811; probably next oldest child
390. Moses 6, b Apr 8, 1806; probably d Jan 12, 1834 (Salis
MA R)
391. John 6, d Sept 17, 1824 (Salis MA R)
392. Thomas 6, d June 6, 1825 (Salis MA R)
393. Ruth 6, d unm Dec 23, 1844 (Salis MA R)
394. Lois 6, d May 5, 1824, unm (Salis MA R)
395. Charlotte 6, m Stephen Osgood, Jr., Mar 20, 1821 (Salis
MA R)

174. Merriam Bagley 5, John 4, John 3, Orlando 2 Orlando 1 ,
b June 6 or 8, 1737; d Oct 5, 1774; m Apr 20, 1757, Oliver
Blaisdell at Second Church, Amesbury, MA, son Samuel & Dorothy
(Barnard), b Apr 15, 1736; adm granted on his estate, Mar 9,
1803. Lived in Amesbury, MA, and was a joiner and ship
carpenter.

Children:(Amesbury MA R unless otherwise noted)
396. Levi 6, b Sept 20, 1757; probably the Levi Blaisdell who
drowned in Merrimac River near Nichol's Creek, Sept 20, 1808
397. Merriam 6, b Sept 10, 1759; living 1806
398. Joseph 6, b June 15, 1761; d Aug 20, 1762
399. Joseph 6, b June 19, 1766; living 1806
400. Dorothy 6, b Feb 17, 1768; m Feb 21, 1789, David Bagley
of Amesbury; d May 26, 1850, ae 82 (also family R)
401. Judith 6, b Nov 11, 1769; d Aug 9, 1839
402. Ruth 6, b Jan or Feb 12, 1769; probably d before 1802;
not mentioned in settlement of father's estate

175. John Bagley 5, John 4, John 3, Orlando 2, Orlando 1 , b
Aug 28, 1738; m Mary Lowell, Dec 6, 1764, by Dr Samuel Deane,
dau Abner & Lydia (Purrington), b Falmouth, ME, July 30, 1728
"ye Sabbath Day", d Jan 14, 1830, ae 91 (Journal of Rev Thomas
Smith and Rev Samuel Deane, Pastors, 1st Church, Portland, ME)
    He was a sargeant and chaise-maker. They lived at
Falmouth, ME, where he belonged to the First Church. A deed,
dated at Falmouth, ME, in 1771, gives, John Bagley, Mary
Bagley, Abner Lowell, Joshua Lowell, John Lowell, all of
Falmouth, being children and heirs of Abner Lowell, late of
said Falmouth, Mariner, deceased.

Children:
403. Abner 6, b Mar 16, 1766 (1st church, Falmouth, ME R); d
1851 (Tombstone, Newburyport, MA). MA R say d Sept 28, 1851,
ae 85
404. John 6, b Mar 18, 1770 (1st church, Falmouth, ME R); d
unm
405. Daniel 6, b Mar, 1772 (1st church, Falmouth, ME R)
406. Mary 6, b Mar 2, 1777 (1st church, Falmouth, ME R); d
Mar 9, 1802, ae 24 (Tombstone, Portland, ME

178. Daniel Bagley 5, John 4, John 3, Orlando 2, Orlando 1 , b
Feb 3, 1745; d 1781; m at Falmouth, ME, Feb 26, 1772, Sarah
Stewart, b 1749, d May 6, 1774, ae 27; m (2) June 5, 1774,
Dorcas Tucker, dau Josiah & Mary (Thrasher?). She m (2)
Abijah Poole of Portland, ME, intentions, Nov 10, 1786; m Dec
14, 1786 (Portland, ME R).

Daniel was a private in the Rev War: Capt Joseph Noyes
Co, enlisted July 11, 1775, roll made up to Dec 31, 1775.
Service 6 mos, 5 dys, at Falmouth.

On Jan 5, 1814, Theophilus Goodridge of Amesbury, MA, and
his wife, Nancy, in right of his said wife, and Betsey Bagley
of said town, sold land in Newton, NH, by land of Joshua
Bagley. Betsey and Nancy are given as dau of Daniel Bagley,
deceased (Rockingham Co, NH Probate R).

Children:
407.   Daniel 6, b May 6, 1774; d 1803, at sea
408.   Hannah 6, b 1779 (ME R); probably d young
409.   Betsey 6 (probably)
410.   Nancy 6, (Probably)
411.   Dorcus 6, b Aug 29, 1781; d July 24, 1875, ae 93 (ME R)
Portland, ME newspaper for 1785 says of Dorcus, dau of Daniel:
"Dorcus Bagley was born in a house on Spring St., opposite the
great spring which gave the street its name and yet flows
filling a large reservoir under the corner of South Street.
Spring Street was then only a lane running from Love Lane now
Central Steet up to the spring from whence washing water was
obtained for all parts of the town, When Miss Bagley was only
six weeks old, her father was lost with his vessel and all
hands on Newburyport bar when entering during the night. By
this misfortune her mother was left a widow with four small
children."

179. Jacob Bagley 5, John 4, John 3, Orlando 2, Orlando 1 , b
Jan 8, 1747; probably d before Sept 27, 1798. Census of 170
gives a Jacob living in Amesbury, MA , with wife and three
females over 16 years of age. This seems to be the only Jacob
to whom this could apply. No other information has been
found. A family source, sometimes unreliable, says he m Mary
and had a son, Jacob, b May 23, 1766 at Amesbury, MA.

180. Moses Bagley 5, John 4, John 3 Orlando 2, Orlando 1 , b
May 2, 1750; d before Nov 30, 1779; m Kezia Person, published
Mar 18, 1775, dau Thomas & Mary (Currier), b Mar 28, 1756, d
Danville, VT (Ames MA & family R). After Moses' death, she m
Joseph Tilton of Louden, NH, Oct 20, 1783, b Sept 7, 1748, at
East Kingston, d Danville, VT, Feb 22, 1825 (Tombstone,
Danville, VT).

Moses was a chaise-maker and lived at Newburyport, MA.
Adm granted on his estate, Nov 30, 1779 to John McCall and
Philip Bagley gave bond, Dec14, 1770 (Essex Co MA Probate R).
On Aug 24, 1784, she had set off her dower rights in the
estate of her late husband, Moses Bagley, late of Newburyport,
chaise-maker.

Children:

412. Thomas 6, b Nov 21, 1775/76 (Ames MA R); d at sea, Nov 19, 1791
413. John 6, b Jan 19, 1778 (Newburyport, MA R)
414. Moses 6, b Feb 19, 1780 (Ames MA R); d Martinico, Aug 14, 1798 (Newburyport, MA R)

182. Aaron Bagley 5, John 4, John 3, Orlando 2, Orlando 1 , b Oct 5, 1753; d July 18, 1833, at West Topsham, VT; m July 12, 1785, Hannah Weed, probably dau Ephraim & Hannah (Barnard), b Sept 2, 1758, d West Topsham, VT, July 12, 1838, ae 80 (Ames MA R & tombstones, W Topsham, VT).

He was a cordwainer in 1781, yeoman in 1787 and 1789, lived in Amesbury and West Topsham, VT. His father's estate gave him some property, Sept 13, 1793 (Essex Co MA Probate R). He was a Rev War soldier; private in Capt John Currier's Co, Col Isaac Merrill's regt and marched on the Lexington Alarm, Apr 19, 1775. Service 7 dys. Also Capt Moses Nowell's Co, Col Titcomb's regt; roll made up from time of arrival at Providence, RI, to May 4, 1777; discharged July 4, 1777; service time two months and nine days, from Apr 21, 1777 (MA War Rolls).

He made his will, Oct 26, 1822; probated 1833; mentions wife, but not by name; sons: Moses, John, Aaron, William and Ephraim, who was executor of the will; dau, Hannah (District of Bradford, VT Probate R).

Children:
415. Moses 6, b Dec 27, 1786 (Ames MA R); d July 14, 1838 (West Topsham VT tombstone)
416. John 6, b July 7, 1788 (Ames MA R); d Jan 19, 1878 (tombstone, Albany, VT)
417. Aaron 6
418. Hannah 6
419. William 6, b Jan 29, 1796; d Sept 19, 1871 (tombstone, Corinth, VT)
420. Ephraim 6, b 1797; d July 25, 1855 (tombstone, West Topsham, VT)

183. Philip Bagley 5, John 4, John 3, Orlando 2, Orlando 1 , b Dec 9 or 19, 1755; d Apr 24, 1844; m Sarah Bigelow of Newburyport, MA, June 17, 1780; buried New Hill Burying ground; chaise-maker and for many years sheriff of Essex Co, MA, and keeper of the jail in Newburyport, MA. Will made Oct 5, 1843 (Essex Co. MA Probate R).

Rev War soldier: private Capt James Sargent's Co, Col James Frye's regt and marched on Lexington Alarm, Apr 19, 1775 (Service not given). Also return of men in camp at Cambridge, May 17 1775; also company return dated Oct, 1775; also order for bounty coat of its equivalent in money, dated Cambridge, Sept 26, 1775 (MA War Rolls). US pensioner on rolls, May 23, 1833, ae 78 (US Pension R).

Children:
421. James 6, b Nov 8, 1780; d at sea, Dec, 1801 (Newburyport, MA R)
422. Philip 6, b Aug 28, 1782 (Newburyport, MA R)

423.   Nancy 6, b Dec 25, 1784; d Dec 28, 1790 (Newburyport, MA R)
424.   Joseph 6, b Jan 3, 1786; d Nov 8, 1809 (Newburyport, MA R)
425.   Charles 6, b July 28, 1788 (Newburyport, MA R); d young
426.   Charles 6, b July 25, 1789 (Newburyport, MA R)
427.   Nancy 6, b Jan 14, 1791 (Newburyport, MA R)
428.   John 6, b Apr 1, 1793; d Oct 21, 1804 (Newburyport, MA R)
429.   Lucy 6, b Apr 13, 1797 (Newburyport, MA R); d Nov 11, 1870 (Edwards Genealogy)

190.   Timothy Bagley 5, Timothy 4, John 3, Orlando 2, Orlando 1, b Oct 26, 1749; d Aug 23, 1825; m Sarah Goodwin, probably dau David & Eleanor (Challis), b Mar 3, 1749 (Ames MA R), d 1849, ae 99 (Candia, NH R).
        Rev War soldier; private Capt Oliver Titcomb's Co, Col Jacob Gerrish's regt of guards; service from Feb 3, 1778 to Apr 2, 1778. Two mos 2 dys, guarding prisoners after surrender of Burgoyne's army. Roll dated Winter Hill (MA War Rolls).

Children: (Ames MA R)
430.   Sarah 6, b Jan 17, 1776
431.   Molly 6, b June 11, 1776 (obviously there is an error but thus given in records)
432.   Hannah 6, b Mar 8, 1779
433.   John 6, b Dec 30, 1782
434.   Charles S. 6, b Nov 3, 1789

191.   Peter Bagley 5, Timothy 4, John 3, Orlando 2, Orlando 1 published to Sarah Martin, Nov 16, 1784 (Ames MA R); moved to Warner, NH, where he was a farmer. In 1793, he signed petition to be exempt from church taxes because he was a Baptist (Warner, NH R). Nov 7, 1808, he sold 1/2 pew in meetinghouse in Warner and land there being given as of Newbury, Orange Co. VT (Hillsboro, Co, NH Deeds). As of June 1, 1840, he was living in Newbury, VT, being 87 years old (Pension Rolls).
        Rev War soldier: private Capt John Currier's Co, Col Isaac Merrill's regt which marched on Lexington Alarm, service 76 dys; also Capt Currier's Co, Col James Frye's regt; receipt for advance pay dated Cambridge, July 1, 1775; also Co return (probably Oct 1775); also, order for bounty coat or its equivalent in money, dated Cambridge, MA, Nov 16, 1775; also sergt in Capt Moses Nowell's Co, Col Titcomb's regt, roll made up from date of arrival at Providence, RI, May 4, 1777; also muster roll from July and Aug, 1778, dated E Greenwich; also muster roll from January-October, 1778; also return of men who served in boats on expedition against Newport; service 7 dys; endorsed 1778; also priv in Capt Jonathan Evan's Co, Col Nathaniel Wade's regt; enl July 20, 1778; disch Jan 1, 1779; service 5 mos 18 dys, at North Kingston, RI (MA War Rolls). Census of 1790 gives 1-2-3.
        In checking cemeteries in Newbury, VT, plat map shows a Bagley lot in older part of cemetery, but there are no stones.

Children: (Warner, NH R)
435.   Elizabeth 6, b Oct 5, 1785
436.   Polly 6, b about 1787; d 1862, unm, at Warner, NH
437.   Sarah 6, b Jan 30, 1788; d 1862?, at Warner, NH
438.   Peter 6, b Jan 18, 1790; d Jan 17, 1865 (Scholarie Co, NY R)
439.   John Martin 6, b Jan 31, 1794

192.   Isaac Bagley 6, Timothy 5, John 3, Orlando 2, Orlando 1
b Nov 6, 1756; d Feb 1, 1839; m Mehitable Bartlett of Newbury, MA, intentions Sept 16, 1780 (Newbury, MA R) and intentions filed Amesbury, MA, Feb 20, 1781. She b Dec 10, 1757, dau Stephen & Ruth (Currier); living 1811 (Essex Antiquarian). Family checks with Census of 1790 and 1810. A blacksmith.

Children: (Ames MA R)
440.   Ruth 6, b June 30, 1781
441.   Lowell 6, b Feb 2, 1784; d Feb 26, 1863 (Tombstone, Ames, MA)
442.   Richard 6, b 1792 (birth not on Ames MA R); d July 6, 1832

199.   Enoch Bagley 5, William 4, Jacob 3, Orlando 2, Orlando 1
b Apr 27, 1740; d Sept 13, 1814; m Mary Webster before 1766, who d Oct 2, 1816 (Ames MA R). He was a shipwright and lived at Amesbury where he and his wife renewed their baptismal covenants, Nov 16, 1766, at First Church (Church R). Family checks with Census of 1790 except for two females. Enoch mentioned in his grandfather's will, Dec 25, 1767 as "son of my son William" (Essex Co MA Probate R). He sold land in York Co, ME, Oct, 1779.

Children: (Ames MAS R)
443.   William 6, b Oct 3, 1766; d Aug, 1835
444.   Hannah 6, b Nov 16, 1768
445.   Mary (Polly) 6, b Feb 10, 1773; named Molly on Ames R); d Apr 3, 1846, unm
446.   Susy 6, b May 31, 1775; d July 30, 1825, unm
447.   Enoch 6, b Dec 12, 1776
448.   John W. 6, b Apr 5, 1779; d Sept 2, 1780
449.   John 6, b Jan 20, 1781
450.   Nabby 6, b Mar 6, 1783
451.   Lucy 6, b Jan 12, 1786; d Oct 8, 1835 (tombstone, Ames MA)

200.   William Bagley 5, William 4, Jacob 3, Orlando 2, Orlando 1, b Dec 26, 1741; d Sept 30, 1808; m (1) Mary Hoyt, Dec 7, 1763, at Kingston, NH (Kingston R), b Amesbury, MA Dec 15, 1747, dau David & Mary (Quimby), of the Ferry in Amesbury; m (2) Hannah Woodman of Kingston, NH, Sept 1, 1782, dau Joshua & Eunice (Sawyer), b Oct 8, 1750, at Kingston; d May 10, 1830 (Ames MA R).

A yeoman, he lived at Amesbury Ferry and later moved to Hawke (now Danville, NH), where he died. Will made Sept 29, 1808; proved Dec 6, 1808 (Rockingham Co, NH Provate R). Wife

Hannah was adm. Family checks with Census of 1790 if not below for Jeremiah is correct.

Children: (Ames MA R excepted as noted)

452. Jeremiah 6, b before 1766 (birth not recorded Ames MA); d Oct 25, 1807 (Ames MA R). It is not certain he was son of William; however, the late William D. Bagley, who d at Amesbury in 1920, said his father, the son of David & Dorothy (Blaisdell) Bagley, claimed that David, son of Jeremiah, was his cousin. This family lived at the Ferry and Jeremiah was b there. No mention of Jeremiah in William's will as are his sons David and Jacob, but William may have settled property on him earlier.

453. Jacob 6, b May 23 or 28, 1766 ; will proved Aug 5, 1801 (Essex Co MA Probate R)

454. David 6, b Oct 23, 1768; d Dec 2 or 3, 1803

455. Mary (Molly) 6, b Jan 9, 1771 (Salis MA R); d Apr 3, 1856 (History of Salisbury, NH)

456. Anna 6, b Apr 16, 1773; d Oct 17, 1776

457. Anne 6, b May 5, 1774; not mentioned in father's will in 1808

458. Betty (Betsey) 6, b Apr 15 or 16, 1776; d Oct 17, 1776

459. Anna (Nancy) 6, b Apr 17, 1781. Family R call this child Nancy as did her father in his will

460. William 6, b May 14, 1783; but family R give Nov 24, 1782; d Nov 24, 1791

461. Eunice 6, b July 19, 1784; d June 4, 1861; unm (Danville, NH R); she quit-claimed rights in her parents' estates (Rockingham Co, NH Deeds).

462. John 6, b Aug 13, 1786; d June 2, 1860

463. Amos 6, b Oct 14, 1788; d young

464. Dolly 6, b Mar 6, 1790; d young

465. William 6, b Oct 15, 1793; d June 23, 1868 (Danville, NH R)

466. Amos 6, b Aug 20, 1795; d Aug 14, 1796

467. Hannah 6, b 1797 (birth not on Ames MA R); d Aug 11, 1834 (Salis MA R)

201. Jerusha Bagley 5, William 4, Jacob 3, Orlando 2, Orlando 1, b Sept 9, 1743; baptized Dec 25, 1743; d Feb 4, 1819, ae 76; m Dec 7, 1763, Ezra Worthen (m not recorded on Ames, Salis or Newbury, MA R), son Charles & Mehitabel (Gould), b Nov 20, 1738, d Dec 7, 1804, ae 60 (Ames MA R). She is mentioned in her grandfather Jacob Bagley's will in 1767 and given as wife of Ezra Worthen (Essex Co MA Probate R).

Children: (Ames MA R)

468. Charles 6, b Oct 16, 1764

469. Susanna 6, b June 18, 1766

470. Anna 6, b Aug 18, 1769

471. Mehitable 6, b Oct 22, 1771

472. Hannah 6, b Mar 2, 1774

473. Polly 6, b May 10, 1776

474. Sarah 6, b Jan 23, 1779

475. Ezra 6, b Feb 11, 1781

221. Miriam Bagley 5, Joseph 4, Joseph 3, Orlando 2 Orlando 1, b Oct 23, 1767; baptized Oct 23, 1767; d Nov 24, 1849; m Mar 15, 1811, Jonathan Martin, son Capt Jonathan & Sarah (Morrill) (Salis MA R), b July 11, 1766, d Salisbury, MA, Mar 4, 1830. This was his second marriage and Miriam Bagley had no children.

222. True Bagley 5, Joseph 4, Joseph 3, Orlando 2, Orlando 1 b Aug 19, 1770; d June or July 28, 1833, ae 63 (Salis MA R); buried Amesbury. There is a rock beside his stone with no inscription. Census of 1810 gives 1M 15-20, 2F 20-30.

224. Stephen Hunt Bagley 5, Abel 4, Joseph 3, Orlando 2, Orlando 1. b Dec 12, 1763; d Jan 26, 1849; m Aug 20, 1786/87, at Kensington, NH, Dorothy Pike (Kensington, NH R), b Kensington, 1767, d May 13, 1832, ae 66 (Tombstones, Salisbury Plains Cemetery, Amesbury, MA, difficult to read in 1957.

Children:
476. Greenleaf 6, b Salisbury, MA, Sept 28, 1789; d May 28, 1873 (Clinton, ME R)
477. Sarah 6
478. Lydia 6, b about 1787; d June 23, 1835 (Salis MA R)
479. Frederick T 6, b 1798, Salisbury, MA (Family R); d Jan 4, 1879 (Clinton, ME R)
480. Alexander 6, b about 1800; d Aug 8, 1822, ae 22 (Tombstone, Salisbury Plains Cemetery, Amesbury, MA. Hamilton, MA records say he d Aug 7, 1822
481. Franklin 6, b about 1803; d Seabrook, NH, June 9, 1873 (Seabrook, NH R)
482. Oliver P. 6, b about 1804, Salisbury, MA; d E Kingston, NH, Feb 22, 1878, ae 75 (NH R)
483. Judith 6, b Oct 6, 1806; d July 12, -----, Salisbury, MA
484. Lucy P. 6, b about 1809; d May 5, 1892 (there is some questionas to whether she is Stephen's dau or wife to son Franklin. No record of marriage to Franklin has been found and settlement of Franklin's estate does not call her widow.)

225. Elias Bagley 5, Abel 4, Joseph 3, Orlando 2, Orlando 1 , b Apr 8, 1765; d 1816, or soon after as his will was made Nov 8, 1816 (Rockingham Co NH Probate R). Will mentions wife Sarah and four children by Sarah who was made guardian of the children, Nov 1, 1820. Inventory $5084.22. Wife was probably Sarah Thompson whom he m Jan 27, 1801; she was probably the Sally Bagley who d in Portsmouth, NH, Nov 21, 1835 (NH R).

Children:
485. William Page 6
486. Sarah Hunt 6
487. Mary 6
488. Elizabeth 6

240. Molly Bagley 6, Orlando 5, Orlando 4, Orlando 3, Orlando 2, Orlando 1, b Aug, 1771. She was willed two red chests by her grandmother Fitts. The John Hayes Genealogy is incorrect when it gives her as marrying Levi Morrill, Apr 15, 1792.

Molly, dau of William Bagley, m Levi Morrill, and she d Salisbury, NH, ae 85, which would make her birth date about 1771.

243. Benjamin Bagley 6, Seth 5, Orlando 4, Orlando 3, Orlando 2, Orlando 1 , b June 16, 1782; d Nov 25, 1825; m Salisbury, MA, Jan 3, 1814, Eunice Fowler (Salis MA R). Tombstone at Salisbury Plains Cemetery, Amesbury, gives same date but age 47 which does not agree with dates. She was b Seabrook, NH, 1789, dau Samuel & Martha (Cilley), d Salisbury, MA, June 11, 1875 (MA R); probably the Widow Bagley who sold land in Salisbury, MA, Aug 10, 1867; George Bagley, a witness (Essex Co MA Deeds).

Children: (Salis MA R)
489. Mary 7, b July 30, 1814
490. Abigail 7, b Oct 4, 1815; d Mar 27, 1816
491. Valentine 7, b Feb 14, 1817; d Apr 12, 1819
492. John 7, b Sept 17, 1818; d Apr 12, 1819
493. Abigail 7, b Mar 27, 1820
494. Thomas 7, b Oct 25, 1821; d Salisbury, MA, Sept 16, 1909
495. Eliza 7, b Jan 17, 1823; d 1881 (Family R)
496. Sally 7, b Feb 17, 1824
497. Betty 7, b Feb 17, 1824
(The Salisbury, MA R give a dau of Benjamin named Sally who d Jan 14, 1825; this probably number 497. As Benjamin d in 1825, there was probably not another dau Sally who m Seth Gage as the Greeley Genealogy states. This might be a daughter of another Benjamin, or it could have been the twin Betty, or a mistake in names)

244. Dorothy Bagley 6, Henry 5, Henry 4, Orlando 3, Orlando 2, Orlando 1, b Oct, 1747; d Feb 27, 1797, Hartland, VT; m Barnard Worthen, June 11, 1767 (Ames MA R), son George, Jr., & Merriam (Barnard), b Sept 25, 1744 (Ames MA R). He m (2) Mrs. Susanna Doke, Jan 10, 1799. After Dorothy's death, he went to Pennsylvania and died there at Brooklyn.

Children: (Ames MA R)
498. Amos 7, b Dec 28, 1767; m Ruth Stockman of Salisbury, MA, intentions, Sept 28, 1792
499. Nabby 7, b Dec 5, 1769
500. Anne 7, b Feb 21, 1772
501. Molly 7, b Jan 13, 1775; d Oct 20, 1795, unm
502. Nancy 7, b Jan 12, 1776
503. Abner 7, b May 17, 1777
504. Dolly 7, b Apr 16, 1778; probably d young
505. Dorothy 7, b Apr 16, 1780; d Dec 29, 1797
506. Winthrop 7, b July 1, 1783
507. Jacob 7, b Apr 16, 1786
508. Ruth 7, b Apr 21, 1789
509. Jonathan 7, b Jan 14, 1792
510. Marian 7, b Nov 15, 1794

245. Sargent Bagley 6, Henry 5, Henry 4, Orlando 3, Orlando 2, Orlando 1, b Jan 8, 1749/50. Family checks with Census of

1790. He m (1) second Church, Amesbury, MA, Mrs Rebecca
(Wells) Challis, May 5, 1776 (Ames MA R); she d Sept 10, 1805
(Ames MA R); he m (2) Mary Patten, Apr 1, 1806 (Ames MA R),
but Ames MA Church R says May 15, while Second Church R say
May 5.
        Rev War soldier in Capt Mathias Hoit's Co, and marched on
the Lexington Alarm, Apr 19, 1775; service 9 dys (MA War
Rolls).

Children: (Ames MA R)
511.   Dorothy 7, b Feb 6, 1777
512.   Sargent 7, b June 29, 1780; d St Johnsbury, VT, Aug 14,
1845 (VT R)
513.   Moses 7, b May 29, 1797; baptized June 4, 1797; d Mar
23, 1824, ae 26 (VT R)
514.   Mary Patten 7, b Nov 15, 1807
515.   Rebecca Challis 7, b Nov 20, 1810

247. Orlando Bagley 6, Henry 5, Henry 4, Orlando 3, Orlando
2, Orlando 1 , b May 30, 1755 (Ames MA R); d in Ohio about
1824. There is some confusion about his marriage. The
Sargent Genealogy says he m Dorcus Sargent, dau Thomas &
Rebecca (Rogers), b Apr 10, 1760 (Ames MA R). Some say she d
Hartland, VT, Jan 7, 1790 (However marriage is not on
Amesbury, MA R nor is death on VT R).
        The Rev Garford Williams of Nicholson, PA, an historian &
Genealogist of that section of PA, where the Orlando Bagley
family settled, quotes Weston's History of Brooklyn, PA, as
saying that Orlando's Bagley's wife was Dorcas Taylor.
Further, Dr William Bagley of Duluth, MN, placed a memorial
stone on the Jesse Bagley lot. The principal speaker for the
occasion was Attorney William Brewster, eminent historian and
Bagley descendant. The inscription is on a large bronze
tablet firmly secured to a large granite stone. It reads as
follows:
        "To honor the Memory of Orlando Bagley and His Wife
Dorcas Taylor Bagley. Orlando Bagley, son of Henry and Lydia
Weed Bagley, was born May 30, 1755, at Amesbury, Mass., and
died in Ohio about 1824. He served as a private in Cat
Mathias Hoit's Company and marched at the first alarm on April
19, 1775, and served nine days. he also served under Capt
Jonnas Kidder in Colonel Moses Nichol's New Hampshire
Militias. Regiment raised to join the Continental Army at
West Point in 1780.
        "Dorcas Taylor married Orlando Bagley in 1778, at
Amesbury, Massachusetts and died in Ohio about 1824. She was
the mother of thirteen children.
        "Tablet placed in 1938 by their great great grandson."
        It would appear that Orlando Bagley had one wife; that
her name was Dorcas Taylor; that the Sargent Genealogy is
incorrect. There is, of course, the possibility that Dorcas
Sargent had previously married a Taylor, but such a marriage
is not on Amesbury, MA, nor on Weare, NH R.
        For a time the Bagleys lived in Weare, NH, and then in
Hartland, VT. In 1804, Orlando sold out in Hartland and
settled in the small town of Brooklyn in eastern PA.

His son, Jesse, said of the trip (History of Susquehanna County, PA, 1873): "We started on Tuesday and were two Sundays on the road. It was March, and the snow in some places was nearly five feet in depth. We settled on the hill east of what is now Mack's Corners.....We went to Tunkhannock and Wilkes Barre for store goods, to Horton's and Tunkhannock to mill, and to Hyde's at the forks of the Wyalusing to our post office.... Esquire Hinds, only, lived where Montrose is." Orlando Bagley had a deed from John B. Wallace, land agent, Nov 10, 1807, for fifty acres of land, free from incumbrance for $150.

The Bagley family were prominent and influential members of the Methodist Church. Says Mrs Blackman in the History of Susquehanna County: In 1806 Christopher Frye who is described as 'rough as a meat-axe' was an early Methodist preacher in Brooklyn. Jacob Tewskbury was class leader in 1809. That year Edward Paine came to the place and was for many years 'the life of the Methodist Society'. Mr. Frye had a rapid increase of members among them being several of the Bagleys, Tewksburys, Saunders, Worthings (Ames MA R spell this Worthen) and others. Orlando Bagley and Dorcas, his wife, joined the M. E. Church in the Methodist Class of Rev Edward Paine in Brooklyn prior to 1811, and most of the family living in Brooklyn joined the Class before 1811 (Personal Record of Rev E Paine). Dr George Pack in his history of "Early Methodismn" speaks kindly of Orlando Bagley and says that the church in Brooklyn was greatly impoverished by the removal of the Bagley and Saunders families to Ohio. Rev Williams says that Orlando Bagley was called "Uncle Bagley". He was pious, good and kind, tender-hearted and humble before God. The family would walk at night, several times a week, from Mack's Corners to Brooklyn to attend Methodist Class meeting. As they walked they sang Methodist hymns and praised God in shouts. At a certain place in the woods, the group would disburse, go apart into the woods to pray and cleanse their souls before walking on together.

Orlando Bagley was enumerated in the Census of 1810 in Brooklyn, self and wife over 45 years; two males 10-16; 1 female 0-10; one female 16-25. His sons: Jesse and Stephen Bagley were married and at the head of a family and so enumerated. Lyman Saunders, son-in-law of Orlando, was enumerated in this Census.

In the fall of 1817, the Bagley and Saunders families sold their land in Brooklyn and settled in Union township, Union County, Ohio. Orlando Bagley and wife deeded their farm at Mack's Corners for $600, 50 acres, on Oct 7, 1817, to Ebenezer Gere of Preston, New London Co, CO. The deed was witnessed by Stephen and Mary Bagley (Montrose Deed Book 2, p 362). Due to the creation of Susquehanna County in 1810, out of Luzerne County, the first deed of Orlando Bagley was recorded in Wilkes-Barre and recorded again with the deed of land sale in Montrose, PA. Stephen Bagley sold his land in Brooklyn in 1814 and may have gone to Ohio about this time and then returned to encourage others to follow him. Probably all the children of Orlando Bagley who lived in Brooklyn went to Ohio but not all at the same time, and some did not settle there for any length of time. At the time of the Bagley settlement in Union County, that county was part of Delaware County and records of that county were burned which makes research difficult.

In the 1820 Census, the families are enumerated in Union township and the following are heads of families: Orlando Bagley, Jesse Bagley, Stephen Bagley, Thomnas Bagley. Betsey L. (Bagley) Saunders (a widow), and Benjamin Sheffield Saunders. Of these Jesse and Thomas Bagley and B. S. Saunders had returned to Brooklyn, PA, before 1825, and Washington, Sally, and Charles Bagley had returned by 1830.

In Union County at that time there were periodic epidemics of ague and many of the Bagley and Saunders families were victims. It is reported that Orlando and Dorcas Bagley and their dau Dorcas; Lyman Saunders and his parents and brothers and perhaps others died (Weston). It is certain that Orlando Bagley and probably his wife and dau were dead before some of the children returned to Brooklyn in 1824.

Jesse Bagley requested letters of adm on the estate of Orlando Bagley, deceased, on Nov 13, 1821, in the Court of Common Pleas at Marysville, Union County (Book 1, p 33). He signed a bond with George Brown and Andrew Gill as sureties in the sum of $400 as orderd by court; and appraisers were appt to inventory estate before Apr 19, 1822. Orlando is called "late of Union County". In the April term the inventory was presented in full and covers three pages of the docket. There is not mention of land or cash except two notes he held against his son Jesse and against Amos Baily of Brooklyn for $52. The total amount of property was $199.64, and signed by George Brown, William Burnham and David Reed. On Nov 1, 1822, Jesse was granted an additional year to settle the estate. On Apr 19, 1824, the estate was finally declared settled.

The writers are especially grateful to Rev Williams for supplying so much information on the Brooklyn branch.

<u>Children:</u> (Compiled from vital records and Rev William's notes)
516. Winthrop 7, b May 11, 1779 (Weare, NH R); apparently did not go to PA
517. Betsey L. 7, b Jan 1;4, 1781 (Weare, NH R)
518. Thomas 7, b May 3, 1784 (Weare, NH R); probably d young
519. Jesse 7, b Apr 21, 1786 (Weare, NH R); d Nov 30, 1874
520. Stephen Holland 7, b 1788/89; probably Hartland, VT
521. Thomas 7, b Mar 14, 1792; d Apr 14, 1792 (Hartland, VT)
522. Dorcas 7, b Feb 24, 1793 (Hartland VT R); apparently d in OH about 1824
523. Thomas 7, b Mar 10, 1794 (Hartland VT R)
524. Dorothy 7, b July 19, 1797 (Hartland VT R); d Apr 19, 1855
525. Charles George 7, b July 11, 1799 (Hartland VT R)
526. Washington 7, b Jan 24, 1802 (Hartland VT R); d July 3, 1848
527. Sally 7, b about 1804 (Brooklyn, PA; probably d before 1830

248.   Thomas Jefferson Bagley 6, Henry 5, Henry 4, Orlando 3, Orlando 2, Orlando 1 , b Feb 26, 1761; d June 19, 1838; m Olive Perkins, Jan 7, 1782 (New England Genealogical Register), b Dec 20, 1763, dau Jonathan & Abigail (Blake). She is supposed to have had Indian blood. Some sources give her name as Olive Perkins Green.   Her sister did marry a Green. Her death certificate says Perkins when she d July 28, 1839, ae 75 (VT R & tombstone). There is no record of any estate for Thomas in Windsor Co, VT.

He was a Rev War soldier for Weare, NH, on pay roll of Capt Jonas Kidder's Co, Col Moses Nichol's regt of militia raised by the State of New Hampshire to join the Continental Army at West Point , 1780. Time of engagement, July 5, 1780; disch Oct 23, 1780 (NH Rev War Rolls). Also in MA service, as private in Col Oliver Titcomb's Co, Col Jacob Gerrish' s regt of guards from Feb 3, 1778 to Apr 2, 1778, 2 months, 2 dys service, guarding prisoners after the surrender of Burgoyne, roll dated Winter Hill. Enl from Amesbury, MA, Apr, 1777, stationed Providence, RI, May 4, 1777; disch July 4, 1777 (MA War Rolls).

He moved to Weare, NH, Feb, 1780, and from there to Hartland, VT, in 1788, and lived the rest of his life there. From Hartland in the Revolutionary War, Her Soldiers, their Homes, their Lives and their Burial Places with Associated History by Rev Dennis Flower: "Thomas Bagley lived at one time in a house, long since demolished, southeast of Clarine Hadley's, on the opposite side of the road, near a large elm tree. The old cellar remains. Arnold G., William W., and Cyrus, the last two named being Civil War veterans are grandsons.

The following from NH Pension Rolls: Jan 27, 1833, Thomas Bagley of Hartland, Windsor Co, VT, born in Amesbury, MA, Feb 26, 1761, deposed that he enlisted from Amesbury, MAss. in April 1777, and was stationed at Providence, RI. Ensign was Charles Wood: service 2 months, 9 dys. In March, 1778, enlisted to help guard Burgoyne's army, under Capt Oliver Titcomb, service 2 months, 9 dys. In Feb, 1780 moved to Weare, NH, and in July 1780, enlisted from there under Capt Kidder. In 1788, moved to Hartland, VT, where he since resided. Rev Moses Tewksbury and Asa West, both of Hartland, testified to soldier's character.

August 17, 1833, Moses Sergeant of Warren, Washington Co, VT, ae 76, testified to service under Capt Kidder with Thomas Bagley. Claim allowed for 6 moths, 26 days.

Apr 4, 1839, Olive Bagley of Hartland, ae 74, deposed: she is the widow of Thomas Bagley, who d June 19, 1838. Signed by mark. (Notice date of birth given by New England Genealogical Register and her deposition do not agree).

A letter from town clerk of Weare, NH, dated Aug 27, 1838, states he can find no record of marriage and has asked Widow Green, sister of Widow Bagley, but can obtain no definite information. Ebenezer Kelly of Hartland, ae 60, deposed, Apr 4, 1839, that he lived in Deering, NH, adjoining the town of Weare, when Thomas Bagley and wife were neighbors about 50 years ago and Bagley moved to Hartland shortly after his father did, and Thomas and Olive had lived together as man

---

and wife ever since until the death of Thomas. Claim allowed and certificate issued Aug 30, 1839. Olive d July 29, 1839, and Jan 16, 1843, Samuel R. Stocker, adm applied for arrears of pension. Town clerk of Hartland certified no record of children could be found (which is interesting because children are certainly on VT records as for Hartland).

Children: (Hartland, VT unless otherwise specified)
528. Abigail 7, b Sept 20, 1782, probably born Weare, but not recorded
529. Hulda 7, b May 11, 1784, probably born Weare, but not recorded
530. Jonathan 7, b Mar 5, 1786, probably born Weare, but not recorded; d July 3, 1867 (tombstone)
531. Thomas 7, b Mar 9, 1788; d May 14, 1863
532. Olive 7, b Sept 25, 1790; d Dec 10, 1879, Lincoln, VT
533. Daniel 7, b Oct 25, 1792; d Dec 10, 1879
534. Perkins 7, b Aug 11, 1795; d June 10, 1800 (tombstone, Hartland, VT)
535. Polly 7, b Sept 18, 1797
536. Asabel Thomas 7, b Nov 4 or 6, 1799; d July 11, 1849
537. Lucy 7, b Feb 10, 1802; d Aug 8, 1873
538. Lois 7, b Jan 20, 1804
539. Jefferson 7, b July 28, 1806; d June 3, 1887 (tombstone)

249. Henry Bagley 6, Henry 5, Henry 4, Orlando 3, Orlando 2, Orlando 1 , b Nov 9, 1763; d Sept 20, 1847, ae 84; m (1) Abigail Swett of Hillsboro, NH, Apr 11, 1785 (Hillsboro NH R); m (2) Margaret Roach (?), who d Mar 16, 1843, ae 82 (tombstone, Windsor, NH). It may be they were never married, the terms of his will suggesting she may have been a common-law wife, no proof of marriage has been found, but she is buried on the same lot with Henry. His will, dated Mar 11, 1842, wherein he is given as of Windsor, NH, mentions oldest son Sargent, second son, Joel, and dau Sally Bagley (Hillsboro Co NH Probate R). He left all his estate to Sally upon the special condition that she provide for the maintenance of Peggy Roach, her mother, and if she refused, the estate should go to Peggy Roach. On Oct 6, 1847, John Swett was appt adm of estate of Henry Bagley of Windsor, lately deceased, yeoman (Hillsboro Co, NH Probate R).
        Henry sold land in Weare, NH, Oct 29, 1787, in Windsor, NH, July 5, 1802; and in Warner, NH, Feb 14, 1840 (Hillsboro Co, NH Deeds). He signed a petition concerning the Mason-Allen Controversy in 1786; and signed a petition in 1790 asking that Campbell's Gore, now Windsor, NH, be made a town (NH Provincial Papers). He is listed on the list of voters for Campbell's Gore, June 9, 1791. The records of the Masonian Proprietors give him as being conveyed a certain lot of land in Windsor, NH, Lot No 9 in the first range originally drawn in the right of Thomas Packer (NH Provincial Papers). Census of 1800 gives 4 males, 4 females, at Windsor. Census of 1790 gives 1-3-1. If these are children of Henry, we do not have them all, but others may have died young if not mentioned in his will.

Children:
540.   Henry 7, b about 1787; d Aug 16, 1808, ae 21 (tombstone, Windsor, NH)
541.   Sargent 7, living 1842 (Probate R)
542.   Joel 7, living 1842 (Probate R)
543.   Sally 7, living 1842 (Probate R)

250.   Winthrop Bagley 6, Henry 5, Henry 4, Orlando 3, Orlando 2, Orlando 1, b Jan 8, 1768 (Ames MA R)

251.   John Bagley 6, Jonathan 5, Henry 4, Orlando 3, Orlando 2, Orlando 1, b Feb 11, 1759; d Aug 29, 1833; m Olive Judson, Jan 29, 1784, dau Timothy & Sarah (Hooker), b Oct 9, 1767, Woodbury, CO, d Oct 25, 1837, ae 70 (tombstone, Durham, NY)
       His deposition for Rev War pension says he was b Newton, MA (Birth recorded both on Newton, NH and Candia, NH records, but this is a common error because of the late settlement of boundary between NH and MA). He lived in Candia, NH, and was a Rev War soldier in MA, as well as NH. He says he was b Feb 11, 1760. War service for MA: priv in Capt Thomas Cogswell's second Co, Col Gerrish's regt, muster roll, dated Aug 1, 1775, enl June 10, 1775, service one month and 22 dys; also Capt Cogswell's Co, Col Loami Baldwin's (late Col Gerrish's regt), return from Aug, 1775; also Co return dated Sewell's Point; also order for bounty coat or its equivalent in money, date Camp Sewell's Point, Nov 9, 1775 ; also,list of men returned as having lost articles at evacuation of NY, Sept 14, 1776; also list of men who agreed to serve six weeks from Dec 31, 1776; dated Trenton; also Capt Cogswell's Co, Col Baldwin's regt list of men who furnished their own arms, sworn at Haverhill, MA, July 31, 1777; also list of men under command of Col Jacobs, formerly Col Baldwin's regt, who returned guns at Chatham (yr not given); service 6 weeks; also Capt Cogswell's Co return of men in service for six weeks (yr not given) (MA W4.Rev War Rolls).
       NH Rev War Rolls: Capt Stephen Dearborn's Co, Col Thomas Stickney's regt, Stark's Brigade, July, 1777, NH regt. Was in the Battle of Bennington; also pay roll for Capt Benjamin Whittier's Co of militia in Col Nichol's regt raised in State of NH in July, 1780, for defense of US at West Point, as sergeant; enl July 6, 1780; disch Oct 24, 1780, time of service 3 months 18 dys.
From NH Pension Rolls: Feb 4, 1833, John Bagley of Durham, Greene Co, NY, born in Newton, MA, Feb 11, 1760, deposed that in June, 1775, at Candia, NH, joined the army at Cambridge, MA, the day of the Battle of Bunker Hill, and was priv in Capt Cogswell's Co, Lt Moses Dustin and 2nd Lt or ensign Amos Cogswell, brother of the captain and served until Dec 31, 1775. He re-enlisted under the same officers for 1776 and in Dec was disch at Trenton, NJ, but immediately upon request of Gen Sullivan volunteered to serve under him and was placed in Capt Mile's Co until Mar. That he continuously served from June, 1775, to the middle of Mar, 1777. Was in battles of White Plains, Trenton, and Princeton. At Trenton was knocked down by gravel thrown up by the striking of a ball discharged from a field piece of the enemy and considerably hurt. Not so

much but that I was engaged in the subsequent battle at Princeton; was disch at Chatham, NC, where Capt Miles was then stationed. In the service of 1777, enl as priv for three months from Candia militia under Capt Lane, whose brother was killed at Bennington. Was in battle of Bennington. Enl again under Capt Whitter in 1780; marched to West Point; promoted top second sergeant and served as such for three months. Rev James Thompson and Barnard Bagley certify as to the soldier's character. Barnard Bagley of Durham, NY, ae 69, deposed that he was brought up within 100 rods of the residence of soldier in Candia, and moved to Durham about the same time he did and knew he was a Rev War soldier, served with him for one term under Capt Whittier. Claimed allowed for 23 months service and certificate 14740, NY agency, issued June 13, 1833, Act of June 7, 1832.

He moved from Candia, NH to Cairo and Durham, NY, by 1784. Granted war pension, State of NH, June 13, 1833. Early travelers west in NY speak in diaries of John Bagley's wheat fields in Cairo, NY. Nov 5, 1793, Edward Griswold, councilor at law in NYC sold John Bagley, yeoman, lands in Durham "now in John Bagley's possession". John had completed payment by Aug 14, 1794. This sale was to settle conflicts between original grantees and the actual settlers. He built the first grist mill in Durham and was captain of first militia company.

John Bagley's will, dated Jan 9, 1833, mentioned his beloved wife, Olive, and provides for her maintenance "as long as she shall remain my widow"; son, Truman; dau, Laura, wife of Ira Day and sets up a trust for his grandchildren: Laura Bagley, Ira B. Day, Henry A. Day, and Edgar T. Day. Ira Day and Olive Bagley were originally appt adms. Before the estate was settled, Olive Bagley and Ira Day died. Prior to this time, Ira Day, on Aug 22, 1833, swore that John Bagley was deceased and that he left a widow, Olive, and three children: Truman of Durham; Laura, wife of Ira Day (Cairo), and John Bagley of Medina, NY. After the death of Ira Day, Horatio L. Day, residuary legatee in the will of John Bagley, May 18, 1842, asked to be made adm of the estate. He states that Laura Bagley, Ira B. Day, Henry A. Day, and Edgar I. Day (Laura supposedly child of Truman and the other three children of Ira Day and Laura Bagley) are infants and that John Bagley, son of the deceased, had moved to Michigan and that he had a dau Delia. The court appt Ira's widow and brother, Horatio, as adms.

Children:
544.   Truman 7, b 1784; d Aug 31, 1871 (NY R)
545.   Sally 7, d Apr 13, 1829 (Family R)
546.   Laura 7, b Nov 17, 1797; d June 8, 1844 (tombstone, Cairo, NY)
547.   John 7, b Jan 21, 1800; d May 3, 1855, in Michigan

233. Dorothea Bagley 6, Jonathan 5, Henry 4, Orlando 3, Orlando 2, Orlando 1, b Nov 19, 1761; d Goffstown, NH, Dec 25, 1849; m (1) William Thornton of Laconia, NH, who d Oct 26, 1844 (tombstone, Thornton, NH); m (2) Feb, 1819, Stephen

Bartlett of Plymouth, NH, probably son of John & Zipporah (Flanders), b May 11, 1784, d May 23, 1823 (Salis MA R & Ply NH R)

Children: (All by Thornton NH R)
548.   William 7, b Jan 13, 1784; m Oct 9, 1805, Mary Bagley, dau Winthrop of Thornton, NH
549.   John 7, b June 25, 1786
550.   Polly 7, b Apr 13, 1788; d unm May 31, 1821 (tombstone, Thornton, NH)
551.   Matthew 7, b Feb 8, 1791
552.   Nathan 7, b Sept 30, 1794 *d 1860 TS Thornton*
553.   Hannah 7, b Mar 27, 1797
554.   James 7, b Apr 3, 1799

254. Winthrop Bagley 6, Jonathan 5, Henry 4, Orlando 3, Orlando 2, Orlando 1, b Aug 19, 1762/63 (Deposition for pension says b Amesbury, MA); d July 21, 1851, ae 88 (tombstone, Thornton, NH). He lived at Candia and later in Thornton, NH. On pension rolls for Grafton Co militia. He bought and sold land in Thornton, Plymouth, Campton, Franconia from 1783 to 1840 (Grafton, Co NH Deeds). He bought Bagley's Island in the Pemigewasset River from Jane Thornton, Nov. 1794. He lived on the place in Thornton occupied by George Blaisdell in 1880. On Jan 7, 1850, Winthrop and his wife Maria conveyed to Tillotson Blaisdell, whose wife Sally was Winthrop's dau, their property in return for the Blaisdell's care during their old age. (Grafton Co Deeds)

He m Maria Dudley of Raymond, NH, dau Gilman & Sarah (Currier), Jan 1, 1787 (Epsom, NH R), b 1761, d Aug 29, 1858, ae 95 (tombstone, Thornton, NH). Quarterly Obituary gives her death date as 1855. His name first appears on the town books of Thornton in 1787, and he was active in town affairs as selectman, tax collector, surveyor of highways and line surveyor. He was a prominent member of the Methodist Church and served as tithingman. A farmer, he was also a tavern keeper and the sign that hung by his tavern was still in the Blaisdell family in 1888.

Rev War soldier, enl at Candia, NH, Mar 1778, Capt Ezekiel Worthen's Co, and served nine months. Also in Col Stephen Peabody's regt in RI where he saw Lafayette. Enl June, 1781, at Campton, NH, under Lt Peter Stearns, serving on the northern frontier 6 months.

NH Pension Rolls: Winthrop Bagley — Maria, widow, of state service: Sept 5, 1832, Winthrop Bagley of Thornton, Grafton Co, NH, born Amesbury, MA, Aug 19, 1762, deposed he enlisted at Candia, NH, under Capt Ezekiel Worthen, Mar, 1778, service 9 months in RI. In June, 1781, at Campton, enl under Lt Peter Stearns, serving on the northern frontier 6 months. That, since the Revolution, he has lived in Thornton where he now resides. Deacon Enoch Gilman and Moody Elliott, testified to soldier's character. Sept 4, 1832, Jonathan Robbins of Plymouth, ae 66, testified to service with Bagley under Lt Peter Stearns in 1783 for 3 months. At the end of this time Robbins engaged a substitute and went home. Enoch Colby of Thornton testified July 2, 1832, to service in a company near

Bagley in 1778 at RI. June 29, 1832, Daniel Heath of Plymouth, NH, testified to service with Lt Peter Stearns with Bagley, under Col Charles Johnson of Haverhill, who allowed them to go home a few days before their time was out, and Bagley and he journeyed together. Jonathan Jewett, ae 72, testified to service with Bagley under Capt Ezekiel Worthen, in 1778. Claim allowed and certified Apr 29, 1833, for 14 months and 15 dys service.

Nov 20, 1851, Maria Bagley of Thornton, ae 90, deposed that she is the widow of Winthrop Bagley who died at Thornton, July 21, 1850, and sends certificate of the clerk at Epsom, Merrimac Co, NH, showing that Jan 1, 1787, Mr. Winthrop Bagley of Candia and Miss Maria Dudley of Raymond were married by Rev M. Hazelton of Epsom. Samuel C. Dudley of Sanbornton, brother of Maria Bagley, certified to marriage of his sister Maria before May, 1788, when he moved to Sanbornton. After the marriage they moved to Thornton and not long afterwards, I visited them. While I was there, my sister gave birth to a dau who afterwards, I think, married Mr Thornton. All this took place before May, 1788. Claim allowed and No 5893, NH agency, Widow, Apr 3, 1853, Act of Feb 2, 1848. Mar 31, 1858. Maria Bagley applied for bounty land; granted.

He made his will, Mar 16, 1848; filed but never probated, Nov 19, 1850 (insolvent) (Grafton Co NH Probate R). John Keniston was made adm of his estate, Sept 5, 1850. Maria Bagley's will proved 3rd Tuesday, 1855. Only child mentioned was Nancy Thornton (Grafton Co NH Probate R).

Children: Thornton, NH R)
555. Mary (Polly) 7, b Dec 29, 1787; d Sept 19, 1822, ae 36 (tombstone, Thornton)
556. Nancy 7, b Oct 13, 1789; d Dec 23, 1857, ae 68 (tombstone, Thornton)
557. Betsey 7, b Aug 6, 1791; d unm, Dec 29, 1849, ae 50. In 1839, her father deeded her land in Thornton, including the whole of Bagley's Island. She is listed as spinster (Grafton Co NH Deeds).
558. Sally 7, b Oct 24, 1793; d May 25, 1854, ae 47 (tombstone, Thornton)
559. Hannah 7, b Nov 16, 1795

255. Cutting Bagley 6, Jonathan 5, Henry 4, Orlando 3, Orlando 2, Orlando 1 , b Jan 5, 1765; d before June 19, 1817, as adm on his estate was granted then to Thomas Bagley of Durham, NY. Bond of Thomas Bagley as adm with John Bagley and Eli Brooks as sureties, filed June 19, 1817. Oath of appraisal of personal property made by appraiser and filed Dec 16, 1817 (Greene Co NY R). He is mentioned in his father's will in 1809. Married Christiana Barker. In 1817, Cutting Bagley of New Durham, Greene Co, NY, conveyed land in Thornton, NH "all that estate that william Thornton of Thornton died with." (Grafton Co NH Deeds). He moved to Durham, NY, and settled next to his brother John in 1784. On Nov 5, 1793, Edward Griswold, Councilor at law for the original grantees sold Cutting land next to John Bagley's land. He also owned a huge tract of land in partnership with

Phineas Tyler (Greene Co NY Deeds).

Since records are lacking, there is a great deal of question about Cutting's children. When Barnard, supposedly brother of Thomas and Augustus (known to be sons), d in 1878, the Watertown, NY Daily Times for June 27, 1878 says that he was one of eight children, six sons and two daughters. All were living in 1875, when one brother died ae 75; two d in 1877, ae 88 and 90. Four were still living when Barnard died. The Census of 1800 gives 8 children.

When Cutting died, he was land poor. On May 6, 1837, Phineas and Sarah Tyler and Thomas and Mary Bagley (son of Cutting) of Durham sold Ebenezer White land in Durham being the land bought by Phineas and Cutting in joint ownership. But there was a tract of land owned by Cutting alone called the undivided tract. At the time of Cutting's death, this tract was divided into eight parts for each of the eight heirs since Cutting died intestate. From time to time Thomas Bagley bought up some of these shares.

Mar 28, 1831, James Wildey and Submit, his wife, of Windham, NY sold to Thomas Bagley "that certain undivided eight part of two pieces of land which Cutting Bagley died cised and possessed of and which the said James and Submit are heirs to which pieces and parcels of land." On July 2, 1825, Henry Bagley of the town of Nunda (Allegheny Co, NY, and Lucy his wife, sold to Thomas Bagley of Durham "a certain undivided eighth part or parcel of land which Cutting Bagley died with and said Henry is an heir." Benedict and Julliette Bagley, and Barnard Bagley, also sold Thomas Bagley two pieces of undivided land. On May 4, 1837, Orrin and Mary A. Day quitclaimed to Thomas Bagley land which was in the possession of Cutting Bagley at the time of his death. This deed was in the interest of Augustus Bagley "one of the heirs of Cutting Bagley, being the one divided up into eight parts of the half undivided part of said premises owned by Cutting Bagley at his decease." It would appear that we thus have five sons and two daus established for Cutting Bagley if the above reasoning is correct.

Cutting was a Rev War soldier. Following taken from Rowley, MA descriptive list of enl men dated Feb 29, 1782, ae 19, 5 ft 6 1/2 inches, complexion, light, hair brown; occupation, farmer; residing Rowley; enlisted Aug 2, 1782; joined Capt Rufus Lincoln's Co, Lt Col Vrook's 7th regt; deserted June 13 (yr not given), from New Windsor.

Children:
560. Thomas 7, b 1790; d Mar 21, 1876 (tombstone, Durham, NY)
561. Benedict 7
562. Henry 7, b 1794; d 1845 (Nunda, NY tombstone)
563. Barnard 7, b Nov 5, 1791 (Durham Church R); d June 26, 1878 (Watertown Times and tombstone, Durham, NY)
564. Submit 7
565. Augustus 7, b about 1797; d Feb 18, 1882 (East Haven, CO)
566. Mary 7
567. Unknown male 7

258. Jonathan Bagley 6, Jonathan 5, Henry 4, Orlando 3, Orlando 2, Orlando 1 , b Nov 11, 1769; mentioned in father's will in 1809; m Elizabeth Hall of Chester, NH, at Candia, NH, Oct 20, 1793 (Candia, NH R); called Lt. Probably the Capt Jonathan of Searsport, ME, who d at Searsmont, Feb 2, 1853, ae 86 (tombstone). Elizabeth, his wife, d Oct 9, 1861, ae 88 (tombstone)

Children:
568. Betsey or Elizabeth 7
569. Hall 7, b Candia, NH; about 1799; living 1880 (US Census)
570. Jonathan or John 7, b about 1806; d Corinth, ME, Sept 27, 1892, ae 86 (Death record gives place of birth as Candia, NH; father as John)

259. William Bagley 6, Jonathan 5, Henry 4, Orlando 3, Orlando 2, Orlando 1, b Dec 9, 1771; d 1815 (DAR R); m Nov 11, 1803, Mary or Molly Fitts of Sandown, NH (NH R), b 1779, d 1922; mentioned in father's will in 1809. Taxed in Candia in 1800 and 1810. He, with Polly Edmunds, was adm of estate of Edward Edmunds in 1802 (Rockingham Co NH Probate R). Census of 1810 gives 1M-5, 1M-5-10, 1 M 30-40; no females mentioned. This might be the William Bagley of Thornton, NH, whose wife Polly, sold land there in 1810 (Grafton Co NH Deeds).

Children:
571. Currier Fitts 7, b June 27, 1805 (Candia, NH R); d 1854 (DAR R). Another source says d 1871
572. Olive Judson 7, b Dec 18, 1808; d Jan 12, 1810
573. Henry 7, b Nov 6, 1810 (Candia, NH R)
574. William 7 (probably)

260. Molly (Polly) Bagley 6, Jonathan 5, Henry 4, Orlando 3, Orlando 2, Orlando 1 , b Nov 13, 1773; m (1) Dec 7, 1790, Edward Edmunds, who d in 1802; m (2) Simeon Ward and is stated in her father's will in 1809 as being his wife. He d Sept 27, 1848, ae 75.

261. Nathan Bagley 6, Jonathan 5, Henry 4, Orlando 3, Orlando 2, Orlando 1 , b Nov 29, 1775; d Sept 27, 1848, ae 75 of typhoid fever; m Sept 13, 1803, Rhoda Witham of Candia, NH, who d May, 1863, ae 79 (NH R). He conveyed land in Candia, Oct 31, 1814 and July 27, 1815 (Rockingham Co NH Deeds). Taxed in Candia in 1810. Moved from Candia to Gilford, NH after 1814. Census of 1830 shows in addition to children on Candia records two girls, aged 15-20, who might have been born in Gilford. In 1860 Rhoda was living at Meredith Bridge (Laconia). In her household is one Elizabeth Burleigh of the right age to have been one of these girls. In 1850 there is an Eliza Cheney in the household (supplied by Helena Wright, librarian, Merrimac Valley Textile Museum, North Andover, MA).

Children: (Candia, NH R)
575. Jefferson 7, b Nov 25, 1803
576. Thomas 7, b 1805; d Jan 1, 1855, ae 50 (Dedham, MA)

577.   Sally 7, b Apr 29, 1806
578.   Mary Osgood 7, b Feb 25, 1808; d Jan, 1863
579.   Henry Osgood 7, b June 29, 1812

262.   Elizabeth Bagley 6, Jonathan 5, Henry 4, Orlando 3,
Orlando 2, Orlando 1 , b Jan 26, 1776; m Oct 29, 1809,
Jeremiah Bennett (Rockingham Co NH Probate R). By his will,
her father left her the use of a room in his house and part of
the farm, dated Mar 19, 1809. Apparently at this time, she
had an illegitimate child, After her marriage in 1812, her
father made a codicil to his will and gave Elizabeth's two
children one dollar each and left Elizabeth a dollar.

Children:
580.   Elizabeth Bagley 7, b Oct 26, 1803 (Candia, NH R)
581.   Ruth Bennett 7, born before 1812

263.   Moses Bagley 6, Jonathan 5, Henry 4, Orlando 3, Orlando
2, Orlando 1, b Nov 6, 1778; d July 1, 1823; m Judith Currier,
b Newton, NH, dau Aaron & Judith, d May 21, 1875, ae 85.   He
was executor of his father's estate by request of the widow,
May 19, 1819 (Rockingham Co NH Probate R) and was tax
collector in Candia in 1819.   His widow apparently moved back
to Newton for she styles herself as of Newton in deeds in
1826, 1836, and 1844.   Census of 1810, for Newton, NH, gives
1M-5, 1M20-30, 1F - 5, 1F 15-20.

Children:
582.   Aaron Currier 7, b Aug 10, 1807 (Newton NH R)
583.   Betsey 7, b Dec 11, 1809 (Newton NH R); d Oct 21, 1855,
ae 35 (tombstone, Newton, NH)
584.   Sally 7, b Aug 2, 1815 (Candia, NH R)

264.   Sarah (Sally) Bagley 6, Jonathan 5, Henry 4, Orlando 2,
Orlando 1 , b July 29, 1781; d before 1809 as her father
mentions her as deceased in his will and left her children
something; m O. Duncan.

266.   Christina Bagley 6, Jonathan 5, Henry 4, Orlando 3,
Orlando 2, Orlando 1, b Aug 15, 1786; m John Bagley of Candia,
NH, Dec 10, 1816 (Candia, NH R), son Timothy and Sarah, b Dec
30, 1782.   In 1809, her father willed her a feather bed
because she had a sickly constitution.   She and her husband
conveyed land in Candia, NH, Mar 20, 1860, given as of
Raymond, NH; also conveyed land in 1864.   Lived for a time in
West Topsham, VT.   For children, see John Bagley.

267.   Ebenezer Bagley 6, David 5, Henry 4, Orlando 3, Orlando
2, Orlando 1, b about 1763; d Nov 29, 1841, ae 77 (tombstone,
Warner, NH).   See note under his father David as to parentage
and proof of lineage.   His wife was Sarah (Salley), b about
1767, d Aug 17, 1841, ae 74 (tombstone, Warner, NH).
Harriman's History of Warner, NH says he came from Amesbury,
MA.   He bought land in Warner for 60 pounds of Jeremiah
Fowler, John Gage, and Abigail, his wife, the original grant
of Thomas Fowler; also purchased land of Peter and Rebecca

Aikin, Jeremiah and Thomas Fowler, Stephen Gould and Daniel and Hannah Aiken, Aug 24, 1791. The Mar 15, 1788 town records of Warner named him among others as persons to name the moderator of the town meeting, and he served on various other committes during his lifetime.

He kept a tavern across the road from the present Bagley homestead and his sons David and Barnard built houses alike, one still standing and the other located on Bagley Hill long since burned. His name is on Bradford, NH inventory of 1801 with 1 poll, 1 horse, 2 oxen, 1 cow, 1 three-year old, and three two-year olds, two acres of mowing and tilling land; ninety acres of wild land and $8.00 in buildings. The Census of 1800 gives 4 males and 3 females. After Ebenezer's death, the farm was sold to Edward Cressey and later burned.

For a while Ebenezer lived in Durham, NY, and served on the militia there. One of his children died and is buried there.

Children:
585.   Barnard 7, b Sept 3, 1795 (Family R); d Aug 3, 1859, ae 63 (Bradford, NH R & tombstone)
586.   Betsey 7, b about 1797; d Nov 18, 1812, ae 21 (tombstone, Warner, NH)
587.   Abigail 7
588.   David 7, b 1800; d 1866, ae 64 (Warner, NH R; the family records give d Feb 10, 1866)
589.   George W. 7, b 1808; d Jan 17, 1828, ae 20 (tombstone, East Durham, NY)

268.   Barnard Bagley 6, David 5, Henry 4, Orlando 3, Orlando 2, Orlando 1 , b Aug, 1764; d Dec 16, 1838, East Durham, NY; m (1) Elizabeth, d Jan 17, 1836 (tombstone, Durham, NY); m (2) Polly Wade, June 28, 1836. She later m Jonas Kilmer, Dec, 1842. She was appointed guardian for her son Henry Barnard Bagley, b Jan 10, 1839.

Dec 28, 1786, Barnard Bagley of Woodbury, CT, "in full satisfaction of Annie Baggle of Woodbury aforesaid and Ann Baggle to her heirs two pieces of land, dwelling house", etc, "left me by my honored father David Bagley, deceased." This was part of the settlement of the estate of David Bagley; the Annis mentioned being his step-mother and the Ann, his half-sister.

His original lot was purchased of John Nielson of New Brunswick, NJ, Apr 22, 1793. Most of the farm was in Big Hollow, Durham. From time to time he is mentioned in deeds as buying or selling land, e.g., Barnard and Polly, his wife, sold land in Durham in Big Hollow, Dec 22, 1836. Apr 30, 1859, Henry B. Bagley and Polly Kilmer of the town of Scholarie, NY, sold land to David Hopson in Big Hollow. There is no wife signing along with Henry Bagley.

His will, dated Aug 19, 1839 (note discrepency in date of death and date of will), mentioned a son Henry Barnard and leaves real estate in the town of Windham, NY, to three nephews, Samuel Bagley of Windham , NY, and David and Barnard Bagley of NH "sons of my deceased brother Ebenezer". Will admitted to probate, Jan 8, 1839 (Greene Co NY R).

Barnard was a Rev War soldier, priv in Co of Capt Brown, Col Grovenor's regt in NH line for 12 months and 25 dys having served near West Point. His pension deposition is the basis for listing him as son of this David Bagley and part evidence for placing Ebenezer Bagley as his brother. Dated June 28, 1832, Barnard Bagley testified that he was b Aug 1764, at Newton, NH; that he enl from Candia, NH, in the company of Capt Brown and served around Portsmouth in 1779. In July, 1780, he says he served in company of Capt Whittier from Kingston, NH to Great Barrington, MA, to Poughkeepsie, NY to West Point. In Mar, 1781, he enl from Southbury, CT, serving near Fairfield. In July, 1781, he served in the regt of Col Grovenor, his residence being in Southbury, CT, and further states he moved to Durham, NY in 1784. In Sept, 1854, Polly Kilmer applied for bounty land in the name of her son, Henry Barnard, who she states, was b July 10, 1837, and who was "the only child Barnard Bagley ever had."

Child:
590.   Henry Barnard 7, b July 10, 1837

269.   Winthrop Bagley 6, David 5, Henry 4, Orlando 3, Orlando 2, Orlando 1, probably b Candia, NH. May have m Lucy Hawkins, Apr 24, 1793, Orford N. (New England Genealogical Register). She was baptized June 5, 1774.
There was a Winthrop Bagley who settled on the southern slope of high peak on the McGlashian farm in Durham, NY, who was head of a band of counterfeiters. They cut a road running from their camp to within a few rods of the Elm Ridge Road running from Big Hollow to East Windham. There is no proof that this is the same Winthrop, but both Barnard and David settled in the vicinity as did their cousin, John Bagley.

270.   David Bagley 6, David 5, Henry 4, Orlando 3, Orlando 2, Orlando 1, probably b Candia, NH. On May 19, 1792 (CT Deeds), David and Winthrop Bagley sold land left them by their father David Bagley. Nov 9, 1789, a David Bagley and wife Eunice among others bought the entire lot No 124 and other land in Coeymans, NY, subject to an annual quit-rent. All the purchasers are stated to be from CO. On June 2, 1794, there is a will for a David Bagley, State of NY, Freehold, County of Albany, in which he wills land left to me and to my brother Winthrop by "my honored father David Bagley". We are not sure these David Bagleys are the same person, but the evidence is certainly suggestive.
Note: There is a David of Candia, NH, who went from Candia, July 26, 1781, for six months' service: men raised by State of New Hampshire to serve in the Continental Army in year 1781 at West Point. Received of Salmuel Folsom muster master the above 49 men at Exeter, Aug 3, 1781, J. Boynton, Lt., Aug 2, 1781. David Bagley of Candia until the last day of Dec next. The above David is the only David who can be placed in Candia at this time who would fit.

Child:
591.   Samuel 7, where this child should go is a mystery. He

was a nephew of Barnard Bagley as stated in Barnard's will and
probably goes either with David or Winthrop or less probably
with Barnard's half-brother Henry. Born about 1788, he was 53
at the time of his death, July 27, 1841 (NY R). Census of
1840 gives him as being between 50 and 69; his wife in a
deposition stated that at the time of his death, he was
between 50 and 55 years old. Of his known children, none was
named for him or any of his uncles.

272.   Anne Bagley 6, David 5, Henry 4, Orlando 3, Orlando 2,
Orlando 1 , b June 28, 1781 (Southbury, CT R); or June 4, 1779
(Webster Reunion Book); d 1852/57. The date would make her
dau of David and Annis (Hickok). Mrs Lucy Brown of Houston TX
says she m Heman Webster and that some of the line runs as
follows: Roswell Webster m Emily P. Harvey; Melvin H. Webster
m Carrie G. Mack; Maude E. Webster m Guy Benjamin Brown; Lucy
Martha Brown m Robert G. Brown; Lucy J. Brown m Shannon E.
Young . Heman Webster, b Nov 7, 1773, Litchfield, CT, d Apr
27, 1850, Morgan Twnship, OH, son Stephen, descendant Gov John
Webster of CT. Marriage date Sept 7, 1802.

Children: (Family R)
592.   Linnus 7
593.   Truman 7
594.   David 7
595.   Jeremiah 7
596.   Harvey 7
597.   Roxanna 7
598.   Merritt 7
599.   Heman 7
600.   Noah 7
601.   Roxwell 7

274.   Harry (Harvey or Henry) Bagley 6, David 5, Henry 4,
Orlando 3, Orlando 2, Orlando 1 probably b Southbury, CT.

275.   David Bagley 6, Samuel 5, Henry 4, Orlando 3, Orlando 2,
Orlando 1 , b Mar 3, 1763; d West Topsham, VT, 1841. There is
some confusion about his wife or wives. We have found Mary,
Sally, Sarah and Sophia as mothers of some of the children.
There is an inscription on Bagley stone in West Topsham, VT
cemetery marked Sophia Andrews. She d Chelsea, VT, Aug 2,
1855, ae 68. She would have been born about 1787 which makes
her too young to have been the mother of David's older
children, but she could have been the mother of the younger
ones. The best guess seems to be that his first wife was Sally
or Sarah and his second or third Sophia Andrews.
     He was a Rev War soldier from Candia, NH, and went for
Candia; West Point Man in 1781; mustered July 26, 1781; priv
Henry Trebout's Co, Col Goose Van Scharck's regt; muster roll
for Jan-Mar, 1781, dated West Point; disch Mar 18, 1781;
substitute for William Reede (NH Rev War R & National
Archives).

Children: (West Topsham, VT R except as noted)
602. Elijah 7, b Sept 29, 1789 ; d May 13, 1846 (tombstone,

Manchester, NH)
603.   David 7, b Mar 1, 1801; d Oct 29, 1882 (tombstone, W Topsham, VT)
604.   Enoch 7, b Oct 27, 1802; d Dec 29, 1868 (tombstone, W Topsham, VT)
605.   Sally 7, b Jan 7, 1805
606.   John Andrews 7, b Oct 26, 1807; d Mar 7, 1890 (Piermont, NH R)
607.   Eliza 7, b Sept 29, 1809
608.   Charles Whitney 7, b Sept 9, 1811; d Jan 21, 1889 (tombstone, Chelsea, VT, which gives birth date as Sept 9, 1810)
609.   Sophia Andrews 7, b June 7, 1812

278. Molly (Mary) Bagley 6, Samuel 5, Henry 4, Orlando 3, Orlando 2, Orlando 1 , b Oct 29, 1768; living 1804 as mentioned in father's will; m Richard Morrill, probably at Warner, NH, June 10, 1788, probably son Daniel, Jr., and Anna (Fitts), b Feb 17, 1767 (Salis MA R), d 1847.

Child:
610.   Ephraim 7

279. Jacob Bagley 6, Samuel 5, Henry 4, Orlando 3, Orlando 2, Orlando 1, b Dec 5, 1770; mentioned in father's will in 1804 probably m Eunice, who d Aug 14, 1832, ae 66 (tombstone, Mad River, Thornton; no stone for Jacob). He m (2) Polly Buckhart, Nov 15, 1832 (Thornton, NH R), *dau Jacob & Polly*

Children:
611.   Jacob 7
612.   James 7
613.   Elkins 7, b about 1805

Note: There is a listing in Campton, NH R that Joseph Bagley pd a school tax. No other record has been found.

280. Samuel Bagley 6, Samuel 5, Henry 4, Orlando 3, Orlando 2, Orlando 1, b Jan 30, 1773; mentioned in father's will in 1804; according to Magazine of American Genealogy this Samuel should have been b in 1766, but this seems inaccurate; m Marion Lowe or Willey, b Mar 9, 1770. There is some confusion about his wife since there was a Samuel who m Lydia Snow in Chester, NH, and his grandson Charles (presumed) uses that name for Samuel's wife, but the deed mentioned below certainly applies to this Samuel and the name is given as Marion. The Census of 1850 calls her Miriam; it is of course possible that he m twice.

      He served in War of 1812. Bought land in Thornton, NH on Mad River Road near Sandwich Notch Road, Mar 24, 1819, and sold his property to John Bagley of Thornton, Mar 19, 1851. John was to provide Samuel and his wife, Marion, with a room in the same house and firewood (Grafton NH Co NH Deeds).

Children:
614.   John 7, b Jan 4, 1796; d Aug 18, 1836

615.   Rhoda (Polly) 7, b about 1799; d Apr 22, 1885, ae 85 (tombstone, Thornton, NH)
616.   Elijah 7, b about 1804; d May 30, 1888, ae 84 (Thornton NH R & tombstone, Mad River)
617.   Mary 7, b 1804/05; d Sept 24, 1884, ae 84 (Thornton NH R)
618.   Sarah Ann 7, b 1813/14; d Jan 1, 1891, ae 73 (Holderness NH tombstone)

281. Mehitable Bagley 6, Samuel 5, Henry 4, Orlando 3, Orlando 2, Orlando 1 b Oct 10, 1774; mentioned in father's will in 1804; d Sept 1, 1812; m John Huse, June 30, 1793 (Ames MA R); he d Sept 30, 1820 (Belfast ME R).

Children:
619.   John Adams 7, b Feb 22, 1802; d July 12, 1805
620.   Emela 7, b Mar 26, 1805
621.   Stephen 7, b Jan 29, 1804
622.   Harriet 7, b Nov 24, 1808

286. James Bagley 6, Jacob 5, Henry 4, Orlando 3, Orlando 2, Orlando 1, b 1769/70; d Aug 1825, ae 56. Death record at Montville, ME, says b NH, probably at Candia; m Abigail Tolbird, June 6, 1799 (Montville ME R), b Jamestown, Eng., d Feb 23, 1860, ae 87 (Montville, ME R). Farmer. Census of Montville for 1810 gives 3M3-5, 1M 20-30, 2F -5, 2F 20-30.

Children: (Montville, ME R except as noted)
623.   Betsey 7, b Sept 7, 1799
624.   Mary (Polly) 7, b May 10, 1801; d 1851
625.   Sophronia 7, b Jan 25, 1803; d Feb 13, 1870 (Family R)
626.   James, Jr., 7, b Dec 20, 1804
627.   Hannah 7, b Mar 1, 1806; d Mar 12, 1806
628.   Levi 7, b June 23, 1807; d Aug 8, 1891 (Family R)
629.   Samuel 7, b Oct 9, 1809; d June 14, 1898 (Family R)
630.   Richard 7, b June 23, 1811 (tombstone, Montville, ME); d Oct 3, 1896 (Liberty, ME R)
631.   Lydia 7, b Nov 7, 1813; d Oct 29, 1899 (Family R)
632.   Lois 7, b Apr 2, 1817; d Feb 10, 1888 (Family R)
633.   Thomas 7, b 1819; d in Mexican War (Family R), 1847
634.   Esther 7, b Feb 24, 1820; d Aug 5, 1853 (Family R)
635.   Rhoda 7, b Jan 13, 1821; d Mar 25, 1900 (Family R)

287. Rhoda Bagley 6, Jacob 5, Henry 4, Orlando 3, Orlando 2, Orlando 1, b 1787/88; d Dec 9, 1870, ae 83; m Elias Davis, Apr 2, 1808 (intentions Nov 1807), at Montville, ME, who d Apr 30, 1852, ae 66 (Family R).

Children: (Family R except as noted)
636.   Sabra 7, b 1811; d Mar 20, 1884
637.   Amanda 7, b Mar 11, 1812; d Mar 18, 1923
638.   Cyrus F. 7, b 1817/18; d Jan 23, 1901 (Montville ME R)
639.   Warren K. 7, b 1827/28; d Mar 2, 1860, ae 42
640.   Abigail 7, b 1825; d Sept 27, 1902, ae 77
641.   Harriet 7, b 1839; d 1900
642.   Samuel Henry 7, b 1821/22; d Aug 3, 1840

643.   Jane 7, b Dec 22, 1845; d June, 1947
644.   Eunice 7
645.   Thomas 7

288.   David Bagley 6, Jacob 5, Henry 4 Orlando 3, Orlando 2,
Orlando 1, b Apr 12, 1793; d Sept 28, 1871, ae 78 (tombstone,
Lee, ME); records say Sept 7, 1871; m Betsey Moor of Harlem,
ME, now China, ME, Jan 1, 1818 (Family R), dau Leonard, a
shoemaker, b Aug 23, 1797, d Feb 11, 1865, ae 67 (tombstone
Lee, ME & Lee R). He lived for a time at Palermo, ME, and
then in Lee, Lot #2 in the 9th Range.

Children: (Lee ME R except as noted)
646.   Mary Anne 7, b Oct 2, 1818
647.   Emily 7, b June 30, 1820
648.   Henry 7, b July 27, 1822;.d Aug 19, 1840, ae 18
(tombstone, but R say d Aug 23)
649.   Jacob 7, b Apr 27, 1825; d 1882 (Family R)
650.   William 7, b May 3, 1828
651.   Lucretia 7, b May 13, 1831
652.   David 7, b Oct 12, 1834
653.   Samuel 7, b Aug 28, 1837; d Apr 29, 1910, ae 73
(tombstone, Lee, ME)

289.   Mary Bagley 6, Jacob 5, Henry 4, Orlando 3, Orlando 2,
Orlando 1, b 1783/84; d Sept 16, 1805; m John Marden of
Chester, NH, Apr 23, 1801, b Feb 18, 1779; lived Palermo, ME.

Children: (Family R)
654.   Male 7, b 1801/02; d Sept 2, 1805, ae 3
655.   Eliza 7, b 1803
656.   Hiram 7, b Sept 10, 1805

290.   Levi Bagley 6, Jacob 5, Henry 4, Orlando 3, Orlando 2,
Orlando 1, d May 3, 1810, ae 65 (this is the best reading
from a broken tombstone, but could not be correct as he had
children born in 1815, more likely about 1774); m Abigail
(Nabby) Brown, July 26, 1798 (Candia NH R), who d Mar 1, 1847,
ae 68 (tombstone, Montville ME, but R give d Mar 1, 1817)

Children: (Montville ME R)
657.   Richard 7, b Nov 22, 1798
658.   Eliza 7, b Dec 30, 1800
659.   Sally 7, b Nov 18, 1804
660.   Charlotte 7, b July 10, 1807
661.   Henry 7, b July 30, 1809
662.   Nancy 7, b June 18, 1813
663.   Harriet 7, b Aug 21, 1815

291.   Henry Bagley 6, Jacob 5, Henry 4, Orlando 3, Orlando 2,
Orlando 1, b 1798/99; d Mar 3, 1871, ae 72. Marriage
certificate gives him as b Chester, NH; m Eliza Moar of
Belfast, ME, June 8, 1823 (Montville ME R). He was a farmer
and lived Searsmont, ME. She d Oct 29, 1884, ae 80
(Montville ME R)

Children:
664. Susan M. 7, 1824/25; d Apr 15, 1853, ae 28, unm (tombstone, Montville, ME)
665. Hiram 7, d May 22, 1861, ae 34, at Randolph, MA; given as m (MA R)
666. Mary E. 7, b 1832/33; d Oct 20, 1850, ae 18, unm (tombstone, Montville, ME)
667. George F. 7, b 1837; d 1913 (tombstone, Montville, ME); vital records give him as d Dec 20, 1913, ae 76, single, b Montville
668. Augustus 7, b Dec 15, 1847; d Jan 15, 1918, by cutting his throat, unm (Montville ME R)

295. Jacob Bagley 6, Jacob 5, Henry 4, Orlando 3, Orlando 2, Orlando 1 , Mr Pierce Lee thinks this Jacob was brother to David who went to Calais, ME, or New Brunswick; however, we think he goes here; b about 1800; m Hannah French of Montville, ME, Oct 29, 1831 (Montville & Portland ME R). The Moses Bagley family went to Montville, ME, with Jacob Bagley, Jr. Some of their children were named Bagley since Hannah Bagley m Moses French, Jr., of Candia, NH, Oct 24, 1799. She b Amesbury and a dau of theirs, Mary, d at Candia, NH, Oct 17, 1893, ae 81 and is buried at Martin's Corner, NH. Census of 1840 gives 2M-5, 2M 5-10, 1M 30--40, 1F -5, 1F 30-40.

Children:
669. Charles Durham 7, b May 17, 1832
670. Joseph Stacey 7, b Dec 5, 1833
671. Moses French 7, b Oct 6, 1835
672. James Madison 7, b July 19, 1837

296. William Bagley 6, Jacob 5, Henry 4, Orlando 3, Orlando 2, Orlando 1 , b 1772, Montville, ME.

313. Nathan Bagley 6, David 5, David 4, Orlando 3, Orlando 2, Orlando 1 , b Mar 13, 1768; d Nov 1, 1845, ae 77; m Betsey Foard, probably baptized Dec 1, 1771, dau William & Mary (Gilbert) (Gloucester MA R), b about 1771, d Sept 19, 1854, ae 82 (tombstone, W Topsham, VT). (MA R say she d Sept 17, 1854, b Haverhill, NH). At the time of their marriage they were both from Newton, NH. A deed from Asa Porter to Nathan Bagley of Warner, NH, dated Nov 5, 1799, conveys land to Nathan in West Topsham, VT (Topsham Land Book).

Children: (West Topsham VT R except as noted)
673. Hannah 7, b Apr 21, 1791 (Warner NH R); d Mar 26, 1841, unm (tombstone, W Topsham)
674. William 7, b Apr 24, 1792 (Warner NH R)
675. Betsey 7, b Dec 13, 1793 (Warner NH R)
676. Rhoda 7, b Feb 6, 1797 (also on Warner NH R which give 1793, an error); d Jan 24, 1843
677. Nathan 7, b May 23, 1799; d May 30, 1881 (tombstone, W Topsham)
678. Marcy G. 7, b Mar 9, 1801; d Sept 27, 1858 (Piermont NH R)
679. Philip 7, b Aug 13, 1802

680.   John F., b Mar 2, 1804
681.   Harriet 7, b Apr 30, 1806
682.   Charlotte 7, b Oct 15, 1809; d May 2, 1886 (Piermont   NH
R)

314.   Jonathan Bagley 6, David 5, David 4, Orlando 3, Orlando
2, Orlando 1, b Aug 13, 1772; d Nov 1, 1860; had, as a
common-law wife, Sally Goodwin, b Feb 9, 1770, d Dec, 1807, ae
37, dau Seth & Mary (tombstone, Bradford, NH). He m July 21,
1808, Mrs Rachel Morgan of Hopkinton, NH, who d Oct 3, 1841,
ae 70, and is buried with Jonathan in the Reuben Moore Yard.
The family cemetery is situated in a large field and is
enclosed by a wooden fence. His common-law wife is not buried
there but all alone in the Old Burial Ground in Bradford, NH.
       He was second selectman of Bradford, July 6, 1815, and
sealer of weights and measures, Mar, 1812 (Bradford NH R) .
He first appears on Bradford records in inventory of 1798
which gives him as having 1 poll, 2 oxen, 1 cow, 2 acres
mowing and tillage and 90 acres of wild land, buildings first
listed in that year, but Jonathan apparently did not have any.
In 1800 he had 1 poll, 2 oxen, 1 cow and a two-year-old, 2
acres mowing and tillage, 80 acres of wild land and $3 worth
of buildings. apparently a log cabin. In 1802, he had
buildings worth $10, probably the 1st part of the home of
Reuben Moore of Bradford, NH, which burned in the late 1960's.

Children: (Bradford NH R)
683.   David 7, b Sept 28, 1797; d Mar 31, 1873, Washington,
NH. There is another David listed with Jonathan & Sally at
Warner as being b Sept 28, 1787, but this seems a mistake. If
correct, he d young.
684.   Worcester 7, b Oct 7, 1799; d Jan 25, 1879 (Newbury NH
R)
685.   Sally 7, b Aug 2, 1801; d Feb 17, 1886, unm
686.   Gilman 7, b Dec 15, 1803; d Mar 26, 1872, unm (Family
Bible gives him as b 1804)
687.   Rachel F. 7, b July 4, 1812

315.   Elizabeth Bagley 6, David 5, David 4, Orlando 3, Orlando
2, Orlando 1, b Sept 16, 1774; probably m James Flanders of
Salisbury, NH, Dec 22, 1797, at Warner, NH (Warner NH R).

316.   Philip Bagley 6, David 5, David 4, Orlando 3, Orlando 2,
Orlando 1, b July 10, 1777 (Warner NH R)

317.   Sarah Bagley 6, David 5, David 4, Orlando 3, Orlando 2,
Orlando 1, b Dec 2, 1779; m Oct 5, 1800, at Warner, NH,
Phineas Bailey, b Dunbarton, NH, 1772; and lived at Orford, NH
& Fairlee, VT. Had nine children of whom two were living in
1858, Major Jerome of Fairlee and Hannah Bagley Mason (History
of Fairlee, VT.

320.   David Bagley 6, David 5, David 4, Orlando 3, Orlando 2,
Orlando 1, b Oct 19, 1794; supposed to have gone to Cayuga Co.
NY.
321.   Joshua Bagley 6, David 5, David 4, Orlando 3, Orlando 2,

Orlando 1, b Dec 29, 1796; d Aug 21, 1886, ae 69, unm. Adm granted Gideman Bean of Warner, Sept term, 1866. Inventory real estate $2900; personal estate $622.39; cash $1554.25; Apr term, 1867, account settled; d intestate (Merrimac Co NH Probate R).

322. Ruth Bagley 6, Joshua 5, David 4, Orlando 3, Orlando 2, Orlando 1, b Mar 7, 1778; d May 13, 1806, ae 28; not mentioned in father's will in 1809; m at Kingston, NH, Jan 20, 1802, Bagley Carter, b Feb 23, 1770 (E Kingston NH R), who d May 26, 1815, ae 41 (tombstone, Newton, NH). Salis MA R say d May 25, 1815.

Children:
688.   Joshua Bagley 7, b Dec 8, 1802 (Salis MA R)
689.   Bagley 7, b May 11, 1806; d July 11, 1806 (tombstone, Newton, NH)

325. Lydia Bagley 6, Joshua 5, David 4, Orlando 3, Orlando 2, Orlando 1, b Oct 2, 1780; d May 31, 1814, ae 34; m Isaac Merrill, intentions May 5, 1804 (Ames MA R). He was executor of her father's will in 1809, and the will states that Lydia is wife to Isaac Merrill (Rockingham Co NH Probate R). He d Mar 13, 1840, ae 59 (tombstone, Newton, NH)

Children:
690.   Isaac 7, b about 1809; d Sept 24, 1853, ae 44 (tombstone, Newton, NH)
691.   Joshua Bagley 7, b 1814; d Aug 3, 1814 (tombstone, Newton, NH)

326. Dolly Bagley 6, Joshua 5, David 4, Orlando 3, Orlando 2, Orlando 1, b Sept 20, 1782; d Apr 11, 1847, ae 64; mentioned in father's will as single but she later m Isaac Merrill, widower of her sister Lydia, Mar 16, 1815.

Children:
692.   Lydia 7, b about 1816; d Apr 18, 1888, ae 72, unm (tombstone, Newton, NH)
693.   Joshua Bagley 7, b about 1821; d Jan 9, 1848, ae 27 (tombstone, Newton, NH)
694.   Polly 7, b about 1830; d June 22, 1869, ae 39, unm (tombstone, Newton, NH)

327. Judith Bagley 6, Joshua 5, David 4, Orlando 3, Orlando 2, Orlando 1, b Jan 17, 1787; mentioned in father's will as single in 1809; later married Bagley Carter, widower of her sister Ruth, intentions, Feb 10, 1810 (Salis MA R).

Children:
695.   Merrill 7, b June 9, 1812 (Salis MA R)
696.   Tappan 7, b July 2, 1814 (Salis MA R)

328. David Bagley 6, Elijah 5, David 4, Orlando 3, Orlando 2, Orlando 1, b Feb 22, 1777; d Oct 5, 1854. Farmer but

previous to War of 1812 sold dry goods for 20 yrs. A Baptist 10 years, he left them for the Freewill Baptists and was a deacon; anti-slavery and member of the Liberty Party in 1845-46, and a candidate for the legislature. He and Hannah Bagley were adm of his father's estate and sold land in Newton, NH, in 1816 (Rockingham Co NH Probate R & Deeds). He m Sally, who d Mar 19, 1847, ae 69 (tombstone, W Topsham, VT); m (2) Salerina, who d Dec 24, 1852, ae 51 (tombstone, W Topsham, VT); probably m (3) Mrs. Jerusha Tillotson, Dec 18, 1853, who d Aug 12, 1872, ae 86 (W Topsham VT R).

There is some confusion as to whether or not the children of David Bagley who m Sophia Andrews and this David Bagley go with the right David. As has been pointed out, David probably had a wife prior to Sophia Andrews and Sophia seems to have been called Sally. Some of the children listed on the records say only child of David & Sally. The Census of 1830 for David Bagley gives 2M 10-15, 1M 15-20, 1M 40-50, 1F 5-10, 1F 15-20, 1F 20-30, and 1F 50-60. This is right for numbers for David and Sophia but not for ages. If it refers to the above David, then we do not have all the children. What we have done is to place them where they seem to go logically, and those buried on the same lot.

Children: (W Topsham VT R except as noted)
697. George K. 7, b about 1816; d May 31, 1882 (Chelsea VT R & tombstone)
698. William A. 7, b about 1815; d May 31, 1884, ae 69 (VT R)
699. Gilman W. 7, b about 1818; d Sept 30, 1904, ae 69 (tombstone)

329. William Bagley 6, Elijah 5, David 4, Orlando 3, Orlando 2, Orlando 1, b July 22, 1779; d before Sept 9, 1809; m Elizabeth Nichols of Amesbury, MA, Apr 14, 1803 (Newton NH R); intentions Feb 19, 1803 (Ames MA R). She was adm of his estate Sept, 1811, and sold to Elijah Bagley of Newton land laid out in the right of Capt David Bagley, deceased, Feb 24, 1812 (Rockingham Co NH Probate R & Deeds). Appt adm of her husband's estate in MA, Sept 7, 1809, and made guardian of his children, Sept 6, 1810 (Essex Co MA Probate R). Census of 1810 for Amesbury, MA, gives 2 males under 5, 1 female 20-30 and 1 female under 5.

Children:
700. John 7, b about 1803
701. Ann 7, b about 1806
702. Eunice 7, b about 1808
703. Elizabeth 7, b about 1809; d Ames, MA, Sept 29, 1889, ae 91; given as dau William & Elizabeth (MA R)
704. William 7, b about 1810; d Mar 2, 1876, ae 65 (MA R)

330. Enoch Bagley 6, Elijah 5, David 4 Orlando 3, Orlando 2, Orlando 1, b Jan 13, 1782; d May 19, 1823; m Sarah Colby, Nov 26, 1808, at Newton, NH (Kingston Church R), who d Aug 7, 1823 (Newton NH R). Elizabeth Bagley, adm of estate sold land to Enoch Bagley, June 16, 1813, in W Topsham, VT, witnessed by Elijah Bagley (Rockingham Co NH Probate R & Deeds). John

Bagley was appt guardian of Enoch's minor children under 14 yrs of age, who were William, Robert, and Susan, in 1823, and on Oct 13, 1834, guardian of Susan. William and Robert conveyed land in Newton, NH, in 1842, as heirs-at-law of Elijah, their grandfather (Rockingham Co NH Deeds).

Children:
705. Nancy 7, b Mar 8, 1809 (Newton NH R)
706. William 7, b about 1811; d Jan 6, 1849, ae 38 (tombstone, Newton, NH)
707. Robert 7, b about 1812; d Dec 4, 1891, ae 79 (tombstone, Newton, NH)
708. Susan 7, b Newton, NH, about 1816 (Census of 1860)

332. Elizabeth Bagley 6, Elijah 5, David 4 Orlando 3, Orlando 2, Orlando 1, b Aug 29, 1787; d Apr 15, 1847; m John Sargent, Nov 30, 1812 (Newton NH R), son David and Sarah (Favour), b June 27, 1791. He m (2), at Newton, NH, Sept 27, 1849, Mrs Lucy Clark. Both d Haverhill, MA, where he was a carpenter. He is buried Newton, NH; in 1842 Elizabeth conveyed land in Newton as one of the heirs-at-law of her father (Rockingham Co NH Deeds).

Children:
709. Elijah Bagley 7, b May 27, 1813; d Dec 27, 1886
710. Sarah 7, b Aug 23, 1817; d 1896
711. John 7, b Aug 25, 1819; d 1850
712. Elizabeth 7, b July 10, 1822; d 1845
713. Mary A. 7, b May 27, 1825; d Aug 11, 1878
714. Harriet M. 7, b Nov 7, 1827

333. Sarah (Sally) Bagley 6, Elijah 5, David 4, Orlando 3, Orlando 2, Orlando 1, b Jan 13, 1790; d Dec 24, 1848, ae 53 (note that date of birth and death do not agree with age); m Daniel Hoit, Feb 22, 1820 (Kingston NH R), son Reuben & Hannah, b May 31, 1788, d July 22, 1834, ae 46 (tombstone, Newton, NH). In 1842, she conveyed land in Newton, as one of the heirs-at-law of her father, under the name of Hoit (Rockingham Co NH Deeds). They resided Newton, NH.

Children:
715. Elijah B. 7, b July, 1821; d Jan 3, 1904 (tombstone, Newton, NH)
716. Sarah E. 7, b Feb, 1823
717. Hannah C. 7, b Mar, 1830
718. Lucina 7, b about 1834; d Jan 25, 1913, ae 79 (tombstone, Newton, NH)

334. Molly (Polly) Bagley 6, Elijah 5, David 4, Orlando 3, Orlando 2, Orlando 1, b July 10, 1792; d Dec 12, 1840; m Benjamin Currier of South Hampton, NH, Oct, 1814 (Newton NH R). He d Mar 5, 1863, ae 71 (tombstone, Newton, NH).

335. John Bagley 6, Valentine 5, Jonathan 4, Orlando 3, Orlando 2, Orlando 1, b Jan 31, 1765; d Apr 19, 1826, ae 61; m Sarah (Sally) Hackett, July 4, 1791, at Second Church,

Salisbury, MA (Salis MA R). Intentions are on Amesbury, MA R as June 17, 1791, and Salis MA R give date of m as July 7, or Aug 9, 1791. She b Feb 23, 1766, d Aug 5, 1845, ae 80, dau Capt William & Anna (Osgood) (Salis MA R).   He was called Captain.

Children: (Salis MA R)
719.   Dolly 7, b Apr 14, 1792
720.   Nancy 7, b Jan 27, 1795
721.   William Hackett 7, b June 2, 1799; d Oct 18, 1856 (tombstone, Ames, MA)
722.   John 7, b Mar 10, 1804; d Aug 26. 1865 (tombstone. Georgetown, MA)
723.   Sarah Ann 7, b Mar 27, 1807

339. Valentine Bagley 6, Valentine 5, Jonathan 4, Orlando 3, Orlando 2, Orlando 1 , b Jan 17, 1773; d Jan 19, 1839; m Hannah Currier, July 24, 1796 (Ames MA R), dau Timothy & Ann (Colley), a twin, b July 27, 1774, d Oct 1, 1859, ae 85 (MA R). He lived in Amesbury, and was the sea captain who was the subject of John Greenleaf Whittier's poem "The Captain's Well". He dug the famous well in 1796.
    Capt Valentine Bagley early took to sea and became a sailor. For some time he was connected with the Brig Mechannis, which sailed from his home. On May 4, 1791, he sailed from Salem, MA, as second mate on the Grand Sachem on an Indian voyage. He arrived at Cape of Good Hope in 166 days; sailed from the Cape, Oct 9, and arrived at Isle de France, Nov 11. Here on Christmas Day, he left the vessel and about a month later shipped as carpenter's mate on the brig Commerce of Boston, John Leach, Master. He arrived Madras, Mar 25, 1792. Here Capt Samuel Johnson took command, and they sailed to Bombay, Apr 28. Capt Johnson, unfamiliar with the coast, sailed farther west than he should have and ran the vessel ashore on the coast of Arabia .
    All efforts to get the vessel off proved unsuccessful, and the crew were obliged to take to boats. The hostility of the natives prevented them from going ashore, and all there was left to do was to stock the boats with everything that was necessary and try for Muscat, the nearest seaport where an European vessel could be found. Thirty-four men embarked in boats. Two days later a yawl had to be abandoned, and the next day the weather compelled them to give up the idea of reaching Muscat by sea. In getting ashore one of the boats capsized and three men were drowned. The next day they were attacked and robbed by Arabs who stripped them of their very shirts on their back and even cut off one man's hair for the ribbon on which it was tied.   Then walking, barefoot and destitute, they started on a 500-mile march across the desert and rocky terrain to Muscat.
    In the desert they suffered many hardships from thirst and exposure and here Capt Valentine vowed that if he ever got home again, he would dig a well for the Lord.   Securing at last some help from some friendly Arabs with camels they reached Muscat on the Gulf of Oman after more than a month of hardship; of the seventeen white men who left the ship, only 8

survived. While on the desert, a companion, Charles Lapham,
fell by the way and was covered with sprays and leaves by a
tree and left to die. It was his request that if Capt Bagley
lived to get home and should have a son, he would name him
Charles Lapham. Capt Bagley was in such destitute condition
that he was not willing to return home but shipped from Muscat
as a carpenter's mate on an Arabian vessel. He made several
voyages. While he was away, his companions published an
account of their sufferings in the desert.

In 1817, in Amesbury, MA, Capt Bagley opened a public
house at Bartlett's Corner where he kept for many years a
tavern in the good old style of those times. A large open yard
was left for public use, and it was a lively place during May
militia training. The signpost read: V. Bagley, 1818. He was
a member of Warren Lodge, AF & AM, Amesbury. He made his
will, Aug 10, 1838; proved Feb 1838 (Essex Co MA Probate R).

Children: (Ames M R)
724. Male 7, d Feb, 1797, infant
725. Charles Lapham 7, b Mar 28, 1798; not mentioned in
father's will 1838
726. Rhoda 7, b Jan 15, 1801; d July, 1801
727. Harriet 7, b Feb 11, 1804; d Apr 9, 1833
728. Edward H. 7, b Oct 9, 1808; d Dec, 1808
729. William E. 7, b June 2, 1812; d May 20, 1845
730. Valentine 7, b Oct 24, 1814; d Nov 8, 1860

340. William Bagley 6, Valentine 5, Jonathan 4, Orlando 3,
Orlando 2, Orlando 1, b May 27, 1780; d July 12, 1812, ae 33.
Ames MA R say that Capt William who d on this date was the son
of William & Susanna which is a mistake as the dates do not
agree. He was called captain & m Sally Worthen, Feb 27, 1803,
dau Ezra & Jerusha (Bagley), b Jan 23, 1779 (AMES MA R) of
Consumption, Jan 16, 1843, ae 64 (Salis MA R). She made her
will, Jan 9, 1843 (Essex Co MA Probate R).

Children: (Ames MA R)
731. Hannah Curier 7, b Dec 15, 1803
732. Daniel Currier 7, b Mar 8, 1806; d Apr 17, 1864
(tombstone, Ames, MA)
733. Paulina 7, b Apr 29, 1808; d May 18, 1881 (Family R)

347. Dorothy B. Bagley 6, Orlando 5, Jonathan 4, Orlando 3,
Orlando 2, Orlando 1, b July 5, 1771; d 1818; mentioned in
father's will in 1807; m Elijah Weed, Feb 26, 1794 (Ames MA
R), son Isaac & Merriam (Clough), b June 10, 1762; d Mar 5,
1823 (Ames MA R).

Children: (Ames MA R)
734. Hannah 7, b Dec 17, 1794; d Dec 9, 1809; buried
Merrimac, MA
735. Elijah B. 7, b Sept 26, 1810
736. Hannah 7, b Dec 18, 1812
737. Anna H. 7, b May 30, 1815

348. David Wells Bagley 6, Orlando 5, Jonathan 4, Orlando 3,

Orlando 2, Orlando 1 , b Oct 25, 1774; mentioned in grandfather's will, Mar 23, 1779, but not in father's will in 1807; m Sally Weed, Jan 29, 1799, probably dau Isaac & Mary (Ring), b June 29, 1774, d Jan 24, 1812 (Ames MA R). He probably m (2) Feb 27, 1815, Dolly Selley of Seabrook, NH (Salis MA R). There is no documentary proof yet found that the David who m Dolly is the same as he who m Sally. However, he is only David who would fit. His wife d three years before the second marriage. While it can be argued that he is not mentioned in his father's will in 1807, which argues for his being dead, there are several instances in which a child was not named in father's will because the father had already provided for him in his own lifetime. Note too that he named the first son by second wife, Orlando.

Children: (Salis MA R)
738.   Mary 7, b Jan 1, 1805 (Ames MA R)
739.   Abigail Jpoy 7, b Nov 7, 1815
740.   Orlando 7, b Aug 30, 1818
741.   Emily Ann 7, b Sept 9, 1821; d Dec 7, 1823
742.   Emily Ann 7, b Sept 20, 1824; d Dec 12, 1824

349. Molly (Mary) Bagley 6, Orlando 5, Jonathan 4, Orlando 3, Orlando 2, Orlando 1 , b Dec 3, 1776; m a Sanborn, as stated in father's will which mentions the children.

Children: (Essex Co MA Probate R)
743.   Sally 7
744.   Orlando Bagley 7
745.   Dorothy 7
746.   Polly 7

350. Hannah Bagley 6, Orlando 5, Jonathan 4, Orlando 3, Orlando 2, Orlando 1 , b Jan 4, 1782; not mentioned in father's will in 1807; m Feb 23, 1806, Moses Hoyt 4th, probably son David & Judith (Currier), b Mar 16, 1777, d June 11, 1840, ae 63 (Ames MA R). He lived on his father's homestead next to Amesbury Town House. Part of family's record was furnished to Miss Florence Norton, a descendant of Orlando 5, by a grandaughter of Hannah Hoyt, so there must have been other children unless Anna m very young.

Child:
747.   Anna 7, b Jan 1, 1807; d Sept 22, 1828 (Ames MA R)

351. Jonathan Bagley 6, Orlando 5, Jonathan 4, Orlando 3, Orlando 2, Orlando 1 , b Jan 8, 1785; d June 23, 1861, ae 75; m Sarah (Sally) Smith, dau Timothy & Ezekia of Sanbornton, NH, intentions, June 27, 1807 (Ames MA R) , m Oct 13, 1807 (History of Sanbornton, NH); she d Sept 3, 1867, ae 83 (tombstone, Shipley Cemetery, Londonderry, NH). The vital records of Londonderry, edited by Danniel Annis say her father was Ezekiel Smith and her mother Sarah. The Sanbornton history says her father was Timothy and that he came to Sanbornton before the Rev War being the only one of the four Smiths in town to sign the Association Test in Apr, 1774.

Nothing more is known of him except he d Feb 11, 1812, and was buried west of the present Obediah Eastman place on Steele Hill. Cemetery has not been found. Sarah, wife of Jonathan, was the last Smith to occupy her father's homestead.

He sold land in Warren, NH, Dec 15, 1825, and in Londonderry, NH, Oct 5, 1826 (Grafton & Rockingham Co Deeds). he sold land in Plymouth in right of his wife, Nov 25, 1843, and may have lived in Plymouth for a time. After his death his heirs sold land in Plymouth; names on the deed are J. R. Bagley, M. J. Bagley, Sarah Bagley, Orlando Bagley, A. F. Bagley, Richard & Sarah Strong, and John & Mahala Greeley, Jr. (Grafton Co NH Deeds). In his father's will, dated May 12, 1807, Jonathan was to carry on the home place; half to his mother; and was executor of his father's will (Essex Co MA Probate R). The Census of 1850 gives him as of Plymouth, NH.

Children:
748. Orlando 7, b Manchester, NH, May, 1809; d July 10, 1867, Biddeford, ME (Manchester, NH R, where he is buried)
749. Mahala 7, b Oct 22, 1882, probably Sanbornton; d May 19, 1914 (tombstone, Hudson, NH)
750. Hannah 7, probably b Sanbornton and probably d young
751. Sarah Ann 7, b Mar, 1817, probably Sanbornton; d Oct 20, 1896 (tombstone, Hudson, NH)
752. Jonathan 7, b Mar 16, 1820, Sanbornton, NH; d July 17, 1900 (Londonderry, NH R)

355. Mary Bagley 6, Israel 5, Thomas 4, Orlando 3, Orlando 2, Orlando 1, b Nov 22, 1768; baptized Apr 7, 1771; m Mar 1, 1787, at Turner, ME, Edward Fifield (History of Durham, ME). He was of Royalsborough, now Durham, as early as 1784; b Kingston, NH, July 10, 1765. They moved to Greenwood, ME, about 1814-1817. She d Oct 8, 1857, Greenwood ME (ME R).

Children: (History of Durham, ME)
753. O. Israel Bagley 7, b Apr 1787; early settler at Ripley, ME
754. John 7, b Dec 17, 1788
755. Elizabeth 7, b May 31, 1791
756. Winthrop 7, b Apr 17, 1793; d Apr 21. 1794
757. Dolly 7, b May 25, 1795
758. Mary Snow 7, b Nov 20, 1796; d Feb 8, 1805

356. Elizabeth Bagley 6, Israel 5, Thomas 4, Orlando 3, Orlando 2, Orlando 1, b Apr 26, 1770; baptized Apr 7, 1771; m Reuben Dwyer, Apr 21, 1794, b Sept 9, 1770.

Children: (History of Durham, ME)
759. O. Israel Bagley 7, b Apr 18, 1796
760. Mary 7, b Mar 25, 1798
761. Reuben 7, b Feb 14, 1800

357. Hannah Bagley 6, Israel 5 Thomas 4, Orlando 3, Orlando 2, Orlando 1, b Durham, ME, June 14, 1773; d Oct, 1843; m July 28, 1793, Enoch Newell, b Feb 14, 1770, son Ebenezer & Catherine (Richards), d Mar 18, 1848.

Children: (History of Durham, ME)
762.   O. Israel Bagley 7, b Apr 5, 1794; d 1846
763.   Enoch 7, b June 19, 1796; d Sept 2, 1825
764.   Hannah 7, b June 1, 1798; d Mar 25, 1805
765.   Lora 7, b Apr 20, 1800; d Mar 22, 1805
766.   Ebenezer 7, b Apr 16, 1802
767.   Edward 7, b Mar 16, 1804; d Oct 6, 1864
768.   Freeman 7
769.   Daniel 7, b Nov 23, 1809; d Jan 13, 1887
770.   Stillman 7, b 1816; d 1847
771.   Mary 7
772.   Hosea 7, b about 1807; m Esther; lived Yarmouth, ME

358.   Susannah Bagley 6, Israel 5, Thomas 4, Orlando 3,
Orlando 2, Orlando 1 , b Mar 9, 1777; d June 5, 1798; m
Francis Harmon, Oct 15, 1797, son Daniel & Sarah (York), b
Standish, ME, June 1, 1772.

Child: (History of Durham, ME)
773.   O. Israel Bagley 7, b Mar 7, 1798; d 1820

359.   Thomas Bagley 6, Israel 5, Thomas 4, Orlando 3, Orlando
2, Orlando 1 , b 1779, Ripley, ME; d Apr 26, 1842, Troy, ME; m
Susannah Gerrish, Mar 22, 1801, b Durham, ME, Mar 9, 1777, dau
George & Mary (Mitchell), at Durham, ME.   He sold land in
Troy, ME, to Jacob & Charles Bagley, Sept 3, 1829; land bought
by Jacob was land purchased from David Millet, who bought the
land from Thomas.   A quit-claim deed says Thomas lived in
Troy, on July 30, 1830.

Children:
774.   Orlando Israel 7, b Durham, ME, Sept 19, 1801; d Mar,
1847 (ME R)
775.   Joseph Mitchell 7, b Mar 16, 1803; d May 16, 1863
(Family R)
776.   George Gerrish 7, b Durham, ME, Jan 20, 1805 (Family R)
777.   Enoch 7 (probably), b about 1806; d Troy, ME, Nov 3,
1892, ae 86 (tombstone, troy, ME).   There is some confusion
about the Enochs of Troy, ME, and we have not found
documentary proof that this Enoch goes with Thomas.   Some
sources give him as son of Israel, Thomas' father.   However,
Israel was having children in the 1770's, while Thomas was
having them in the 1800's.   On source says that Israel's son,
Enoch, m Merriam Hoyt, but this was Israel's brother.   A
descendant of this line says that Thomas had a son Enoch.
778.   Thomas 7 (Family R)
779.   Mary 7, b Dec 14, 1810; d Dec 17, 1887, Thorndike, ME
(Family R)
780.   Susan J. 7, b 1813; d Nov 6, 1841 (Family R)
781.   Orzilla 7, b 1815; d July 13, 1891; buried Grove
Cemetery, Belfast, ME, but no stone (Family R)
782.   Hannah J. 7, b 1819; d May, 1871, Chicopee, MA (Family
R)

783.   Jeremiah 7, d in Cuba (Family R)
784.   James G. 7, b 1822; d at sea, 1868, ae 46 (Family R)

361.   Rhoda Bagley 6, Thomas 5 Thomas 4, Orlando 3, Orlando 2
Orlando 1 , b May 18, 1774; m Jan 17, 1793, William Proctor,
at Second Church, Salisbury, MA (Salis MA R).

Children:
785.   William 7, b Aug 21, 1793 (Salis MA R)
786.   James 7, b Feb 10, 1795 (Salis MA R)
787.   John 7, b Apr 21, 1796; d June 8, 1803
788.   Thomas 7, b Feb 5, 1798; d Sept 23, 1802
789.   Amos 7, b Jan 23, 1800; d July 19, 1800
790.   Rhoda 7, b May 16, 1801; d July 1, 1801
791.   Amos 7, b May 10, 1802; m Lydia Richards
792.   John 7, b Aug 13, 1804; d Dec 30, 1883
793.   Sally 7, b Mar 23, 1806; d Jan 16, 1892; m Thomas
Cilley, Nov 27, 1825 ?
794.   Rhoda 7, b Aug 16, 1807; d Jan 4, 1895; m Timothy Dane,
Feb 2, 1834
795.   Sylvia 7, b Mar 31, 1809; d Jan 4, 1895
796.   Thomas 7, b Jan 14, 1811
797.   Jonathan 7, b Jan 10, 1813; d Mar 1, 1817

362.   Polly Bagley 6, Thomas 5, Thomas 4, Orlando 3, Orlando
2, Orlando 1 , b May 2, 1776; d Sept 26, 1804; m John Sanborn
of Sanbornton, NH, Aug 21, 1796 (Ames MA R), b Sept 21, 1773,
styled Jr., and also "Dote", son Josiah & his second wife.
They lived in Sanbornton. After his wife's death he moved
down East and went to sea, hence the name "Mariner".

Children:
798.   Sarah Shaw 7, b Sept 8, 1797
799.   Orlando Bagley 7, b Oct 8, 1799
800.   Dolly Wood 7, b Feb 7, 1802

363.   Sukey or Susan Bagley 6, Thomas 5, Thomas 4, Orlando 3,
Orlando 2, Orlando 1 , b Jan 20, 1779; m Stephen Brown, Aug
11, 1801, son Jacob II, baptized Aug 29, 1773; d Dec 27, 1823
(Ipswich MA R).

Children: (Kensington NH R)
801.   Joseph 7, b Mar 9, 1803; d Kensington, Apr 18, 1887; m
Mary Anne Weare
802.   Amos Bagley 7, b Mar 11, 1804; m Sophia Boardman
803.   Polly 7, b Feb 18, 1806' m Joseph Weare, May 30, 1829
804.   Nancy 7, b Oct 10, 1807; d Kensington, Mar 28, 1838
805.   John 7, b Dec 25, 1811; d Brentwood, NH, May 23, 1882
806.   Stephen 7, b Feb 4, 1817; d July 7, 1900
807.   Moses 7, b July 13, 1818
808.   Jonathan 7, b July 13, 1818; m Lucy Weare
809.   Susan Rebecca 7, b Dec 27, 1825; d Oct 19, 1844

364.   Ruth Bagley 6, Thomas 5, Thomas 4, Orlando 3, Orlando 2,
Orlando 1 , b Aug 10, 1783; d Jan 13, 1824; probably m Feb 15,

1804, Joshua Page, d Dec 3, 1847, ae 78 (Salis MA R).   He probably m (2) Nov 26, 1824, Sarah Greeley.

Child:
810.   Thomas 7, b Mar 1, 1805; probably m (1) Mary Hunt, Nov 6, 1831; m (2) Eliza Goodwin, Dec 29, 1845. He is given as widower, ae 40 and she ae 30 which must be a mistake since she was b Aug 19, 1809 (Salis MA R)

365.   Amos Bagley 6, Thomas 5, Thomas 4, Orlando 3, Orlando 2, Orlando 1 , b Aug 1, 1788; d Aug 8, 1811, intentions to Sally Fowler, May 18, 1811 (Salis MA R).

366.   Joseph Bagley 6, Thomas 5, Thomas 4, Orlando 3, Orlando 2, Orlando 1 , b June 18, 1792 (Salis MA R)

380.   Jonathan Bagley 6, Enoch 5, Thomas 4 Orlando 3, Orlando 2, Orlando 1 , b June 8, 1782; d Feb 28, 1881, ae 99; m Oct 4, 1804, Eunice Reed, dau Abram & _____ (Brown). She d Aug 27, 1865, ae 85 (tombstone, Troy, ME). They sold land in Troy, ME, Apr 23, 1828, Enoch, Jr., a witness. On Census of 1850.

Children: (Troy ME R)
811.   John 7, b Apr 22, 1810; d July 6, 1871
812.   Hannah 7, b July, 1813; d Feb 6, 1852
813. Polly 7 also called Mary, d 1839 (Family R)
814.   Susan 7, b 1817; d 1889 (Family R)
815.   Newell B. 7, b June 11, 1820; d June 4, 1906, ae 86 (tombstone, Troy, ME)
816.   Levi 7, b 1806; d Aug 8, 1873
817.   Ralph 7, b 1824; d Caribou, ME, Apr 11, 1897 (ME R)

381.   Enoch Bagley 6, Enoch 5, Thomas 4, Orlando 3, Orlando 2, Orlando 1 , b Jan 8, 1788; d Feb 16, 1864; m (1) Rachel Reed, Apr 2, 1811 (Waldo Co ME R), b 1788, d 1834 (tombstone, Troy, ME); m (2) July 26, 1835, Mahala Myrick, b 1809, d 1872 (tombstone, Troy, ME).

Children: (Troy ME R or tombstones)
818.   Jane 7, b Sept 23, 1811, twin; d 1841
819.   Isaac 7, b Sept 23, 1811, twin
820.   David S. 7, b Apr 15, 1815
821.   Merriam 7, b May 11, 1817; d 1833, unm
822.   William 7, b May 16, 1821
823.   Reuben 7, b Dec 16, 1822; d Bangor, ME, Jan 9, 1897 (ME R)
824.   George W. 7, b May 27, 1825
825.   Enoch 7, b about 1837; d 1915
826.   Samuel G. 7, b 1839; d 1862
827.   Sewell H. 7, b 1843; d Lewiston, ME, Oct 28, 1899 (ME R)
828.   Sarah H. 7, b 1844; d Aug 22, 1845
829.   Moses W. 7, b about 1846 (4 yrs old Census 1850)
830.   Philmore (Filmore) 7, b 1851; d 1883
Census of 1850 gives Enoch & Mahala; Enoch, ae 13; Samuel C.; ae 11; Sarah H, ae 8; Moses W., ae 4

382. Ruth Bagley 6, Enoch 5, Thomas 4, Orlando 3, Orlando 2, Orlando 1 , b Feb, 1790; d Dec 19, 1831; m John Work, b 1792, Winthrop, ME, d Boston, MA, Oct 22, 1873. They sold land to Hiram Whitehouse and she relinguished dower rights, Apr 26, 1831. He m (2) Betsey Reed); m (3) Mrs Phebe Coffin.

Children: (Troy ME R)
831. Philander 7, b Oct 12, 1810
832. Mathy Jane 7, b Mar 2, 1812
833. Thusey or Susan 7, b Oct 28, 1813
834. Thomas 7, b May 25, 1815
835. Rufus 7, b Feb 15, 1817
836. Abigail 7, b Dec 11, 1818
837. Henry or Hanson 7, b Jan 12, 1821
838. Horace 7, b July 22, 1826
839. John 7, b July 22, 1826
840. Moses 7, bb May 8, 1828
841. Mary 7, b Apr 17, 1830

383. Israel Bagley 6, Enoch 5, Thomas 4, Orlando 3, Orlando 2, Orlando 1 , b July 1, 1793; d Mar 26, 1868, ae 78; m (1) Cynthia Rogers, d Jan 16, 1831, ae 38 (tombstone, Troy, ME); m (2) Azuba Gerrish, May 8, 1844 (Troy ME R), d Nov 17, 1854 (tombstone, Troy, ME). He was a captain and constable of Troy in 1833. Appt guardian of Susanna & Louisa Craig, minor heirs of Peter Craig, Aug 3, 1844. On Census of 1850 .

Children: (Troy ME R)
842. Luther 7, b Nov 5, 1815; d Aug 30, 1873
843. Pauline 7, b Jan 21, 1821; d Sept 19, 1898
844. Louis 7, b Sept 15, 1830; d Sept 15, 1834 (tombstone, Troy, ME)

384. Thomas H. Bagley 6, Enoch 5, Thomas 4, Orlando 3, Orlando 2, Orlando 1 , b 1797; d Oct 18, 1877; m a Fairbanks; supposed to have died in St James, New Brunswick (Family R).

385. Moses Bagley 6, Enoch 5, Thomas 4, Orlando 3, Orlando 2, Orlando 1 , b 1793 or 1798; d Sept 12, 1869 or 1871 (discrepency between ME R & History of Durham, ME; m (1) Kezia Getchell, b Oct 15, 1803, d Lincoln, ME, Feb 12, 1846 (ME R); m (2) Nov 1846, Charlotte C. Spencer of Lincoln, ME, dau John Tufts, b Peru, ME, d May 15, 1892, ae 72 (Canaan, NH R). On Census of 1850.

Children: (ME R)
845. Dennis 7, b Lincoln, ME, Oct 23, 1826; d W Bangor, ME, Oct 23, 1904
846. Sarah P. 7, b Lincoln, ME, Oct 7, 1833
847. Sylvia 7, b Lincoln, ME, Mar 24, 1834
848. Merriam 7
849. Augustus K., b 1850
850. Elbridge L. 7, b 1854
851. Charles N. 7, b 1856; probably d young (Census of 1860)
852. Aahut 7, b 1859
853. Charles E. 7, b Lincoln, ME, Jan 5, 1860; d Carmel, ME,

Sept 23, 1933
854.   Lila A. 7, b Lincoln, ME, Feb 13, 1861; d June 19, 1887

Census of 1860 gives children as Augustus K., ae 10; Elbridge
L., ae 6; Charles N., ae 4; Aahut, ae 1

386. Reuben Bagley 6, Enoch 5, Thomas 4, Orlando 3, Orlando
2, Orlando 1 , b Sept or Oct 1, 1802; d May 11, 1892,
Wakefield, MA; m Mar 8, 1830, Sarah Campbell, b 1812, d July
14, 1887, Stoneham, MA, dau John & Rebecca. Alderman in
Bangor, ME. Sold land to James McLaughlin, Oct, 1836. Reuben
is given as a housewright. Other land in Bangor was sold May
25, 1834. Francis' death certificate gives his mother as
Sarah Brewster. On Census of 1850, Bangor, ME.

Children:
855.   Francis Marion 7, b Mar 2, 1831 (Me R)
856.   Hellen Maria 7, b Mar 14, 1837 (Bangor ME R)
857.   Edward 7, b about 1849
858.   Henry C. 7, b about 1844; d May 24, 1919, ae 75,
Winchester, MA (Bangor ME R)
859.   Sarah H. 7, d Apr 23, 1836, ae 4 mos (Bangor ME R)

Census of 1860 gives Reuben, ae 57; Sarah, ae 48; Edward, ae
11; Henry C., ae 16)

387. Sarah (Sally Bagley 6, Enoch 5, Thomas 4, Orlando 3,
Orlando 2, Orlando 1 , b Feb 23, 1805; d Oct 24, 1882; m Feb
23, 1827 (Troy ME R), Charles Smith of Readville, ME, b May
11, 1799, Readville, d May 18, 1854

Children: (Troy ME R)
860.   David 7, b June 3, 1830; d Nov 26, 1901
861.   Marion 7, b Oct 1, 1831
862.   Lucy 7, b May 12, 1833
863.   Elizabeth 7, b Nov 24, 1834
864.   Sarah 7, b July 14, 1836
865.   Charles 7, b Apr 14, 1837; d Nov 30, 1916
866.   Hester Ann 7, b Apr 30, 1839
867.   Francis 7, b Mar 11, 1843
868.   Graham 7, b Nov 29, 1844
869.   Ardella Cordelia 7, b Jan 26, 1848
870.   Mary 7, b about 1850

403. Abner Bagley 6, John 5, John 4, John 3, Orlando 2,
Orlando 1 , b Mar 16, 1766; d Sept 28, 1851; m intentions May
7, 1801, Sarah Hodge (Newburyport MA R);he given as of
Portland, ME. She b Nov 15, 1770, d consumption Sept 5, 1849
(Newburyport mA R), dau Michael & Sarah. He, with his brother
John, was one of the incorporators of Second Congregational
Church Society of Falmouth, ME. He deeded land to his son
John, July 31, 1821; John residing in New York City. On
Census of 1850 for Newburyport, MA.

Children:
871.   John S. 7, b 1804; d Mar 24, 1880; resided NYC in 1876

(MA R & tombstone, Newburyport, MA)
872.   Mary 7, b 1805; d Mar 31, 1884, ae 77 (Danvers MA R &
tombstone, Newburyport, MA).   She was a teacher & d unm.   Her
will, dated Sept 14, 1875 - Henry Kimball, adm June 30, 1884 -
mentions her sister, Sarah, brother John & children of Michael
Hodge Bagley; also children of John A & Charles Hodge (Essex
Co MA Probate R).
873.   Sarah S. 7, b 1808; d 1881 (tombstone, Newburyport, MA),
unm.   Will, dated Sept 14, 1875, mentions sister, Mary;
brother John of Brooklyn, NY; his children: John A. & Charles
Hodge Bagley; Michael Hodge Bagley's wife and four sons of
Meadville, PA (Essex Co MA Probate R).
874.   Michael Hodge 7, b Portland, ME; d Easton, MA, Oct 29,
1874, ae 63 (MA R); lived Meadville, PA.

404. John Bagley 6, John 5, John 4, John 3, Orlando 2,
Orlando 1 , b Mar 18, 1770; native of Portland, ME.   He was
the first ME native admittted to the bar in Cumberland Co.   He
did not long continue in practice of law but engaged in
commerce for a short time and d unm (History of Portland, ME.,
by Willis).   History of Cumberland Co., ME says he left the
bar in 1797.   He was one of the incorporators of the Second
Congregational Church in Falmouth, ME.

405. Daniel Bagley 6, John 5, John 4, John 3, Orlando 2,
Orlando 1 , b Mar 1, 1772; said to have settled in Palermo,
ME.   A check of records and cemeteries shows no trace.

406. Mary Bagley 6, John 5, John 4, John 3, Orlando 2,
Orlando 1 , b Mar 2, 1777; m Dec 18, 1801, James D. Hopkins, a
lawyer.   Buried   Old Cemetery, Portland, ME.   "God   Hath
Withdrawn the spirits and here mingle the ashes of the wives
of James D. Hopkins; Mary Hopkins, dau of John & Mary Bagley,
d Mar 9, 1802, ae 24 years".

407. Daniel Bagley 6, Daniel 5, John 4, John 3,   Orlando 2,
Orlando 1 , b May 6, 1774; supposed to have died at sea in
1803; m Thankful Burnham, Nov 20, 1800, Portland, ME, dau John
& Abigail (Stickney).   She m (2) Nov 22, 1807, David Brown
(Judson Genealogy by Peleg Tallman).

Children: (Portland ME R)
875.   John Stickney 7, b Aug 18,1801 (Portland R give John B)
876.   Harriet 7, b Jan 6, 1803; d Sept 30, 1848
877.   John Burnham 7, b Aug 11, 1804; d Nov 8, 1889

408. Hannah Bagley 7, Daniel 5, John 4, John 3, Orlando 2,
Orlando 1 , b 1779; m May 12, 1798, Capt William Crabtree.

Child:
878.   Eliza 7, b Dec 7, 1818, Falmouth, ME; d Oct 21, 1882,
Boston; m Silas Whitten, a builder in Boston, b Sept 25, 1816,
Falmouth, ME, d Apr 29, 1890.

410. Nancy Bagley 6, Daniel 5, John 4, John 3, Orlando 2,
Orlando 1, wife of Theophilus Goodridge in 1814 (Rockingham Co

NH Deeds).

412. Thomas Bagley 6, Moses 5, John 4, John 3, Orlando 2, Orlando 1 , b Nov 21, 1775/76; d at sea, Nov 19, 1798, ae 23 (Newburyport MA R). Adm on his estate granted to Ebenezer Pearson, Mar 4, 1799 (Essex Co MA Probate R).

413. John Bagley 6, Moses 5, John 4, John 3, Orlando 2, Orlando 1 , b Jan 25, 1778.

414. Moses Bagley 6, Aaron 5, John 4, John 3, Orlando 2, Orlando 1 , b Dec 27, 1786; d July 14, 1938, ae 51; m Dec 6, 1812, Mary Streeter of W Topsham, VT (W Topsham VT R). His father left him the sum of three dollars in his will, Oct 26, 1822, to be paid within three years of his decease (District of Bradford VT Probate R). No record of his estate in Bradford, VT R. Served in Capt Walbert's Co, Col Fifield's regt, attached militia in US service, 2 mos 23 dys in 1812. Volunteered to go to Plattsburgh, Sept, 1814, service in Capt Amos Stiles' Co, Reference Book 52, AGO, p 36, Box 53, AGO, p 33; buried in Washington, VT.

Children:
879. Russell S. 7, b June 12, 1815 (Washington VT R)
880. Mary E. 7, b Nov 21, 1823 (Washington VT R)
881. Eleanor N. 7, b about 1824; d May 5, 1896, ae 72, at Haverhill, MA; a teacher, b Washington, VT (MA R).

416. John Bagley 6, Aaron 5, John 4, John 3, Orlando 2, Orlando 1 , b July 7, 1788; d Jan 19, 1879, ae 89; m Mary Downing, Feb 5, 1812 (Barre VT R), d Apr 2, 1877, ae 84 (tombstone, Albany, VT). From Probate Records of Orleans Co, VT. John Bagley who d in 1878; d intestate, and application to sell with consent of all heirs was made. Andrew McClary, guardian of Burnham and Charles Bagley; John Bagley; Samuel Bagley; Charles and Mary J. Lawrence. This seems very odd. We have found no sons named Charles and Burnham. Perhaps John had a son we do not find who had these sons and who had died before John Bagley did. Another odd thing is that Gideon is not listed as an heir altho he was living.

Children: (Vt R excepted as noted)
882. Betty Noyes 7, b Dec 5, 1812; d Dec 15, 1818
883. John 7, b June 11, 1814, Orange, VT; d Aug 8, 1880, ae 66 (tombstone, Albany, VT)
884. Samuel Downing 7, b Nov 10, 1816, Washington, VT; d Lebanon, NH, Feb 11, 1895 (NH R)
885. Gideon Downing 7, b Apr 12, 1821; d Nov 12, 1887, ae 66 (tombstone, Albany, VT)
886. Dorothy 7, b Jan 24, 1818
887. Mary Jane 7, b Feb 12, 1824

417. Aaron Bagley 6, Aaron 5, John 4, John 3, Orlando 2, Orlando 1 , his father left him $10 to be paid after his deceased within three years, Oct 26, 1822 (District of Bradford VT Probate R). Believed to be the Aaron Bagley

listed as from Barre, VT, who volunteered to go to Plattsburgh in War of 1812, Sept, 1814, in Capt Ellis' Co. Pension Certificate 3299. He is thought to have settled in Cambridge, NY, at least for a time, In cemetery at Cambridge is grave for Lydia Bagley, wife of Aaron Bagley, who d May 24, 1835, ae 43. Buried on same lot with Lydia is Sarah, wife of Andrew W. Culver, who d Dec 5, 1838, ae 29.

Child:
888. William 7, d Aug 30, 1825, ae 9 mos (Cambridge, NY tombstone)

418. Hannah Bagley 6, Aaron 5, John 4, John 3, Orlando 2, Orlando 1, mentioned in father's will, Oct 26, 1822. Left her fifty dollars to be paid after his decease; also "one equal half of all my household furniture after the decease of my said wife, together with one half of beds and bedding excepting my iron ware, my writing desk and one bed suitable bedding therefor & one bedstead, also the left of the middle front room in my house and a sufficient supply of wood for fuel and use of my oven and cellar at pleasure, so long as she remains a single woman."

419. William Bagley 6, Aaron 5, John 4, John 3, Orlando 2, Orlando 1, b Jan 29, 1796; d Sept 19, 1871; m (1) Sally Burroughs, Aug 30, 1821, dau Thomas & Amy of Newbury, VT, b May 10, 1800, d Jan 31, 1844, ae 43 (Corinth VT R); m (2) Apr 22, 1845, Ruth Meserve, dau James & Lydia, b Mar 24, 1808, d Oct 22, 1899 (tombstone, Corinth, VT). Census of 1850 gives him as of Corinth, VT. Ruth's will, dated Nov 30, 1898; proved Nov 14, 1899, gives everything to her niece, Sarah Ellen Meserve; no children mentioned. Possibly she had been previously married to a Freeman.

Children:
889. Augusta 7, b Feb 7, 1822 (Corinth VT R); d Mar 25, 1835, ae 14 (tombstone, Corinth, VT, says "Only daughter")
890. Augustus Y. 7, b Feb 5, 1824, Corinth, VT; d Graesmere, NH, Nov 27, 1903 (NH R)

420. Ephraim Bagley 6, Aaron 5, John 4, John 3, Orlando 2, Orlando 1, b about 1797; d July 25, 1855; m Jan 6, 1825, Betsey Banfield of Newbury, VT, dau George & Anna (Sanborn), of Newburyport, MA and W Topsham, VT. She d Apr 14, 1848, ae 52 (tombstone, W Topsham, VT). He m (2) Mrs Persis Barnett, May 9, 1850 (VT R), dau Robert and Betsey (Varnum), b Feb 15, 1807, d May 27, 1892. Was executor of father's estate and was left the residue from it.

Children: (West Topsham VT R except as noted)
891. Infant 7, d Nov 13, 1825 (tombstone, W Topham)
892. Elizabeth 7, b Apr 1, 1827; d Apr 21, 1827 (Tombstone, W Topsham)
893. Eleanor 7, b Apr 22, 1828
894. Abner 7, b Oct 24, 1830
895. Elizabeth 7, b Mar, 1833; d Sept 24, 1833 (tombstone, W

Topsham)
896.   Ephraim 7, b Oct 27, 1834; d Boston, MA, Mar 10, 1896,
ae 61 (MA R)
897.   Moses 7, b June 4, 1839; d Worcester, MA, Nov 20, 1893,
ae 54 (MA R)

422.   Philip Bagley 6, Philip 5, John 4, John 3, Orlando 2,
Orlando 1 , b Aug 28, 1786

424.   Joseph Bagley 6, Philip 5, John 4, John 3, Orlando 2,
Orlando 1 , b Jan 3, 1786; d Nov 8, 1809, by drowning. A
merchant; m Mary Folsom Giddings of Exeter, NH, Oct 11, 1808
(Newburyport MA R), b Aug 15, 1786, d Aug 9, 1824, ae 37
(Newburyport MA R & tombstone), dau Nathaniel & Anne Folsom
(Exeter NH R). Adm on his estate granted to Philip Bagley
Sept 7, 1810 (Esex Co MA Probate R).

Child:
898.   Mary 7, b Aug 12, 1809 (Newburyport MA R)

426.   Charles Bagley 6, Philip 5, John 4, John 3, Orlando 2,
Orlando 1 , b Jan 14, 1791; probably m Charlotte Clark, Feb 2,
1836; called Captain.

427.   Nancy Bagley 6, Philip 5, John 4, John 3, Orlando 2,
Orlando 1 , b Jan 14, 1791; m Dr John Thurston of Castine, ME,
Mar 8, 1811 (Newburyport MA R).

429.   Lucy Bagley 6, Philip 5, John 4, John 3, Orlando 2,
Orlando 1 , b Apr 13, 1797; d Nov 11, 1870; single in 1856,
and probably conveyed land in Seabrook to Franklin Bagley on
Sept 8 of that year. She m Rev E. W. Hooker, Dec 28, 1857,
and was his third wife. No children. He d Mar 31, 1875, at
Ft Atkinson, Wis.

430.   Sarah Bagley 6, Timothy 5, Timothy 4, John 3, Orlando 2,
Orlando 1 , b Jan 17, 1776; m Nicholas French, Jr., at Candia,
NH, Aug 16, 1797 (NH R). They went to Montville, ME.

Children: (All b Candia, NH)
899.   Charles Sargent 7, b Nov 23, 1797
900.   True 7, b Sept 2, 1799
901.   Sally, b Mar 19, 1801
902.   Joseph 7, b May 28, 1805
903.   Levinor 7, b Sept 5, 1807
904.   Belinda 7, b June 17, 1809
905.   Maryanne 7, b June 17, 1811
906.   Louise 7, b May 16, 1813; d Aug 5, 1813
907.   Nicholas Gilman 7, b Mar 9, 1816
908.   John 7, b Aug 14, 1819

431.   Molly Begley 6, Timothy 5, Timothy 4, John 3, Orlando 2,
Orlando 1 , b June 11, 1776; probably m Thomas Dearborn, Aug
28, 1794 (Candia NH R). Could have m Stephen Jones, Mar 28,
1797 (South Hampton NH R). Note there is a mistake in the
records either for her birth or that of her sister Sarah.

433. John Bagley 6, Timothy 5, Timothy 4, John 3, Orlando 2, Orlando 1 , b Dec 30, 1782; probably m Christina Bagley, Dec 10, 1816 (Candia NH R), dau Jonathan & Anne (Favour), b Aug 15, 1786. he and his wife conveyed land in Candia, NH, given as of Raymond, H, in 1860 and 1864 (Rockingham Co NH Deed). They lived for a time in W Topsham, VT.

Children:
909.   Henry 7, b Mar 14, 1821 (W Tophsam VT R)
910.   Sarah Ann 7, b Dec 6, 1822 (W Topsham VT R)
911.   Jonathan 7, b Apr 26, 1826

434. Charles S. Bagley 6, Timothy 5, Timothy 4, John 3, Orlando 2, Orlando 1 , b Nov 3, 1789; m Lydia Davidson, Feb 4,1813 (Goffstown NH R), b Mar 15, 1788, dau Nathaniel & Lydia (Eaton) in Hanock, NH. She m (2) Robert Nichols and d Sept 14, 1873. He was a clothier and lived in Goffstown and then in Candia, NH and erected a clothing mill about 60 rods from the highway. He also owned a fulling mill in Chester, NH, which he bought from Alfred Sanborn in 1807. This was sold in 1809; he conveyed land June 5, 1818, and Aug 7, 1819 (Rockingham Co NH Deeds).

Children:
912.   Nathaniel Gilman 7, b July 19, 1813 (Goffstown NH R);   d Aug 16, 1909 (Sharon NH R)
913.   Maria 7, b Jan 30, 1820 (Goffstown NH R); d Nov 14, 1921, ae 94. Death certificate gives her birth as June 10, 1827; a school teacher
914.   Sally 7, died prior to Aug 6, 1909 (Worcester Co MA Probate R)

438. Peter Bagley 6, Peter 5, Timothy 4, John 3, Orlando 2, Orlando 1 , b Jan 18, 1790; moved to Newbury, VT, and then to Broome, Scholaries Co, NY; d Jan 17, 1865 (NY R); m Mar 2, 1824, Dorothy Morrill of Newbury, VT, by JP Edmund George West (W Topsham VT R). His wife given as Polly, d Jan 8, 1867, ae 74 (NY R). We do not know if this was a second wife or a nickname for Dorothy.

Children:
915.   Benjamin 7, b 1813, Broome, NY (Church of Latter Day Saints R); d between Jan 5, & Feb 25, 1894
916.   Harrison 7, b 1819, Broome, NY; d May 2, 1888, in Freehold, NY (Church of Latter Days Saints R)
(See also Daniel of New Baltimore, NY in Notes on Bagley Lines)

439. John Martin Bagley 6, Peter 5, Timothy 4, John 3, Orlando 2, Orlando 1 , b Jan 31, 1794.

440. Ruth Bagley 6, Isaac 5, Timothy 4, John 3, Orlando 2, Orlando 1 , b June 30, 1781; m Nathan Nutter, Sept 18, 1806 (Ames MA R). He was lost at sea, July 27, 1842, ae 60 (Ames MA R).

Children: (Ames MA R)
917. Charles 7, b Jan 5, 1808; m Lydia Anne David, widow, Oct 23, 1847
918. Alonzo 7, b Aug 23, 1809; m Dorothy Jackman, intentions, Apr 24, 1837; she d 1847, and he m (2) Elizabeth Blumley, May 24, 1849
919. Alvira 7, b Mar 24, 1811; m Philip Osgood of Boston, Sept 18, 1836
920. Mary Ann 7, b Apr 2, 1814; d Jan 26, 1833, unm
921. John 7, b June 17, 1816
922. Nathan 7, b Aug 21, 1818
923. Ruth 7, b about 1823 (birth not on Ames MA R); m Edwin M. Currier, Jan 25, 1846; given as son Nathan & Ruth

441. Lowell Bagley 6, Isaac 5, Timothy 4, John 3, Orlando 2, Orlando 1 , b Feb 2, 1784; d Feb 26, 1863; m Sally Osgood, Nov 26, 1811 (Salis MA R), intentions Nov 3, 1811 on Ames MA R, b May 12, 1791, dau Samuel & Anna, d Jan 6, 1876 (tombstone, Ames, MA). Member of Warren Lodge, AF & AM, and Justice of Peace in Amesbury. Wife made adm of his estate, Nov 3, 1863. She made her will, proved Mar 24, 1879, with dau Sarah, adm, Aug 24, 1879 (Essex Co MA Probate R).

Children:
924. Mary Fowler 7, b May 22, 1816; d Oct 1, 1864, unm (tombstone & Ames MA R)
925. Emeline 7, b Oct 22, 1812 (Ames MA R); d Dec 29, 1892 (Ames MA tombstone)
926. Sarah Osgood 7, b Sept 4, 1820; d unm Aug 22, 1905 (tombstone, Ames, MA). She was a faith healer and was the Sarah Bagley who took in Mary Baker Eddy, founder of the Christian Science Faith, and introduced her to John Greenleaf Whittier, the poet. Richard Kennedy of Boston was appt adm Nov 6, 1905 (Essex Co MA Probate R).

442. Richard Bagley 6, Isaac 5, Timothy 4, John 3, Orlando 2, Orlando 1 , b 1792; d July 6, 1832; m (1) Sarah Bailey, May 13, 1820, b about 1797, d Oct 29, 1826, ae 29 (Ames MA R); m (2) Jane Stavers, Feb 19, 1829 (Newburyport MA R), b about Mar 10, 1809, dau John & Betsey (Swazey) (Newburyport MA R); she probably m (2) James Foot, intentions Aug 9, 1834 (Ames MA R). Adm on Richard's estate granted to Lowell Bagley, Nov 7, 1832. Widow Jane of Salisbury, MA appt guardian of son Richard, 2 years old, Dec 11, 1832 (Essex Co MA Probate R).

Child:
927. Richard 7, b 1830 (Probate R); d May 1, 1877, ae 48 (tombstone, Ames, MA)

443. William Bagley 6, Enoch 5, William 4, Jacob 3, Orlando 2, Orlando 1 , b Oct 3, 1766; d Aug 3, 1835; was no compos mentis and supported by the town and cared for by sisters, Susy & Polly. The following from Merrill's History of Amesbury, Mass. "1826. At the annual meeting it was voted to raise fifty dollars in addition to the sum already raised to

Children: (Ames MA R)
917.   Charles 7, b Jan 5, 1808; m Lydia Anne David, widow, Oct 23, 1847
918.   Alonzo 7, b Aug 23, 1809; m Dorothy Jackman, intentions, Apr 24, 1837; she d 1847, and he m (2) Elizabeth Blumley, May 24, 1849
919.   Alvira 7, b Mar 24, 1811; m Philip Osgood of Boston, Sept 18, 1836
920.   Mary Ann 7, b Apr 2, 1814; d Jan 26, 1833, unm
921.   John 7, b June 17, 1816
922.   Nathan 7, b Aug 21, 1818
923.   Ruth 7, b about 1823 (birth not on Ames MA R); m Edwin M. Currier, Jan 25, 1846; given as son Nathan & Ruth

441.   Lowell Bagley 6, Isaac 5, Timothy 4, John 3, Orlando 2, Orlando 1 , b Feb 2, 1784; d Feb 26, 1863; m Sally Osgood, Nov 26, 1811 (Salis MA R), intentions Nov 3, 1811 on Ames MA R, b May 12, 1791, dau Samuel & Anna, d Jan 6, 1876 (tombstone, Ames, MA). Member of Warren Lodge, AF & AM, and Justice of Peace in Amesbury. Wife made adm of his estate, Nov 3, 1863. She made her will, proved Mar 24, 1879, with dau Sarah, adm, Aug 24, 1879 (Essex Co MA Probate R).

Children:
924.   Mary Fowler 7, b May 22, 1816; d Oct 1, 1864, unm (tombstone & Ames MA R)
925.   Emeline 7, b Oct 22, 1812 (Ames MA R); d Dec 29, 1892 (Ames MA tombstone)
926.   Sarah Osgood 7, b Sept 4, 1820; d unm Aug 22, 1905 (tombstone, Ames, MA). She was a faith healer and was the Sarah Bagley who took in Mary Baker Eddy, founder of the Christian Science Faith, and introduced her to John Greenleaf Whittier, the poet. Richard Kennedy of Boston was appt adm Nov 6, 1905 (Essex Co MA Probate R).

442.   Richard Bagley 6, Isaac 5, Timothy 4, John 3, Orlando 2, Orlando 1 , b 1792; d July 6, 1832; m (1) Sarah Bailey, May 13, 1820, b about 1797, d Oct 29, 1826, ae 29 (Ames MA R); m (2) Jane Stavers, Feb 19, 1829 (Newburyport MA R), b about Mar 10, 1809, dau John & Betsey (Swazey) (Newburyport MA R); she probably m (2) James Foot, intentions Aug 9, 1834 (Ames MA R). Adm on Richard's estate granted to Lowell Bagley, Nov 7, 1832. Widow Jane of Salisbury, MA appt guardian of son Richard, 2 years old, Dec 11, 1832 (Essex Co MA Probate R).

Child:
927.   Richard 7, b 1830 (Probate R); d May 1, 1877, ae 48 (tombstone, Ames, MA)

443.   William Bagley 6, Enoch 5, William 4, Jacob 3, Orlando 2, Orlando 1 , b Oct 3, 1766; d Aug 3, 1835; was no compos mentis and supported by the town and cared for by sisters, Susy & Polly. The following from Merrill's History of Amesbury, Mass. "1826. At the annual meeting it was voted to raise fifty dollars in addition to the sum already raised to

support the poor and applied toward the support of the Bagley boys. There were three brothers and a nephew non compos; viz; William, Enoch and John Bagley and Thomas Lane. These were for many years maintained by Susan and Polly Bagley, sisters of the Bagley boys and aunts to Thomas Lane and lived on Ferry Street. They were constant attendants at church, occupying the long front seat in the west Gallery of the Sandy Hill meetinghouse. Their oddities were sometimes very amusing, but people were very kind to them. During the latter part of their lives, the town supported them."

444. Hannah Bagley 6, Enoch 5, William 4, Jacob 3, Orlando 2, Orlando 1 , b Nov 16, 1768; m Feb 12, 1792, Thomas Lane (Salis MA R), d Feb 1, 1797, ae 30 (Ames MA R). Paid his father-in-law for land in Amesbury, Sept 13, 1793. She petitioned for the right to sell and settle her husband's estate in 1798 (Essex Co MA Probate R).

Child:
928. Thomas 7 (see above)

447. Enoch Bagley 6, Enoch 5, William 4, Jacob 3, Orlando 2, Orlando 1 , b Dec 12, 1776 (see above)

449. John Bagley 6, Enoch 5, William 4, Jacob 3, Orlando 2, Orlando 1 , b Jan 20, 1781 (see above)

451. Lucy Bagley 6, Enoch 5, William 4, Jacob 3, Orlando 2, Orlando 1 , b Jan 12, 1786; d Oct 8, 1835; m John Patten Sargent of Haverhill, MA, Dec 4, 1809 (Ames MA R), b Feb 25, 1784, d Feb 8, 1855, Dover, NH; a brick manuf in later years at Dover. Children not recorded on Ames or Salis MA R.

Children: (From Sargent Genealogy)
929. John G. 7, b Oct 13, 1810
930. Abigail 7, b Dec 1, 1812
931. Sarah S. 7, b Nov 7, 1814
932. Mary B. 7, b Jan 20, 1817
933 Amos 7, b Sept 19, 1819; d Aug 10, 1848, Kittery, ME; buried Elliott, ME
934. Susan B. 7, b Nov 22, 1821
935. Lucy A. 7, b Jan 13, 1825

452. Jeremiah Bagley 6, William 5, William 4, Jacob 3, Orlando 2, Orlando 1 , b about 1766; d Oct 25, 1807; m July 5, 1795, Betty Bailey (Ames MA R), b Jan 29, 1771, dau Daniel & Anna (Blaisdell) (Ames MA R). A shipwright, he lived in Ames in 1798. She m (2) Mr. Goodrich.

Children: (Ames MA R)
936. William 7, b Mar 30, 1796; d July 4, 1882 (tombstone, Ames, MA)
937. Daniel 7, b Sept 5, 1800; d May 14, 1879 (Raymond NH R)
938. Joseph 7, n Aug 30, 1803
939. Sarah 7, b June 5, 1806

453.   Jacob Bagley 6, William 5, William 4, Jacob 3, Orlando
2, Orlando 1 , b May 23 or 28, 1766; d before Aug 5, 1801; m
Anne Randall, Apr 21, 1785, probably dau Capt Isaac & Anne
(Colley), b Jan 25, 1767 (Ames MA R). In his will, Jacob left
1/2 pew in the meetinghouse. Will made Apr 26, 1801; proved
Aug 5, 1801; wife Anne was adm (Essex Co MA Probate R).
Jacob's father, in his will, left money to children of son,
Jacob, deceased (Rockingham Co NH Probate R). Jacob was
styled Gentleman and captain.

Anne Randall's father kept a tavern at Mudnock, Amesbury
Ferry, at the time of her marriage to Jacob, and at the time
Gen Washington came to Amesbury, he came up from west of the
junction of Merrimac and Powow Rivers, on a barge built for
the occasion by the citizens of Newburyport. The landing was
close to the Randall Tavern and Washington took lunch there.

Children: (Ames MA R)
940.   Betsey 7, b May 20, 1786
941.   Dorothy 7, b Dec 15, 1789; d Jan 18, 1824
942.   Rebecca 7, b Jan 6, 1788
943.   Jacob 7, b Sept 14, 1791; d young
944.   George W. 7, b Oct 27, 1793; d Feb 12, 1843 (tombstone,
Nashua, NH)
945.   Randall 7, b July 22, 1795
946.   Jacob 7, b Apr 9, 1797
947.   Ignatius 7, b Jan 11, 1799; d about 1879 (Family R)
948.   Ann 7, b Nov 4, 1800

454.   David Bagley 6, William 5, William 4, Jacob 3, Orlando
2, Orlando 1 , b Oct 23, 1768; d Dec 2 or 3, 1803; buried
Amesbury, MA; m Dorothy Blaisdell, Feb 21, 1790 (Second Church
Ames MA R). Ames MA R give intentions as Feb 6, 1789 and
marriage as Feb 21, 1789. She b Feb 17, 1768, d May 26, 1850,
ae 82 (Family R), dau Oliver & Merriam (Bagley) (Ames MA R).
She m (2) Stephen Gordon "Major Fifer", Oct 11, 1806 (Ames MA
R), b June 12, 1780 (Family R). Adm on estate of David Bagley
granted to Jacob Brown; d intestate; estate allowed Apr 10,
1805 (Essex Co MA Probate R). Left pew in East Parish
meetinghouse. In David's father's will, he left David's
children money because David was deceased (Rockingham Co NH
Probate R).

Children: (Ames MA R)
949.   Mary 7, b Jan 13, 1790; d June 7, 1843 (Family R)
950.   Levi 7, b Nov 2, 1791; d young
951.   Levi 7, b Oct 13, 1793; d Oct, 1872 (Family R)
952.   Merriam 7, b Feb 4, 1793 ?; d Sept 30, 1803
953.   William 7, b Oct 17, 1794; d Aug 21, 1869 (MA R)
954.   Frederick 7, b Dec 13, 1797; d Feb 13, 1868 (MA R)
955.   Joseph 7, b Nov 2, 1800; d young of accident in nail
factory
956.   David 7, b July 28, 1804; d Feb 26, 1886 (Family R)

455.   Mary (Molly) Bagley 6, William 5, William 4, Jacob 3,
Orlando 2, Orlando 1 , b Jan 9, 1771; d Apr 3, 1856; m Levi
Morrill, Apr 15, 1792 (Salis MA R), b Oct 15, 1764, d Feb 19,

1858, ae 93, son Henry & Eleanor (Currier) (Salis & Bradford NH R). He was a blacksmith, farmer, scythe maker and maker of fine tools. In her father's will in 1808, Mary was willed $7, under the name of Mary Morrill (Rockingham Co NH Probate R).

Children: (History of Salisbury, NH, by Dearborn)
957. Clarissa 7, b Salisbury, NH, Jan 9, 1794; d Lowell, MA, Jan 2, 1893, ae 98; buried Nashua, NH; m Mar 9, 1823, George W. Bagley of Amesbury, MA (Ames MA R give 1723 which is an error), son Jacob & Anne (Randall), b Oct 27, 1793, d Feb 12, 1842
958. Henry 7, b Salisbury, NH, Jan 24, 1796; d Dec 7, 1808
959. William B. 7, b Feb 11, 1798; d in Maine
960. John M. 7, b Aug 11, 1800; d in Maine
961. Jacob B. 7, b Aug 17, 1802; d young
962. Levi 7, b Aug 20, 1805; d June 6, 1879
963. Daniel O. 7, b June 19, 1807; d young
964. Benjamin F. 7, b Aug 12, 1810
965. Daniel B. 7, b Dec 31, 1815; d Feb 19, 1862

459. Anna (Nancy) Bagley 6, William 5, William 4, Jacob 3, Orlando 2, Orlando 1 , b Apr 17, 1781; family records and her father's will in 1808 refer to her as Nancy Woodman; m at Kingston, NH First Church, June 10, or July 28, 1805, to John Woodman. Church records say July 28 by Rev Elisha Thayer; town records give June 10.

Children: (East Kingston NH R)
966. Dolly 7, b Feb 18, 1806
967. William 7, b May 31, 1808
968. Stephen 7, b Mar 16, 1812
969. Harriet 7, b Oct 6, 1818

462. John Bagley 6, William 5, William 4, Jacob 3, Orlando 2, Orlando 1 , b Aug 13, 1786; d June 2, 1860; m Mary Allen of Plaistow, NH, Mar 22, 1806 (Danvers MA R), b Plaistow, Mar 3, 1789, dau David & Elizabeth (Fisk) (Danvers MA R), d Nov 9, 1874, ae 85, at Peabody, MA (MA R give her parents on death certificate as Francis & Elizabeth Allen). Corinth VT R sometimes call his wife Elizabeth. In a deed, dated Mar 9,1831, giving himself as of Corinth. VT., he conveyed all rights in his late father's and mother's estate to William Bagley of Danville, NH (Rockingham Co NH Probate R). This is the John Bagley of Hawke who sold land in Grafton, NH, June 15, 1812 and who sold land in the same town in 1813 and 1819 (Grafton Co NH Deeds). John Bagley of Grafton, NH, and Mary Ellen, his wife, with Elizabeth Allen, widow, of Plaistow, NH, sold land in Plaistow, Jan 25, 1814 (Rockingham Co NH Deeds). He made his will, July 18, 1856; proved July 3, 1860 (Essex Co MA Probate R). On Census of 1850 for Danvers, MA.

Children:
970. Amos 7, b July 8, 1807; d Jan 25, 1808. Some records give this child as b Plaistow, NH. Danvers, MA R, where John Bagley was careful to record his whole family, give place of birth and death as Hawke (now Danville), NH.

971.   Louisa 7, b Sept 23, 1808; d Sept 24, 1808, b Plaistow (Danvers MA R)

972.   William 7, b Sept 30, 1809; d Apr 19, 1810 .   Record gives b Plaistow, NH; d Hawke, NH (Danvers MA R)

973.   Elizabeth Allen 7, b Sept 17, 1812, Plaistow, NH; mentioned in father's will in 1856; d Mar 22, 1895, ae 82 (Peabody MA R)

974.   Mary Osgood 7, b May 19, 1814, Grafton, NH (Danvers MA R); also recorded Corinth, VT)

975.   Francis Allen 7, b July 22, 1816, Grafton, NH; d Feb 18, 1825, Corinth, VT (Danvers MA R)

976.   Dorothy A. 7, b Jan 24, 1818, Grafton, NH; also recorded Corinth, VT (Danvers MA R); her father's will in 1856 leaves money to the town of Danvers, MA, as reimbursement for the care of his insane dau Dorothy. She d Jan 24, 1857, ae 39 (Danvers MA R)

977.   Almond Fisk 7, b Mar 30, 1819, Grafton, NH; also recorded Corinth, VT; mentioned in father's will in 1856; d Apr 15, 1862, ae 53, (Wenham MA R)

978.   Sarah Whittier 7, b Apr 11, 1820, Grafton, NH; also recorded Corinth, VT (Danvers MA R); mentioned in father's will in 1856

979.   John 7, b June 13, 1822 (Danvers MA R); records give this child as b Corinth, NH which is probably a mistake for Corinth, VT

980.   Julia Anne 7, b July 8, 1824, Grafton, NH; d Sept 11, 1825, Corinth, VT (Danvers MA R)

981.   Lydia Drew 7, b Aug 31, 1826 (Danvers MA R); records give this child as b Corinth, NH, probably a mistake for Corinth, VT

982.   Harriet Jane 7, b Jan 26, 1829 (Danvers MA R); records give this child as b Corinth, NH, probably a mistake for Corinth, VT

983.   Francis Allen 7, b Feb 17, 1831; d May 13, 1853, ae 22, unm (Danvers MA R); records give this child as b Corinth, NH, probably mistake for Corinth, VT

465. William B. Bagley 6, William 5, William 4, Jacob 3, Orlando 2, Orlando 1 , b Oct 15, 1793; d June 23, 1868; m at Hawke (now Danville), NH, Mar 16, 1820, intentions Aug 20, 1819 (Ames MAR), Sarah Merrill, b Oct 16, 1796, d Dec 10, 1891 (Danville NH R), dau Benjamin & Sarah (Eastman) (Ames MA R). William bought land in Deerfield, NH, May 7, 1833, and he and his wife sold land in Danville, in 1835, 1846, 1860, and 1863 (Rockingham Co NH Deeds). He sold land in Grafton, NH, Feb 21, 1816 and 1820 (Grafton Co NH Deeds). On July 9, 1868, William Patton of Kingston, NH, was made adm of his estate worth about $8000 (Rockingham Co NH Probate R). On Census of 1850 for Danville.

Children: (Danville NH R)

984.   Emeline 7, b 1821; d Hampstead, NH, Nov 6, 1896; buried Danville

985.   Harriet 7, b 1823

986.   William M. 7, b 1823; d 1852 (tombstone, Danville, NH)

987.   Julia 7, b 1825

988.   Andrew J. 7, b Feb 24, 1829; d Feb 27, 1914
989.   John 7, b Feb 8, 1833; d Feb 6, 1909
990.   Sarah M. 7, b 1835; d Jan 1, 1916, Haverhill, MA, unm.
Will made Dec 20, 1913, mentions nieces and nephew and brother
Andrew J., and sister, Hannah Lovejoy (Rocking Co NH Probate
R)
991.   Isaiah 7, b 1835; d 1864 (tombstone, Danville, NH)
992.   Eliza E. 7, d Oct 27, 1863, ae 24, unm (tombstone,
Danville). William Patten of Kingston, NH, was adm of her
estate.   Another adm was appt for her property in   MA
(Rockingham Co NH Probate R). She was also known as Ellen.
993.   Irene T. 7, b 1842; d 1846 (tombstone, Danville, NH)
994.   Hannah 7, b about 1831; living 1914 (Rockingham Co NH
Probate R)

467. Hannah Bagley 6, William 5, William 4, Jacob 3, Orlando
2, Orlando 1 , b 1797; d Aug 11, 1824 (Salis MA R); m Zebedee
or Zebulon Morrill of Salisbury, MA, Jan 9, 1823 (Ames MA R);
probably son David & Susanna (Pillsbury), b Apr 5, 1795 (Salis
MA R). Her father's will in 1808 leaves her an equal share
with her sister Eunice "when she comes of age or should marry"
(Rockingham Co NH Probate R). Zebedee was styled "Captain".

Child:
995.   William Bagley 7, b June 22, 1823 (Salis MA R)

476. Greenleaf Bagley 6, Stephen 5, Abel 4, Joseph 3, Orlando
2, Orlando 1 , , b Sept 28, 1789 (Family R); d May 28, 1873
(Clinton ME R); m June 23, 1813, at Hampton Falls, NH (NH R),
Hannah True, b Nov 28, 1791, at Seabrook, NH, d Jan 28, 1876
(Clinton ME R). His son's death certificate gives Greenleaf
as b Salisbury, MA, and Hannah as b Seabrook, NH, but not on
vital records. He went to Clinton, ME., He was a War of 1812
veteran, Capt J. Moore's Co, Lt Col Monroe's regt, priv from
Sept 12 to Sept 27, 1814. Known as Captain.   On Census of
1850 for Clinton, ME.

Children: (Clinton ME R except as noted)
996.   Abner T. 7, b Oct 28, 1841; d Feb 12, 1882, ae 67
997.   Jane 7 (Family R)
998.   Dorothy P. 7, b Dec 7, 1816 (Family R)
999.   Stephen Hunt 7, b Dec 10, 1818; d Nov 11, 1867, ae 48
(MA R)
1000. Mary J. 7, b Feb 22, 1824 (Family R)
1001. John F. 7, b Feb 7, 1821; d Somerville, MA, June 4,
1898 (MA R)
1002. Simeon O. 7, b Aug 15, 1826 (Family R); d before 1873
1003. Abigail A. 7, b Aug 23, 1829 (Family R)
1004. Moses A. 7, b June 19, 1832; d June 11, 1909, ae 75-10
(MA R)
1005. Elenor M. 7, b Jan 17, 1833 (Family R)
1006. Charles M. 7, b Apr 12, 1839; d Jan 11, 1873, ae 33
(Charlestown MA R)
1007. Asa 7, b 1838; probably d before 1873

477. Sarah Bagley 6, Stephen 5, Abel 4, Joseph 3, Orlando 2,

Orlando 1 , m Mar 25, 1799, at Seabrook, NH, Bryant Eaton (Seabrook NH R). Must have d before 1873 as not mentioned as heir-at-law of Franklin Bagley.

Child:
1008. Ann 7, one of the heirs-at-law of Franklin Bagley in 1873.

478. Lydia Bagley 6, Stephen 5, Abel 4, Joseph 3, Orlando 2, Orlando 1, b about 1787; d June 23, 1835, ae 48; m June 2, 1819 (Salis MA R). Rev Theophilus B. Adams, b Beverley, MA; wounded War of 1812; ordained Baptist minister at New London, NH; preached in Wilmot, Acworth and Unity, NH. First wife was Jemima Moulton and Lucy was his second wife (History of New London, NH).

Children: (History of New London, NH)
1009. Jemima 7, d young from consumption
1010. Dorothy 7, m Putnam George (d before 1873 as not mentioned as heir-at-law of Franklin Bagley nor are any George children)
1011. Harrison H. 7, m Lydia Osgood (heir-at-law of Franklin Bagley, 1873)
1012. Judith 7, d unm, before 1873
1013. Carver P. 7, d unm, before 1873
1014. Louisa 7, d unm, before 1873
1015. John B. 7, d young, before 1873

479. Frederick T. Bagley 6, Stephen 5, Abel 4, Joseph 3, Orlando 2, Orlando 1 , b 1798, Salisbury, MA (Family R); d Jan 4, 1879 (Clinton ME R); m Oct 10, 1819, at Clinton, ME, Mary Tammie Richardson, b 1797, Clinton, ME, d there Feb 24, 1862, dau John 7. He probably m (2) Margaret Wing of Ripley, ME, intentions, July 2, 1875 (Clinton, ME R). Census of 1850 gives him as residing Sebastic, ME.

Children: (Clinton ME R except as noted)
1016. Greenleaf 7, b Jan 24, 1822; d Parkman, ME, Nov 27, 1903 (ME R)
1017. Jonathan 7, b 1824; d Sept 6, 1905, ae 81 (ME R)
1018. Lucy Ann 7, b 1828, Clinton, ME (Family R)
1019. Alexander 7, b Aug, 1834; d Feb 5, 1865; buried on same lot with mother, Mary
1020. Oliver 7, b 1837; d Feb 5, 1865; buried same lot with mother, Mary
1021. Franklin 7, b 1836; d June 25, 1908, ae 78 (Family R)
1022. Name unknown, female 7, b & d Clinton, ME (Family R)

480. Alexander Bagley 6, Stephen 5, Abel 4, Joseph 3, Orlando 2, Orlando 1, b about 1800; d Aug 8, 1822, ae 22 (tombstone Salisbury Plains Cemetery Amesbury, MA. Hamilton MA R say he died Aug 7, 1822.

481. Franklin Bagley 6, Stephen 5, Abel 4, Joseph 3, Orlando 2, Orlando 1 , b about 1804, Salisbury, MA (Death certificate d June 9, 1873, Seabrook, NH (MA R); buried Salisbury Plains

Cemetery, Amesbury, MA). Census of 1850 for Seabrook, NH gives Franklin, ae 54, and Lucy, ae 50. Lucy d May 25, 1892 and is buried on the same lot with Franklin. No record of marriage has been found, and it is presumed she was the maiden sister of Franklin by that name. She is mentioned as an heir-at-law of Franklin Bagley, but never as wife, and there is no mention of dower rights. Originally styled "Husbandman", he lived in Boston and evidently prospered since at his death he is styled "Gentleman". NH deeds show, he , as Gentleman of Boston, gave land to Lucy P. Bagley and James Titcomb, June 4, 1849, and at the same time gave land to Betsey Gove, widow of Stephen Gove, of Seabrook, deceased. He sold land in Seabrook, Jan 6, 1855. He d intestate.

Oct 23, 1873, the following persons, heirs-at-law of Franklin Bagley, conveyed land in Seabrook, NH: Oliver Bagley & Elizabeth of East Kingston, NH (his brother and wife); Lucy P. Bagley (Franklin's sister, see above); Bryant Carter of Seabrook (we have not placed him); Ann Eaton of Seabrook (dau of Franklin's sister Sarah); Eleanor Walton and Jonathan Walton of Seabrook (dau of Greenleaf, Franklin's brother, and her husband); Nelson G. Frost of Seabrook (surviving child of Judith, Franklin's sister); Emily and Daniel Bailey of Seabrook (dau Judith); Jane Evans and John Evans of South Hampton, NH (child of Judith); Alexander Brown of Haverhill, MA (not placed); Harrison & Lydia H. Adams of Newburyport, MA (son of Lydia, Franklin's sister); John T. Bagley & Mary M. Bagley of E Somerville, MA (Franklin's brother and wife); Greenleaf Bagley (Franklin's brother's son); Frederick T. Bagley of Clinton, ME (Franklin's brother); Abner T. Bagley of Clinton, ME (son of Greenleaf, Franklin's brother); Dorothy & Abner True of Clinton, ME (dau of Greenleaf, Franklin's brother; Hartley B. & Mary J. Libby of Baranka, ME (dau of Greenleaf, Franklin's brother).

482. Oliver P. Bagley 6, Stephen 5, Abel 4, Joseph 3, Orlando 2, Orlando 1 , b Salisbury, MA about 1803; d East Kingston, NH, Feb 22, 1878, ae 75; m intentions Feb 5, 1837 (Salis MA R) Elizabeth Currier, d Sept 8, 1900, ae 84 (MA R), at Amesbury, given as dau of James & Sarah. Census of 1850 gives him as of Francestown, NH.

Children: (MA R)
1023. Jacob Currier 7, b Salisbury, MA, Jan 12, 1841; d there June 18, 1864, ae 23
1024. Sarah Elizabeth 7, b Feb 6, 1847; d Jan 31, 1867 (MA R call this child Susan Elizabeth)

483. Judith Bagley 6, Stephen 5, Abel 4, Joseph 3, Orlando 2, Orlando 1 , b Oct 9, 1808, probably Salisbury, MA; m Oct 11, 1835, Newell Frost (Salis MA R), b Salisbury, MA, Jan 8, 1808, d there Aug 1, 1854 (Salis MA R). Judith must have died before 1873 as her surviving children were heirs-at-law of Franklin Bagley but she was not.

Children: (Salis MA R)
1025. Emily Donelson 7, b Nov 17, 1838; m Daniel Bailey of

Salisbury, MA. Heir-at-law of Franklin Bagley in 1873
1026. Dolly Pike 7, b July 11, 1840; d Dec 16, 1844
1027. Jane Newell 7, b Nov 4, 1841; m John Evans of So uth
Hampton, NH. Heir-at-law of Franklin Bagley in 1873
1028. Newell Frost 7, b July 1, 1843; d Folly Island, SC, Nov
1, 1863, Co C, 40th MA Regt
1029. Polly Pike 7, b Apr 20, 1845; d Salisbury, MA, 1869
1030. Nelson Greeley 7, b July 1, 1847; heir-at-law of
Franklin Bagley in 1873

485. William Page Bagley 6, Elias 5, Abel 4, Joseph 3,
Orlando 2, Orlando 1 , Pn Sept 25, 1821, he, given as of
Richmond Co, GA, sold his share of his father's estate
(Rockingham Co NH Probate R). Probably m Mary G. Pickett,
June 13, 1831 (Richmond Co GA R).

486. Sarah Hunt Bagley 6, Elias 5 Abel 4, Joseph 3, Orlando
2, Orlando 1 , probably the Sarah Bagley who m Daniel Wyett,
Sept 25, 1843 (South Church, Portsmouth, NH R).

491. Valentine Bagley 7, Benjamin 6, Seth 5, Orlando 4,
Orlando 3, Orlando 2, Orlando 1 , b Feb 14, 1817; m at
Seabrook, NH, Feb 14, 1852, Elizabeth Fowler, dau Abram &
Abigail (Seabrook NH R), d Sept 6, 1902, ae 75 (Seabrook NH
R). He was living in 1867 (Rockingham Co NH R). Census of
1860 gives Valentine, ae 49; Elizabeth, ae 33; John S., ae 8;
and Morris, ae 3.

Children:
1031. John S. 8, b 1853/54, Seabrook, NH; d Jan 7, 1896
(Seabrook NH R)
1032. Valentine 8, b 1853/54; d Apr 21, 1926 (Lynn MA R)
1033. Morris H. 8, b 1858; d Jan 19, 1909, ae 51 (tombstone,
Seabrook, NH)
1034. Mary C. 8, b about 1861 (Census of 1870 gives as 9)
1035. Charles H. 8, b about 1864 (Census of 1870 gives ae 6)
1036. Lizzie 8, b Mar 31, 1866 (Seabrook NH R)
1037. Melissa T. 8, b Dec 16, 1868 (Seabrook NH R)

493. Abigail Bagley 7, Benjamin 6, Seth 5, Orlando 4, Orlando
3, Orlando 2, Orlando 1 , b Mar 27, 1820 (Salis MA R); m
      Gorman.

494. Thomas Bagley 7, Benjamin 6, Seth 5, Orlando 4, Orlando
3, Orlando 2, Orlando 1 , b Oct 25, 1821 (Salis MA R); m Sept
7, 1845, Hannah Remick, b 1826, d June 30, 1890 (Newburport MA
R). Death record says ae 59, dau William & Eliza. He d Sept
16, 1909, ae 84, Salisbury, MA. Record gives his father and
Valentine and mother as Eunice Fowler; carriage maker. Census
of 1850 gives him in Salisbury, MA.

Children:
1038. Hannah 8, b Dec 15, 1845 (Salis MA R)
1039. Thomas W. 8, b Nov 19, 1847 (Salis MA R); d Mar 21,
1921
1040. John H. 7, b about 1848; d Woodstock, NH, 1902, ae 54

1041. Sarah E. 8, b Feb 19, 1853; d Feb 10, 1874
1042. James 8, b Nov 8, 1860; d Newton, NH, Aug 13, 1932 (NH R)
1043. Sally 8, b June 26, 1863 (Family R)
1044. Frank B. 8, b 1853 (Salis MA); d Mar 7, 1907, ae 53 (Ames MA R)
1045. Elizabeth 8, b 1855, Salisbury, MA (Census of 1870 gives ae 15)
1046. Ellen 8, b 1855, Salisbury, MA (Census of 1870 gives ae 12)
1047. Charles 8, b 1861, Salisbury, MA (Census of 1870 gives ae 9)
1048. Susan 8, b June 26, 1863 (MA R)
1049. Eliza 8, b 1867 (Census of 1870 gives ae 3)

496. Sally Bagley 7, Benjamin 6, Seth 5, Orlando 4, Orland 3, Orlando 2, Orlando 1 , b Feb 17, 1824; m Seth Gage, June 21, 1845, Lowell, MA, son Iaac & Anna, b Waterville, ME, d Amesbury, MA, June 27, 1881 (Family R).

Children:
1050. Anne E. 8, b May 4, 1848 (Salis MA R)
1051. Sarah M. 8, b June 21, 1854; d Jan 14, 1867
1052. Seth H. 8, b Jan 28, 1856
1053. Rosetta F. 8, b Sept 23, 1858
1054. Alice L. 8, b Dec 7, 1861
1055. Clara 8, b Mar 18, 1863; d Dec 9, 1880
1056. Charles B. 8, b July 10, 1867; d young

512. Sargent Bagley 7, Sargent 6, Henry 5, Henry 4, Orlando 3, Orlando 2, Orlando 1 , b June 29, 1780; d St Johnsbury, VT, Aug 14, 1845; m July 10, 1807, Betsey Kelley (Ames MA R), probably dau Stephen & Louisa (Sargent), b Oct 22, 1784 (death certificate says 1787), d St Johnsbury, VT, July 30, 1843, ae 56 (VT R). Paid taxes in Weare, NH in 1810. On June 12, 1827, Sargent and Betsey sold land in Newton, NH (Rockingham Co NH Deeds). This was apparently a Kelley estate as other Kelleys are mentioned. Sargent and wife are given as of Bradford, VT. Supposed to have had five children.

Children:
1057. Ira Atwood 8, b Feb 6, 1813; d May 28, 1880 (VT R)
1058. Rebecca Challis 8, b Dec 13, 1810; d St Johnsbury, VT, about 1866 (VT R)
1059. Eliza 8, b Feb 20, 1816; d Sept 3, 1869

513. Moses Bagley 7, Sargent 6, Henry 5, Henry 4, Orlando 3, Orlando 2, Orlando 1 , b May 29, 1797; baptized June 4, 1797; m May 15, 1823, Rebecca Jewett (St Johnsbury VT R), dau Luther & Betsey (Adams). He d Mar 24, 1824 (VT R); a medical doctor.

Child:
1060. Nancy E. 8, b Nov 30, 1823, Washington, VT (VT R)

514. Mary Patten Bagley 7, Sargent 6, Henry 5, Henry 4,

Orlando 3, Orlando 2, Orlando 1 , b Nov 15, 1807;   probably   m
Kimball Snow, July 21, 1842, St Johnsbury, VT (VT R).

516.   Winthrop Bagley 7, Orlando 6, Henry 5, Henry 4,   Orlando
3, Orlando 2, Orlando 1 , b May 11, 1779; d Aug 31,   1814,   ae
39, Windsor, VT; m Apr 28, 1803, at Windsor, VT,   Susannah
Willis, d Mar 11, 1818, ae 38 .
     Feb 1, 1820, Judge Luther Mills was appt   guardian   to
Susan Bagley of Windsor, a minor under the age of 14, heir   to
estate of Winthrop Bagley.   May 22, 1822, Ebenezer Shedd   of
Windsor was appt guardian of Albert Bagley of Windsor, a minor
and heir to estate of Susan Bagley, late of Windsor, deceased.
Feb 8, 1823, Judge Truman Harkans of Rutland, VT, was   appt
guardian of Susannah Bagley of Windsor, VT, a minor above   the
age of 14, and one of the heirs of the estate of Winthrop
Bagley, late of Windsor, deceased.

Children:
1061.   Caroline 8, b Windsor, VT, Nov 24, 1803 (Family R)
1062.   Gilman 8, b Windsor, VT, Dec 19, 1805; d Feb 1, 1806
1063.   Susannah 8, b Windsor, VT, Aug 7, 1807 (Family R)
1064.   Albert 8, b Windsor, VT, Aug 14, 1809; d Aug 31, 1810
(Family R)
1065.   Maria 8, b Windsor, VT, Oct 27, 1811; d Mar   17,   1876,
Westfield, NY.   Another record gives her as b Mendon, VT)
1066.   Albert Gilman 8, b Windsor, VT, Apr 10, 1814

Note: There is another Winthrop Bagley,   often   confused   with
this one. He is on   the   1810 Census   of   Candia, NH.   His
parentage cannot be traced from Candia Records.   His   marriage
certificate gives him as of Candia and styles him   Lieutenant.
He m Jane Pillsbury, Apr 4, 1805, b Nov 2, 1781,   d Sept   17,
1861, ae 79, at Cambridge, MA, the dau of Benjamin & Bridgett.
He is believed to have gone to Stanstead, QUE. Later his wife
and at least one child, Betsey Ann, returned   to   the   States.
Betsey Ann was born Feb 2, 1814, Deerfield, NH,   and   died   at
Cambridge, MA, May 6, 1884.   She m Samuel   Dustin   of
Stanstead, QUE (MA R)

517.   Betsey L. Bagley 7, Orlando 6, Henry 5, Henry 4, Orlando
3, Orlando 2, Orlando 1 , b Jan 14, 1791, Weare, NH;   went   to
Brooklyn, PA, about 1804, where she m in 1806 Lyman Saunders,
son Joshua & Mary (Taylor).   They went to OH in 1817 where   he
d of ague before 1820 and left her with small   children;   none
of them returned to Brooklyn, PA. He b about 1780,   Westerly,
RI, d about 1819 in Union Township, Union Co,   OH.   Names   of
children not found.
     Lyman Saunders had a deed from John B. Wallace of land in
the vicinity of Mack's Corners, now Lindaville (Weston).   He
was a blacksmith and assisted his father who lived with   or
near him. Census of 1810 for Bridgewater Township,   Luzerne
Co, PA, gives self and wife, ae 26-45; 2 females 0-10.   She
was a member of Rev Edward Paine's Methodist Class in Brooklyn
in 1811.
     Census of 1820 lists her in Union Township, Union Co, OH,
living near Lyman's brothers, Thomas and B,   Sheffield

Saunders.

Lyman Saunders of Waterford Township, Susquehanna Co, PA, deed to Rev Edward Paine, on Oct 7, 1817, for $1000, sixty acres of land, Betsey granted her right of dower and signed the deed; recorded Sept 25, 1819, Montrose Deed Book 3, p 357.

519. Jesse Bagley 7, Orlando 6, Henry 5, Henry 4, Orlando 3, Orlando 2 Orlando 1 , b Apr 21, 1786; d Nov 30, 1874, ae 89; m Polly Saunders, dau John (Weston gives birth as Apr 2, but monument gives 21). Weston says Phally Saunders, dau Joshua & Mary (Taylor). He went to Hartland, VT, with his father, Orlando and his grandfather Henry and the older children after stopping at Weare, NH. He moved to Brooklyn, PA, in 1804, in company with the Tewksburys and wrote an account of his trip which was published, now in Newberry Library, Chicago, in the county directory of Rockingam Co, which says: "We started on Tuesday and were two Sundays on the road; we settled on a hill which is now east of Mack's Corners. We went to Tuckhannock and Wilkes Barre for store goods, to Horten's and Tunkhannock to mill, and to Hyde's at the Forks to the Post Office. Esquire Hind lived where Montrose now is." On account says he dropped dead in the Methodist Church, but this is disputed, correctly, we think by Rev Williams, since he d at Lanesboro where he lived in the home of his son. At his death, only a granddaughter remained in Brooklyn.

He and his wife were members of Rev Edward Paine's Methodist Class in Brooklyn in 1811 and listed as married. They named a son for Rev Paine. Jesse was a member of the committee to build the first Methodist Church in Brooklyn (Weston).

He and his family went to OH in 1817 with their parents, where their son Horace was born in 1818. He is listed as a head of family in the Census of 1820 for Union Township, Union Co, OH. The family returned to Brooklyn, apparently by 1824.

The date of the marriage of Jesse and Polly is recorded in a Wilkes-Barre newspaper for Jan 8, 1808, and is printed in the Proceedings of the Wyoming History Society, Wilkes-Barre, PA. Their ceremony occurred in Bridgewater of which Brooklyn was then a part. The finding of this date crowds the first four children into a four-year period.

In 1806, he was a captain in the local militia; in the War of 1812 served in the Danville Expedition under Col Frederick Bailey as a first sargeant. Weston says he was promoted to captain. This service is confirmed in PA archives. However, he was not a pensioner for his service in the War of 1812, nor for service in the PA militia.

Records of the Commonwealth of PA say: "One Jesse Bagley performed a tour of duty which included the period Nov 2 to Nov 29, 1814, as a first sergeant, Capt Frederick Bailey's Co, detached from the 129th Regt, 2nd Brigade, 9th Div, PA militia in the service of the USA which was discharged at Danville, Nov 22, 1814, according to a company return dated Nov 16, 1814.

"One Jesse Bagley performed a tour of duty which included the period Nov 2 to Nov 29, 1814, as a sergeant, Capt Frederick Bailey's Co, 129th Regt, 2nd Brigade, 9th Div, PA militia in the service of USA which was discharged at Danville under order of Col James Montgomery in which capacity he received 90/cents as pay according to an undated receipt roll. Residence in all instances as ascribed as Susquehanna County."

He seems to have been a shoemaker, hotel keeper, school teacher and woodchopper. He is mentioned as teaching school at Mack's Corner very early. He was constable in 1831, (Weston) .

He and his wife and two daughters, Harriet R. and Mary Eliza, are buried in the Old Cemetery, Brooklyn.

Children:
1067. Henry W. 8, b 1808, Brooklyn, PA
1068. Daniel B. 8, b May 30, 1809; d Aug 6, 1843
1069. Alice 8, b 1810, Brooklyn, PA
1070. Loren Lathrop 8, b June 8, 1811, Brooklyn, PA; d Apr 14, 1872, Carbondale, PA
1071. Harriet 8, d young
1072. Edward Paine 8, b 1816, Brooklyn, PA
1073. Horace 8, b 1818, Union County, OH
1074. Mary Eliza 8, b Jan 17, 1824, Brooklyn, PA; d Sept 14, 1875, residence of Samuel Yeomans, Carbondale, PA, of consumption
1076. Jesse H. 8, b 1826, Brooklyn, PA
1077. William Albert 8
1078. Lucy Caroline 8, b Oct 2, 1830, Brooklyn, PA; d Apr 2, 1888, Mauch Chunk, PA; buried there
1079. John W. 8, b 1832, Brooklyn, PA; d June 19, 1863
1080. James Everett 8, b 1836, Brooklyn, PA; d Oct 2, 1864

520. Stephen Holland Bagley 7, Orlando 6, Henry 5, Henry 4, Orlando 3, Orlando 2, Orlando 1 , b 1788/89; probably Hartland, VT; probably d in OH; m Brooklyn, PA, about 1809, Mary Saunders, dau Joshua & Mary (Taylor), b about 1790, Westerly, RI. Names of all children not found. Weston says he was son of Orlando Bagley.

He and his wife are listed in Census of 1810 for Brooklyn, PA, both ae 16-26 and alone. They were members of Rev Edward Paine's Methodist Class in Brooklyn, in 1811, and listed as married.

He sold his farm at Mack's Corners in Brooklyn Township on Apr 5, 1814 for $514 to Capt Stephen Williams. Mary Bagley, wife of Stephen, signed off her dower rights (Susquehanna County, PA Deed Book 1, p 244. They went with the rest of Orlando Bagley's family to Union County, OH, in the fall of 1817 and did not return to Brooklyn, PA.

Child:
1081. Maria or Marion 8, probably dau Stephen above 14 years of age when in 1826, her Uncle Thomas, was made her guardian.

522. Dorcas Bagley 7, Orlando 6, Henry 5, Henry 4, Orlando 3, Orlando 2, Orlando 1 , b Feb 24, 1793, Hartland, VT. Member of Rev Edward Paine's Methodist Class in Brooklyn, PA, in 1811, and listed as single. Known to have been unmarried in 1817. Went to OH with her parents in 1817 and did not return

to Brooklyn; is thought to have died of the ague in OH.

523.   Thomas Bagley 7, Orlando 6, Henry 5, Henry 4, Orlando 3,
Orlando 2, Orlando 1 , b Mar 10, 1794, Hartland, VT; d Mar 12,
1876, Springville, PA; m about 1824, Abiah Lane, b Sept 29,
1794, d July 31, 1856, dau Gershom Flagg Lane & Lydia
(Thomas). Gershom was a Rev War soldier. Thomas was a
veteran of the War of 1812 in Capt Bailey's Co of Montgomery
County, PA, militia. He was a farmer and a shoemaker.

He went to OH at the same time as his father and was
enumerated in the 1820 Census of Oh with his father and
brother Jesse in Union Township. Returned to PA about 1822.
Lived at Springville, after his marriage, and upon his return
from OH, settled in Auburn Township , Susquehanna Co, PA,
Census of 1850 lists family as Thomas, ae 56, farmer, b VT;
Biah, ae 56, housewife, b MA; Juliette, ae 17, b PA; Roxanna,
ae 12, b PA. He is not listed in 1860 Census for Auburn,
Brooklyn, Dimock, Lathrop or Springville.

He and his wife were deeply religious "being remarkable
for their piety and power in religious exhortations and able
to quote the Scripture at will." They organized the Craig
Hill Methodist Church in Auburn, and he was class leader for
many years.

Thomas was appt guardian for Maria Bagley, over fourteen
years of age, and posted $600 bond on Jan 30, 1826. Maria was
probably the daughter of Stephen and Mary Bagley. She was
probably m by 1850.

In 1812-1814, a cotton factory was built in Brooklyn and
put in operation. Thomas Bagley and Samuel Yeomans went to
Philadelphia with two ox-teams and brought the machinery to
Brooklyn, takinbg 23 days for the trip (Weston).

Children: (from Lane Genealogies and Garrison)
1082. Julia Etta 8, b Jan 19, 1818, VT; d Feb 24, 1819
Springville, PA
1083. Eliza Emily 8, b Mar 4, 1820, OH
1084. Miriam Ophelia 8, b Nov 23, 1823, Springville, PA; d
Jan 13, 1921
1085. James Henry 8, b Jan 20, 1826, Springville, PA; d July
29, 1917
1086. Hannah Mary 8, b Dec 11, 1828, Springville, PA; d Sept
11, 1897
1087. Sarah Martha 8, b June 17, 1830, Springville, PA; d Apr
21, 1902
1088. Julie Etta 8, b Nov 23, 1832, Springville, PA; d July
9, 1878
1089. Cinthia Sophronia 8, b Mar 23, 1836, Springville, PA; d
Feb 4, 1857
1090. Roxiena 8, b Jan, 1838, Springville, PA; d July 12,
1920

525. Dorothy Bagley 7, Orlando 6, Henry 5, Henry 4, Orlando 3, Orlando 2, Orlando 1 , b July 19, 1797, Hartland, VT; d Apr 19, 1885, Brooklyn, PA, ae 87-9; buried Old Cemetery, Brooklyn; m July 39, 1816, Brooklyn, PA, by Rev Elisha Bibbins, pastor Methodist Church, Brooklyn, Benjamin Sheffield Saunders, son Joshua & Mary (Taylor), b about 1794, Charlestown, RI, d Feb 8, 1859, Brooklyn, ae 64; buried Old Cemetery, Brooklyn.

They spent most of their lives in Brooklyn, except for the time they spent in OH, with their parents, going there in fall of 1817, and returning to Brooklyn in 1822. Their eldest child, Lydia, was about six weeks old when they went to OH, and was carried there on a pillow; their second child, Ruth, was born in OH in 1820. Sheffield Saunders is on the 1820 Census of Union Township, Union Co, OH, near his brother, Thomas, and near the widow of his brother Lyman, Betsey L. (Bagley) Saunders.

Benjamin drove the stage on the Milford and Oswego Turnpike for a time after his return from OH and is listed as a miller in the 1850 and 1860 Census.

He and his wife, Dolly, are on Rev Edward Paine's 1811 Methodist Class list, both being listed as single at that time. They were members of the Brooklyn Methodist Church until their deaths.

He was appt in Orphans Court in Susquehanna County as guardian of Mary A. Bagley, dau Washington Bagley. She was raised with this family and is listed with them on the Census. She was willed some household goods by her aunt, Dorothy (Bagley) Saunders. Dolly Saunders names her children in her will: Catherine Hall to have the family Bible; Ruth Tewksbury, a history book; Emeline Bagley, a small Bible; Mary Shappe, a history book; Henrietta Kent, an illustrated book; Lydia Brooks and all the others to have one dollar; Eliza Tewksbury to have all the rest and mark the family monument with the name of Perry D. Saunders, her son. Will dated May 4, 1878, Will Box 5, p 274, Montrose, PA.

Children:
1091. Lydia Weed 8, b Aug 29, 1817; d May 1, 1879; m Feb 24, 1841, Henry Knapp Nutt; m (2) ____Brooks. A Mrs Arthur Brundage of Syracue, NY, joined the DAR on war service of Orlando Bagley and Joshua Saunders, a granddaughter of Lydia Nutt
1092. Ruth A. 8, b Mar 15, 1820; d Aug 8, 1895; m Sept 30, 1841, Isaac S. Tewksbury
1093. Mary M. 8, m Oct 13, 1842, George P. Shappe of Elmira, NY
1094. Henrietta 8, m George J. Kent, son Justis and Ann (Stuart)
1095. Catherine 8, m ____ Hall
1096. Emeline 8, b about 1830; m James Bagley, son Thomas & Abiah (Lane)
1097. Eliza A. 8, b 1932; d 1902; m Ephraim S. Tewskbury, b 1830, d 1896. After the death of her husband, Dorothy Saunders lived and died at the home of her dau Eliza

1098.   Benjamin Orlando 8, b June 4, 1836, Brooklyn, PA; d Apr
4, 1838; buried Old Cemetery, Brooklyn, PA
1099.   Charles George 8, b June 29, 1837, Brooklyn, PA; d Dec
29, 1839; buried Old Cemetery
1100.   Perry Duward 8, b Feb 6, 1841, Brooklyn, PA; d May 6,
1864, ae 23-6. Killed in the Battle of Wilderness, Civil War;
body not returned to Brooklyn. Co F, 141 regt, PA Vols Inf.
Accidently shot from Union side.

525. Charles George Bagley 7, Orlando 6, Henry 5, Henry 4,
Orlando 3, Orlando 2, Orlando 1 , b July 11, 1799, Hartland,
VT. For legal purposes he went by name of Charles George, but
was commonly called George. Married in Brooklyn about 1824,
Phebe Lawrence, dau William & Amy. In 1850 they were living
in Springville Township and owned property. Weston says the
family went West after 1850. He owned land in Springville
Township, deed dated Oct 1, 1831, and land in Dimock Township
in 1845. He sold land in Dimock Aug 12, 1834.
     Census of 1850 gives him in Springville Township where he
states himself as ae 50 and b in VT. His daughter Amy and her
husband, Joshua Jackson lived next door.

Children: (Census of 1850)
1101.   Amy F. 8, b about 1827
1102.   Orlando 8, b about 1829
1103.   Sarah 8, b about 1832
1104.   Elizabeth A. 8, b about 1838
1105.   Lucy A. 8, b about 1841
1106.   Adelaide 8, b about 1844
1107.   Clark 8, b about 1846
1108.   George W. 8, b May 1, 1850

526. Washington Bagley 7, Orlando 6, Henry 5, Henry 4,
Orlando 3, Orlando 2, Orlando 1 , b Jan 24, 1802, Hartland,
VT; d Brooklyn, PA, July 3, 1848, of an axe injury; m
Brooklyn, PA, Dec 24, 1834, Lydia Morgan Williams, dau Capt
Stephen & Mary (Williams) Williams.
     He had a furniture shop in Brooklyn and used the town
brook to run his lathe. He and his nephew, Daniel B. Bagley,
made chairs and other fine furniture which is still highly
prized.
     Adm on his estate opened July 13, 1848, with renunciation
of widow and letters were granted to Amos G. Bailey (Will Book
1). Estate not settled until Aug 22, 1850 in Orphans Court.
Court was petitioned to allow the guardians and adm to sell
Washington Bagley's house and barn and five acres, all in need
of care and attention on Jan 22, 1855. Land sold to Ezra S.
Kent, the highest bidder, for $293, Nov 29, 1856.
     Adm on estate of Lydia M. Bagley began in Orphans Court
with the application for guardians of her minor children.
Three children were too young to choose guardians so the court
appt Samuel Allen Newton for Ann Eliza; Robert Gere for Ellen
L; Benjamin Sheffield Saunders for Mary A. Sarah Roxanna,
being over fourteen years, chose her uncle, Benjamin S.
Saunders. Later Samuel Allen Newton resigned as guardian for
Ann Eliza and her uncle Amos Williams of Springville was appt.

Census of 1850 for Brooklyn, PA gives Lydia M. Bagley, ae 35; Roxena, ae 14; Ann Eliza, ae 5; Mary A., ae 2. Census of 1860 for Springville shows Ann E., ae 15, servant in house of Ezra Strickland. Census of 1860 for Springville gives Mary A., ae 12, servant in the house of Dorothy Saunders.

Estate of Ellen L. Bagley, deceased, adm Robert W. Gere, her guardian on June 5, 1858, amount $59. 21 (Will Book 2). Estate settled on Aug 24, 1858. Final account made Aug 28, 1860 include some of the following: M. L Mack for coffin $9.50; I. Tewskbury for digging grave $3; Dr Richardson for service $1; G. W. Palmer for gravestone $20.

Children:
1109.   Sarah Roxena 8, b Apr 2, 1836; d Jan 19, 1891, Dimock, PA
1110.   Ann Eliza 8, unm in 1860
1111.   Ellen M. 8, d unm; buried with her parents, 1858
1112.   Mary A. 8, b May 24, 1848, Brooklyn, PA; d Nov 237, 1915, Kingston, PA

527.   Sally Bagley 7, Orlando 6, Henry 5, Henry 4, Orlando 3, Orlando 2, Orlando 1 , b about 1804, Brooklyn, PA; probably d before 1830; m about 1826, Brooklyn, PA, Luke A. Williams, son Latham & Lucy (Stanton), b about 1802, Groton, CO, d Sept 6, 1829, Brooklyn, PA.

Sally went to Ohio with her parents in 1817, but returned to Brooklyn about 1826 when she m Luke Williams. She does not appear on the 1830 Census as head of a family. She and her husband do not have headstones in Brooklyn Cemetery. Latham Williams, father, was appt adm of estate of Luke A. Williams, deceased, late of Brooklyn, on Aug 29, 1832. No account of widow, no renunciation with her signature, no inventory, no final account, only adm's bond with the signature of Latham Williams (Will Book 1, p 104). Luke Williams, deceased, late of Brooklyn, left one son Henry Mason Williams, ae 3 yrs. Isaac Williams of Brooklyn appt guardian on Apr 20, 1832, and he signed a bond for $300. There is no mention of the mother of Henry Williams (Orphans Court 1, p 240). Later in 1832, Washington Bagley, uncle and next of kin, requested the court to appoint a guardian for his nephew, Henry Mason Williams, under age fourteen, and son of Luke A. Williams, deceased. The court appt Ami Ely as guardian, Sept 4, 1832 (Orphans Court 1, p 249). There is no mention of Henry's mother, nor of the resignation of Isaac Williams as guardian. It is possible that Henry Williams lived with the family of Washington Bagley, but there is no mention of this in above materials.

Child:
1113.   Henry Mason Williams 8, b 1829, Brooklyn, PA; m Lurena N. Saunders, dau Aaron & Polly (Crandall), b June 25, 1830, Lathrop Township, d Feb 12, 1912, Carbondale, PA; buried Evergreen Cemetery, Brooklyn. A dau of theirs, Sarah G. Williams, b June 19, 1853, Brooklyn, PA, m William T. Daley, son Charles G. & Lucy L. (Wilcox). Their children were Grace A., who m Earl Tiffany, son of Mather; and Charles H. Daley,

who m Ruth Lee.

528.   Abigail Bagley 7, Thomas 6, Henry 5, Henry 4, Orlando 3, Orlando 2, Orlando 1 , b Sept 20, 1782; probably m Edmund Kelley, Apr 24, 1807 (VT R)

Child:
1114.   Salvin K. 8

530.   Jonathan Bagley 7, Thomas 6, Henry 5, Henry 4, Orlando 3, Orlando 2, Orlando 1 , b Mar 5, 1786 (probably Weare, NH); d July 3, 1867, ae 81, being thrown from a horse; m Lydia Small, Apr 5, 1812, b June 6, 1796, d Jan 29, 1877, ae 81 (VT R).   Census of 1850 gives Hartland, VT.

Children: (Hartland VT R except as noted)
1115.   Frederick 8, b Apr 12, 1813
1116.   Clarissa 8, b Sept 7, 1814
1117.   Aaron 8, b Nov 2, 1815; d Apr 13, 1898 (tombstone, Granville, VT)
1118.   George Dwight 8, b Apr 15, 1817; d Apr 2, 1852, ae 35
1119.   Edwin 8, b Dec 5, 1819; d Dec 19, 1819 (tombstone, Hartland, VT)
1120.   Emmeline 8, b Nov 7, 1821; d July 6, 1872
1121.   Lucy Ann 8, b July 26, 1820
1122.   Alonzo 8, b Dec 26, 1823
1123.   Simeon 8, b Aug 14, 1829; d Sept 30, 1856 (tombstone, Hartland, VT)
1124.   Lucia 8, b Mar 14, 1827; d 1898 (tombstone, Hartland, VT)
1125.   Laura 8, b Mar 14, 1827; d Jan 6, 1904 (tombstone, Hartland, VT)
1126.   Charlotte 8, b Nov 14, 1833; d Mar 22, 1897 (tombstone, Hartland, VT)
1127.   Ellen 8, b May 4, 1836; d Jan 9, 1918 (tombstone, Hartland, VT)
1128.   Sanford Boutwell 8, b Apr 11, 1841; d 1923 (tombstone, Hartland, VT)
1129.   Julia 8, b Apr 25, 1831; d Feb 14, 1853

531.   Thomas Bagley 7, Thomas 6, Henry 5, Henry 4 Orlando 3, Orlando 2, Orlando 1 , b Mar 9, 1788; d May 14, 1863; m Nancy Marsh, May 25, 1817, dau John & Emily (Wells), d Dec 10, 1878, ae 83 (VT R).   Served in War of 1812, Capt R. R. Brown's Co. Pension certificate of Widow Nancy No 9065.   Buried Sheddsville, VT.   Census of 1850 shows W. Windsor, VT.

Children: (Hartland VT R except as noted)
1130.   Nancy Ann 8, b Feb 24, 1818; d June 15, 1903
1131.   Emily Sophia 8, b July 10, 1819; d Oct 2, 1854
1132.   Charlotte 8, b Feb 1, 1821; d 1854
1133.   Lois Maria 8, b Mar 7, 1823; d Oct 15, 1863
1134.   Mary 8, b Oct 9, 1824; d 1897
1135.   Edward 8, b Apr 12, 1827; d Apr 22, 1827
1136.   Ellen 8, b Apr 12, 1827

1137.   Marcia 8, b Oct 16, 1828; d Mar 29, 1911 (Family R)
1138.   John Parker 8, b Feb 24, 1837; d Apr 16, 1862
1139.   Edwin E. 8, b Feb 25, 1831; d Mar 25, 1907

532.   Olive Bagley 7, Thomas 6, Henry 5, Henry 4, Orlando 3,
Orlando 2, Orlando 1 , b Hartland, VT, Sept 25, 1790; d May
14, 1863; m Elisha Rice, Sept 7, 1818 (VT R).

533.   Daniel Bagley 7, Thomas 6, Henry 5, Henry 4, Orlando 3,
Orlando 2, Orlando 1 , b Hartland, VT, Oct 25, 1792; d Dec 10,
1879, Lincoln, VT, given as of Warren, VT; m Betsey Blaisdell,
dau Silas, Mar 14, 1816, d Lincoln, VT, July 8, 1880, ae 87
(VT R). Death certificate gives him as son Thomas and Olive.
Believed to be the Daniel, given as of Hartland, VT, who with
Betsey, his wife, conveyed land in Weare, NH, Feb 8, 1827, and
who released property rights in Weare as heirs-at-law of Capt
Hadley, Feb 19, 1833 (Hillsboro NH Probate R). Enl in War of
1812, July 4, 1812; served to Jan 5, 1814. Engaged in
Chautauqua River Battle, Capt Phineas Williams' Co, 11th regt,
from Jan to Feb 26, 1813.

Children: (VT R)
1140.   Mary 8, b 1824, Warren, VT; d Jan 28, 1887, ae 63,
Lincoln, VT
1141.   George 8, b about 1821; d Lincoln, VT, Jan 24, 1896, ae
65
1142.   Silas W. 8, b about 1837, Dumerston, VT; d Lincoln, VT,
June 9, 1899 (Census of 1860 gives him as 38)
1143.   Walter A. 8, b Hartland, VT, about 1825; d Warren, VT,
Apr 10, 1895, ae 85

534.   Perkins Bagley 7, Thomas 6, Henry 5, Henry 4, Orlando 3,
Orlando 2, Orlando 1 , b Hartland, VT, Aug 11, 1795; d June
10, 1880, ae 84; m (1) Edith Smith, d Apr 8, 1827, ae 27
(Hartland VT R); m (2) Apr 1, 1828, Mary Rogers, dau William &
Mary (Landry), b Feb 19, 1807, Hartland, VT, d May 2, 1885, ae
78 (Hartland VT R). In War of 1812 in Capt Bacon's Co;
received a pension. Census of 1850 gives Hartland.

Children: (Hartland VT R except as noted)
1144.   Helen 8, d young
1145.   Lucian 8, b about 1827; d Aug 4, 1848
1146.   Arnold 8, b Nov 10, 1829; d Mar 21, 1910, unm
1147.   Roderick 8, b about 1831; d Saginaw, Mich., Nov 14,
1849
1148.   Frederick Hatch 8, b about 1834; probably son Perkins;
d Sept 29, 1849; buried Gallup Cemetery, Hartland, VT
1149.   Helen 8, b Aug 3, 1838; d Sept 29, 1849
1150.   Olive 8, b about 1836; d Aug 19, 1857
1151.   William Washington 8, b Aug 3, 1838; d Mar 11, 1926
(Claremont NH R)
1152.   Thomas 8, b Aug 6, 1844; d May 8, 1849
1153.   Cyrus Ransom 8, b Dec 20, 1847; d Feb 20, 1911, ae 63
1154.   Thomas W. 8, b 1849; d young

536. Asabel Bagley 7, Thomas 6, Henry 5, Henry 4, Orlando 3,

Orlando 2, Orlando 1 , b Hartland, VT, Nov 4 or 6, 1799; d July 11, 1849, ae 50; m Mary Marcy, dau William & _____ (Pike) of Cornish, VT, Mar 25, 1827, who d Apr 12, 1844, ae 37 (tombstone Jenneysville, VT). Windsor Co VT R say that Asabel Bagley d July 11, 1849 and left no will and an adm was appt upon request of Jane Frances Bagley, dau and only heir of said deceased, there being no widow.

Child:
1155. Jane Frances 8

537. Lucy Bagley 7, Thomas 6, Henry 5, Henry 4, Orlando 3, Orlando 2, Orlando 1 , b Hartland, VT, Feb 10, 1802; d Aug 8, 1873, Hartland, VT; m (1) Josiah Brown, Feb 4, 1827, son David & Sally, b Nov 23, 1803 or 09, Hartland, VT, d Mar 7, 1827, Hartland; she m (2) June 30, 1829, Charles E. Colston, son William & Sarah, b 1785, Hartland, d there Mar 4, 1864 (VT R).

Children: (Hartland VT R)
1156. Lucinda Brown 8, b Apr, 1827; d July, 1828
1157. Albert 8, b May 16, 1830
1158. Lucinda 8, b Apr 10, 1832; d Nov 22, 1894; m Jan 23, 1858, Edwin H. Bagley
1159. Theodore 8, b Feb 27, 1837
1160. John F. 8, b Jan 13, 1846; d May 2, 1921; m Eliza Gay

539. Jefferson Bagley 7, Thomas 6, Henry 5, Henry 4, Orlando 3, Orlando 2, Orlando 1 , b Hartland, VT, July 28, 1806; d June 3, 1887, ae 80; m 1836, Fidelia Gallup, dau Joseph & Rebecca (Huckins), b Mar 24, 1814, Melbourne QUE. Another source says she was dau of Josiah Huckins & Mary (Randall), b Mar 21, 1814, Hartland, VT, d Nov 12, 1881, ae 67 (Hartland VT R).

Child:
1161. Henry Jefferson 8, b Sept 13, 1837 (Hartland VT R)

541. Sargent Bagley 7, Henry 6, Henry 5, Henry 4, Orlando 3, Orlando 2, Orlando 1 , probably m Lydia Goff of Washington, NH, Jan 23, 1812 (NH R). Conveyed land Mar 18, 1811, given as of Weare, NH (Hillsboro Co NH Deeds). Living in 1842 as mentioned in father's will.

542. Joel Bagley 7, Henry 6, Henry 5, Henry 4, Orlando 3, Orlando 2, Orlando 1 , living 1842 as mentioned in father's will; m Betsey Farnsworth of Roxbury, NH, at Keene, NH, Jan 21, 1815 (Keene NH R). Not on Census of 1850 for NH.

543. Sally Bagley 7, Henry 6, Henry 5, Henry 4, Orlando 3, Orlando 2, Orlando 1 , living 1842 as mentioned in father's will in that year as single; however she m 1842, Nathaniel W. Sawyer, b June 6, 1812, son Enoch & Sarah (Little) of Hampstead, NH, d Apr 18, 1851 (Descendants of George Little, and History of Goffstown, NH). The History of Antrim, NH says that Nathaniel Sawyer, son of Samuel & Susanna (Read), b June 12, 1812, m Sarah Bagley of Windsor in 1842 and died in that

town. His widow lived alone on the farm for eleven years when
she fell and broke her hip. It was mid-winter and she was
alone. She managed to crawl to the house, and she lay there
several days without help. Finally, a neighbor came. She
sold her property and moved to Antrim. He was a veteran of
the Seminole War. No children.

544. Truman Bagley 7, John 6, Jonathan 5, Henry 4, Orlando 3,
Orlando 2, Orlando 1 , mentioned in father's will, probated
Sept 14, 1833; b about 1790; d Aug 31, 1871 (Family R &
Census); m Rebecca, who d Apr 4, 1839; buried Durham, NY.
Census of 1860 gives him as ae 70, Cairo, NY, and Ellen
Conley, ae 18, b Ireland, was the only other member of the
household. Census of 1870 gives Truman, ae 82, b NY, resident
of Cairo, in the town poorhouse.

Child:
1162. Laura 8, mentioned as infant, in litigation over the
estate of her grandfather, John Bagley

546. Laura Bagley 7, John 6, Jonathan 5, Henry 4, Orlando 3,
Orlando 2, Orlando 1 , b Nov 11, 1797; d June 8, 1844
(tombstone, Cairo, NY); m Ira T. Day, d May 11, 1842, ae 51
(tombstone, Cairo). On June 4, 1842, Laura Day was appt
guardian of Ira T. Day, her son, a minor over 14 yrs.   From
other court records it would appear that the following were
the children of Ira and Laura (Bagley) Day (Greene Co NY R).

Children:
1163. Ira T. 8
1164. Henry 8
1165. Edgar 8, was 12, Apr 21, 1842

547. John Bagley 7, John 6, Jonathan 5, Henry 4, Orlando 3,
Orlando 2, Orlando 1 , b Jan 21, 1800; d May 3, 1855; m Mary
Smith, Mar 9, 1825, b Aug, 1802, d Detroit, Mich., Oct 6, 1855
(American Biography). Lived Medina, NY, for a time, and then
moved to Mich. In July, 1826, he and his wife sold land in
Windham, NY, to Bennet Osborne, "he being in possession."   It
appears that a leather factory stood on this land (Greene Co
NY R). They are supposed to have had seven children.

Children:
1166. Delia 8, mentioned in court litigation as dau of John
1167. Olive 8, b Jan 1, 1830 (Durham NY Church R)
1168. John Judson 8, b July 24, 1832; d July 27, 1881

555. Mary (Polly) Bagley 7, Winthrop 6, Jonathan 5, Henry 4,
Orlando 3, Orlando 2, Orlando 1 , b Dec 29, 1787; d Sept 19,
1822, ae 36; m Oct 9, 1806, William Thornton, son William &
Dorothy (Bagley) of Thornton, NH (NH R), b 1785 (DAR), d Dec
22, 1854 (tombstone, Thornton, NH). He m (2) May 19, 1823,
Harriet Elliott (Thornton NH R).

Children: (Thornton NH R)
1169. Lucinda 8, b Oct 21, 1806; d Nov 5, 1806

1170.   Cenae 8, b Feb 23, 1809; d Mar 28, 1809
1171.   Milton 8, b Oct 20, 1809
1172.   Freeman 8, b Feb 17, 1811
1173.   Cynthia 8, b Feb 23, 1813; d 1856 (DAR)
1174.   Lavinia 8, b Sept 12, 1814
1175.   George Washington 8, b Mar 13, 1819
1176.   Levi 8, b Dec 30, 1820

556.   Nancy Bagley 7, Winthrop 6, Jonathan 5, Henry 4, Orlando 3, Orlando 2, Orlando 1 , b Oct 13, 1789; d Dec 25, 186_, ae 68 (tombstone, Thornton, NH illegible); m Joseph E. Dow, Oct 4, 1825 (Thornton NH R), son Moses & Phebe (Emerson), b Haverhill, NH, Dec 28, 1777, grad Dartmouth College, 1799, admitted to bar at Haverhill, NH, Sept term, 1802, and in Caledonia Co, VT, in 1803. Practicing a few years in Haverhill, he moved to Littleton, NH, in 1807, being the first lawyer in the town. In 1811, he moved to Franconia, NH, where he resided until 1830, holding office and being useful in town affairs. He lived a few years in Thornton, retiring to Franconia where he d Aug 25, 1857. Nancy Bagley was his second wife, his first having died Mar 28, 1824 (History of Littleton, NH, by Stearns). In 1858 when Nancy's mother died, Nancy was the only surviving child of Winthrop & Maria Bagley.

Child:
1177.   Joseph 8, b about 1828; d a printer in Boston, Sept 20, 1854, ae 26 (tombstone, Thornton, NH)

558.   Sally Bagley 7, Winthrop 6, Jonathan 5, Henry 4, Orlando 3, Orlando 2, Orlando 1 , b Oct 24, 1793; d May 25, 1854, ae 57; m Tillotson Blaisdell of Campton, NH, Mar 16, 1820 (Thornton NH R), d July 9, 1877, ae 77 (tombstone, Thornton, NH).

Children:
1178.   Franklin 8, d Feb 26, 1868 (tombstone, Thornton, NH)
1179.   Emily 8, d Jan 26, 1897, ae 63 (tombstone, Thornton, NH)
1180.   Mary M. 8, b about 1824 (Census of 1850 gives ae 26)

560.   Hannah Bagley 7, Winthrop 6, Jonathan 5, Henry 4, Orlando 3, Orlando 2, Orlando 1 , b Nov 16, 1795; d before 1858; m James Tyler of Franconia, NH, Oct 7, 1816 (Thornton, NH R).

Children: (NH R)
1181.   Benjamin 8
1182.   Fanny 8
1183.   Harriet 8
1184.   Winthrop 8
1185.   William 8
1186.   Russell 8
1187.   Perley 8

560.   Thomas Bagley 7, Cutting 6, Jonathan 5, Henry 4, Orlando 3, Orlando 2, Orlando 1 , b 1790; d Mar 21, 1876 (Greene Co NY

R); m 1823, Mary Daley, d Sept 22, 1875. She deeded land in Cairo, NY, as one of the heirs of Edward Daley, deceased (Greene Co NY R). He d intestate and the records mention a son Mercedes Bagley (Marcus Elmore), a resident of Jerseyville, Jersey Co, IL. Thomas left 1500 acres of land in Durham, NY. Census of 1850 gives Thomas, ae 60; Mary, ae 50, and the children listed below. Census of 1870 for Durham, NY, gives Thomas, ae 80, and Mary, ae 70.

Children:
1188. Marcus Elmore (Mercedes), b Aug 18, 1828; d after 1912 (Family R)
1189. Harry 8, b about 1835 (ae 15, Census of 1850); d July 28, 1912, Freehold, NY (Family R)
1190. Nancy 8, d June 9, 1840, ae 14 (tombstone, Durham, NY)
1191. Mary 8, b about 1837 (ae 13, Census of 1850)
1192. Nancy 8, b about 1843 (ae 7, Census of 1850); d Feb 17, 1854, ae 11 (tombstone, Durham, NY)

Also given in this household is Helen Van Sturmberg, ae 20, but whether hired help or married dau is undetermined.

561. Benedict Bagley 7, Cutting 6, Jonathan 5, Henry 4, Orlando 3, Orlando 2, Orlando 1 , See discussion of this family under Cutting Bagley; m Juliette. Name is mentioned in several deeds for Durham, NY. No record of children found.

562. Henry Bagley 7, Cutting 6, Jonathan 5, Henry 4, Orlando 3, Orlando 2, Orlando 1 , b 1794; d 1885 (Nunda, NY tombstone); m (1) Lucy, who d before 1835; m (2) Eliza, buried with Henry at Nunda, NY, b 1806, d 1883. Lucy and Henry sold land in Cairo, NY, in 1820.

Children: (tombstones, Nunda, NY)
1193. George H. 8, b Aug 8, 1818; d Feb 21, 1871
1194. Eliza A. 8, b 1822; d 1839
1195. Delia H. 8, b 1826; d 1841
1196. Leverett 8, b 1841; d 1841
1197. Nancy W. 8, b 1835; d 1837
1198. Augustus E. 8, b 1837; d 1837

563. Barnard Bagley 7, Cutting 6, Jonathan 5, Henry 4, Orlando 3, Orlando 2, Orlando 1 , b Durham, NY, Nov 5, 1791 (Church R); d Watertown, NY, June 26, 1878; buried Durham, NY. Settled in Antwerp, NY, in 1812, where he taught school and took contracts for building roads. Went to Watertown in 1815 or 1816 and studied law with Charles E. Clark; admitted to bar in 1826. Town supervisor for Pamelia, NY; member of legislature, 1849. Active in civic and county affairs. Married (1) Polly Ann Griffen; m (2) Zurviah Gates, dau Jacob & Zurviah (Harris), widow of Lawyer Wright. Census of 1850 gives Barnard, ae 60; Zurviah, ae 50; George A., ae 24, a lawyer.

Children:
1199. Barnard 8, died prior to his father and probably before

1850 (Watertown Daily Times for June 27, 1878)
1200.   George A. 8, b July 22, 1826; d May 1912, Watertown, NY

564.   Submit Bagley 7, Cutting 6, Jonathan 5, Henry 4, Orlando
3, Orlando 2, Orlando 1 , m James Wildey of Windham, NY.

565.   Augustus Bagley 7, Cutting 6, Jonathan 5, Henry 4,
Orlando 3, Orlando 2, Orlando 1 , b 1797; d Feb 18, 1882; m
Emeline Bradley, b 1805, d Aug 2, 1884, ae 80 (East Haven CO
R).   Census of 1850 gives him as of East Haven, CO.

Children:
1201.   Leverett S. 8, b Jan 23, 1832; d Oct 1, 1905 (East
Haven, CO R)
1202.   Grace 8, b about 1841 (Census of 1850 gives as 9)

567.   Unknown Male Bagley 7, Cutting 6, Jonathan 5, Henry 4,
Orlando 3, Orlando 2, Orlando 1 See discussion of this family
under Cutting Bagley. A guess is the name might have been
Leverett since brothers Henry and Augustus both named sons
Leverett.

568.   Elizabeth Bagley 7, Jonathan 6, Jonathan 5, Henry 4,
Orlando 3, Orlando 2, Orlando 1 , m Samuel Harriman of
Montville, ME, Mar 13, 1836 (ME R).

Child:
1203.   Mayo E. 8, d May 5, 1897, ae 59 (Montville ME R)

569.   Hall Bagley 7, Jonathan 6, Jonathan 5, Henry 4, Orlando
3, Orlando 2, Orlando 1 , b Candia, NH, about 1799; d Aug 11,
1885 (tombstone, Corinth, ME & ME R); m Eunice Carter, Nov 16,
1823, Montville, ME, b Bridgton, ME, 1800; d Charlestown, E,
Jan 26, 1895, ae 95, dau Rufus & Eunice (Hall). Census of
1880 for Charlestown, ME gives Hall, ae 81; Eunice, ae 80. He
and his wife were sealed in the Church of Jesus Christ of
Latter Day Saints as of the town of Garland, ME, May 3, 1844.
Children are from ME R, Census of 1880, and family R).

Children:
1204.   Ambrose 8, b Charlestown, ME, Aug 2, 1837; d there Apr
15, 1916
1205.   George 8, d Dec 1, 1869, ae 40-1-2
1206.   Elethier 8

570.   Jonathan or John Bagley 7, Jonathan 6, Jonathan 5, Henry
4, Orlando 3, Orlando 2, Orlando 1 Death record gives b
Candia, NH, father John, 1806; d Corinth, ME, Sept 27, 1892,
ae 86. He may have m (2) Mrs Margaret N. Gray of Dover, ME,
at Bangor, Jan 16, 1883, by Charles A. Plumer (Bangor ME R).

Child:
1207.   Charles H. 8, b about 1848; d Mar 3, 1889, ae 41-7-17
(Family R)

571.   Currier Fitts Bagley 7, William 6, Jonathan 5, Henry 4,

Orlando 3, Orlando 2, Orlando 1 , b 1805; d 1854 (DAR); m 1831, Maria Louisa Roach, dau William, b 1808, d 1871 (DAR). The DAR records must be incorrect here as MA R say he died at Boston, Sept 26, 1871, ae 66, b Candia, NH, a merchant. Further, the MA R say he m (2) Submit J. Page, b Benton, NH, dau Caleb & Louisa, who d Barnstable, MA, Aug 26, 1891, ae 68. Census of 1850 gives him as of Cambridge, MA.

Children:
1208.   William Chase 8, b Aug 19, 1833; d 1911
1209.   Francis Herbert 8, b Jan 16, 1840; d 1878
1210.   Sidney Currier 8, b Aug 18, 1842; d 1919
1211.   Richard E. 8, d Dec 1, 1866, ae 8 mos (Boston MA R)

573.   Henry Bagley 7, William 6, Jonathan 5, Henry 4, Orlando 3, Orlando 2, Orlando 1 , b Nov 6, 1810.

574.   William Bagley 7, William 6, Jonathan 5, Henry 4, Orlando 3, Orlando 2, Orlando 1 , this William is supposed to have had a son of the same name, but we can find no proof.

576.   Thomas Bagley 7, Nathan 6, Jonathan 5, Henry 4, Orlando 3, Orlando 2, Orlando 1 , b 1805, Candia, NH; d Jan 1, 1855, of lung fever, ae 50 (Dedham, MA R); m intentions Apr 10, 1831 (Walpole MA R), Harriet Sumner, d about 1883, at Braintree, MA (M R). When estate of Thomas was probated in 1855, she was made guardian of Clinton, Lewis and Sumner (Norfolk Co MA Probate R).

Children: (Walpole MA R except as noted)
1212.   Harriet J. 8, d Aug 12, 1845, ae 11 (Dedham MA R)
1213.   Clinton 8, b Dec 16, 1838 (Pension R); d Feb 18, 1901, ae 64 (Walpole MA R)
1214.   Sumner 8, b about 1840; d Apr 8, 1911
1215.   Lewis 8, b about 1847; d Jan 15, 1878, ae 31

578.   Mary Osgood Bagley 7, Nathan 6, Jonathan 5, Henry 4, Orlando 3, Orlando 2, Orlando 1 , b Feb 25, 1808 (Candia NH R); d Jan, 1865; m William Horne of Tuftonboro, NH, July 1, 1829, at Meredith. He d 1851/52. Will states he was a cabinet maker. He left furniture and a turning lathe to his wife Mary Jane. His business was left to his brother, Isaiah, who m Mary Jane, Nov, 1832.

579.   Henry Osgood Bagley 7, Nathan 6, Jonathan 5, Henry 4, Orlando 3, Orlando 2, Orlando 1 , b June 10, 1812 (Candia NH R); d Meredith, NH, 1854; probably m Sally Gilman, b about 1810.   Horace Langley and Lyman Gilman, his brothers-in-law, were executors. Census of 1850 for Meredith Bridge gives Henry, ae 38, b Candia, engineer; Sally, ae 40, b NH; Frank P., ae 8 mos, b MA; George H., ae 5; and Rhoda, mother of Henry, ae 66.
     This family worked in work seasons in mills at Lowell, MA. In slack times they returned to Meredith Bridge. Sarah is supposed to have been an early advocate of women's rights and organized a newspaper for women mill workers and organized

a strike in the Lowell mills.

Rhoda Witham Bagley had a sister, Polly Witham Morse, who lived in Dedham, MA.

Children: (Census of 1850)
1216. George H. 8, b about 1845
1217. Frank P., b MA, about 1849

580. Elizabeth Bagley 7, Elizabeth 6, Jonathan 5, Henry 4, Orlando 3, Orlando 2, Orlando 1 , b Oct 26, 1803. Records list this birth under Elizabeth's father, Jonathan as a grandchild (Candia NH R). Moses Dudley of Raymond, NH was appt her guardian, a minor under 14 years of age, Oct 20, 1809 (Rockingham Co NH Probate R).

582. Aaron Currier Bagley 7, Moses 6, Jonathan 5, Henry 4, Orlando 3, Orlando 2, Orlando 1 , b Aug 10, 1807; m Sere (another source says Jacashel Currier). He sold land in Candia, NH, in 1831, 1840, and 1850 (Rockingham Co NH Deeds). Census of 1850 gives Candia, NH.

Child:
1218. Augusta Ann 8, b & d Mar 14, 1831 (South Hampton NH R)

583. Betsey Bagley 7, Moses 6, Jonathan 5, Henry 4, Orlando 3, Orlando 2, Orlando 1 , b Dec 11, 1809. Called Nancy, she m Sylvester Rowe, b Jan 10, 1820, d Feb 28, 1899 (tombstone & Newton NH R).

584. Sally Bagley 7, Moses 6, Jonathan 5, Henry 4, Orlando 3, Orlando 2, Orlando 1 , b Aug 2, 1815; m Benjamin Carter, son Thomas W. & Elizabeth (Webster). Mar 12, 1835 , b Aug 2, 1807, Newton, NH.

Children:
1219. Marilla L. 8, b July 9, 1837; m (1) Thomas P. Ellis; m (2) Edward Johnson of Newburyport, MA, Aug 1, 1883 (MA R)
1220. Sylvester B. 8, b Exeter, NH, June 23, 1845; m Sept 21, 1869, Margaret M. Orne

585. Barnard Bagley 7, Ebenezer 6, David 5, Henry 4, Orlando 3, Orlando 2, Orlando 1 , b Sept 3, 1795; d Aug 3, 1859, ae 63. Death record, Bradford, NH, says he was b Warner, NH; m Hannah Ellis of Broom, Scholarie Co, NY, Dec 26, 1826 (Family R), b Fulton Co, NY, Oct 21, 1807, d Nov 2, 1894 (Family R). Bradford NH R say she d Nov 1, but tombstone gives d Nov 2, 1894, ae 87.

Barnard was in the War of 1812 from NY, where he then lived. Was in lumber business in NY for a time and later returned to Bradford, NH. He and his wife Hannah sold land in Durham, NY, in 1822, and on May 16, 1827, given as Broome, Scholarie Co (Greene Co NY R). Barnard is given as Barnard II, but not as junior.

He d intestate and adm was granted to Mason W. Tappan of Bradford, NH, Sept, 1859. Inventory of Oct term of court, 1859, showed real estate valued at $2000, and personal estate valued at $849.24. At Nov term of court, permission was granted to sell personal estate (Merrimac Co NH Probate R). Hannah was appt guardian of Barnard's minor children, Aug term of court, 1859: Samuel, over 14 yrs of age; Ellen C. and Frank B, under 14 yrs of age (Merrimac Co NH Probate R).

Hannah Bagley was a litle woman. When one of her children was born, it was in early forenoon. She took care of the birth in every detail and then went to the cellar, got some salt pork and potatoes and made dinner for her men (Mr. Everett Bagley of Warner, NH). She made her will, June, 1886; proved Nov 13, 1894; mentions dau Mrs. Harriet A. Roby of Claremont; dau Mrs Sarah Burrill of Melvin Mills, Warner, NH; son George Washington Bagley of Lowell, MA; son David Wesley Bagley of So Sutton, NH; grandsons, Arthur and Elvar Rowe, children of my deceased dau, the late Ellen C. Rowe of Newport, NH; grandchildren, Orson, Orrin, Alice May and Flora Bell Bagley, all children of my deceased son Samuel, late of Sutton; and Frank Barnard Bagley. Inventory of real estate was $100, and personal estate $531.40. Adm granted to Benjamin L. Heath of Warner, NH (Merrimac Co NH Probate R).

Children: (Family R except as noted)
1221. George W. 8, b Jan 26, 1828; d Mar 4, 1899 (Sutton NH R)
1222. Harriet C. Amelia 8, b Mar 7, 1830
1223. David Wesley 8, b Mar 11, 1832; d Nov 20, 1898 (Sutton NH R). Family R say d 1899
1224. Caroline 8, b Jan 30, 1834; d Nov 3, 1853, unm (tombstone)
1225. Sarah Majory 8, b Oct 17/18, 1838; d Jan 26, 1920 (tombstone says b Dec 19, 1837, d Jan, 1920)
1226. Samuel 8, b Apr 4, 1841; d Jan 31, 1881 (Sutton NH R say d Jan 30, 1881)
1227. James Francis 8, b Sept or Oct 25, 1845; d Jan 27, 1846
1228. Ellen Cochran 8, b Dec 8, 1847; d Apr 25, 1883
1229. Francis Barnard 8, b Feb 21, 1851; d Jan 24, 1916

586. Betsey Bagley 7, Ebenezer 6, David 5, Henry 4, Orlando 3, Orlando 2, Orlando 1, d Nov 18, 1818, ae 21; m Cummings Marshall, son Richard, d Dec 23, 1877, ae 81 (Family R).

587. Abigail Bagley 7, Ebenezer 6, David 5, Henry 4, Orlando 3, Orlando 2, Orlando 1, m May 21, 1815, at Bradford, NH, by Rev William Dodge, Robert Cressey, b 1797 (Groton NH R give this m as May 21, 1816).

Children:
1230. Laura 8, b 1816; d 1823 (tombstone)
1231. Barnard S. 8, b 1819; d in armed forces at Ft Snelling
1232. Betsey Ann 8, b 1823; d Aug 9, 1866; m Amos Davis, b Mar 29, 1815, d Aug 8, 1889, m Dec 25, 1845, and had one son Charles C. Davis, b Apr 13, 1860, d June 3, 1922, m Apr 27, 1885, Lizzie Danforth (Family R)

588. David Bagley 7, Ebenezer 6, David 5, Henry 4, Orlando 3, Orlando 2, Orlando 1, b Aug 4, 1800, Warner, NH; d 1866, ae

65 (Warner NH R mistakenly give him as son Barnard). Family R say d Feb 10, 1866; m (1) Margaret Brown of Wilmot, NH, Sept 12, 1822, dau Samuel & Comfort, b Nov 4, 1801, d Jan 29, 1841, ae 39 (tombstone, Warner, NH); m (2) Apr 20, 1842, Judith Cheney of Bradford, NH (NH R).

A farmer, he made his will Feb 8, 1866; filed Mar term of court, 1866; mentions wife Judith; second son George W.; eldest son David; dau Harriet Melvin, wife of Proctor D. Melvin; grandchildren: Warren T., Camilla A., and David O., children George W. Bagley; Margaret F. Melvin and Richard E. Melvin (probably for Edson), and Walter Melvin, children of Proctor D. Melvin (Merrimac Co NH Probate R). George W. Bagley of Warner appt adm Mar, 1866.

Judith Bagley d before May 1872 as her will was a filed on that date. Mentions children of first husband and stepchildren, George Bagley and Susan Bagley. Adm granted to John W. Morse, of Bradford, July term of court, 1872 (Merrimac Co NH Probate R).

Children: (all by Margaret Brown)
1233. David 8, b Mar 29, 1823; d Apr 10, 1885, Sumter, GA (Family R)
1234. Harriet 8, b Oct 24, 1826; d Sept 29, 1908 (Family R)
1235. Betsey 8, b Aug 7, 1830; d Nov 7, 1855, unm (Family R)
1236. George W. 8, b June 10, 1834; d Apr 16, 1909 (tombstone, Bradford, NH). Death R says born June 10, 1833.

590. Henry Barnard Bagley 7, Barnard 6, David 5, Henry 4, Orlando 3, Orlando 2, Orlando 1 , b July 10, 1837. As late as Apr 30, 1859, Polly Kilmer and Henry B. Bagley sold land in Durham, NY; no wife given for Henry.

591. Samuel Bagley 7, David 6, David 5, Henry 4, Orlando 3, Orlando 2, Orlando 1 , d Aug, 1841, ae between 50 and 55, which makes him b about 1795 (Greene Co NH R); m Laura or Louise (he calls her both names in his will). He is mentioned in Barnard Bagley's will as a nephew in 1841, and his own will was probated Sept 15, 1841. Given as of Windham, NY. George W. Clark appt special guardian for the children. Children compiled from will with birth dates estimated from age given in Census of 1850.

Children:
1237. Thomas Newton 8, b about 1830
1238. Harriet 8, b about 1832 (ae 18)
1239. Dolly or Sally 8, b about 1834 (ae 16)
1240. Horace 8, b about 1836 (ae 14)
1241. Sanford 8, b about 1837 (ae 13)
1242. Susannah 8, b about 1839 (ae 11)
1243. Candace or Condolence 8, b about 1841 (ae 8)
(See Horace of Durham, NY in Notes on Bagley Lines)

602. Elijah Bagley 7, David 6, Samuel 5, Henry 4, Orlando 3, Orlando 2, Orlando 1 , b Sept 29, 1797; m Dec 30, 1824, Hannah Mills of W Topsham, VT (VT R); d Manchester, NH, May 13, 1846 (tombstone). Died intestate and his widow declined adm of

estate which was granted to Frederick Stark of Bedford, NH, Aug 4, 1846. He left land in Bedford, NH (Hillsboro Co NH Probate R).

Child:
1244. John 8, b W Topsham, VT, 1826; d 1882 (tombstone, Manchester (Family buried in cemetery junction South William St. and Huse Road).

603. David Bagley 7, David 6, Samuel 5, Henry 4, Orlando 3, Orlando 2, Orlando 1 , b Mar 7, 1801; d Oct 29, 1882, ae 83; m (1) Lois Bullard, Dec 15, 1825, dau Ebenezer & Jemima (Mann), d Dec 14, 1841, ae 36; m (2) Ploomey Simpson, dau John & Charlotte, b Bradford, VT, and d July 1, 1869, ae 57; m (3) Voda Page of Corinth, VT, dau Jonathan & Jerusha (Rowland Tillotson, Apr 5, 1870 (all W Topsham VT R or tombstones). Voda d Manchester, NH, Mar 10, 1888, ae 50 (NH R). Census of 1860 gives David, ae 59; Ploomy, ae 46; Orasmus, ae 18; Gilman, ae 16; Jackson, ae 11. Census also calls David, David, Jr.

Children: (W Topsham VT R & tombstones except as noted)
1245. David 8, b Feb 11, 1827; d Nov 11, 1903 (Canaan NH R)
1246. Gilman 8, b Jan 2, 1829; d Aug 26, 1830
1247. Mary Jane 8, d Mar 12, 1852
1248. Mary 8, b 1833; d Aug 1, 1852
1249. William 8, b 1839; d June 18, 1918, ae 80
1250. Orasmus 8, b Orange, VT, 1841; d May 14, 1895
1251. Gilman 8, b Feb 5, 1845; d Mar 31, 1904
1252. Jackson 8, b 1849

604. Enoch Bagley 7, David 6, Samuel 5, Henry 4, Orlando 3, Orlando 2, Orlando 1 , b Oct 27, 1802; d Dec 29, 1868, ae 66; m Fanny Jewell, Dec 18, 1826 (Well's History of Newbury, VT), dau Solomon & Abigail (Corliss), b July 26, 1802, d Oct 3, 1864, ae 63 (tombstone, W Topsham).

Children : (W Topsham R & tombstones)
1253. Jane E. 8, b Sept 15, 1831; living 1898
1254. Sarah A. 8, b 1829; d June 17, 1893, unm. Her will, probated June 30, 1893, mentions brother, Newell C.; sister, Jane Kidder. Newell was executor (Orange Co VT Probate R).
1255. Newell 8, b Oct 15, 1836; d Apr 24, 1901; lived on homestead in W Topsham, the third generation to live in it.
1256. Charles G. 8, b 1839/40; d Chicago of small pox in Civil War, Mar 3, 1863, ae 24
1257. Enoch 8, b 1843/44; d Nov 24, 1882, ae 39

605. Sally Bagley 7, David 6, Samuel 5, Henry 4, Orlando 3, Orlando 2, Orlando 1 , b Jan 7, 1805; probably m Elijah B. Minard, Feb 21, 1831, W Topsham, VT. Another record gives his name as Miner, but his pension record says Minard.

606. John Andrews Bagley 7, David 6, Samuel 5, Henry 4, Orlando 3, Orlando 2, Orlando 1 , b Oct 26, 1807; d Mar 7, 1890; m Charlotte Bagley, Dec 4, 1828 (W Topsham VT R), dau

Nathan & Betsey Foard), b Oct 15, 1809, W Topsham, VT (Death R says, Haverhill, NH), d May 2, 1886, ae 76 (Piermont NH R). Bought land in Haverhill, NH, in 1832 and 1841, and in Bath, NH, in 1841. Sold land in Piermont, NH in 1867 (Grafton Co NH Deeds). He made his will, Feb 18, 1884; mentions son, George K.; grandson, Lang Bagley, alias Merrill; and a dau, Emma C. Underhill; and wife Charlotte. Dau Emma was appt adm, Apr 28, 1890 (Grafton Co NH Probate R). Some of the children are recorded on Hopkinton, MA R; some are buried at Haverhill Center, NH, and some at Piermont, NH.

Children:
1258. Emma C. 8, b Mar 4, 1849
1259. Sally 8, b 1829; d Mar 10, 1835 (tombstone, Haverhill Center)
1260. Frederick C. 8, b Feb 15, 1832, W Topsham VT (Hopkinton MA R)
1261. Daniel 8, b Haverhill, NH, about 1837; d Boston, MA, Oct 7, 1876, ae 39, a boatmaker (MA R)
1262. John M. 8, b about 1840; d Jan 16, 1843 (tombstone, Haverhill Center)
1263. Frank M. 8, b about 1843; d Lynn, MA, June 24, 1883, ae 40 (MA R)
1264. George K. 8, b Craftsbury, VT, 1846
1265. John Oscar 8, b Sept 1, 1845; d Sept 19, 1848 (Hopkinton, MA R)
1266. Charlotte 8, b Mar 4, 1849, Haverhill, NH (Hopkinton MA R)
1267. Charles 8, b Hopkinton, MA; d there Sept 19, 1852, ae 40 mos (MA R)

607. Eliza Bagley 7, David 6, Samuel 5, Henry 4, Orlando 3, Orlando 2, Orlando 1 , b Sept 29, 1809; m Dec 7, 1826, Stephen David or Davis (W Topsham, VT R).

Child:
1268. Jonathan Sanborn 8

608. Charles W. Bagley 7, David 6, Samuel 5, Henry 4, Orlando 3, Orlando 2, Orlando 1 , b Sept 9, 1811; d June 21, 1889, at Chelsea, VT; a medical doctor; m Alvira Hilliard, Dec 21, 1830, d July 6, 1844, ae 39 (VT R); m (2) Charlotte Magoon, Oct 15, 1844 (W Topsham VT R), dau Jonathan & Dorothy (Eastman), b Oct 20, 1811, d Sept 2, 1888 (tombstone, Chelsea, VT). Census of 1850 gives Topsham, VT.

Children:
1269. Charles 8, b Dec 3, 1845; d For Monroe, VA, Apr 11, 1864 (tombstone, Chelsea, VT), the only son
1270. Alvira 8, b 1832 (Census of 1850 gives her as 12)
1271. Rebecca Sophia 8, d Mar 7, 1912 (tombstone, Chelsea, VT)
1272. Betty Maria 8, b Nov 4, 1853

609. Sophia Andrews Bagley 7, David 6, Samuel 5, Henry 4, Orlando 3, Orlando 2, Orlando 1 , b June 7, 1812; m May 8,

1836, Thomas H. Minard (W Topsham VT R); the NH pension rolls call him Hazen A. S. Minard.

611. Jacob Bagley 7, Jacob 6, Samuel 5, Henry 4, Orlando 3, Orlando 2, Orlando 1. A Jacob, Jr., sold land Feb, 1829 (Grafton Co NH Deeds). He may have been son of Jacob & Eunice; no other record found.

612. James Bagley 7, Jacob 6, Samuel 5, Henry 4, Orlando 3, Orlando 2, Orlando 1, sold land in Grafton Co, NH, in 1829 (Grafton Co NH Deeds). He probably m Polly Abbott of Raymond, NH, at Candia, NH, Dec 25, 1817 (Candia NH R).

613. Elkins Bagley 7, Jacob 6, Samuel 5, Henry 4, Orlando 3, Orlando 2, Orlando 1, b about 1805, probably Candia, NH. he was a farmer and sold land May, 1838, Nov, 1842 in Thornton and Campton (Grafton Co NH Deeds). Married Lavinia Cobb of Thornton, NH, at Campton, NH (Campton NH R). He probaly d prior to 1867 when a Mrs Louisa Bagley of Thornton, NH (one of her daus' death certificate gives this name as does US Census; whether she is the same as Lavinia or whether Elkins m again is not known) m Daniel Blaisdell on May 4, at Gilford, NH (NH Vital Records in Newspapers). Following children were compiled from NH R, Census of 1850 and Census of 1860. Census of 1850 gives Elkins, ae 45; Louisa, ae 43; Melinda, ae 14; Harold, ae 12; Henry, ae 4; Martha J., ae 1; and Martin, ae 1.

Children:
1273. Malinda 8, b Thornton, NH, Aug 23, 1837; d Laconia, NH, dec 29, 1914, unm (NH R)
1274. Harold D. 8, b about 1838; d National Soldiers Home, June 11, 1920, ae 79 (ME R)
1275. Abigail 8, b about 1840; probably d young
1276. Abbie C. 8, b May 10, 1842; d June 15, 1917 (NH R). Not listed on Census of 1850 but probably lived elsewhere (see Elijah)
1277. Elkins, Jr. 8, b about 1845 (may have d before 1860 as not listed on Census in that yr)
1278. Henry 8, b about 1848
1279. Martin J. 8, b Thornton, NH, May 4, 1849; d Laconia, NH, Apr 16, 1925 (NH R)
1280. Martha J. 8 b about 1850, supposed to have been a twin; she is on Census of 1850, but Mary J. is not. Could Mary J. have died?
1281. Mary J., b about 1850, supposed to have been twin
1282. Lavinia 8, b about 1854

614. John Bagley 7, Samuel 6, Samuel 5, Henry 4, Orlando 3, Orlando 2, Orlando 1, b Jan 4, 1796; d Aug, 1836; m Dec 21, 1826, Sarah Hunnewell of Boston, MA, d Jan 15, 1864, ae 64 (tombstones, Mad River, Thornton, NH).

Children:
1283. George W. 8, b Jan 16, 1828; d Aug 21, 1892, ae 64 (Boscawen NH R)
1284. Lafayette 8, b 1833/34; d Nov 11, 1895, ae 68 (Boscawen

NH R). On Census of 1850 he is listed as 19 in household of Elijah Bagley; since John, son of Elijah is listed as 19, it is probable that Lafayette was living with his uncle and that he is the son of John.

1285.   Mary A. 8, b 1835/36; d Mar 31, 1893, ae 56 (Thornton NH R)

1286.   Charles 8, There is some question as to whether or not he is the son of John. His service record in the Civil War is so confused (see over) that one is not sure which information to trust. He is given on vital records of NH, as having d Sandwich, NH, June 7, 1884, ae 46. If this is correct, John was probably not the father since he d Aug, 1836; however, 1838, depending on days could be right. Elistment record gives birth date as 1843. His death certificate gives John as father but no mother. Census of 1850 gives him as ae 7. His marriage certificate gives his father as Samuel, b Chester, and his mother as Lydia Snow. His grandfather was Samuel, b Chester, and his grandmother, Miriam, seems also to have been called Lydia. Likewise the Census of 1850 gives Charles, ae 7, as living in the house of Samuel and Miriam, he being 80 and she 89. The best conclusion seems to be that he might be John's son, but that at least he was b Thornton and was brought up by Samuel and Miriam, at least for a time.

615. Rhoda (Polly) Bagley 7, Samuel 6, Samuel 5, Henry 4, Orlando 3, Orlando 2, Orlando 1 , b 1799/1800; d Apr 22, 1885, ae 85; m Langdon Foss, Oct 29, 1823 (NH R), who d May 19, 1886, ae 83 (tombstones for both, Mad River, Thornton, NH)

Child: (May have been others)
1287.   Eliza Ann 8, b 1833; d Jan 27, 1844 (tombstone)

Near the Foss stones is a stone for Carrie Bagley, d Jan 27, 1854; we do not known her parentage, but she may have been dau of Rhoda and Langdon and her middle name was Bagley.

616. Elijah Bagley 7, Samuel 6, Samuel 5, Henry 4, Orlando 3, Orlando 2, Orlando 1 , b 1804/05; d May 30, 1888, ae 84, North Woodstock, NH, widower; m Serena Foss of Thornton, NH, b 1808/09, d Nov 7, 1875, ae 67 (tombstone). As to the children listed below, sources are insufficient; it may be that Lafayette should go under John, above, and Abbie C. under Elkins should go with Elijah and see discussion of Charles. For instance, Abbie C. lived in No Woodstock and Elijah died there. The Census of of 1850 gives Lafayette and Abigail in the household of Elijah, but other sources give them as above.

Children:
1288.   John S. 8, b 1832/33; d Jan 6, 1899, ae 68 (Thornton, NH R)
1289.   James O. 8, b Aug 24, 1833; d Nov 22, 1898, ae 60 (Thornton NH R)
1290.   Augusta 8, b about 1842 (Census of 1850 gives ae 6)

617. Mary S. Bagley 7, Samuel 6, Samuel 5, Henry 4, Orlando 3, Orlando 2, Orlando 1 , b 1804/05; d Sept 24, 1888, ae 84; m

John Dearborn of Chester, NH, Oct 28, 1829, at Campton, NH (NH R), who d Oct 18, 1867, ae 63-4 (both buried Blair Cemetery , Campton, NH).

Children:
1291.   Charles 8, b Feb 16, 1833; d Apr 2, 1908; m Lucasta Follansbee, d July 21, 1977, ae 35-8; m (2) Elmira E., d May 12, 1894, ae 46-3; buried Campton
1292.   Esther C. 8, b Campton; d Meredith, NH, Dec 10, 1885, ae 47; a _____ Blake
1293.   Martine Rogers 8, m David Percival in 1865

618.   Sarah Ann Bagley 7, Samuel 6, Samuel 5, Henry 4, Orlando 3, Orlando 2, Orlando 1 , b 1818-19; d June 1, 1891, ae 73; m Thomas Caldon, intentions, May 27, 1839, Thornton, NH, d Dec 22, 1878, ae 65, son Robert of Meredith (tombstones, Trinity, Holderness, NH).

Children:
1294.   Marilla Jane 8, b Aug 20, 1840, Campton, NH; d Jan 26, 1897; m James Sanborn
1295.   Amanda Malvina 8, b June 8, 1842, Campton, NH; m James Keeble
1296.   Sophia Sophronia 8, b Jan 11, 1844, Campton, NH; m John Huckins
1297.   Betton Francis 8, b June 11, 1846; d Dec 24, 1846
1298.   Bagley Lyford 8, b Jan 29, 1848; d Jan 1, 1894; m Amanda Coffin Carson
1299.   Nancy Jane 8, b Dec 25, 1856, Campton, NH; m George Ordway in 1866
1300.   Ella Belle 8, b Dec 25, 1856, Campton, NH; m Emerson Getchell
1301.   Edith F. 8, b June 9, 1860, Campton, NH; m (1) William Gould of Plymouth, NH; m (2) Otis Young, Jr., of Plymouth

623.   Betsey Bagley 7, Jacob 6, Jacob 5, Henry 4, Orlando 3, Orlando 2, Orlando 1 , b Sept 7, 1799; m _____ Doyle; two children (Family R).

624.   Mary (Polly) Bagley 7, James 6, Jacob 5, Henry 4, Orlando 3, Orlando 2, Orlando 1 , m Feb 23, 1823, Jacob Leeman (Montville ME R), who d 1845; m (2) _____ Sawyer (Family R).

Children: (Family R)
1302.   Mary 8, b Nov 11, 1823; d Sept 23, 1968
1303.   Catherine 8, b Aug 24, 1825
1304.   Jacob 8, b Nov 11, 1827; d Feb 17, 1879
1305.   Henry 8, b Oct 15, 1829; d Mar 1, 1920
1306.   Adam 8, b Dec 15, 1831; d Apr 4, 1861
1307.   Elijah 8, b Apr 23, 1834; d Apr 17, 1849
1308.   James 8, b Apr 23, 1836; d Apr 9, 1893
1309.   Anne 8, b Jan 1, 1839; d 1875

625.   Sophronia Bagley 7, James 6, Jacob 5, Henry 4, Orlando 3, Orlando 2, Orlando 1 , b Jan 25, 1803, Montville, ME; d Feb 13, 1870 (Family R); m Michael Overlock of Waldeboro, ME, Nov

20, 1821 (Montville ME R).

Children: (Family R)
1310.   Abigail 8, b Jan 11, 1824
1311.   James 8, b Nov 24, 1825
1312.   Lydia 8, b Oct 1, 1827
1313.   Mary 8
1314.   Nancy 8, b Dec 29, 1831; d Oct 13, 1896
1315.   Bickford 8, b Feb 1, 1834; d Feb 24, 1869
1316.   Ansel 8
1317.   Rufus 8, b 1845; d Dec 11, 1864, at Salisbury Prison during Civil War
1318.   Rhoda 8, probably d young

626.   James Bagley, Jr., 7, James 6, Jacob 5, Henry 4, Orlando 3, Orlando 2, Orlando 1 , b Dec 20, 1804; m Rachel Kelley, dau David & Dorcus. He probably d before 1860 as his wife is given on Census in Jonesport as head of family.

Children:
1319.   Martha Ann 8, b Jonesport, ME, June 6, 1827 (ME R); d Beaver Island, Mich., July, 1853 (Family)
1320.   James 8, b Jonesport, mE, July 28, 1829 (ME R)
1321.   David 8, b 1831 (Family R); not on Washington Co Census after 1850
1322.   Richard 8, b Jonesport, ME, July 21, 1833 (Family R); d Nov 28, 1899, ae 65 (ME R)
1323.   Elmira 8, b 1835 (Family R)
1324.   Cordelia Ann 8, b 1837; Census of 1850 gives her as living in home of Andrew and Susan Smith
1325.   Abijah 8, b Jonesport, ME, July, 1841; d there Jan 25, 1916 (Family R)
1326.   Abigail 8, b 1843 (Family R)
1327.   Esther Jan 8, b 1845 (Family R)

628.   Levi Bagley 7, James 6, Jacob 5, Henry 4, Orlando 3, Orlando 2, Orlando 1 , b June 23, 1807; d Aug 8, 1891; m Catherine Overlock, Dec 24, 1829, dau John and Marguerite, b Nov 13, 1810, d Sept 6, 1903 (Liberty ME R). Death notice says b Washington, ME.

Children:
1328.   Nancy 8, b Dec 27, 1830; d Oct 30, 1900 (Family R)
1329.   Christiana 8, b Nov 17, 1833 (Family R); d unm Apr 18, 1860 (Montville ME R)
1330.   Mary, Melissa or Melvira 8, b Mar 13, 1837; d Mar 10, 1865 (Family R)
1331.   Sarah A. 8, b Oct 25, 1841 (Family R); d Jan 7, 1872, ae 31 (Montville ME R)
1332.   Sophronia 8, b May 14, 1846 (Family R); d Feb 15, 1929 (Liberty ME R)
1333.   David 8, b Jan 11, 1850 (Family R); d July 3, 1856, ae 5 (Liberty ME R)

629.   Samuel Bagley 7, James 6, Jacob 5, Henry 4, Orlando 3, Orlando 2, Orlando 1 , b Oct 9, 1809; d June 4, 1898; m

Mehitable Clark, Feb 25, 1835, dau Joel & Deborah (Stiles), b Nov 14, 1814 (Family R), d May 18, 1903 (Liberty ME R). Census of 1840 for Liberty, ME, gives 1M-5, 1M-20, 2F 20-30, 2F -5. He lived for a time in Lebanon, NH.

Children: (Family R)
1334.   Shephard 8, b Aug 28, 1836; d Nov 28, 1903
1335.   Philema 8, b Dec 2, 1837; d Oct 19, 1851
1336.   Hannah 8, b Jan 6, 1840; d Dec 23, 1915
1337.   Alonzo 8, b June 8, 1842; d 1905
1338.   Abigail 8, b June 4, 1847; d Apr 11, 1914
1339.   Augustus M. 8, b May 10, 1850; d July 25, 1889
1340.   Charles 8, b Aug 15, 1852; d Feb 22, 1921 (Liberty ME R)

630.   Richard Bagley 7, James 6, Jacob 5, Henry 4, Orlando 3, Orlando 2, Orlando 1 , b June 13, 1811; d Oct. 1896; m Christiana Speed, Sept 14, 1838 (ME R), b July 26, 1816, d Feb 3, 1900, b Washington, ME, dau David & Sarah (Mills) (tombstone & Liberty ME R). Family checks with Census of 1850 and 1860.

Children:
1341.   Levi 8, b about 1839
1342.   Harriet 8, b about 1847
1343.   Charles H. 8, b June 4, 1855 (Family R); d Aug 6, 1926 (Liberty ME R)

631.   Lydia Bagley 7, James 6, Jacob 5, Henry 4, Orlando 3, Orlando 2, Orlando 1 , b Nov 27, 1813; d Oct 29, 1899; m Apr 14, 1835, Edward Bridges of Edgecomb or Liberty, ME, Apr 14, 1835, intentions Mar 29, 1835 (Montville mE R), b Feb 11, 1813, d Jan 9, 1895 ?.

Children: (Family R)
1344.   Vestula 8, b Sept 28, 1836; d May 21, 1921; m Charles White of Derry, NH, 1865
1345.   Susa or Sara 8, b June 26, 1838; d Apr 13, 1932
1346.   Samuel 8, b Mar 8, 1840; d May 16, 1923
1347.   Lydia 8, b Feb 22, 1842; d July 5, 1909
1348.   Rhoda 8, b Aug 11, 1843; d Dec 7, 1925 (Montville ME R)
1349.   Lois 8, b Nov 27, 1847; d Jan 31, 1890
1350.   George Wilmot 8, b Dec 20, 1852; d May 30, 1882

632.   Lois Bagley 7, James 6, Jacob 5, Henry 4, Orlando 3, Orlando 2, Orlando 1 , b Apr 2, 1817; d Feb 10, 1888; m (1) _____ Stinson; m (2) _____ Tibbetts, Aug 19, 1837, b Apr 8, 1816 (Family R).

Children: (Family R)
1351.   John 8, b 1838; d Aug 21, 1862
1352.   Vida 8
1353.   Hannah 8, b July 15, 1841; d Apr 15, 1861
1354.   Abbie 8
1355.   Cyrus 8, b 1849; d 1915 or 1918

633. Thomas Bagley 7, James 6, Jacob 5, Henry 4, Orlando 3, Orlando 2, Orlando 1 , b 1819; d in Mexican War (Family R); m Marin B. Kelley, dau David, b 1814, d 1898 (Family R).

Child:
1356. Sylvestania 8, only child (ME R); family records say this child was Sylvestin K., b about 1837 (Census of 1850); d before 1880.

634. Esther Bagley 7, James 6, Jacob 5, Henry 4, Orlando 3, Orlando 2, Orlando 1 , b Feb 24, 1820; d Aug 5, 1853; m Shelbourne Rowe; no children (Family R).

635. Rhoda Bagley 7, James 6, Jacob 5, Henry 4, Orlando 3, Orlando 2, Orlando 1 , b Jan 13, 1821; d Mar 25, 1900; m May 30, 1839, Ezra Cox, b June 20, 1814, d Apr 25, 1876 (Family R).

Children:
1357. levi 8, b Oct 21, 1840; d June 8, 1902
1358. Elmina 8, b Jan 4, 1845; d Aug 27, 1929
1359. Antoinette 8, b Aug 22, 1847; d Nov 20, 1930
1360. Charles M. 8, b Mar 12, 1850; d Feb 12, 1869

646. Mary Anne Bagley 7, David 6, Jacob 5, Henry 4, Orlando 3, Orlando 2, Orlando 1 , b Oct 2, 1817; m Nathan Lee (ME R).

Children: (Census of 1850)
1361. Rebecca 8, ae 15, b about 1835
1362. Pashase 8, ae 13, b about 1837
1363. Emily 8, ae 1, b about 1849
1364. Adeline 8, ae 1, b about 1849

647. Emily Bagley 7, David 6, Jacob 5, Henry 4, Orlando 3, Orlando 2, Orlando 1 , b June 30, 1820 (Lee ME R); m William Rich.

648. Henry Bagley 7, David 6, Jacob 5, Henry 4, Orlando 3, Orlando 2, Orlando 1 , b July 27, 1822; d Aug 23, 1840 (Lee ME R) tombstone, Lee, ME gives Aug 19.

649. Jacob Bagley 7, David 6, Jacob 5, Henry 4, Orlando 3, Orlando 2, Orlando 1 , b Apr 27, 1825; m Frances Lee, dau Stephen, b July 20, 1829, d June 10, 1862 (Lee ME R); m (2) Sophia Dennis, dau Samuel, Apr 7, 1863 (Prentice ME R), d May 4, 1914, ae 76 (Prentice ME R).

Children:
1365. Jacob F. 8, b Jan 8, 1851; d July 6, 1862 (Lee ME R)
1366. Stephen 8, b July 1, 1852 (Lee ME R); d Jan 5, 1925, ae 69 (Montville ME R); tombstone, Lee, ME says 1855-1925
1367. Emma J. 8, b Dec 5, 1856; d July 9, 1862 (Lee ME R)
1368. Ella 8, b Dec 5, 1859; d July 9, 1862 (Lee ME R)
1369. Harry 8, b Feb 9, 1864; d Jan 12, 1934, twin (Prentice ME R)
1370. Victor 8, b Feb 10, 1864, twin; d at birth

1371.   Victor 8, b Feb, 1869; d 1940 (Family R)
1372.   Jacob 8, b Feb 16, 1873; d June 16, 1936, unm (Prentice ME R)
1373.   Vernon 8, b June, 1876 (Family R); d Apr 23, 1899, unm (Prentice ME R)
1374.   Veniene 8, b July, 1878 (Family R)

650.   William Bagley 7, David 6, Jacob 5, Henry 4, Orlando 3, Orlando 2, Orlando 1 , b May 3, 1828; m Sylvina Augusta Jackson, dau Godfrey & Cyrena (Hall) of Lee, ME, b May 23, 1834, d Lincoln, ME, Dec 24, 1909, ae 75 (ME R).

Children: (Lee ME R)
1375.   Emeline 8, b July 17, 1857
1376.   William E. 8, b Mar 22, 1858; d unm, on West Coast
1377.   Leila A. 8, b Feb 14, 1861; d Fall River, MA, June 19, 1887, ae 26 (MA R)
1378.   Jacob 8, b Jan 26, 1863

651.   Lucretia Bagley 7, David 6, Jacob 5, Henry 4, Orlando 3, Orlando 2, Orlando 1 , b May 13, 1831; m Jonathan Tilton.

652.   David Bagley 7, David 6, Jacob 5, Henry 4, Orlando 3, Orlando 2, Orlando 1 , b Oct 12, 1834; m and went to Mich.; at least one child.

Child:
1379.   Frank 8, a lawyer, in Hart, Mich., 1942

653.   Samuel Bagley 7, David 6, Jacob 5, Henry 4, Orlando 3, Orlando 2, Orlando 1 , b Aug 29, 1837; d Apr 29, 1910, ae 73; m Lovinia Neil, b Jan 2, 1842 (Lee ME R), d Aug 20, 1894, ae 52 (tombstone, Lee, ME).

Children: (Lee ME R)
1380.   Lucretia 8, b Oct 25, 1865; living Census of 1880
1381.   Lizzie 8, b Apr 14, 1866; living Census of 1880
1382.   Samuel (Sand or Land) 8, b Apr 30, 1869; living Census of 1880. There is a Samuel, b Lee, ME, Apr 30, 1875, son of Samuel & Lovinia, who d at Lincoln, ME, June 17, 1932 (ME R). Either there is a mistake in date, or the first Samuel died, and another son was named Samuel in 1875
1383.   Oasie 8, b June 11, 1875; living Census of 1880
1384.   David F. 8, b June 8, 1877; d Jan 28, 1919 (tombstone, Lee, ME, gives 1873-1919)
1385.   Hattie R. 8, b Jan 9, 1882, twin
1386.   Lillie R. 8, b Jan 9, 1882, twin

657.   Richard Bagley 7, Levi 6, Jacob 5, Henry 4, Orlando 3, Orlando 2, Orlando 1 , b Nov 22, 1798.

658.   Eliza or Elizabeth Bagley 7, Levi 6, Jacob 5, Henry 4, Orlando 3, Orlando 2, Orlando 1 , b Dec 30, 1800; probably m Martin Ulhman of Montville, ME, June 12, 1824 (Montville ME R).

659. Sally Bagley 7, Levi 6, Jacob 5, Henry 4, Orlando 3, Orlando 2, Orlando 1 , b Nov 8, 1804; m John Edmunds, Apr 29, 1823 (Montville ME R), son John & Charlotte (Bagley), d Feb 15, 1892, ae 61 (Family R).

Child:
1387. John 8

661. Henry Bagley 7, Levi 6, Jacob 5, Henry 4, Orlando 3, Orlando 2, Orlando 1 , b July 30, 1809; m Shuah Neal of Belmont, ME, Nov 28, 1830 (ME R).

665. Hiram Bagley 7, Henry 6, Jacob 5, Henry 4, Orlando 3, Orlando 2, Orlando 1 , b about 1827, Montville, ME; d Randolph, MA, May 22, 1861; m Susan Lyons, b Randolph, MA (MA R). He was a shoe maker. Census of 1850 gives Haverhill, MA.

Children:
1388. Eliza 8, d Jan 1, 1861, ae 7 mos (Randolph MA R)
1389. H. Augustus 8, b Dec 22, 1848; d Jan 15, 1922, ae 73 (ME R)

669. Charles Durham Bagley 7, Jacob 6, Jacob 5, Henry 4, Orlando 3, Orlando 2, Orlando 1 , b May 17, 1832.

670. Joseph Stacy Bagley 7, Jacob 6, Jacob 5, Henry 4, Orlando 3, Orlando 2, Orlando 1, b Dec 5, 1833.

671. Moses French Bagley 7, Jacob 6, Jacob 5, Henry 4, Orlando 3, Orlando 2, Orlando 1, b Oct 6, 1835.

672. James Madison Bagley 7, Jacob 6, Jacob 5, Henry 4, Orlando 3, Orlando 2, Orlando 1, b July 19, 1837.

674. William Bagley 7, Nathan 6, David 5, David 4, Orlando 3, Orlando 2, Orlando 1, b Apr 24, 1792; probably m Amelia Howes, Oct 17, 1819 (Washington VT R).

675. Betsey Bagley 7, Nathan 6, David 5, David 4, Orlando 3, Orlando 2, Orlando 1, b Dec 13, 1793; m Frederick Carr, Feb 14, 1821, son Capt Daniel & Elizabeth (Worth), Bath, NH, b N Haverill, Mar 22, 1799, d Jan 11, 1833. No children.

676. Rhoda Bagley 7, Nathan 6, David 5, David 4, Orlando 3, Orlando 2, Orlando 1, b Jan 6, 1797; d Jan 24, 1843, W Topsham; m Feb 9, 1823, Deacon Daniel Carr, b Jan 31, 1799, son Capt Daniel & Elizabeth (Bailey). He m (2) Hannah Sawyer of Bath, NH, Apr 11, 1843, and d Apr 13, 1879; his second wife d late in 1887.

Children: From (History of Haverhill, NH)
1390. Infant son 8, b Oct 5, 1824, at birth
1391. Daniel 8, b dec 14, 1827; d Jan 13, 1827
1392. Nathan Bagley 8, b July 24, 1827
1393. Francis Bagley 8, b Apr 27, 1829; m Helen E. Carr, dau John & Susan (Rider), b May 5, 1832, d Feb 6, 1876

1394. Charles Frederick 8, b Jan 10, 1831; m Kate Melissa Eaton, at N Haverhill, NH, Nov 29, 1855
1395. George Edwin 8, b Oct 7, 1832; m Mary Ann Foster of Bath, NH, Feb 28, 1860, b Bath, Dec 20, 1837
1396. Jackson 8, b Dec 25, 1834; d Oct 11, 1863; m Rosoetta Colburn, dau David of Cabot, VT, May 29, 1856, b June 9, 1826
1397. Harriet Bagley 8, b Aug 7, 1838; d Oct 18, 1842
1398. Charlotte Bagley 8, b Aug 23, 1839; d Feb 8, 1840

677. Nathan Bagley 7, Nathan 6, David 5, David 4, Orlando 3, Orlando 2, Orlando 1, b May 23, 1799; d May 30, 1881, ae 82, of old age; m Nancy, d Oct 6, 1875, ae 73 (W Topsham VT R & tombstones).

Children: (W Topsham VT R)
1399. Hannah 8, b June 28, 1828; d Apr 13, 1870 (tombstone)
1400. Jonathan J. 8, b Mar, 1830; d Mar, 1831; given as John F. on records)
1401. Nancy 8, b 1832; d May, 1833 (tombstone)
1402. Emily 8, b Nov, 1825; d Nov 28, 1842 (tombstone)
1403. Adoniram Jefferson 8, b June 15, 1837; d Sept, 1862, ae 25 (tombstone); probably the Civil War soldier who d of small pox in Chicago
1404. Charlotte 8, b 1838; d Dec 2, 1848 (tombstone)
1405. SallyAnn (Sarah), b July 12, 1840; d July 7, 1867, unm
1406. Mary G. 8, b May 2, 1842; d Dec 25, 1874, ae 32, of consumption (tombstone gives death date as Sept 30)
1407. Caroline 8, b Oct 2, 1844; d Aug, 1852, ae 7

678. Marcy or Mary Bagley 7, Nathan 6, David 5, David 4, Orlando 3, Orlando 2, Orlando 1, b Mar 9, 1801 (Piermont History says Mar 20); d Sept 27, 1858; m Simeon Underhill, b Feb 14, 1800, Piermont, NH, d July 21, 1869, Piermont, son Nathaniel & Esther (Carr). He m (2) Sophronia Dodge.

Children: (History of Piermont, NH)
1408. Charlotte 8, b Mar 27, 1825, Piermont; d Sept 14, 1885; m Charles Rogers in 1857
1409. Betsey 8, b Apr 1, 1827, Bradford, VT; d Jan 12, 1898; m James Blatt
1410. Emily 8, b July 10, 1829, Newbury, VT; d Feb 13, 1851
1411. Mary 8, b Oct 5, 1831, Barre, VT; d Dec 6, 1907; m Ivory Simpson, May 15, 1854
1412. Nathaniel 8, b Jan 23, 1834, Barre, VT; d Dec 25, 1844
1413. Hazen 8, b Apr 2, 1836, Piermont, NH; d June 10, 1839
1414. Ellen 8, b Sept 14, 1839, Piermont, NH; m June 10, 1866, James Jordon or Gordon
1415. William 8, b Oct 28, m 1841, Piermont, NH; d May 3, 1916; m Nov 25, 1869, Helen Gilmore or Gilman
1416. Jason E. 8, b Feb 12, 1845, Piermont, NH; d Feb 26, 1886, unm

679. Philip Bagley 7, Nathan 6, David 5, David 4, Orlando 3, Orlando 2, Orlando 1 , b Aug 13, 1802; probably m Sophia Hale, Jan 7, 1829 (VT R). Not on Census of 1850 for W Topsham, VT.

Child:
1417. Caroline 8, b 1829/30; d Mar 25, 1831, ae 16 mos (W Topsham, VT tombstone)

680. John F. Bagley 7, Nathan 6, David 5, David 4, Orlando 3, Orlando 2, Orlando 1, b Mar 2, 1804.

682. Charlotte Bagley 7, Nathan 6, David 5 David 4, Orlando 3, Orlando 2, Orlando 1, b Oct 15, 1809; d Piermont, NH, May 2, 1886; m John A. Bagley, Dec 4, 1828 (W Topsham VT R), son David & Sophia (Andrews), b Oct 26, 1807 (W Topsham VT R), d Mar 7, 1890 (Piermont NH R). See John Andrews Bagley for children.

683. David Bagley 7, Jonathan 6, David 5, David 4, Orlando 3, Orlando 2, Orlando 1, b Sept 28, 1797; d Washington, NH, Mar 31, 1873, ae 75; m Dec 6, 1818, Susan Hart (Bradford NH R), b 1792, d Washington, NH, Oct 15, 1870, ae 77, dau John & Mary. Resided at Bradford, NH, until 1817, when he went to Hopkinton, NH, and resided on Major Brook's place; later he lived in Greenfield, NH, and then went to Washington, NH, in 1856, where he d and is buried (Census of 1850 gives Greenfield).

Children:
1418. David E. 8, b June 15, 1823 (Family R); d June 28, 1897, ae 75 (Bradford NH R)
1419. Jason 8, b 1824; d Nashua, NH, Apr 21, 1896, ae 76 (Nashua NH R give b Bradford, NH).
1420. Aratus 8, b 1828; d Washington, NH, July 28, 1870, ae 42, unm (Washington NH records give him as b Bradford, MA which is a mistake)
1421. Sarah G. 8, b about 1830; d Dec 30, 1906, ae 75 (Washington NH R)

684. Worcester Bagley 7, Jonathan 6, David 5, David 4, Orlando 3, Orlando 2, Orlando 1, b Oct 7, 1799; d Jan 25, 1879; m (1) Polly Peaslee, b Bradford, NH, d Apr 13, 1845, ae 45 (tombstone, Newbury, NH). Probably m (2) Isore Peaslee, dau Samuel & Hannah, Winchendon, MA, Mar 1, 1843 (Winchendon MA R), d Apr 13, 1868, ae 57 (Newbury NH R). On Census of 1850 for Newbury, NH.

Children:
1422. Samuel A. 8, b Feb 26, 1830 (Family R); d July 3, 1906, ae 76, at Hartland, VT (VT R)
1423. Joel 8, b 1834; d Jan 4, 1889, ae 52 (tombstone, Nashua, NH). Farmer & unm. Census of 1850 gives for Newbury, NH.
1424. Ira 8, b Winchendon, MA, about 1838; d May 26, 1885, ae 47 (Nashua NH R)
1425. Sarah E. 8
1426. David M. 8
1427. Henry M. 8
1428. Orlando T. 8
1429. Charles S. 8

687. Rachel F. Bagley 7, Jonathan 6, David 5, David 4, Orlando 3, Orlando 2, Orlando 1, b July 4, 1812; probably m Jan 5, 1835, Smith Morgan of Bridgewater, NH (Bradford NH R).

Children:
1383A.   Jeremiah 8
1384B.   Jonathan 8
1384C.   Rachel 8
1384D.   Abigail 8
1384E.   Sarah 8
1384F.   David 8
1384G.   Henry 8
1384H.   Orlando 8
1384I.   Charles 8

697. George K. Bagley 7, David 6, Elijah 5, David 4, Orlando 3, Orlando 2, Orlando 1, b about 1816; d May 31, 1882, Chelsea, VT; m Susan Worthley, Dec 5, 1837, b Weare, NH, dau Thomas & Elizabeth, d Chelsea, VT, Dec 6, 1885 (Chelsea VT R); a medical doctor.

Children:
1430.   George A. 8, b about 1843, W Topsham, VT; d May 10, 1872 (Chelsea VT R)
1431.   Sarah M. 8, b about 1852 (Census of 1860 gives ae 8)
1432.   Thomas M. 8, d Apr 27, 1854, ae 12 (tombstone, Chelsea, VT)
1433.   Ella B. 8, d Mar 16, 1854, ae 15 (tombstone, Chelsea, VT)
1434.   Louisa 8, b about 1856 (Census of 1860 gives ae 4)

698. William Andrew Bagley 7, David 6, Elijah 5, David 4, Orlando 3, Orlando 2, Orlando 1, b W Topsham, VT, about 1815; d May 31, 1884, ae 69. Death certificate gives b W Topsham, son David & Sarah; m Anna, b about 1815, dau Jonathan & Jerusha Tillotson, at W Topsham, d Apr 30, 1876, ae 61 (tombstone & W Topsham VT R). She had previously been m to a Mittson. Adm granted on his estate, but no heirs mentioned (Bradford District, Orange Co VT R).

Child:
1435.   Eva Belle 8, b July 28, 1845; not mentioned in father's will in 1876

699. Gilman W. Bagley 7, David 6, Elijah 5, David 4, Orlando 3, Orlando 2, Orlando 1, b W Topsham, VT, about 1818; d there, Sept 30, 1904, ae 86; m (1) Sarah Rogers of W Topsham, June 16, 1841, d Oct 1, 1847; m (2) Elizabeth Kidder, dau Andrew & Hannah, Apr 16, 1848, b May 21, 1821, W Fairlee, VT, d W Topsham, Dec 29, 1890 (W Topsham VT R). He lived W Topsham, VT, until 1875, when he and his wife went to live with their son in Bradford, VT, but moved back to W Topsham in 1880. He was a farmer and shoemaker, selectman of W Topsham and possessed a liberal education.

Child:
1436. Victor 8, b Oct 7, 1849; probably d in Kansas City, MO

700. John Bagley 7, William 6, Elijah 5, David 4, Orlando 3, Orlando 2, Orlando 1 , b 1803. Given on Essex Co, MA Probate records of guardianship. Probably d young since he is not one of the heirs-at-law of Elijah Bagley, his grandfather, in 1842.

702. Eunice Bagley 7, William 6, Elijah 5, David 4, Orlando 3, Orlando 2, Orlando 1 , b 1808. Given on Essex Co, MA Probate R of guardianship; m Feb 2, 1832, Daniel Gould (Ames MA R). They conveyed land in Newton, NH, in 1842, as heirs-at-law of her grandfather, Elijah Bagley (Rockingham Co NH Deeds).

Children:
1437. Ellen Maria 8, b Aug 18, 1836 (Ames MA R)
1438. Daniel Warren 8, b Oct 18, 1840 (Ames MA R)

704. William Bagley 7, William 6, Elijah 5, David 4, Orlando 3, Orlando 2, Orlando 1 , b 1810; d Mar 2, 1876, ae 65 (MA R); given on Essex Co, MA Probate R of guardianship; m Ann Tenney Nov 12, 1833 (Ames MA R), dau John and Ann (Sargent), d Nov 29, 1880, ae 69 (MA R). Carriage maker at River village, Amesbury.

Children: (Ames MA R)
1439. Lucia 8, b about 1835 (Census of 1850 gives ae 15)
1440. John Tenney 8, b Jan 7, 1838; d Sept 15, 1900, ae 63 (Wakefield MA R)
1441. William Johnson 8, b Apr 13, 1839
1442. Laura Francette 8, b Apr 13, 1841; d Mar 23, 1862
1443. Albert Augustus 8, b Mar 14, 1844; d Mar 11, 1846
1444. Emma Augusta 8, b Apr 15, 1847; d Oct 7, 1848
1445. Emma Augusta 8, b Apr 4, 1849/50; d Feb 1, 1863

705. Nancy Bagley 7, Enoch 6, Elijah 5, David 4, Orlando 3, Orlando 2, Orlando 1 , b Mar 8, 1809; called Ann; probably m Ebenezer Davis, June 9, 1831 (NH R). They conveyed land in Newton, NH, in 1842, as heirs-at law of her grandfather, Elijah Bagley (Rockingham Co NH Deeds).

706. William Bagley 7, Enoch 6, Elijah 5, David 4, Orlando 3, Orlando 2, Orlando 1, b 1811; d Jan 6, 1849, ae 35 (tombstone, Newton, NH); m Nancy Sargent, dau Jonathan & Mary (Currier), b Aug 6, 1808, d Jan 2, 1849, ae 33. On Jan 10, 1849, Robert Bagley was appt adm of William's estate; inventory made Feb 12, 1849; filed Feb 21, 1849 (Rockingham Co NH Probate R). On Apr 2, 1850, Joseph Harris was appt guardian of William N. Bagley, child of William of Newton, deceased. On Apr 15, 1852, Zebediah Hoit was appt guardian of Sarah A. Bagley, minor child of William, deceased, and on Jan 13, 1849, he was appt guardian of Sally Ann, child of William, deceased (Rockingham Co NH Probate R).

Children:
1446. William N. 8, b 1839/40; d Mar 6, 1914, ae 76 (tombstone, Sandwich, NH)
1447. Sarah A. 8, living 1852
1448. Alice R. 8, probably d before 1852 as no guardian appt for her
1449. Sally Ann 8, living 1849

707. Robert Bagley 7, Enoch 6, Elijah 5, David 4, Orlando 3, Orlando 2, Orlando 1 , b about 1812; d Dec 4, 1891, ae 79 (tombstone, Newton, NH). MA R say died Dec 2, 1892, ae 79. Census of 1860 for Essex Co, MA gives him as ae 55, b NH. His wife is given as Sophia, ae 44, b MA. Melvin Bagley of Merrimac, MA was appt adm of his estate, July 10, 1893 (Essex Co MA Probate R). It is probable that his second wife was Lydia Hoyt, dau Thomas, b 1820, Merrimac, MA, d Dec 4, 1889, ae 69 (MA R).

Children:
1450. Albert 7, b about 1846 (Census of 1860)
1451. Alphonse 8, b about 1848; d Dec 6, 1872, ae 24, Ames MA R); father given as Robert of Newton and Lydia, b Amesbury, MA
1452. Melvin 8, b about 1852 (Census of 1860); d Haverhill, MA, Feb 4, 1918, ae 65; buried Newton, NH (NH R)

708. Susan Bagley 7, Enoch 6, Elijah 5, David 4, Orlando 3, Orlando 2, Orlando 1 , b Newton, NH, about 1816 (Census of 1860); m Mar 10, 1836, James B. Hoit, son John & Sally (Young). In 1841 and 1843, she and her husband conveyed land in Newton as heirs-at-law of her grandfather, Elijah (Rockingham Co NH Deeds). James Hoit was b Newton, NH, 1815.

Children: (Census of 1860
1453. Susan A. 8, b Ames, MA about 1838
1454. Roxanna 8, b Ames, MA about 1848
1455. Clara J. 8, b Ames, MA about 1850

719. Dolly Bagley 7, John 6, Valentine 5, Jonathan 4, Orlando 3, Orlando 2, Orlando 1 , b Apr 14, 1792; m John Carey.

720. Nancy Bagley 7, John 6, Valentine 5, Jonathan 4, Orlando 3, Orlando 2, Orlando 1 , b Jan 27, 1795; m Dudley Evans, Apr 8, 1819 (Salis MA R), son Ezekiel & Sarah (Carr) (Salis MA R), b Mar 10, 1793.

Children: (Salis MA R)
1456. John Quincy 8, b July 17, 1819
1457. Ezekiel 8, b Aug 16, 1821
1458. Dudley Carr 8, b Dec 31, 1823
1459. Benjamin E. 8, b Oct, 1826
1460. Sarah Ann 8, b Mar 6, 1829

721. William Hackett Bagley 7, John 6, Valentine 5, Jonathan 4, Orlando 3, Orlando 2, Orlando 1 , b June 2, 1799; d Oct 18, 1856, ae 57; m Hannah Swett, Aug 7, 1822 (Salis MA R), b Sept

13, 1801 (Family R), d Jan 28, 1885, ae 83, dau Enoch & Merriam (Swett) (MA R).

Member of Warren Lodge of Masons, Amesbury, MA. Man of superior abilities and most excellent character, high-minded and honorable and greatly esteemed. He built many vessels, some of the ships of great size. He built the US frigate Alliance for tribute to the government of the Dey of Algiers. He draughted and superintended the building of the frigate Essex at Salem, MA. He was a devoted Christian and deacon of the Rocky Hill Church for 30 years. The last of his life he was partially paralyzed by a fall from a vessel when he was a young man. This was the day of flint and steel and his family was obliged to wet the cloth to prevent his setting fire in the night. At one time he went as far as the chain bridge with a lantern in search of fire to obtain light, and at another time as far for a pair of tongs for the same purpose. He lived in Hannah Bagley's house which was built by his father.

Adm on Hannah (Swett) Bagley's estate granted Apr 20, 1885 (Essex Co MA Probate R0.

Children: (Salis MA R)
1461. Hiram A. 8, b Apr 10, 1823; d Nov 11, 1911, Worcester, MA (tombstone at Georgetown, MA)
1462. Timothy H. 8, b Jan 29, 1825; d Sept 3, 1915 (tombstone, Ams, MA)
1463. Sarah B. 8, b Apr 2, 1827
1464. Hannah Swett 8, b Jan 23, 1829; d Feb 10, 1921, at Exeter, NH (Folsom Genealogy)
1465. Dolly P. 8, b Oct 20, 1831
1466. Nancy 8, b Dec 15, 1833

722. John Bagley 7, John 6, Valentine 5, Jonathan 4, Orlando 3, Orlando 2, Orlando 1 ,b Mar 10, 1804; d Aug 26, 1865; m Dec 27, 1832, Eliza Bickford (Salis MA R), dau Paul & Martha (Mansfield); m (2) Lydia Adams, whose maiden name was Walton and who had been previously m to Levi Waitt, intentions, Feb 15, 1834 (Ames MA R), b 1821, d 1904 (tombstone, Georgetown, MA). Lydia was appt adm of his estate, Dec 19, 1865 (Essex Co MA Probate R). She made her will, July 27, 1883; mentions a son Albert H. Waitt. She bequeathed the John Bagley pitcher to her son John A. Bagley of Lincoln, NB. Her dau Isabelle O. Bagley was adm.

Children:
1467. Harriet 8, b Oct 24, 1833 (Salis MA R); not mentioned in will in 1883
1468. Ann Elizabeth 8, b Apr 29, 1836 (Salis MA R); not mentioned in will in 1883
1469. John A. 8, b about 1855 (Census of 1870 gives ae 15); living Lincoln, NB, in 1883
1470. Isabelle 8, b about 1854 (Census of 1870 gives ae 16), unm in 1883

723. Sarah Ann Bagley 7, John 6, Valentine 5, Jonathan 4, Orlando 3, Orlando 2, Orlando 1 , b Mar 7, 1807; m George

Keniston, Sept 10, 1828 (Salis MA R); probably son John & Nancy, b Sept 13, 1805 (Salis MA R).

Children: (Salis MA R)
1471.   Paul 8, b June 5, 1831; d June 30, 1832
1472.   Ellen 8, b Sept 28, 1833
1473.   Angelina Eliza 8, b July 7, 1836; d Feb 20, 1839

725.   Charles Lapham Bagley 7, Valentine 6, Valentine 5, Jonathan 4, Orlando 3, Orlando 2, Orlando 1 , b Mar 28, 1798; m Rhoda Silloway, Amesbury, MA, Oct 11, 1829 (Ames MA R). Not mentioned in father's will in 1838, nor are any children of his.

727.   Harriet Bagley 7, Valentine 6, Valentine 5, Jonathan 4, Orlando 3, Orlando 2, Orlando 1 , b Feb 11, 1804; d Apr 9, 1833; m Henry Morrill, intentions, Apr 16, 1831 (Ames MA R), probably the Henry Morrill of Amesbury, MA, buried June 10, 1845, ae 47, son Capt Ephraim & Mary (Barnard), b Aug 15, 1900 (No children on Amesbury of Salisbury, MA records).

729.   William F. Bagley 7, Valentine 6, Valentine 5, Jonathan 4, Orlando 3, Orlando 2, Orlando 1 , b June 2, 1812; d May 20, 1845; m Betsey Wells, intentions, Jan 31, 1835 (Ames MA R). Thomas J. Clark was adm of his estate, 1850. Daniel C. Bagley was appt guardian of Harriet, Mar 26, 1850, and John Wells, guardian of Charles Lapham, Mar 26, 1850 (Essex Co MA Probate R).

Children: (Ames MA R except as noted)
1474.   Harriet 8, b Jan 15, 18361; d Jan 23, 1852
1475.   Charles Lapham 8, b Mar 1, 1842; d Moretown, VT, Jan 16, 1931, ae 88 (VT R)
1476.   Mary Catherine 8, b Mar 10, 1844; d Feb 12, 1846

730.   Valentine Bagley 7, Valentine 6, Valentine 5, Jonathan 4, Orlando 3, Orlando 2, Orlando 1 , b Oct 24, 1814; d Nov 8, 1860, Amesbury, MA; m Mary C. J. Whitten of Newburyport, MA, intentions, Sept 25, 1847 (Ames MA R); married Oct 10, 1847 (Salis MA R), b 1819, dau David & Mary. A shoemaker.

Child:
1477.   Hannah 8, b about 1850 (Census of 1850)

731.   Hannah Currier Bagley 7, William 6, Valentine 5, Jonathan 4, Orlando 3, Orlando 2, Orlando 1 , b Dec 15, 1803; probably m Harrison Howland of Chester, NH.

732.   Daniel Currier Bagley 7, William 6, Valentine 5, Jonathan 4, Orlando 3, Orlando 2, Orlando 1 , b Mar 8, 1806; d Apr 17, 1864, ae 58; m Abigail Bayley, Aug 8, 1831 (Ames MA R), dau William & Elizabeth (Ordway), b July 15, 1808, d Sept 29, 1889, ae 81 (Ames MA R). Machinist. Will signed Nov 1, 1860; proved July 5, 1864; mentions wife, Abigail; dau Ella M, adopted (Essex Co MA Probate R). Her will mentions a dau Abby B. King; and adopted dau Ella M (Essex Co MA Probate R). May

2, 1872, Abigail Bagley conveyed land in South Hampton, NH., to Ellen Maria Bagley and Edward A. Childs (Rockingham Co NH Deeds). On May 27, 1862, Daniel and Abigail Bagley, Hannah, wife Harrison Howland; Betsey Boardman, wife of William Boardman, and Orlando S., all of Amesbury, MA, conveyed land in South Hampton, NH (Essex Co MA Deeds).

Note: William Boardman's first wife was Nancy; they had a son Bagley W., b Feb 17, 1811; his second wife appears to have been Betsey; they had two children: Daniel Bagley Boardman, b Feb 11, 1841, d Sept 9, 1841; and Elizabeth Bagley Boardman, d Oct, 1842, ae 4. The use of the name Bagley and deed mentioned above would imply that Betsey Bagley was probably a sister to Daniel or a daughter, or at least close enough to be an heir-at-law, but we have not found where she fits in the line.

Children:
1478. Edward 8, adopted son, b 1834; d May 5, 1855, ae 21, a trimmer (tombstone, Ames, MA, and Boston MA R)
1479. Anna 8, adopted dau; d May 24, 1849 (tombstone, Ames, MA)
1480. Another adopted hild on tombstone, Amesbury, MA, but no name of dates
1481. Abby B. 8, not known if adopted or not, in mother's will but not in father's. Did Abigail adopte her after Daniel's death?
1482. Ella M. 8, adopted dau

733. Paulina Bagley 7, William 6, Valentined 5, Jonathan 4, Orlando 3, Orlando 2, Orlando 1 , b Apr 29, 1808; d May 18, 1881; m Abel Jones, intentions, Feb 21, 1824 (Salis MA R).

Children: (Salis MA R)
1483. Lois Downing 8, b Aug 3, 1827
1484. Daniel Bagley 8, b Aug 27, 1829; d Mar 16, 1886; m Hannah Rowell
1485. Hannah Elizabeth 8, b Oct 11, 1832; d Oct 24, 1834
1486. Hannah Elizabeth 8, b Mar 18, 1837
1487. William 8, b Jan 23, 1839; d Mar, 1839 (Family R)
1488. William Valentine 8, b Oct 21, 1844

740. Orlando Bagley 7, David Wells 6, Orlando 5, Jonathan 4, Orlando 3, Orlando 2, Orlando 1 , b Aug 30, 1818 (Salis MA R).

748. Orlando Bagley 7, Jonathan 6, Orlando 5, Jonathan 4, Orlando 3, Orlando 2, Orlando 1 , b May, 1809, Manchester, NH; d July 10, 1867, ae 58, Biddeford, E; buried Manchester, NH.; m Arvilla Foster of Manchester, NH, at Pembroke,NH, June 16, 1840 (Pembroke NH R). She d New Gloucester, ME, Apr 14, 1896, ae 78; buried Manchester. Census of 1850 gives Biddeford, ME. Probate R of Alfred Co, ME, says he d July 11, 1867. There is no mention of children in the estate, only of the widow, Arvilla.

Children:

1489. Frank O. 8, d Manchester, NH, July 28, 1846, ae dys (Manchester NH R); buried Manchester

1490. George B. 8, b about 1852, Biddeford, ME; d Boston, MA, June 28, 1897, ae 454, newspaper editor; given as m; definitely given as son of Orlando and Arvilla. It seems odd he is not mentioned in father's estate. The family tradition also is that Orlando Bagley had only one son, Frank, who d in infancy.

749. Mahala Bagley 7, Jonathan 6, Orlando 5, Jonathan 4, Orlando 3, Orlando 2, Orlando 1 b Oct 22, 1822; d May 19, 1914, ae 91; m John Greeley, d Aug 13, 1877; lived and buried Hudson, NH. No children.

751. Sarah Ann Bagley 7, Jonathan 6, Orlando 5, Jonathan 4, Orlando 3, Orlando 2, Orlando 1 , b Mar 1817; probably Sanbornton, NH; d Oct 20, 1896; m Richard N. Strong, at Plymouth, NH, Aug, 1841, b June 27, 1812, d Oct 28, 1880; both buried Hudson, NH. At one time they owned a considerable part of what is now High Street, Derry, NH, and developed it as a residential section. No children.

752. Jonathan Russell Bagley 7, Jonathan 6, Orlando 5, Jonathan 4, Orlando 3, Orlando 2, Orlando 1 , b Sanbornton, NH, Feb, 1820; d July 17, 1900, ae 80, West Derry, NH, where he resided 22 years in a house he built on High Street; m Martha Jane Howland of Franconia, NH, Nov 8, 1842, at Franconia, his residence given as Plymouth, NH, dau Russell and Lavinia (Spooner). She b 1824; d Dec 25, 1891, ae 67 (tombstone, Shipley Cemetery, Londonderry, NH). They resided Plymouth, Manchester, Londonderry, Windham and Derry, NH. At one time he was in charge of the county poor farm in Londonderry and held several offices in the town.

A Civil War soldier, enl July 23, 1861, as priv; appt captain, Sept 20, 1861; mustered in to date Sept 18, as captain; resigned Jan 13, 1862. Enl state service, Manchester Mechanic's Phalanx, Apr 25, 1861, as second lieutenant; elected captain of Captain Jonathan Bagley's Company, on or about June 12, 1861; paid as capt to July 12, 1861 (Civil War Rolls of NH). Census of 1850 gives Manchester.

Children:
1491. Frank Russell 8, b Mar 31, 1856; d Apr 15, 1927 (NH R)
1492. Willette 8, d Jan, 1920
1493. Willis H. 8, d Manchester, NH, Aug 19, 1850, ae 5 (NH R); buried Manchester

774. Orlando Israel Bagley 7, Thomas 6, Israel 5, Thomas 4, Orlando 3, Orlando 2, Orlando 1 b Durham, ME, Sept 19, 1801; d Mar 5, 1847; probably the Orlando listed as Orlando I., who sold land to his brother, Joseph, below, in 1838. Census of 1840 gives 1M 30-40, 1F 30-40, 1M 10-15; 1F 5-10. His wife was Sally, and she was adm of his estate, July 1, 1847, with Benjamin Bagley as witness (ME R).

Children:

1494.   Arvilla 8, b 1826; d 1891 (Family R)
1495.   Orlando, Jr., 8, b 1834; d Feb 27, 1899; no m given (ME R)

775.   Joseph Bagley 7, Thomas 6, Israel 5, Thomas 4, Orlando 3, Orlando 2, Orlando 1 , b Mar 16, 1803; d May 16, 1863; m Apr 13, 1829, Louisa Blethen, b Apr 4, 1808, d June 25, 1885, Thorndike, ME. No children. She m (2) Nathan Ward. On July 14, 1838, Joseph and Louisa bought land of Orlando Bagley, Joseph being given as of Thorndike, ME.

776.   George C. Bagley 7, Thomas 6, Israel 5, Thomas 4, Orlando 3, Orlando 2, Orlando 1 , b Jan 20, 1805, Durham, ME.

777.   Enoch Bagley 7, Thomas 6, Israel 5, Thomas 4, Orlando 3, Orlando 2, Orlando 1 , b about 1806; d Troy, ME, Nov 3, 1892, ae 86; m Marian Reed, who d July 1, 1899, ae 82 (tombstones, Troy, ME).

Child:
1496.   Charles 8, b about 1828; d Aug 8, 1894; given as of Durham, ME (ME R). Mr Frederick Weymouth of West Valley, NY, who did much work on Troy, ME families thinks this child should go with Enoch and Rachel Reed.

778.   Thomas Bagley 7, Thomas 6, Israel 5, Thomas 4, Orlando 3, Orlando 2, Orlando 1 , went to Raymond, IL. Apparently some of his children were b in Thorndike, ME, since in a letter from his son James to Aunt Annie (Hannah), James mentions that he remembers the old Thorndike well. Died before 1875, see Ella Susan, below.

Children: (Not necessarily in order; from family records
1497.   Thomas 8, lived Los Gatos, Colo., in 1898
1498.   Charles 8
1499.   Male 8
1500.   Joseph 8
1501.   John 8
1502.   Martha 8
1503.   Eva 8
1504.   Amy 8
1505.   Andrew 8
1506.   James 8

Note: There is a Thomas Jefferson Bagley, who may be the Thomas above, b about 1795, Troy, ME, who m Abigail Sinkler, b Mar 26, 1798, Vasselboro, ME, d May, 1829, Winona, MN, dau Joshua & Abigail (Pattee). Vasselboro ME R give the following children: Jefferson, b 1820, m Nancy Smith, b about 1824, Vasselboro, ME, and had Ella, b 1844, at Vasselboro; Hester, b 1822; William, b 1825; information supplied gy James Sinclair, a relative.

779.   Mary Bagley 7, Thomas 6, Israel 5, Thomas 4, Orlando 3, Orlando 2, Orlando 1 , b Dec 14, 1810; d Dec 17, 1887, Thorndike, ME; m 1830, Philip Blethen (Family R).

780. Susan Bagley 7, Thomas 6, Israel 5, Thomas 4, Orlando 3, Orlando 2, Orlando 1 , b 1813; d Nov 6, 1841; m Henry Patterson (Family R).

781. Orzilla Bagley 7, Thomas 6, Israel 5, Thomas 4, Orlando 3, Orlando 2, Orlando 1 , b 1815; d July 13, 1891; buried Grove Cemetery, Belfast, ME, but no stone; m Henry Patterson as his second wife, Dec 14, 1843 (Family R).

782. Hannah J. Bagley 7, Thomas 6, Israel 5, Thomas 4, Orlando 3, Orlando 2, Orlando 1 , b 1819; d May, 1871, Chicopee, MA; m (1) William Patterson; m (2) William Howe of Holyoke, MA (From Republican Journal, Belfast, ME)

783. Jeremiah Bagley 7, Thomas 6, Israel 5, Thomas 4, Orlando 3, Orlando 2, Orlando 1 ,m Hannah Shute, Sept 24, 1838, Belfast, ME, who was ae 13, d Aug 18, 1865, Belfast, ME. He sold land to Joseph Bagley, Oct 11, 1839, with Sarah Shute as a witness. They went to VA where their two youngest children were born. Hannah came back to Belfast when Flora was three weeks old. Jeremiah went to Cuba for his health where he died.

Children: (Family R)
1507.   Dwight Preston 8, b 1839
1508.   Pearl 8, b 1843; lost at sea 1895
1509.   Abbie 8, b 1844
1510.   Harriet 8, b 1848 (Census of 1860, Belfast, ME)
1511.   Flora 8, b 1850

784. James G. Bagley 7, Thomas 6, Israel 5, Thomas 4, Orlando 3, Orlando 2, Orlando 1 , b 1822; d Sept 30, 1868, ae 46 (tombstone, Waldeboro, ME); m (1) Cynthia Rand of Belfast, ME (Belfast ME R); m (20 Elsie Walter, June 27, 1857, N Waldeboro, ME, b 1840, d 1922; buried No 4 Cemetery, Albion, ME., with second husband, John Carter. James is supposed to have d at sea in 1868. History of Belfast, ME says James G. Bagley, captain of the Boston brig Sussex sailed from Boston, Dec 19, 1850; arrived San Francisco, Apr 5, 1851. Time 107 days - 2 days short of record.

Children:
1512.   James 8, b June 16, 1857, Waldeboro, ME; d Monroe, ME, Dec 22, 1933 (tombstone, Monroe, ME)
1513.   Ella Susan 8, b 1861; d 1930 (Family R)
1514.   Frank H. 8, b July 27, 1866; d Aug 10, 1925 (Family R)
1515.   Edward T. 8, b Waldeboro, ME, June 23, 1867; d Albion, ME, Nov 17, 1935

811. John Bagley 7, Jonathan 6, Enoch 5, Thomas 4, Orlando 3, Orlando 2, Orlando 1 , b Apr 22, 1810; d July 6, 1871; m Mar 5, 1831, Lucy Hall of Thorndike, ME (ME R).

Children:
1516.   Truman 8, b July 9, 1831 (Census of 1850 gives ae 19)

1517.   Amanda 8, b Aug 17, 1832 (Troy ME R) (Census   of   1850
gives ae 17)
1518.   James 8, b Apr 3, 1835 (Troy   ME   R) (Census   of   1850
gives ae 15). Mr Weymouth gives this child as Jane
1519.   Achsah 8, b about 1839 (Census of 1850 gives ae 11)
1520.   Melvina 8, b Aug 17, 1839 (Troy ME R).   Not   on   Census
of 1850 altho she grew to womanhood and m; perhaps   in   some
other household
1521.   Sarah H. 8, b about 1843 (Census of 1850 gives ae 6)
1522.   John, Jr. 8, b about 1846 (Census of 1850 gives ae 3)
1523.   George L. 8, b Troy, ME, July 12, 1850; d Dec 25,   1923
(Troy ME R).

812.   Hannah Bagley 7, Jonathan 6, Enoch 5, Thomas 4,   Orlando
3, Orlando 2, Orlando 1 , b July, 1813; d Feb 6, 1852; m   Mar
3, 1835, Sumner Gerrish.

813.   Polly (Mary) Bagley 7, Jonathan 6, Enoch   5,   Thomas   4,
Orlando 3, Orlando 2, Orlando 1 , d Sept 30, 1839; m   Apr   14,
1830, Illustrious Nutt (Troy ME R).

Children:
1524A.   Almira 8
1524B.   Valentine 8

814.   Susan Bagley 7, Jonathan 6, Enoch 5, Thomas   4,   Orlando
3, Orlando 2, Orlando 1 , b 1817; d 1889; m Sept 2, 1834, Moses
Hollis, Jr. (Troy ME R).

815.   Newell B. Bagley 7,   Jonathan   6,   Enoch   5,   Thomas   4,
Orlando 3, Orlando 2, Orlando 1 , b June 11, 1820; d   June   4,
1906, ae 86; m Mary E. Knowles, June 6, 1850, b Feb 10,   1828,
d July 13, 1918 (Troy ME R and tombstones).   Town treasurer of
Troy, ME.

816.   Levi Bagley 7, Jonathan 6, Enoch 5, Thomas 4, Orlando 3,
Orlando 2, Orlando 1 , b 1806; d Aug 8, 1873; m Abiail   Coombs
of Bradford, ME, b in Scotland.

Children:
1524.   Benjamin 8, b Orrington, ME, Nov 13,   1834;   d   Dexter,
ME, June 28, 1917 (ME R)
1525.   Newell 8, b Milo, ME; d Belfast, ME, Nov 7, 1906, ae 61
(ME R)
1526.   John H. 8, b Troy or Milo, ME, Mar 27, 1842; d July 13,
1914 (Troy ME R)
1527.   Levi 8,   b   1844;   d   Dec   14,   1900 (Troy   ME   R   and
tombstone)
1528.   Luther 9, b 1848; family tradition is that he   went   to
Aroostock Co. ME
1529.   Susan 8, b 1850 (Family R)
1530.   Sarah 8, b 1852 (Family R)
1531.   Alice 8, b 1854 (Family R)
1532.   Mary 8, b 1856 (Family R)

817.   Ralph Bagley 7, Jonathan 6, Enoch 5, Thomas   4,   Orlando

3, Orlando 2, Orlando 1 , b 1823; d Caribou, ME, Apr 14, 1897, ae 74; m Lucy Whitehouse, Troy, ME, Oct 12, 1848.   Death certificate gives his father as Jonathan and   mother   as   Mary Nutt.

Children:
1533.   Lucius Augustus 8, d Caribou, ME, Nov 24, 1940 (ME R)
1534.   J. C. Freemont 8, b Troy, ME, Sept 11, 1856; d Madison, ME, Jan 1, 1917 (ME R)
1535.   George S. 8, b Troy, ME, Dec 14, 1857; d Pittston, ME; residence Winthrop, ME, Sept 27, 1942, single (ME R)
1536.   Mattie 8, b 1860 (probably goes here; Troy ME R)

818.   Jane Bagley 7, Enoch 6,   Enoch 5, Thomas 4, Orlando 3, Orlando 2, Orlando 1 , b Sept 23, 1811; d 1841; m Jonathan Fernald of Troy, ME, b 1809, d 1866 (tombstone) Apr 21, 1833. He probably m (2) Martha Fales, b 1823, d 1867 (tombstone, Troy, ME).   No children by Jane Bagley.

819. Isaac Bagley 7, Enoch 6, Enoch 5, Thomas 4, Orlando 3, Orlando 2, Orlando 1 , b Sept 23, 1811; twin.

823. Reuben Bagley 7, Enoch 6, Enoch 5, Thomas 4, Orlando 3, Orlando 2, Orlando 1 ,b Dec 16, 1822; d Jan 19, 1897, ae 73; m Sarah E. Powers, dau James & Hannah (Jackman), b Garland, ME, d Sept 25, 1903, ae 74. Alderman, Bangor, ME. Census of 1880 gives Reuben, ae 57, Sarah, ae 52; Lilla, ae 28.

Child: (May have been others)
1537. Belinda or Lilla 8, b about 1853

824. George W. Bagley 7, Enoch 6, Enoch 5, Thomas 4, Orlando 3 Orlando 2, Orlando 1 , b May 27, 1825; one source says he d 1839, but he was probably the George W., given on the Census of 1850 whose wife was Louisa, he given as ae 32; and she, ae 24. Mr Weymouth gives two sons named George W. for Enoch, one by his first wife, b 1825, and another George W. by his second wife, 1837, who m Feb 23, 1871, Sarah Heald. He does not have definite proof but thinks it likely. We have found some instances of this situation occurring in other families. It is possible that George W. m again in 1871, but we have found no record of Louisa's death. The George W., who m Sarah Heald, had a child Medwin, b 1874, Troy, ME. We put this child in here so he does not get lost, without being sure just which George he goes with.

Child:
1538. Medwin 8, b 1874 (Troy ME R)

825. Enoch Bagley 7, Enoch 6, m Enoch 5, Thomas 4, Orlando 3, Orlando 2, Orlando 1 , b 1837; d 1915; m Feb 21, 1861, Sylvia Fletcher (Troy ME R), d 1876 (tombstone, Troy, ME).

Child:
1539. Franz S. 8, b 1862, Waldo, ME; d Brookfield, MA, Nov 25, 1930, ae 68; buried Troy, ME (MA R & tombstone).

826. Samuel S. Bagley 7, Enoch 6, Enoch 5, Thomas 4, Orlando 3, Orlando 2, Orlando 1 , b 1839; d 1862.

827. Sewell H. Bagley 7, Enoch 6, Enoch 5, Thomas 4, Orlando 3, Orlando 2, Orlando 1 , b about 1843; d Lewiston, ME, Oct 28, 1899; m Azuba Myrick, Sept 11, 1864 (Troy ME R).

829. Moses W. Bagley 7, Enoch 6, Enoch 5, Thomas 4, Orlando 3, Orlando 2, Orlando 1 , b about 1846.

830. Philmore (Filmore) Bagley 7, Enoch 6, Enoch 5, Thomas 4, Orlando 3, Orlando 2, Orlando 1 , b 1851; d 1883; a medical doctor.

842. Luther Bagley 7, Israel 6, Enoch 5, Thomas 4, Orlando 3, Orlando 2, Orlando 1 , b Nov 5, 1815; d Aug 30, 1873; m (1) Susan Kezer, Jan 6, 1841, d June 1, 1847 or 40; m (2) Hannah D. Gilfrey, Nov 6, 1849, dau Samuel & Betsey (Whitney), b

Gorham, ME, d Apr 4, 1905, ae 86 (ME R).

Children:
1540. Cynthia L. 8, d July 6, 1849 (ME R). There is some mistake here as the Census of 1850? gives a Cynthia in Luther's household, making her 7 or b about 1843. For the sake of clarity we put in two Cynthias with this note.
1541. Cynthia L. 8, b about 1843; d Jan 22, 1906, ae 63 (tombstone, Troy, ME)
1542. Edmund 8, b Troy, ME, Dec 25, 1850; d May 20, 1880 (tombstone, Troy, ME)
1543. Arthur Willis 8, b July 25, 1856; d Nov 3, 1889, ae 33, at Detroit, ME (tombstone, Troy, ME)

843. Pauline Bagley 7, Israel 6, Enoch 5, Thomas 4, Orlando 3, Orlando 2, Orlando 1 , b Jan 21, 1821; d Sept 19, 1898; m Oct 12, 1844, Rufus Burnham Stone (Troy ME R), b 1815, d 1894 (DAR).

Child:
1544. Alzoria P. 8, b 1847 (DAR)

845. Dennis Bagley 7, Moses 6, Enoch 5, Thomas 4, Orlando 3, Orlando 2, Orlando 1 , b Lincoln, ME., Oct 23, 1826; d W Bangor, ME, Oct 25, 1904; m (1) Sarah O. Kyle b Oct 7, 1833, d Oct 7, 1855; m (2) Rebecca Bailey, Lincoln, ME, Oct 4, 1856. Census of 1880 gives Dennis, ae 55; Rebecca, ae 55; and Ida, ae 24.

Children:
1545. Ida 8, b 1856 (Census of 1880 gives, ae 24)
1546. Daisy A. 8, b Lincoln, ME, 1875 (ME R); probably died before 1880 as not on Census

849. Augustus K. Bagley 7, Moses 6, Enoch 5, Thomas 4, Orlando 3, Orlando 2, Orlando 1 , b 1850.

850. Elbridge L. Bagley 7, Moses 6, Enoch 5, Thomas 4, Orlando 3, Orlando 2, Orlando 1 , b 1854.

852. Aahut Bagley 7, Moses 6, Enoch 5, Thomas 4, Orlando 3, Orlando 2, Orlando 1 , b 1859.

853. Charles E. Bagley 7, Moses 6, Enoch 5, Thomas 4, Orlando 3, Orlando 2, Orlando 1 , b Lincoln, ME, Jan 5, 1860; d Carmel, ME, Sept 24, 1933 (ME R).

855. Francis Marion Bagley 7, Reuben 6, Enoch 5, Thomas 4, Orlando 3, Orlando 2, Orlando 1 , b Mar 2, 1831; d Mapleton, ME, Jan 21, 1901; m (1) Lizzie A. French, d July 3, 1868, ae 34 (Bangor ME R); m (2) Lydia A. Hewes, Feb 7, 1870 (Bangor ME R).

Children: (Family R)
1547. Addie Helen 8, b Apr 15, 1856; d Oct 14, 1911, ae 55, Northboro, MA (MA R)

1548.   Henry Reuben 8, b Sept 25, 1858; d Oct 29, 1924
1549.   Walter Francis 8, b Apr 1, 1861; d Dec 24, 1940
1550.   Willie Douglas 8
1551.   Luella Marion 8, b Jan 23, 1871; d June 21, 1961
1552.   George Adelbert 8, b Oct 31, 1872, Bangor, ME; d May
11, 1935
1553.   Fred Hewes 8, b Jan 3, 1874; d Apr 18, 1939 (VT R &
tombstones, N Bennington, VT)
1554.   William Campbell 8, b Apr 3, 1876; d Apr 7, 1912
1555.   Charles Edgar 8, b May 2, 1878; d Waterville, ME, Mar
10, 1946
1556.   Arthur Stanley 8, b Feb 10, 1881, Mapleton, ME; d July
28, 1924

856. Hellen Maria Bagley 7, Reuben 6, Enoch 5, Thomas 4,
Orlando 3, Orlando 2, Orlando 1 , b Mar 14, 1837; m Harrison
Hasey of Glenbonia, ME. He was killed in Civil War in 1865,
and she m (2) Lyman Smith of Willimantic, CO. (Family R).

Child:
1557.   Harry Campbell 8, m Arlene Hussey of Denver, Colo.

857. Edward Bagley 7, Reuben 6, Enoch 5, Thomas 4, Orlando 3,
Orlando 2, Orlando 1 , b about 1849.

858. Henry Clay Bagley 7, Reuben 6, Enoch 5, Thomas 4,
Orlando 3, Orlando 2, Orlando 1 , b about 1844 (Census of 1860
gives ae 16); d May 24, 1919, ae 75, at Winchester, MA; m
Theresa A. Stewart, Mar 31, 1869, d Winchester, MA, Mar 15,
1934, ae 89, b Bangor, ME, dau Simon & Dorcas (Malone).
Resided part of his life at Bangor and was a member of 31 Vol
Regt in Civil War (Bangor ME R).

Children:
1558.   Bertha Alice 8 (Family R)
1559.   Amy Campbell 8, (Family R)

871. John S. Bagley 7,, Abner 6, John 5, John 4 , John 3,
Orlando 2, Orlando 1 , b Apr 27, 1804; d Mar 24, 1880; m (1)
Margaret A., b 1813, d 1843 (tombstone, Newburyport, MA); m
(2) Margaret Harper, Jan 27, 1846, b Apr 21, 1811, d Aug 14,
1896 (tombstone), dau William. He is given in his sisters'
wills as being in Brooklyn, NY.

Children:
1560.   John A. 8, b 1833; d 1896 (tombstone, Newburyport, MA)
1561.   Charles H. 8
1562.   Walter Jackson 8, b Jan 19, 1852; d Aug 23, 1902 (MA R)

874. Michael Hodge Bagley 7, Abner 6, John 4, John 4, John 3,
Orlando 2, Orlando 1 b Portland, ME; d Oct 29, 1874, ae 63, at
Easton, MA (MA R); m Margaret Huslet, dau Hazlett & Elisa, b
Pittsburgh, PA, d Nov 13, 1884, ae 75, at Easton, MA. Lived
for a time in Meadsville, PA. Census of 1860 gives wife as b
ME. On her death certificate, she is given as wife of Henry
A., but this is unlikely since she was b in 1809-10, and age

agrees with Michael's wife on Census of 1860.

Children:
1563.   Rebecca H. 8, b about 1840 (Census of 1860 gives ae 20)
1564.   Charles Hazlett 8, b about 1843 (Census of 1860 gives ae 17)
1565.   Henry Abner 8, b Meadsville, PA; d Dec 7, 1874, ae 27, at Easton, MA (MA R)
1566.   Sarah E. 8, b Meadsville, PA; d Dec 7, 1874, ae 27, at Easton, MA (MA R)
1567.   Frederick Sewell 8, b about 1852 (Census of 1860 gives ae 8)
1568.   Herman 8, b about 1855 (Census of 1860 gives ae 5)

875.   John Stickney Bagley 7, Daniel 6, Daniel 5, John 4, John 3, Orlando 2, Orlando 1, b Aug 10, 1801 (Portland ME R call this child John Burnham; if so he probably d young as another child by that name was b 1804.

876.   Harriet Bagley 7, Daniel 6, Daniel 5, John 4, John 3, Orlando 2, Orlando 1, b Jan 6, 1803; d Sept 30, 1848; m Oct, 1822, at Portland, ME, John Bradley Hudson, b Mar 6, 1799, son John & Mercy (Bradley), d July 24, 1880.

Children:
1569.   Daniel Bagley 8, b July 29, 1823; d Jan 20, 1824 (Portland ME R)
1570.   Sarah Love 8, b Feb 27, 1825; m Timothy Everett; d Feb 23, 1911
1571.   George Clark 8, b Aug 7, 1827; m Estella Boyden; d Jan 4, 1901
1572.   Harriet Bagley 8, b Dec 22, 1829; m Francis Henry Fassett; d Dec 26, 1916
1573.   John Bradley 8, b Feb 27, 18932; d Nov 11, 1903, unm
1574.   Caroline Chapman 8, b May 9, 1834; m Isaac Henry Dupee; d July 16, 1920
1575.   Maria May 8, b Oct 26, 1837; m Peleg Tallman; d Apr 9, 1910, Syracuse, NY
1576.   Walter Corey 8, b May 24, 1841; d Sept 21, 1851

877.   John Burnham Bagley 7, Daniel 6, Daniel 5, John 4, John 3, Orlando 2, Orlando 1, b Aug 11, 1804; d Portland, ME, Nov 8, 1889, ae 89; a baker; m (1) Mary (Margaret) Harriet Cummings of Freeport, intentions, Dec 15, 1827 (ME R), dau Enoch & Lydia (Reed), d Nov 30, 1853; m (2) July 23, 1856, Caroline A. Gage; m (3) Sarah Fields, Oct 10, 1865.   He and his wife Mary sold land in Portland to Lewis Dela, Sept 23, 1847 (ME R).

Children: (Portland ME R except as noted)
1577.   Frances C. n Jan 2, 1829
1578.   Leah Harper 8, b Feb 8, 1830; d Sept 1, 1830
1579.   Ellen 8, b Feb 5, 1831
1580.   Harriet R. 8, b Aug, 1832
1581.   Daniel 8, b July 27, 1834
1582.   Mary 8, b Aug 21, 1836

1583. George W. 8, b Feb 5, 1838; probably d there, Oct 13, 1871
1584. John B., Jr. 8, b Nov 7, 1839; d Nov, 1890
1585. David 8, b Oct 5, 1841; probably d young
1586. Lewis Dela 8, b Aug 6, 1844; d Aug 9, 1844
1587. Maria Griffiths 8, b Oct, 1845; d Oct 31, 1849
1588. David Burnham 8, b Mar 6, 1846; d May 8, 1846
1589. Asa 8, b Oct 20, 1947
1590. Enoch Cummings 8, b Sept 10, 1849; d Oct 10, 1864
1591. Phebe Cummings 8, b Feb 23, 1850
1592. Maretta 8, b May 13, 1858

879. Russell S. Bagley 7, Moses 6, Aaron 5, John 4, John 3, Orlando 2, Orlando 1 , b June 12, 1815; m Lucy Hancock of Washington, VT, Nov 27, 1834 (VT R); d Northfield, VT, ae 46, Dec 24, 1863; a painter (VT R).

Children:
1593. Elon H. 8, d Dec 30, 1863, ae 26, b Washington, VT; d Charlestown, MA (MA R)
1594. Ellen E. 8, b about 1841 (Census of 1850 gives ae 9)
1594A. Russell, b 1843; Washington, VT; d Apr 6, 1899, ae 56

883. John Bagley 7, John 6, Aaron 5, John 4, John 3 Orlando 2, Orlando 1 , b June 11, 1814, Orange, VT; d Aug 3, 1880, ae 66; m Hannah Bailey, Mar 4, 1850, d Mar 17, 1895, Holland, MA (VT R), dau Moses. There is some confusion about his m. One record from Holland, MA, says he m Hannah, July 16, 1880, when he was 66, his second m. He is definitely given as son of John Bagley and Mary Downing. She was dau of Moses Bailey. On marriage certificates of his sons, Moses and Henry, both give their parents as John Bagley and Hannah Bailey. He left no will but accounts mention wife Hannah, who survived him. William Nelson Bagley, son of Moses, says his father was b Apr 27, 1842; if so, this date is before John's marriage to Hannah Bailey as given on VT R) .

Children:
1595. Moses O. 8, b about 1853; d Randolph, VT, Feb 15, 1895, ae 52 (VT R) (See above for different birthdate)
1596. Edwin E. 8, b May 30, 1857; d Jan 29, 1922, ae 64 (NH R)
1597. Ella A. 8, b Washington, VT, Apr 7, 1855 (VT R)
1598. Henry 8, b Dec 31, 1847; d Sept 13, 1921, ae 72 (Montpelier VT R)
1599. George W. 8, b Oct 18, 1845; d Dec 29, 1902 (Brimfield MA R)
1600. Andrew 8, b Mar 22, 1850; d June 2, 1918, ae 68 (Holland MA R)
1601. Richard 8, b Dec 8, 1840 (VT R); d North Dakota, Feb 5, 1931 (pension R says he deposed he was b Dec 8, 1841)
1602. Elizabeth N. 8, b Feb 8, 1844 (VT R)
1603. Ezra N. 8, b Jan 3, 1853 (VT R)
1604. William 8, b Sept 23, 1838; d 1911; buried Preston, CO

884. Samuel Downing Bagley 7, John 6, Aaron 5, John 4, John

3. Orlando 2, Orlando 1 , b Nov 10, 1816; d Lebanon, NH, Feb 11, 1895, b Washington, VT; m Roxanna Richardson, Nov 10, 1837 (VT R), d Feb 21, 1866, ae 48 (tombstone, W Topsham, VT)

Children:
1605. Loren Richardson 8, b May 23, 1845 (History of Littleton, NH); d Littleton, NH, Sept 19, 1912. Death certificate gives b May 9, 1846, ae at death 66-4-10 (NH R)
1606. Robert 8, b 1846; d 1888 (tombstone, E Haverhill, NH)
1607. Addison 8, b 1849; d May 24, 1882, ae 32 (Haverhill NH R)
1608. Carlos Coolidge 8, b 1850; d July 27, 1929 (Bradford VT R)
1609. Royal 8, b Feb 2, 1852; d Manchester, NH, July 17, 1915 (NH R say b Newport, NH)
1610. Wallace 8, b Feb 24, 1856; d May 24, 1927 (VT R)

885. Gideon Bagley 7, John 6, Aaron 5, John 4, John 3, Orlando 2, Orlando 1 , b Apr 14, 1821, Orange, VT; d Nov 12, 1887, ae 66; m Luseba H. Smith, Nov 28, 1841, Albany, VT, d July 22, 1903, ae 78 (tombstone, Albany, VT). Lived at Craftsbury and Albany, VT.

Children:
1611. Hollis 8, b about 1842 (Census of 1850 gives ae 8)
1612. Emily 8, b about 1844 (Census of 1850 gives ae 6)
1613. Eliza 8, b about 1848 (Census of 1850 gives ae 2)
1614. Hellen 8, b about 1854

887. Mary Jane Bagley 7, John 6, Aaron 5, John 4, John 3, Orlando 2, Orlando 1 , b Feb 12, 1824; m Charles Lawrence, Jan 1, 1857 (VT R); given as heirs-at-law of her father John Bagley, who d intestate in 1878 (Orleans Co VT Probate R).

890. Augustus Y. Bagley 7, William 6, Aaron 5, John 4, John 3, Orlando 2, Orlando 1 , b Feb 5, 1824; d Nov 27, 1903, at Grasmere, NH; m Groton, NH, Nov 8, 1848, Diantha R. Phelps, d Groton, NH, Feb 7, 1866, ae 56, dau Nathan & Rebecca (Otis). Town clerk of Groton, 1876. Given as of Manchester at time of marriage.

Children:
1615. Nellie B. 8, b Sept 17, 1860, Groton, NH; d there Nov 21, 1863 (NH R)
1616. Elmo 8, b about 1866, Groton, NH

894. Abner Bagley 7, Ephraim 6, Aaron 5, John 4, John 3, Orlando 2, Orlando 1 , b Oct 24, 1830; m Sabrina Moody.

Children: (Manchester VT R)
1617. Elizabeth 8, b Dec 9, 1862
1618. Celia 8, b Sept 11, 1865

896. Ephraim Bagley 7, Ephraim 6, Aaron 5, John 3, Orlando 2, Orlando 1 , b W Topsham, VT, Oct 27, 1834; d Boston, MA, Mar 10, 1876, ae 61; m Adelia T. Hall, dau Benjamin, b ME, d

Boston, MA, May 16, 1906, ae 66 (MA R).

Children:
1619.   Carrie 8, b Worcester, MA; d Boston, MA, June 26, 1952,
ae 88-11-17 (MA R)
1620.   Arthur H. 8, b VT; d July 22, 1870, ae 5 (MA R)
1621.   Maude A. 8, b Worcester, MA; d Boston, MA, Jan 21,
1872, ae 4 (MA R)

897. Moses Bagley 7, Ephraim 6, Aaron 5, John 4, John 3,
Orlando 2, Orlando 1, b June 4, 1834; d Worcester, MA, Nov 20,
1893, ae 54 (MA R); m Mary T. Tinkham, dau Jesse & Hannah
(Eddy) of Enfield, NH, d Apr 17, 1908 (Worcester MA R).

Children:
1622.   Stillborn 8, b & d Dec 31, 1871 (MA R)
1623.   Hattie M. 8, b Worcester, MA; d there Feb 26, 1930, ae
54, a bookkeeper (MA R).   Her will, filed Mar 19, 1930,
mentions an aunt, Hannah M. Whittemore; cousin, Jennie E.
Smith, wife Cyrus Smith of Athol, MA; George W. Stewart of
Hingham, MA; Dorothy Stewart of Hingham, MA ; Ida Smith;
Fannie A. Spring, a cousin of West Haven, CO.   Some of the
above had died before the will was probated since Fannie S.
Spring states she is the only heir-at-law of the deceased and
had no objection to George Stewart's being appt adm (Worcester
Co MA Probate R).

909. Henry Bagley 7, John 6, Timothy 5, Timothy 4, John 3,
Orlando 2, Orlando 1, b Mar 14, 1821.

911. Jonathan Bagley 7, John 6, Timothy 5, Timothy 4, John 3,
Orlando 2, Orlando 1, b Apr 26, 1826.

912. Nathaniel Gilman Bagley 7, Charles 6, Timothy 5, Timothy
4, John 3, Orlando 2, Orlando 1, b July 19, 1813; d Aug 6,
1909, Sharon, NH; m Celestia Appleton of Sharon, at New
Ipswich, NH, June 26, 1848, d 1859. Sold land in Sharon in
1837-43-46 (Hillsboro Co NH Deeds). Ran a tavern in New
Ipswich and sold liquor but never drank himself. Census of
1850 calls him Gilman.
     His will was signed Feb 23, 1886; filed Sept 13, 1909.
Sister Lydia named adm, Aug 26, 1909; names son, David
Appleton; Mary E. Bennett, wife of Dr Bennett, and dau of Mary
and Edward Appleton Preston of New Ipswich, NH; William
Preston and Guy Preston, brothers of Mary Bennett; and his
sister Lydia Maria Bagley and Sally Pillsbury.

Children:
1624.   David Appleton 8, mentioned in father's will in 1886,
but when the will was filed in 1909, Lydia Maria, sister of
Nathaniel was the only surviving heir (Worcester Co MA Probate
R) since Nathaniel died in Fitchburg).
1625.   Maria Celestia 8, d Winchendon, MA, Nov 20, 1885, ae
32, a teacher (MA R)
1626.   Lydia Maria 8, b Mar 29, 1852; d prior to 1886

913. Maria (Lydia Maria) Bagley 7, Charles 6, Timothy 5, Timothy 4, John 3, Orlando 2, Orlando 1 , b Jan 30, 1820 (NH R); d Nov 14, 1921, ae 94. Her death certificate gives birth as June 10, 1827, a teacher; buried Goffstown, NH.   Henry A. Cutter was appt conservator of her estate and property, July, 1916 (Hillsboro CO NH Probate R).   Mentioned in brother's will in 1886 and in 1909 was sole surviving heir.

914. Sally Bagley 7, Charles 6, Timothy 5, Timothy 4, John 3, Orlando 2, Orlando 1 , m Levi Pillsbury and d before 1909 when her brother's will was filed altho living 1886 when it was signed.

Children: (Worcester CO MA Probate R)
1627.   Charles W. 8
1628.   Ella 8, m an Adams

915. Benjamin Bagley 7, Peter 6, Peter 5, Timothy 4, John 3, Orlando 2, Orlando 1 , b 1813, Broome, NY; d between Jan 5, and Feb 25, 1884; m Elizabeth, b 1816-1824, at Broome, NY. Given as of New Baltimore, NY, he made his will Jan 5, 1884; proven Feb 25, 1884. Danforth Bagley & Anson Greene were adms. Wife given as Elizabeth; lists son Danforth; daus Julia Travis, Sabrina Travis, Alvaretta Powell and Priscilla.   Adms sold land in New Baltimore, Mar 28, 1884.

Children:
1629.   Julia A. 8, b 1847, Broome, NY
1630.   Labina or Sabrina 8, b 1848, Broome, NY
1631.   Danforth 8, n 1850, Broome, NY
1632.   Alvaretta 8, b 1857, Broome, NY
1633.   Rosetta 8, b 1857, Broome, NY; must have died before 1884 as not mentioned in father's will, nor are any of her children
1634.   Priscilla 8, not on list of children in record of Church of Jesus Christ of Latter Day Saints, but mentioned in father's will as Priscilla Bagley, unless this is another name for Rosetta

916. Harrison Bagley 7, Peter 6, Peter 5, Timothy 4, John 3, Orlando 2, Orlando 1 , b 1819, Broome, NY; d May 2, 1888, Freehold, NY; m Mary, b 1823, Broome, NY. Apparently Mary died and he m Sally Travis, dau of William, since in Mar, 1848, Harrison and his wife Sally Maria, given as of Middleburgh, Scholarie Co, NY, sold land in the estate of William Travis, late of New Baltimore. He bought land in New Baltimore, Mar 23, 1866. Phebe Meeks quit-claimed land to him in New Baltimore, Dec 15, 1860. He bought land of heirs of Benjamin Bagley in New Baltimore, Mar 28, 1884.

Child:
1635.   Emma 8, b 1860, Broome, NY; given as his sole heir in 1888 (NY Probate R)

925. Emeline Bagley 7, Lowell 6, Isaac 5, Timothy 4, John 3, Orlando 2, Orlando 1 , b Oct 22, 1812; d Dec 29, 1892; m James

Whittier, intentions, May 29, 1840 (Ames MA R), b Aug 4, 1816, d May 15, 1899 (tombstones, Amesbury, MA), son James & Mary (Sargent).

Children: (Tombstones, Amesbury, MA)
1636.   Wendell B. 8, b Feb 3, 1842; d Sept 8, 1842
1637.   Adelia E. 8, b Sept 6, 1847; d Aug 5, 1849

927.   Richard Bagley 7, Richard 6, Isaac 5, Timothy 4, John 3, Orlando 2, Orlando 1 , b 1830; d May 1, 1877, ae 48; m Mary A., b Epping, NH, d Jan 18, 1855, ae 50 (tombstone, Newburyport, MA).

Child:
1638.   Charles Oscar 8, d Oct 13, 1851, ae 1 mo (tombstone, Newburyport, MA which says "only child")

936.   William Bagley 7, Jeremiah 6, William 5, William 4, Jacob 3, Orlando 2, Orlando 1 , b Mar 30, 1796; d July 4, 1882, ae 86; m Mary T. Day, intentions, Oct, 1825 (Ames MA R); m at Stratford, NH, Nov 14, 1825, by Rev Enoch Place, she b Boscawen, NH, d Feb 5, 1881, ae 81 (tombstone, Amesbury, MA). member of Warren Lodge of Masons at Amesbury, MA. There is a stone on cemetery lot which says Mary E., not dated.

Children: (Ames MA R)
1639.   Mary 8, b Apr 14, 1826
1640.   David Winkley 8, b Jan 16, 1829; d Apr 24, 1888

937.   Daniel Bagley 7, Jeremiah 6, William 5, William 4, Jacob 3, Orlando 2, Orlando 1 , b Sept 5, 1800; d May 14, 1879, ae 79. Raymond NH R say he d unm but are not correct. He m Eleanor Spinney, Dec 1, 1831 (Hampstead NH R), b 1803, d 1872 (Raymond, NH tombstone), dau Stephen & Annie G., both b Elliott, ME (Raymond NH R give date as Sept 1, 1872, ae 72).

Children:
1641.   Daniel 8, b July 1, 1832; d July 16, 1916, Amesbury, MA (tombstone & MA R)
1642.   Lydia 8, b Jan, 1837; d Sept, 1840 (tombstone, Raymond, NH)
1643.   Lorenda Frances 8, b 1839; d Apr, 1841 (tombstone, Raymond, NH; vital records from Jonathan Swain's notebook says she d Apr 5)
1644.   Clarenda Olive 8, b 1839; d 1846 (tombstone); twin to Lorenda

938.   Joseph Bagley 7, Jeremiah 6, William 5, William 4, Jacob 3, Orlando 2, Orlando 1 , b Aug 30, 1803.

941.   Dorothy Bagley 7, Jacob 6, William 5, William 4, Jacob 3, Orlando 2, Orlando 1 , b Dec 15, 1789; d Jan 17, 1824; m Mar 12, 1812, John Blaisdell, son John & Molly (Bailey), b Mar 11, 1789, d Apr 16,m 1831, ae 41 (Ames MA R).

Children: (Ames MA R)

1645.   William 8, b Aug 5, 1812
1646.   Mary 8, b Nov 15, 1813
1647.   Randall B. 8, b Dec 19, 1815
1648.   Ann 8, b Oct 27, 1818

944.   George Bagley 7, Jacob 6, William 5, William 4, Jacob 3,
Orlando 2, Orlando 1 , b Oct 27, 1793; d Feb 12, 1842; m
Clarissa Morrill, intentions, Jan 11, 1823; m Mar 9, 1823
(History of Salisbury, NH), b Jan 9, 1794, d Jan 3, 1893
(tombstone, Nashua, NH). Nashua R say she d Lowell, MA, Jan
2, 1893, ae 98, dau Levi & Mary of Amesbury, MA.

Children:
1649.   Susan B. 8, d 1820 (tombstone)
1650.   Mary E. 8, d 1821 (tombstone)
1651.   Mary Jane 8, b Jan 20, 1824 (Ames MA R)
1652.   George 8, b May 27, 1826 (Ames MA R); d June 3, 1847
(tombstone, Nashua, NH.
1653.   Eliza A., d 1827 (tombstone)
1654.   Frances 8, d 1828 (tombstone)

945.   Randall Bagley 7, Jacob 6, William 5, William 4, Jacob
3, Orlando 2, Orlando 1 , b July 22, 1795.

946.   Jacob Bagley 7, Jacob 6, William 5, William 4, Jacob 3,
Orlando 2, Orlando 1 , b Apr 9, 1797; one source says he m
Hannah Dearborn and that numbers 669, 670, 671, and 672 are
their children.

947.   Ignatius Bagley 7, Jacob 6, William 5, William 4, Jacob
3, Orlando 2, Orlando 1 , b Jan 11, 1799; d about 1879; m (1)
May 26, 1818, Susan (Sukey) Fowler (Salis MA R), dau Jacob &
Elizabeth, b June 6, 1797, d May 14, 1843, ae 44 (Nashville NH
R, now Nashua); m (2) Cynthia E. Johnson of Nashua, NH (NH R).
Moved from Amesbury to Nashua and had a store of meat and
provisions in the early 1800's. In 1830 he opened a book
store and circulating library; mayor of Nashua about 1843.
Member Warren Lodge of Masons, Amesbury, MA.

Children:
1655.   Susan F. 8, b Dec 6, 1817; d Feb 3, 1849 (Ames MA R)
1656.   Jacob 8, b Sept 25, 1823; d Mar 28, 1904 (tombstone,
Nashua., NH)
1657.   Caroline 8
1658.   Charles 8
1659.   Mary 8

948.   Ann Bagley 7, Jacob 6, William 5, William 4, Jacob 3,
Orlando 2, Orlando 1, b Nov 4, 1800; m July 9, 1826, Joseph
Mann (Ames MA R).

Children: (Ames MA R)
1660.   George 8, b Oct 27, 1827
1661.   Ann 8, b Apr 29, 1829

949.   Mary Bagley 7, David 6, William 5, William 4, Jacob 3,

Orlando 2, Orlando 1 , b Jan 13, 1790; d June 7, 1843; m (1)
James Kendrick, Nov 3, 1816 (Ames MA R), d Sept 16, 1829; m
(2) Jacob Currier, Nov 4, 1840 (Ames MA R), b Jan 31, 1792
(Salis MA R), son Daniel & Sarah (Chase), d June 5, 1865
(Family R).

Children:
1662. Maria 8, b Apr 5, 1817; d Dec 25, 1891 (Ames MA &
Family R)
1663. Hannah T. 8, b Sept 24, 1818 (Ames MA R)
1664. John 8, b Dec 29, 1822; d Aug 13, 1899 (Family R)
1665. William 8, b June 29, 1826; d July 5, 1880 (Family R)

951. Levi Bagley 7, David 6, William 5, William 4, Jacob 3,
Orlando 2, Orlando 1 , b Oct 13, 1793; d Oct, 1872; left
Amesbury at ae 12 and lived with his uncle in Coeymans, NY.
The only time he ever came home was when he was 21.   He and
his brother, William, came together, all the way on horseback.
He returned to Coeymans and in a few years went to
Mississippi, and was not heard from for over 40 years (Family
R).

Children: (Family R)
1666. David 8
1667. Martha 8
1668. Levi 8

953. William Bagley 7, David 6, William 5 William 4, Jacob 3,
Orlando 2, Orlando 1 , b Oct 17, 1794; d Aug 21, 1869; m
Elizabeth Boardman in Albany, NY, Nov 4, 1829 (Family R), dau
Rev William & Rachel of Willimantic, CO, b Oct 19, 1808, d Jan
3, 1891 (Boardman Genealogy). After his wife's death his
remains were taken to Brooklyn, NY. William left Amesbury two
years after his brother, Levi, and lived with his uncle in
Coeymans, NY, and moved to Albany in 1823 where he was a dry
goods merchant.

Children: (Boardman Genealogy & Family R)
1669. William 8, b Aug 27, 1830; d Oct 29, 1907
1670. Margaret 8, b Feb 5, 1833
1671. Mary 8, b June 24, 1835
1672. Charles 8, b Aug 13, 1842

954. Frederick Bagley 7, David 6, William 5, William 4, Jacob
3, Orlando 2, Orlando 1 , b Dec 13, 1797; d Feb 13, 1868, ae
70; m Dec 13, 1825, Betsey Fowler (Salis MA R), dau Robert &
Betsey (Morrill), b Apr 1, 1799 (Salis MA R), d Oct 13, 1862,
ae 63 (tombstone, Amesbury, MA). He was a silversmith and
lived in Salisbury, MA, for a time in a house her father
bought for them and then moved to a farm at Allen's Corner and
from there to a house at the corner of Main & School Streets
in Amesbury, MA, where he lived until his death.   He was a
great reader and his favorite books besides the Bible were
those containing Whittier's poems He was a great lover of
nature and planted two elms beside his house, one was killed
by leaking of a gas main, and the other living in 1898 (since

gone), called Bagley's elm (Family R).

Soldier in War of 1812 for South Hampton, NH, leaving there Sept 17, 1814, for Portsmouth. His will, signed Jan 28, 1868; proved Mar 3, 1868 (Essex Co MA Probate R) mentions a son George Frederick and a dau Mary Bagley Carey. It is thought these children were b in Salisbury, MA, but not on record there.

Children: (Ames MA R and tombstones, Ames)
1673. Susan E. 8, b Oct 9, 1827; d Apr 6, 1856
1674. George F. 8, b Sept 9, 1829; d Apr 2, 1908
1675. Mary K. 8, b Jan 23, 1833; d Nov 14, 1920
1676. Abby K. 8, b Nov 10, 1841; d Sept 18, 1842

956. David Bagley 7, David 6, William 5, William 4, Jacob 3, Orlando 2, Orlando 1 , ,b July 28, 1804; d Feb 26, 1886; m Sarah Ann Brown of Seabrook, NH, Jan 2, 1831 (Ames MA R), b Sept 30, 1812, d Mar 15, 1898, ae 84 (tombstone, Amesbury, MA), dau Jeremiah & Nancy. Always lived in Amesbury where he was a trader. At his death he had been married for 55 years with no death in the family in all that time. Will made May 6, 1864. In it, styled "Gentleman", he mentions wife, Sarah Ann; children: Elizabeth S. Greeley, wife Nathaniel, now of Newburyport; a dau Ann S. Bagley; and a son, William D. (Essex Co MA Probate R). Sold land in Rockingham Co, NH, Nov 24, 1836, and Jan 23, 1833 (Rockingham Co NH Deeds).

Children: (tombstones, Ames MA)
1677. Elizabeth S. 8, b Nov 3, 1832; d Aug 12, 1888
1678. Ann 8, b Sept 22, 1837; d Nov 21, 1917
1679. William D. 8, b July 12, 1843; d Mar 17, 1920

973. Elizabeth Allen Bagley 7, John 6, William 5, William 4, Jacob 3, Orlando 2, Orlando 1 , b Sept 17, 1812, Plaistow, NH; mentioned in father's will in 1856; d Mar 22, 1895, ae 82, Peabody, MA R). Note: Danvers MA R give an Elizabeth A. Philbrick, born Elizabeth A. Bagley, dau of John Bagley, both parents b VT, d Feb 24, 1917, ae 64; she does not seem to be this Elizabeth but we can not place her.

974. Mary Osgood Bagley 7, John 6, William 5, William 4, Jacob 3, Orlando 2, Orlando 1 , b May 19, 1814, Grafton, NH; birth also recorded Corinth, VT, which gives date as May 9. Her father's will in 1856 gives her as deceased. M Apr 23, 1845, Samuel Seamond Stevens, Danvers, MA, age given as 31; his age, 30, probably son Samuel Seamonds Stevens, b Lebanon, NH, July 27, 1812 (Danvers MA R).

Children: (Danvers MA R except last)
1680. Mary Elizabeth 8, b Mar 12, 1846
1681. Hannah Jane 8, b Feb 19, 1849
1682. Ellen P. 8, given as her child in John Bagley's will; the other two children given as of Samuel Stevens & Mary Osgood Bagley.

977. Almond Fisk Bagley 7, John 6, William 5, William 4,

Jacob 3, Orlando 2, Orlando 1 , b Mar 30, 1819 (Mar 13, duplicate Danvers MA) record of birth says be Grafton, NH; also recorded Corinth, VT; d Apr 15, 1872, ae 53, Wenham, MA (MA R); m Louisa Nason, Mar 13, 1843 (Danvers MA R), b Buxton, ME, Juyly 6, 1820, d Beverly, MA, June 21, 1902, ae 81, dau Gee & Martha (Webber). Bought land in Springfield, ME, Mar 15, 1858; mentioned in father's will in 1856 which gives the following children: Frank, George, Charles W. & Emeline.

Children: (Danvers MA R)
1683. Franklin Augustus 8, b July 6, 1844
1684. George A. 8, b May 3, 1847; d Lynn, MA, Feb 15, 1910, ae 62 (MA R)
1685. Charles Warren 8, b Sept 12, 1849
1686. Emeline 8, b Sept 11, 1852

978. Sarah Whittier Bagley 7, John 6, William 5, William 4, Jacob 3, Orlando 2, Orlando 1 , b Apr 11, 1820. Records give b Grafton, NH; also recorded Danvers, MA, & Corinth, VT; m Samuel Swett of Marblehead, MA, Apr 12, 1841. Father's will in 1856 mentions the following children: Lucy O., Ann E., Joseph H., and Sarah A.

Children: (Danvers MA R)
1687. Lucy Osborne 8, b July 21, 1841
1688. Ann Eliza 8, b Mar 9, 1844
1689. Joseph Henry 8, b Dec 30, 1845
1690. Sarah A. 8

979. John A. Bagley 7, John 6, William 5, William 4, Jacob 3, Orlando 2, Orlando 1 , b June 13, 1822, Grafton, NH; also recorded Danvers, MA & Corinth, VT; m at Salem, MA, Dec 30, 1845, Judith Ann Stone (Danvers MA R), b Lynn, MA, Oct 20, 1827, d Peabody, MA, Nov 11, 1908, ae 81, dau Nathaniel & Judith (Lanphear). he probably d in 1890 when Daniel Crowley was made adm of estate of John Bagley, late of Salem, MA (Essex Co MA Probate R). His father's will gives the following children: John, Henry, William, Jenney and Isette.

Children:
1691. John 8, b Peabody; d Ipswich, MA, Oct 11, 1932, ae 63 (MA R)
1692. Henry 8, b July 15, 1846 (Danvers MA R); d July 12, 1891, ae 45 (MA R)
1693. William Wallis 8, b Jan 25, 1849 (Danvers MA R); d S Danvers, MA, Feb 22, 1865 (MA R)
1694. Jenney Lind 8, b Sept 14, 1850 (Danvers MA R)
1695. Preston Brooks 8, b Peabody, MA, 1857; d Oct 27, 1932, ae 75 (Salem MA R)
1696. Gustave T. 8, b Peabody, MA, 1861; d there Oct 15, 1936, ae 75 (MA R)
1697. Isette W. 8

981. Lydia Drew Bagley 7, John 6, William 5, William 4, Jacob 3, Orlando 2, Orlando 1 , b Aug 31, 1826, Corinth, VT; also recorded Danvers, MA; m _____Potter and her father's will

listed the following children: John E., Lydia M.; Harriet A., Eva, and Mary T.

Children: (John Bagley's will)
1698.   Mary T. 8
1699.   John E. 8
1700.   Lydia M. 8
1701.   Harriet A. 8
1702.   Eva 8

984.   Emeline Bagley 7, William 6, William 5, William 4, Jacob 3, Orlando 2, Orlando 1 , b Danville, NH, 1821; d Hampstead, NH, 1896; buried Danville; m Alonzo Ferrin, b 1822, Plymouth, VT, d 1880 in Winnebago Co, IL (Ferrin Genealogy)

985.   Harriet Bagley 7, William 6, William 5, William 4, Jacob 3, Orlando 2, Orlando 1 , b 1823; m Stephen Merrick of Danville, NH, Mar 4, 1841.

Children: (From Census of 1850)
1703.   Ellen 8, ae 9, b about 1841
1704.   Edward 8, ae 6, b about 1844
1705.   Joseph 8, ae 4, b about 1846
1706.   William 8, ae 2, b about 1848
1707.   Henry W. 8, ae 2, b about 1848

986.   William M. Bagley 7, William 6, William 5, William 4, Jacob 3, Orlando 2, Orlando 1 , b 1823; d 1852 (tombstone, Danville, NH).

988.   Andrew J. Bagley 7, William 6, William 5, William 4, Jacob 3, Orlando 2, Orlando 1 , b Feb 24, 1829; d Feb 27, 1914. Will dated Aug 29, 1913; proved Mar 24, 1914, mentions sister, Sarah M. Bagley; niece Mary Metivier; nephew John Metivier of Danville; nephew Harold of Haverhill, MA; Harold's son William of Haverhill; niece, Eunice B. Brown of Pittsfield, NH; niece, Iva M. Odney of Haverhill; niece, Harriet Webster (Rockingham Co NH Probate R). He was a cooper and single.

989.   John H. Bagley 7, William 6, William 5, William 4, Jacob 3, Orlando 2, Orlando 1,b Feb 8, 1833; lived all his life in Danville, NH, and d there Feb 6, 1909; a farmer; m Ellen or Ella Stevens, b about 1852 (given as ae 34 on dau's birth certificate in 1886).

Children:
1708.   Eva M. 8
1709.   Sarah 8, d Sept 20, 1882, ae 4 mos (Danville NH R)
1710.   Harold Sanford 8, b May 27, 1883; d Feb 8, 1976 (NH R)
1711.   William H. 8, b June 27, 1886, Danville, NH; living 1976 in Arizona
1712.   Ina Montrose 8, b June 27, 1886; d Danville, NH, single (NH R)
Note: John Bagley was 53 in 1886; his wife, b Peabody, MA was 34, so it is possible that Eva M. may have been a child of a

146

first marriage.

991. Isaiah 7, William 6, William 5, William 4, Jacob 3, Orlando 2, Orlando 1 , b 1836; d 1864; served in Civil War, 2nd regt, ZNH Vol Inf, b Danville, ae 24, enl May 21, 1861, priv, mustered in June 6, 1861. Captured Aug 2, 1862 at Bull Run by 2nd VA; paroled; deserted Dec 11,1863, Columbus, OH; returned Mar 21, 1864; sentenced to be confined at hard labor for 3 years; unexpired portion sentence remitted Oct 24, 1865; discharged Nov 30, 1865, Fredericksburg (Ayling Register NH Soldiers in Civil War). This seems odd but is correct. He d of illness and after his death the sentence was remitted, and he was discharged (National Archives).

994. Hannah Bagley 7, William 6, William 5, William 4, Jacob 3, Orlando 2, Orlando 1 , b 1831; living 1914; m ____ Lovejoy. Conveyed land in Danville, NH, Nov 17, 1868 (Rockingham Co NH Deeds).

Child:
1713. N. Grace 8

996. Abner T. Bagley 7, Greenleaf 6, Stephen 5, Abel 4, Joseph 3, Orlando 2, Orlando 1 , b Oct 28, 1814, Amesbury, MA; d Feb 12, 1882, ae 67 (Clinton ME R); m (1) Ann Stinson of Clinton, ME, July 16, 1839 (Clinton ME R), d June 3, 1842 (tombstone); m (2) Ruth North of Clinton, ME, Oct 16, 1842, b 1812, d Clinton, ME, Feb 17, 1868 (Clinton ME R).

Children:
1714. Sewell 8, b about 1841, Clinton, ME
1715. Abner 8, b Amesbury, MA, about 1843; probably d Newbury, MA, Oct 4, 1886 (MA R)
1716. Benjamin Green 8, b Feb 16, 1845; d July 23, 1910 (Worcester MA R)
1717. Samuel 8, b Feb 19, 1864; d Feb 19, 1864 (tombstone, Clinton, ME)
1718. Hannah 8, b 1847

997. Jane Bagley 7, Greenleaf 6, Stephen 5, Abel 4, Joseph 3, Orlando 2, Orlando 1 ,probably died before 1873, as not mentioned as heir-at-law of Franklin Bagley, her uncle.

998. Dorothy Bagley 7, Greenleaf 6, Stephen 5, Abel 4, Joseph 3, Orlando 2, Orlando 1 , b Dec 7, 1816 (Family R); m Feb 2, 1840, Abner True, son Abner of Clinton, ME (Kennebunk, ME History; also source of children below).

Children:
1719. Franklin 8 [handwritten annotation]
1720. Abner 8 [handwritten annotation]
1721. Horace 8, d 1883 [handwritten annotation]
1722. Elvira 8 [handwritten annotation]
1723. Mary 8 [handwritten annotation]
1724. Lenora 8, m Moses Hodgdon, Danvers, MA, July 10, 1895, son Moses & Eliza (Daniels), b Rochester, NH

1725.   Bessie B. 8 *[handwritten: n Betsey]* *[handwritten: Sept 27 1856, m Sept 11 1868 William Gifford]*
1726.   Isadore 8, d 1864 *[handwritten: Aug 8 1858]*

999.   Stephen Hunt Bagley 7, Greenleaf 6, Stephen 5, Abel 4,
Joseph 3, Orlando 2, Orlando 1 , b Dec 10, 1818, Clinton, ME;
d Nov 11, 1867, ae 48 (MA R); m Elvira M. Merrill or Morrill,
Dec 5, 1847, dau Samuel & Susan (Greeley) True, b Salisbury,
MA, about 1817, d May 10, 1874 (MA R).   She was divorced
having m first Joseph Merrill or Morrill, Jr., Dec 29, 1833.
At the time of her m to Stephen Bagley, she is given as ae 29;
he ae 28. The Census of 1850 gives two of his father's
children: Asa and Eleanor, in his household.   There also is an
error in the age of Elvira. He was a stage coach driver.

Children:
1727.   Charles 8, b Feb 9, 1851; d Oct 9, 1852 (MA R)
1728.   Fred 8, b Oct 25, 1853; probably d before 1873 as not
listed as heir-at-law of Franklin Bagley

1000.   Mary J. Bagley 7, Greenleaf 6, Stephen 5, Abel 4,
Joseph 3, Orlando 2, Orlando 1 , b Feb 22, 1824 (Family R); m
Dec 25, 1851, Edmund Ward or Edward Ward.   Another source
gives d Feb 5, 1860, and marriage date Dec 19, 1857. We think
he died Feb 5, 1860 and she m (2) Hartley B. Libby of Baranka,
ME, since Hartley and Mary J. are given as heirs-at-law of
Franklin Bagley in 1873.

1001.   John F. Bagley 7, Greenleaf 6, Stephen 5, Abel 4,
Joseph 3, Orlando 2, Orlando 1 , b Feb 7, 1821, Clinton, ME; d
Somerville, MA, June 4, 1898, ae 77; m Mary Morrill, dau Isaac
& Mary (Pope), b Danville, VT, d Melrose, MA, May 3, 1908, ae
85 (MA R). He was a carpenter.

Children:
1729.   Mary 8, b about 1850, Clinton, ME; d Braintree, MA,
June 1, 1937, ae 87 (MA R)
1730.   Clara M. 8, b about 1853, Somerville, MA; d July 5,
1889, ae 44, a teacher (MA R)
1731.   Herbert D. 8, d Somerville, MA, Oct 15, 1873, ae 7 (MA
R)

1002.   Simeon O. Bagley 7, Greenleaf 6, Stephen 5, Abel 4,
Joseph 3, Orlando 2, Orlando 1 , b Aug 15, 1826 (Family R);
probably d before 1873 as not listed as heir-at-law of
Franklin Bagley.

1003.   Abigail A. Bagley 7, Greenleaf 6, Stephen 5, Abel 4,
Joseph 3, Orlando 2, Orlando 1 , b Aug 23, 1829 (Family R);
probably d before 1873 as not listed as heir-at-law of
Franklin Bagley.

1004.   Moses Bagley 7, Greenleaf 6, Stephen 5, Abel 4, Joseph
3, Orlando 2, Orlando 1 , b June 19, 1832, Clinton, ME; d June
11, 1908, ae 75, at Boston, MA (MA R). His wife's name was
Emily.

1005. Elenor Bagley 7, Greenleaf 6, Stephen 5, Abel 4, Joseph 3, Orlando 2, Orlando 1 , b Jan 17, 1835; m Jonathan Walton, Jr., Jan 22, 1866 (MA R); living 1873.

1006. Charles H. Bagley 7, Greenleaf 6, Stephen 5, Abel 4, Joseph 3, Orlando 2, Orlando 1 , b Apr 112, 1839, Clinton, ME; d Jan 11, 1873, ae 33, Charlestown, MA; an engineer.

1007. Asa Bagley 7, Greenleaf 6, Stephen 5, Abel 4, Joseph 3, Orlando 2, Orlando 1 , b about 1838 (Census of 1850); probably d before 1873 as not mentioned as heir-at-law of Franklin Bagley,

1016. Greenleaf Bagley 7, Frederick 6, Stephen 5, Abel 4, Joseph 3, Orlando 2, Orlando 1 , b Jan 24, 1822, Clinton, ME; d Parkman, ME, Nov 27, 1903 (ME R); m at Benton, ME, Dec 29, 1848, Henrietta Brown, dau Asa, Jr., & Lydia (Stinson), b Feb 13, 1828, Clinton, ME, d Dec 15, 1903, Pittsfield, ME. Mrs. Nellie Wakefield of Parkman, ME says of her grandfather and grandmother: "He was one of the great rivermen of his day and sent the last raft of logs over Clinton dam. He and a couple of brothers cleared the land and built log cabins in Clinton. In the winter the men went to Greenville, ME, to work in the big woods. They didn't come out till spring. They never took their families. Henrietta, his wife and my grandmother, were there alone with two children when two bears came up and were about to break into a small roughly-built shelter for a cow and a heifer. She carried out fire brands and coals, throwing them on the snow near the building. After a while, the bears went away. There was nothing but trees on their land. They cut, burnt, and planted where they could. They found a line of bees, my Granddad and my great uncle. In his sleep, Green got up and went barefooted right to the tree over the smutty ground and marked the tree. When Grandma woke up and saw the dirty bed, she was very unhappy. After breakfast, he and his brother went out and found the marked tree where he had cut a mark in his sleep."

For a time this family went to Eau Clair, WS to lumber. Greenleaf and his son George carried supplies by mule train to the logging camps. Two of his daus married in WS.

Children: (Family R except as noted)
1732. Martha 8, b 1851, Clinton, ME; d May 3, 1938
1733. Lydia 8, b Apr 20, 1852, Clinton, ME; d Jan 9, 1902
1734. Filone 8, b May 12, 1854, Clinton, ME; d Oct 15, 1896
1735. George Orrin 8, b Mar 25, 1856, Clinton, ME; d June 25, 1940
1736. Harlow 8, b Oct 28, 1859, Clinton, ME; d Jan 13, 1939 (ME R)
1737. Alphes 8, b Mar 5, 1863, Clinton, ME; d Jan 5, 1903, Augusta, ME; never m
1738. Arthur 8, b June 5, 1864, Clinton, ME; d Aug 24, 1933
1739. Alton 8, b 1866, Burnham, ME; d May 5, 1904 (ME R)
1740. Amanda 8, b Aug 15, 1869, Burnham, ME; d Oct 3, 1940 (ME R)

1017. Jonathan Bagley 7, Frederick 6, Stephen 5, Abel 4, Joseph 3, Orlando 2, Orlando 1 , b 1824, Clinton, ME; d there Sept 6, 1905, ae 81; Civil War veteran; m Dec 25, 1851, Benton, ME, Lovey Ethia Smiley. No record has been found of her death. There is a George E. Bagley, who d Jan 27, 1874, ae 14; buried Benton, ME, given on the records as son of Jonathan Bagley & Harriet Brown. A Harriet N. Bagley, wife Jonathan Bagley, d Jan 19, 1892, ae 64, given as dau Jeremiah and Nellie (Garland), b Benton; buried Burnham, ME. To add to this confusion, there is apparently another Jonathan Bagley who m Harriet Brown, dau Asa Brown, Jr., & Lydia (Stinson). Mrs. Wakefield thinks the boy George is their son. If may be we are talking about the same Jonathan and some mistake was made on vital records; however, nothing is proven except as above.

Children:
1741. Charles 8, b Jan 12, 1862, Benton, ME; d Thorndike, ME, June 20, 1929 (ME R)
1742. Nellie 8, b Jan 2, 1868
1743. Mary 8

1018. Lucy Ann Bagley 7, Frederick 6, Stephen 5, Abel 4, Joseph 3, Orlando 2, Orlando 1 , b Clinton, ME, 1828; m Oct 29, 1848, Andrew Brown, son Asa, Jr., & Lydia (Stinson), b 1831, d Dec 23, 1891 (ME 7 Family R).

Children: (Family R)
1744. Eli 8
1745. D. 8
1246. Susie 8
1747. Parker 8
1748. Arthur 8

1019. Alexander Bagley 7, Frederick 6, Stephen 5, Abel 4, Joseph 3, Orlando 2, Orlando 1 , b Aug, 1834, Clinton, ME; d July 19, 1908, Ripley, ME; m June 17, 1869, Ripley, ME, Mary Bunker, b Athens, ME, Oct 13, 1830, d Sept 13, 1908, dau Robert & Mary (Alexander), No children. Civil War veteran.

1020. Oliver Bagley 7, Frederick 6, Stephen 5, Abel 4, Joseph 3, Orlando 2, Orlando 1, b 1837, Clinton, ME; d Feb 5, 1865, Clinton, ME; m intentions Aug 13, 1860, Lettice Hunter. No children. Civil War veteran.

1021. Franklin Bagley 7, Frederick 6, Stephen 5, Abel 4, Joseph 3, Orlando 2, Orlando 1, b 1836, Clinton, ME; d June 25, 1908, Clinton, ME; m (1) Dec 11, 1856, Lydia Smiley; may have m (2) Mrs. Deborah Morrill of Benton, May 12, 1867, at Benton, ME (ME R). Civil War veteran.

1023. Jacob Currier Bagley 7, Oliver 6, Stephen 5, Abel 4, Joseph 3, Orlando 2, Orlando 1 , b Salisbury, MA, Jan 12, 1841; d there June 18, 1864; a shoemaker (MA R).

1031. John S. Bagley 8, Valentine 7, Benjamin 6, Seth 5,

Orlando 4, Orlando 3, Orlando 2, Orlando 1 , b 1853/54, probably at Seabrook, NH, altho no record there; d Jan 7, 1896, ae 44; a shoemaker and single (MA R).

1032. Valentine Bagley 8, Valentine 7, Benjamin 6, Seth 5, Orlando 4, Orlando 3, Orlando 2, Orlando 1 , b 1853/54, probably at Seabrook, NH, altho no record there; d Apr 21, 1926, Lynn, MA; m (1) Oct 29, 1873, Seabrook, Clemmie Eaton, dau Samuel, b 1855; m (2) Adeline J. Hyland, dau James & Mary (Campbell) of New Brunswick, d Feb 6, 1952, ae 89, Lynn, MA (MA R). His will, dated May 28, 1917; probated Sept 10, 1940, mentions wife, Adeline J; son, Leon; son Alfred; son Samuel; a dau of Leon's, Rena Estes Bagley, sometimes known as Rena Estes MacCauley.

Children:
1749. Evidell 9, b Nov 14, 1873; d Feb 19, 1888, ae 4 (Seabrook NH & MA R)
1750. Leon 9, b 1876 (Seabrook NH R); d Boston, May 30, 1939, ae 63 (MA R)
1751. Annugine 9, b Aug 11, 1878 (Seabrook NH R); d Salisbury, MA, May 7, 1890, ae 12 (MA R)
1752. Alfred C. 9, b Nov 14, 1879; d Feb 8, 1924 (Seabrook NH R & Newburyport MA R); buried Seabrook
1753. Samuel 9, b Jan 23, 1882; d Concord, NH State Hospital, Sept 3, 1949 (NH R)

1033. Morris H. Bagley 8, Valentine 7, Benjamin 6, Seth 5, Orlando 4, Orlando 3, Orlando 2, Orlando 1 , b Oct 19, 1857, Seabrook, NH; d Jan 19, 1909, ae 51; m E Salisbury, Aug 4, 1885, Mrs Effie A. Fowler (Salis MA R), b Gosport, NH, 1850, dau Robert & Huldah (Downs), d Aug 16, 1914, ae 64 (tombstone, Seabrook, NH). Fisherman.

Children:
1754. Frederick 9, b June 3, 1886; d Oct 25, 1890, ae 4 (Seabrook, NH tombstone & NH R which do not name this child)
1755. Lawrence 9, b Oct 11, 1892 (Seabrook , NH R); d Apr 10, 1940, Brentwood, NH (NH R)

1035. Charles H. Bagley 8, Valentine 7, Benjamin 6, Seth 4, Orlando 4, Orlando 3, Orlando 2, Orlando 1 , b about 1864 (ae 6, census of 1870).

1036. Lizzie Bagley 8, Valentine 7, Benjamin 6, Seth 5, Orlando 4, Orlando 3, Orlando 2, Orlando 1 , b Mar 31, 1866; m Nov 20, 1886, William H. Eaton of Seabrook, NH (NH R).

1039. Thomas W. Bagley 8, Thomas 7, Benjamin 6, Seth 5, Orlando 4, Orlando 3, Orlando 2, Orlando 1 , b Nov 18, 1847 (death record says b Nov 17, 1841); d Mar 21, 1921; m July 22, 1880, Kingston, NH, Maria C. Primrose, b 1856, Lawrence, MA, dau Edwin & Hannah, d Nov 5, 1895, ae 39; name given as Almira (Newton NH R). Will made Mar 8, 1921, mentions son, William E; dau Mildred (Rockingham Co NH Probate R). Son's death certificate gives parents as Thomas, b Salisbury, MA, and

Annie Lyons, b England.

Children:
1756.   William E. 9, b about 1881; d Charlestown, MA,   Dec 8,
1937; ae 56; buried Newton, NH (MA & NH R)
1757.   Mildred 9, b Aug 30, 1896 (Newton NH R) (Something is
wrong with the birthdate here unless Thomas had a second wife)

1040.   John H. Bagley 8, Thomas 7, Benjamin 6, Seth 5, Orlando
4, Orlando 3, Orlando 2, Orlando 1 , b about 1848; d
Woodstock, NH, 1904, ae 54 (NH R).

Child:
1758.   John L. 9, b Amesbury, MA, feb 9, 1873; d Standish, ME,
Mar 15, 1948 (ME R)

1041.   Sarah E. Bagley 8, Thomas 7, Benjamin 6, Seth 5,
Orlando 4, Orlando 3, Orlando 2, Orlando 1 , b Feb 19, 1853; d
Feb 10, 1874; m John Newsome (Family R).

1042.   James Bagley 8, Thomas 7, Benjamin 6, Seth 5, Orlando
4, Orlando 3, Orlando 2, Orlando 1 , b Saugus, MA, Nov 10,
1860; d Newton, NH, Aug 13, 1932, ae 71; buried Amesbury, MA
(Newton NH R); m Elseba E., dau Thomas & Esther Dort, b Philly
Harbor, Nova Scotia, Aug 17, 1861, d Newton, NH, Dec 22, 1923,
ae 62 (Newton NH R). Her will, dated Newton, Sept 29, 1923,
mentions a brother, James Dort; sister, Annie Davenport,
whereabouts unknown; and an adopted dau, Wilda S. Bagley,
never legally adopted, called niece (Rockingham Co NH Probate
R).

1044.   Frank Bagley 8, Thomas 7, Benjamin 6, Seth 5, Orlando
4, Orlando 3, Orlando 2, Orlando 1 , b 1853, Salisbury, MA; d
Mar 7, 1907, ae 53 (Ames MA R).

1047.   Charles Bagley 8, Thomas 7, Benjamin 6, Seth 4, Orlando
3, Orlando 2, Orlando 1 , b 1861, Salisbury, MA (MA R).

1057 Ira Atwood Bagley 8, Sargent 7, Sargent 6, Henry 5,
Henry 4, Orlando 3, Orlando 2, Orlando 1 , b Feb 6, 1813; d
May 28, 1880; m Cynthia H. Hill, dau Thomas of Colebrook, NH;
she probably m (2) Aaron Smith of Danville, VT, July 27, 1882
(VT R). Ira is supposed to have had six children.

Children: (St Johnsbury VT R except as noted)
1759.   Curtis Henry 9, Oct 28, 1844; d Lynn, MA, May 11, 1922
(MA R)
1760.   Leon G. 9, b July 2, 1855; d Apr 8, 1944, Rutland, VT
(VT R)
1761.   Kate Rose 9, b Mar 23, 1858
1762.   Mary B. 9, b Feb 26, 1862
1763.   Charles 9, b Apr 16, 1868; d May 6, 1935 (VT R)

1058.   Rebecca Challis Bagley 8, Sargent 7, Sargent 6, Henry
5, Henry 4, Orlando 3, Orlando 2, Orlando 1 , b Dec 13, 1810;
d Nov 29, 1857, St Johnsbury, VT; m Leonard Shorey, Oct 19,

1829, b Apr 19, 1804, St Johnsbury, VT; d there Nov 31, 1860, son Abel (VT R).

Children: (St Johnsbury VT R)
1764. Mary 9, b July 9, 1830
1765. Russell 9, b Oct 17, 1831; d 1858
1766. Moses 9, b July 18, 1832; m Jan, 1863, Charlotte Frost
1767. Malvina 9, b May 31, 1836; m July 13, 1863, Calvin Bowker
1768. Isabell 9, b Feb 3, 1829; d 1854

1059. Eliza Bagley 8, Sargent 7, Sargent 6, Henry 5, Henry 4, Orlando 3, Orlando 2, Orlando 1 , b Feb 20, 1816; d Sept 3, 1869; m Dec 5, 1829, Ephraim Brewster, b Oct 10, 1812, Woodstock, VT, son Dr Ephraim & Augusta (Crofts), d Craftsbury, VT, Sept, 1870.

Child:
1769. Ephraim 9, b Nov 10, 1842; d Annapolis, MD, Dec 5, 1864, Co F, 1st VT Cavalry, Civil War

1065. Maria Bagley 8, Winthrop 7, Orlando 6, Henry 5, Henry 4, Orlando 3, Orlando 2, Orlando 1 , Windsor, VT, Oct 27, 1811; d Mar 17, 1876, Westfield, NY; m Elisha Ticknor, 1836, at Westfield, NY, b Feb 3, 1802, Broome, NY, son Elias 5, Elisha 4, John 3, William 2, William 1, who originally settled in Scituate, MA. Elisha was one of the first settlers in Westfield, NY, and d there Oct 28, 1894.

Children:
1770. Della Maria 9, b Jan 20, 1832; d 1918; m July 3, 1851, Ira Edgar Hopkins, who d June 27, 1902, Ripley, NY; four children.
1771. Lydia Barton 9, b Mar 8, 1835; d unm, Westfield, NY
1772. Albert Gilbert 9, b Apr 13, 1838; m Jan 10, 1866, Westfield, NY, Phebe Rood Bowen, b July 9, 1841, Collins, NY, dau Jennings & Amy Dillingham (Wood), and had four childre: (1) Lillia Malvina, b Mar 27, 1867, who m George Arthur Boardman; (2) Frederick Emerson, b June 7, 1869, who Dec 17, 1890, Ripley, NY, Alice Belle Abbey and had four children including Hazel Marie, b Nov 30, 1927, Westfield, NY, who m at Erie PA, Wesley J. Gallup on Feb 4, 1956, son Arch C. & Esther (Carvey) of Independence, PA. Mrs. Gallup supplied much information on this line. Albert & Phebe had (3) Cora Alice, b Aug 4, d Sept, 1871, at Westfield, NY; and (4) Bertha Florence, b Apr 15, 1875, who m Henry Scott Abbey and had four children.
1773. Fannie Louise 9, b Apr 16, 1841; m Mar 16, 1870, Ripley, NY, Ansel Burdick Jones, b Sept 1, 1842, Westfield, NY; five children
1774. George Washington 9, b Jan 31, 1844; m (1) Jan 27, 1869, Helen S. Hills, who d Apr 27, 1871; m (2) May 28, 1876, Alice N. Northway. No children.
1775. Almira 9, b Jan 16, 1847; m Mar 16, 1870, at Ripley, NY, Charles Stephen Northway

1067. Henry W. Bagley 8, Jesse 7, Orlando 6, Henry 5, Henry 4, Orlando 3, Orlando 2, Orlando 1, b 1808, Brooklyn, PA; m before 1840, Brooklyn, Mary Skidmore, dau Joseph & Thirza (Noble). Weston says he moved to Hyde Park, PA (now a section of Scranton), b 1889.

1840 Census of Brooklyn, PA, gives Henry W, ae 30-40; wife, ae 20-30; son ae 0-5. Not on Census of 1850 for Brooklyn. Descendants of Thomas Noble of Westfield Mass., by Lucius Boltwood, 1878, p 653, says "Mary Skidmore, dau Thirza Noble and Joseph Skidmore m Henry Bagley and settled in New York City."

Child: (at least)
1776. Male 9, ae 0-5, Census of 1840, Brooklyn, PA

1068. Daniel Boone Bagley 8, Jesse 7, Orlando 6, Henry 5, Henry 4, Orlando 3, Orlando 2, Orlando 1, May 30, 1809, Brooklyn, PA; d Aug 29, 1843, Brooklyn; m Nov 3, 1831, Brooklyn, Sally Fish, dau Anthony & Hannah (Chipman), b Dec 4, 1806, Groton, CO, d Apr 24, 1888, Brooklyn; both buried Old Cemetery.

Weston says Daniel had a deed for land in 1831 and for 26 acres in 1833 (both in Brooklyn). Post office was kept in his house from 1838 to 1841 and from 1842 to 1861. D. B. Bagley was postmaster during this time until his death, and Mrs Bagley held the office the rest of the time. A carpenter, he and his Uncle Washington Bagley, had a lathe and chair factory for several years. Mrs Sally Bagley was a teacher and came with her father from Groton, Co, in 1841.

Sally Bagley, widow of Daniel B. Bagley, late of Brooklyn, petitioned Orphans Court, Apr 22, 1844, for guardians for her minor children: Charles V. and Levira Bagley, both under 14 yrs. Bond of $400 was posted for each and Asa Fish, their uncle, was appt guardian for both.

Daniel is listed in 1840 Census of Brooklyn: self and wife, each 30-40; son 5-10; dau 0-5. Sally (Fish) Bagley, widow is listed in 1850 Census for Brooklyn: Sally Bagley, ae 43, b CO, widow; Levira Bagley, ae 15, dau, b PA; Charles V. is not listed. Sally (Fish) Bagley, widow D. B. Bagley, is listed in 1860 Census of Brooklyn: Sally Bagley, ae 54; A. Chamberlain, ae 28, physician; Levira, wife, ae 24; Emma D., dau, ae 2.

Some of the material from Tuck, Miller, Kilmer, Bagley Families by Marion Miller Bagley and dau of Mary W. Bagley, and St Charles Biographical Directory and Census Report by J. F. Wilcox, and DAR records.

Children:
1777. Charles Vandenburg 9, b Mar 4, 1833, Brooklyn, PA; d Mar 10, 1898, Aurora, IL
1778. Levira 9, b Oct 27, 1836, Brooklyn, PA; d there Mar 4, 1905

1067. Alice Bagley 8, Jesse 7, Orlando 6, Henry 5, Henry 4, Orlando 3, Orlando 2, Orlando 1, b 1810, Brooklyn, PA; m there Samuel L. Kellam, son Elisha & Fannie (Bush). Weston says family moved to Carbondale, PA; not on 1850 Census for Brooklyn.

Children:
1779.   Hellen Josephine 9, b Feb 13, 1837; d Brooklyn, PA, Mar 8, 1837
1780.   Everett Manley 9, b Dec 3, 1838, Brooklyn, PA; d there Aug 26, 1939
1781.   William Osker 9, b July 15, 1847, Brooklyn, PA; d there Nov 10, 1849
1782.   Luther 9 (Weston)

1070.   Loren Lathrop Bagley 8, Jesse 7, Orlando 6, Henry 5, Henry 4, Orlando 3, Orlando 2, Orlando 1, b June 8, 1811, Brooklyn, PA; d Apr 14, 1872, Carbondale, PA; m Aug 6, 1834, Brooklyn, PA, Mary Emily Mack, dau Elisha & Taphena (Lord), b July 27, 1813, Brooklyn, PA, d Dec 31, 1890, Carbondale, PA.

     He is listed in 1840 Census for Brooklyn, PA; self and wife, each 20-30; two daus 0-5. 1850 Census gives Loren, ae 39; Mary Emily, ae 37; Mary R., ae 15; Viola M., ae 11; Elvira, ae 9; all b PA.

Children:
1783.   Mary Rosella 9, b Apr 6, 1836, Brooklyn, PA
1784.   Viola Melvina 9, b Dec 22, 1838, Brooklyn, PA
1785.   Isadore Phally 9, b Dec 22, 1838; twin to Viola; d Jan 5, 1839, ae 2 wks
1786.   Emily Elvira 9, b Feb 11, 1841, Brooklyn, PA
1787.   Emma Eliza 9, b June 20, 1850, Brooklyn, PA
1788.   Arthur Legrand 9, b Feb 26, 1852, Brooklyn, PA; d Mar, 1864, Carbondale, PA

1072.   Edward Paine Bagley 8, Jesse 7, Orlando 6, Henry 5, Henry 4, Orlando 3, Orlando 2, Orlando 1, b about 1816, Brooklyn, PA; m Elmira Barnes; Weston lists him as son of Jesse and as a Civil War soldier.

     Dr. Carey Comfort Worthing, a grandson of Barnard & Dorothy (Bagley) stated in 1888 that "Edward P. Bagley and I built the fires in Brooklyn schoolhouse in 1830 for the ashes. These were sold to the ashery and had money to buy our school books." (Weston)

     Enl papers in National Archives say he enl Camp Curtis, Nov 9, 1862, ae 44, and was mustered out Aug 7, 1863. Served in Draft militia, Co H, 177th regt. Neither he nor his wife applied for federal pension.

     On 1870 Census of Lanesboro, PA: Edward, ae 53, laborer, b PA; Elmira, wife, ae 53, housekeeper; Francina Quick, ae 29, dressmaker. Census of 1880 gives Edward, ae 63, teamster, b PA, father, b NH; mother, b RI; Elmira, wife, ae 63, b PA, father, b CO, mother, b PA. He is not listed at Lanesboro at time of 1850 or 1860 Census nor in Brooklyn. No adm or probate of his estate or that of his wife in Montrose, PA.

Child: (may have been others)
1789.   Daniel Boone 9, b Sept 12, 1844, Harford, PA; d Aug 29, 1909, Great Bend, PA; buried Binghampton, NY

1073. Horace Bagley 8, Jesse 7, Orlando 6, Henry 5, Henry 4, Orlando 3, Orlando 2, Orlando 1 , b Union Township, OH, about 1818; m Nov 4, 1841, Brooklyn, PA, Ann Adams, dau Walter & Anna (Ring). Weston says she was sister to Reuben French Ring. Their homestead in MA once owned by their grandfather, was sold to Daniel Webster and became part of the Marshfield, estate. For a time they lived in the old Andrew Tracy place in Brooklyn.

Not listed on 1840 or 1850 Census for Brooklyn. It appears that after the death of his mother, he moved to Carbondale and to Mauch Chunk, PA; and is not listed in Susquehanna County at all after 1845.

1076. Jesse Harrison Bagley 8, Jesse 7, Orlando 6, Henry 5, Henry 4, Orlando 3, Orlando 2, Orlando 1 , b about 1826, Brooklyn, PA; m Ann Weston, dau Samuel and his second wife, Eliza (Baker), dau Elisha. Born shortly after family came back from OH, in 1824/25 (Weston) and was living in Carbondale in 1889. Among list of unidentified soldiers who can not be placed in their companies or regiments in Civil War. Stocker lists J. J. Bagley. No pension file in Washington.

Not listed in 1840 or 1850 Census for Brooklyn, as head of family. Seems to have left Brooklyn after 1845 and may have spent the rest of his life in Carbondale, PA. Carbondale Census of 1880 gives Jesse H, ae 54; wife Ann E, ae 52, b PA; Grace W., dau, ae 7, b PA

Child: (may have been others)
1790. Grace W. 9, ae 7, Census of 1880

1077. William Albert Bagley 8, Jesse 7, Orlando 5, Henry 5, Henry 4, Orlando 3, Orlando 2, Orlando 1 , not listed on any census for Brooklyn, PA. Weston says he was a soldier from Elmira, NY, and was a prisoner at Salisbury. Enrollment papers not on file nor is any application for pension.

1079. John W. Bagley 8, Jesse 7, Orlando 6, Henry 5, Henry 4, Orlando 3, Orlando 2, Orlando 1 , b about 1832, Brooklyn, PA; d June 19, 1863, Fairfax Seminary, VA, during Civil War; buried Alexandria, VA; m Rebecca Jane Babcock, Mar 4, 1855, Jackson, PA, by Rev R. B. Lamb, at home of Albert Babcock. She b about 1834, d sometimes after Apr 10, 1920, Alton Place, Jamestown, NY; buried there. She m (2) Sept 18, 1878, George H. Stark at Montrose, by Rev Luther Peck; m (3) Jan 23, 1870, Thompson, PA, Silas A. Spencer, who d Feb 20, 1920, Jamestown, NY.

He served in Co B, 17the PA Cavalry, mustered in at Montrose, PA, Sept 15, 1862 (Stocker). Pension files further states he was mustered in at Harrisburg, PA, Sept 21, 1862, and d in hospital at Fairfax, VA, June 19, 1863.

His widow applied for pension, Oct 25, 1863, and gave address at N Jackson, Susquehanna Co, PA. She states her husband left three children: Horace D., ae 6; John L., ae 4, and Cassius M. C., ae 2. Pensions granted to widow and orphans but her pension terminated on Sept 4, 1867 when she remarried. Nov 9, 1868, she asked for pensions for her minor children in her capacity as their guardian. Apr 10, 1920, Rebecca J. Spencer asked that her pension on service of John W. Bagley be restored. Witnesses to her request were her sons John L. & Horace D. Bagley.

On Apr 23, 1868, Elery Washburn, a good friend, petitioned Oprhans Court in Montrose for guardians of minor children of John W. Bagley, late of the county, all under 14 yrs of age. Rebecca J. Stark, their mother, was appt and posted bonds in the amount of $200 in each case.

Children:
1791. Flora 9, d as infant
1792. Horace Dever 9, b Feb 26, 1857, Susquehanna Co, PA; d Aug 21, 1929, Jamestown, NY
1793. John Lincoln 9, b Feb 28, 1859; d 1923, Jamestown, NY
1794. Cassius M. 9, b July 6, 1861; supposed to have died as a child, killed by a train. However, Gerald Lewis Bagley thinks that while at the Civil War Orphans' Home with his two brothers, Cassius ran away and was never heard from.

1080. James Everett Bagley 8, Jesse 7, Orlando 6, Henry 5, Henry 4, Orlando 3, Orlando 2, Orlando 1 , b about 1836, Brooklyn, PA; killed in action near Poplar Grove Church, VA, Oct 2, 1864; buried Petersburg, VA, near where he fell; m Aug 12, 1858, in So Canaan, Wayne Co, PA, by Rev William M. Griffing, Caroline E. Monk of Carbondale, PA. he was probably named for the Rev Dr James Everett, a very prominent Presiding Elder of the Methodist Church who made numerous visits to the church at Brooklyn.

History of the 141st Regiment, Pennsylvania Volunteers, 1862-1865, by David Craft says "Company G, Corporal James E. Bagley, mustered in Aug 25, 1862, killed. James Bagley, a coporal of Company G and one of the color guard was killed, shot through the heart, and was buried by his comrades near where he fell, He was a moulder by trade and at his enlistment was in the employment of the Delaware and Hudson Canal Company at Honesdale. He left a wife who afterwards married J. R. Seagraves, also of Company G, and had two children, Bagley was about twenty-five years of age."

His widow applied for a pension and Rev Dr Ira Taylor Walker said in a sworn statement that he officiated at the marriage of John T. R. Seagraves and Mrs. Caroline E. Bagley in Wayne Co, PA, Jan 1, 1867. On Jan 17, 1865, Caroline A. Bagley in the Court of Wayne Co, PA, stated that "Nina Adelia Bagley is the only child born to her by the said James E. Bagley, now living."

On Nov 8, 1873, Honesdale, Wayne Co, PA, in Orphans Court, George E. Waller, was appt guardian of Nina A. Bagley, "minor child of James E. Bagley, late of Co G, 141st Regt, PA Vols, deceased; the mother of the said Nina A. Bagley is now living in Damascus Township and had intermarried with one John T. R. Seagraves."

Child:
1795. Nina Adelia 9, b Oct 17, 1861, Honesdale, PA

1081. Maria Bagley 8, Stephen 7, Orlando 6, Henry 5, Henry 4, Orlando 3, Orlando 2, Orlando 1 ,probably dau of Stephen above 14 yrs of age in 1826, when her Uncle Thomas was made her guardian. Since she is not on Census of 1850 with this family she had either died, married, or lived elsewhere.

On July 27, 1842, Rev Found m Spencer Evans and Miss Miram Bagley, both of Auburn, PA, at Auburn. Thomas and Abiah Bagley were witnesses. Family descendants give Miram's birthdate as Nov 23, 1823, and date of death as Jan 13, 1921. One of Miram's children was named Thomas and another, Sarah Abiah. Either Miram is not Maria, or there is something wrong with the information.

Children: (May have been others)
1796. Thomas 9
1797. Sarah Abiah 9

1083. Eliza Bagley 8, Thomas 7, Orlando 6, Henry 5, Henry 4, Orlando 3, Orlando 2, Orlando 1 b Mar 4, 1820, OH; m Hiram J. Baker, b 1820, d 1905, Towanda, PA.

Children:
1798. Miriam S. 9, b Oct 1, 1843; d June 28, 1914; m Sept 8, 1866, Thomas Adams
1799. Nancy A. 9, b Auburn, PA; d Sept 15, 1906; m Jan 2, 1866, Nathan Wells King
1880. Orlando 9, b Sept 11, 1849, Craig Hill, PA; d Mar 25, 1929; m Edith Kintner
1801. Ira 9, b Jan 1, 1852; d Aug 28, 1923; m Ida Kintner
1802. Hopi 9, d Nov 18, 1929; m Harry Lake
1803. Ruel A. 9, b Aug 26, 1855; d Apr 6, 1948; m Mar 30, 1860, Jennie Milligen
1804. Annie 9, b Oct 15, 1853; d June 30, 1931; m Charles B. Rosengrant
1805. Phoebe 9, d Mar 8, 1931; m Philander A. Wakefield
1806. Rosie 9, d Mar 14, 1941; m (1) Christopher Wakefield; m (2) Lemuel Rutan
1807. Samuel 9, b July 7, 1866, Auburn, PA; d Apr 13, 1952; m Mar 16, 1908, Falvia Loveless

1084. Miriam Ophelia Bagley 8, Thomas 7, Orlando 6, Henry 5, Henry 4, Orlando 3, Orlando 2, Orlando 1 , b Nov 23, 1823, Springville, PA; d Jan 13, 1921; m July 27, 1842, Spencer Evans, b Mauch Chunk, PA, Apr 15, 1821, d July 22, 1904.

Children:
1808. Sarah Abiah 9, b Dec 16, 1846; d June 24, 1911; m Oct 4, 1865, Francis M. Thompson
1809. Thomas Simeon 9, b Sept 22, 1848, Auburn, PA; d Mar 31, 1852
1810. Estella Louisa 9, b May 13, 1850, Auburn, PA; d Mar 4, 1852
1811. Amelia Ann 9, b Auburn Center, PA; d Jan 31, 1940; m Dec 30, 1880, Silas Jagger
1812. Julia Etta 9, b July 20, 1854; d Aug 19, 1856

158

1813.   Emma Eliza 9, b Aug 29, 1856, Vose, PA; d Aug 16, 1906; m Dec 25, 1880, William Ace

1814.   Clementine B. 9, b Dec 5, 1835, Dimock, PA; d Dec 17, 1958; m Sept 30, 1885, Amos Hollister

1815.   Miranda 9, b Dec 5, 1858, Dimock, PA; d Mar 16, 1892; m Charles E. Jagger, Jan 24, 1880

1816.   Harriet N. 9, b Jan 4, 1881, Auburn, PA; d June 13, 1907; m July 18, 1878, Willis E. Bullock

1817.   William Livingston, b Jan 9, 1863, Auburn, PA; d Jan 25, 1954; m Dec 15, 1889, Effie Whited

1818.   Clara Minnie 9, b May, 1869, Auburn, PA; d Nov 8, 1901; m Feb 6, 1888, Danford Wakefield

1085.   James Henry Bagley 8, Thomas 7, Orlando 6, Henry 5, Henry 4, Orlando 3, Orlando 2, Orlando 1 , b Jan 20, 1826, Springville, PA; d July 29, 1917, Meshoppen, PA; m (1) Emeline Saunders, dau Benjamin & Dorothy (Bagley), and hence his first cousin; they were divorced Nov 20, 1867; he m (2) Phebe A. Manning, b May 5, 1816, d Jan 9, 1880; he m (3) Eliza (Saunders) Lyman, b June 6, 1816, d Apr 16, 1907, the widow of Landers Lyman. Weston says she was a cousin of Emeline Saunders Bagley.

Children: (Lane Genealogy & Garrison) (All by Emeline Saunders except Dora who was dau Phebe)
1819.   Charles Lyman 9, b Mar 13, 1849; d Aug 23, 1933
1820.   Mary E. 9, b June 4, 1851; d Dec 29, 1876
1821.   Sarah Elizabeth 9, b Sept 11, 1853, Washington, PA; d Mar 8, 1924
1822.   Lydia Frances 9, b Oct 30, 1855, Washington, PA; d Oct 30, 1860
1823.   Harriet L. 9, b July 14, 1857, Washington, PA; d May 1, 1887
1824.   Thomas Sheffield 9, b Sept 1, 1860, Washington, PA; d Sept 17, 1946
1825.   Dora 9, b July 14, 1872; d July 13, 1925

1086.   Hannah Mary Bagley 8, Thomas 7, Orlando 6, Henry 5, Henry 4, Orlando 3, Orlando 2, Orlando 1 , b Dec 11, 1828, Springville, PA; d Sept 11, 1897; m John Rowe, b 1816/1817, who lived at Russell Hill, PA.

Children:
1826.   William Edgar 9, b 1850; d May 27, 1708; m Emma A. Lee
1827.   Mary Eliza 9, b Aug 1, 1853, Washington, PA; d Dec 14, 1916; m (1) Henrick Gay; m (2) Elias Felker
1828.   Thomas Henry 9, b Aug 28, 1856; d Mar 8, 1935; m Marian Ellen Lowe
1829.   James Olin 9, b Mar 1, 1861, Meshoppen, PA; d Jan 7, 1924; m Mary Martin

1087.   Sarah Martha Bagley 8, Thomas 7, Orlando 6, Henry 5, Henry 4, Orlando 3, Orlando 2, Orlando 1 , b June 17, 1830, Springville, PA; d Apr 21, 1902, Sepo, IL; m Feb, 1849, at Tunkhannock, PA, Thomas S. Hadsell, who d 1885.

Children: (Supposed to have had 11 children; five died in infancy)
1830. Hannah 9; m _____Slater
1831. Lois 9; m _____Sigley
1832. Emma 9; m _____Slater
1833. Emily 9
1834. George 9
1835. Fannie 9; d ae 15
1836. John W. 9

1088. Juliette Etta Bagley 8, Thomas 7, Orlando 6, Henry 5, Henry 4, Orlando 3, Orlando 2, Orlando 1   b Nov 23, 1832, Springville, PA; d July 9, 1878; m Theophilis Prevost, b Dec 17, 1824, d Nov 6, 1883.

Children:
1837. Adelaide 9, d Apr 16, 1902; m John E. Siegfred
1838. John 9, d June 12, 1914; m Hattie Treeble
1839. Lewis 9
1840. Fred 9, d May 30, 1916; m Mary Nuttenburg; lived El Centro, CA
1841. Sarah 9; m George Appleman
1842. George H. 9, b Sept 20, 1875; d Apr 7, 1876
1843. Minnie 9, d July 9, 1941, High Grove, CA; m Wilbur J. Cogswell, 1905

1089. Roxiena Bagley 8, Thomas 7, Orlando 6, Henry 5, Henry 4, Orlando 3, Orlando 2, Orlando 1, b Jan, 1838, Springville, PA; d July 12, 1920, Danville, PA; m Lewis Carney, b Jan 18, 1838.

Children:
1844. Ella 9
1845. Bertha 9; d ae 3

1101. Amy F. Bagley 8, Charles G. 7, Orlando 6, Henry 5, Henry 4, Orlando 3, Orlando 2, Orlando 1, b about 1827; m Joshua Jackson; lived Springville, PA.

Child: (May have been others)
1846. Burr 9 (Census of 1850)

1102. Orlando Bagley 8, Charles G. 7, Orlando 6, Henry 5, Henry 4, Orlando 3, Orlando 2, Orlando 1, b about 1829.

1107. Clark Bagley 8, Charles G. 7, Orlando 6, Henry 5, Henry 4, Orlando 3, Orlando 2, Orlando 1, b about 1846.

1108. George W. Bagley 8, Charles G. 7, Orlando 6, Henry 5, Henry 4, Orlando 3, Orlando 2, Orlando 1, b May 1, 1850.

1109. Sarah Roxena Bagley 8, Washington 7, Orlando 6, Henry 5, Henry 4, Orlando 3, Orlando 2, Orlando 1, b Apr 2, 1836, Brooklyn, PA; d Jan 19, 1891, Dimock, PA; buried Dimock; m about 1865, James W. Gavett, son Libbeus & Mary Squier), b Oct 30, 1842, Dimock, PA, d there Apr 29, 1925. Civil War soldier;

enl Aug 29, 1864, Co B, 2nd Regt, PA Vols; discharged June 23, 1865, Salisbury, NC.

Children:
1847. Judson H. 9, b Apr 5, 1866, Dimock, PA; d 1936, Springville, PA; m Mar 3, 1887, Savanna C. Shoemaker, 1866-1948. No children. Spent lives on farm near Springville, PA.
1848. Minnie E. 9, b Apr 27, 1869, Dimock, PA; m Sept 23, 1893, Lloyd Edward Squier, b Oct 18, 1868, son Sylvenius King Squier & Mary Ann (Harrington). Moved to VA with a large family and d there.
1848A. Lydia Mary 9, b July 29, 1875, Dimock, PA; d there Feb 15, 1956; m Jan 1, 1895, Amherst Henry Button, b Aug 15, 1867, d Dimock, PA, Oct 26, 1945, son Elhanon & Betsey M. (Lindsay); three children

1110. Ann Eliza Bagley 8, Washington 7, Orlando 6, Henry 5, Henry 4, Orlando 3, Orlando 2, Orlando 1 , unm in 1860. Soon after the death of her father, she went to Springville Township at Lynn to live with her Uncle Amos Williams. He d in 1865, and she may have lived with his widow. No other record. No tombstone with family.

1073. Mary A. Bagley 8, Washington 7, Orlando 6, Henry 5, Henry 4, Orlando 3, Orlando 2, Orlando 1, b May 24, 1848, Brooklyn, PA; d Nov 27, 1915, Kingston, PA; m June 29, 1872, Binghampton, NY, by Rev Lyman Wright, Charles M. Brewster, son Erastus & Submit, b June 20, 1842, Harford, PA, d Feb 1, 1905, Hop Bottom, PA; buried Evergreen Cemetery, Brooklyn, PA. His second wife.

He was a soldier in Civil War, Co A, 107the Regt, PA Vols, from Mar 1, 1862; discharged Dec 24, 1862, with loss of an eye (National Archives).

Child:
1849. William P. 9, b June 23, 1877, Brooklyn, PA; d Aug 29, 1962, Kingston, PA; unm; buried with his parents in Evergreen Cemetery, Brooklyn, PA. Attorney and member of Luzerne Co Bar Assoc; admitted June 14, 1900. An eminent historian, he was author of History of the Certified Township, Kingston, PA, 1769-1929; A Short Account of the Fourteenth Commonweath; The Pennsylvania and New York Frontier; History of from 1720 to the Close of the American Revolution; The Origin and Influence of the Pilgrims; The Beginning of the Anthracite Coal Industry. "The Connecticut Claim", an Address delivered by him in 1939 before the Wyoming Monument on the anniversary of the Wyoming Massacre was so well received it was put into a booklet form. He did considerable work in tracing some of the descendants of Orlando Bagley, but this work was lost in the Wilkes-Barre flood.

He was a generous benefactor of the Hoyt Memorial Library in Kingston, PA, and a large wing was added to the library in his memory - the Brewster Room was to house his personal papers. The big flood in the Wyoming Valley in 1972 destroyed

161

the papers.

1115. Frederick Bagley 8, Jonathan 7, Thomas 7, Henry 5, Henry 4, Orlando 3, Orlando 2, Orlando 1 , b Apr 12, 1813, Hartland, VT; m Lucinda Crosby, Dec 21, 1838 (Hartland VT R), who d Oct 17, 1860, ae 46 (Hartland VT R). Her tombstone on the same lot with Asabel Bagley at Jenneysville, says Oct 27, 1860, ae 48.

Children:
1850. Frederick Rush 9, b Oct, 1841; d Apr 14, 1937, ae 95, unm (Hartland VT R)
1851. Ella 9, b Dec 7, 1853; d Mar 14, 1934, ae 80 (Hartland VT R)
1852. Lydia 9, b about 1845
1853. Joanne 9, b about 1849
1854. Marion 9, b about 1853

1116. Clarissa Bagley 8, Jonathan 7, Thomas 6, Henry 5, Henry 4, Orlando 3, Orlando 2, Orlando 1 , b Sept 1, 1814; m Erastus Symes, Jan 4, 1842 (VT R).

1117. Aaron Bagley 8, Jonathan 7, Thomas 6, Henry 5, Henry 4, Orlando 3, Orlando 2, Orlando 1 , b Nov 2, 1815; d Apr 13, 1898, ae 82; m Eliza Robinson, May 8, 1848 VT R), dau Luther & Polly (Moore), b Bridgewater, VT, Nov 23, 1824 (Family R), d Ocr 19, 1892, ae 67. Their tombstones at Granville, VT, read "father is resting", and "Mother is resting."

Children:
1855. Cyrene Rodney 9, b Apr 22,1847; d Feb 10, 1921 (tombston (Granville, VT)
1856. Henri Clinton 9,. b June 11, 1850 (Family R)

1118. George Dwight Bagley 8, Jonathan 7, Thomas 6, Henry 5, Henry 4, Orlando 3, Orlando 2, Orlando 1 , b Apr 15, 1817; d Apr 2, 1852, ae 35; m Oct 4, 1841, Adeline Rogers (VT R), b about 1816, dau William & Chloe (Peabody), d Nov 3, 1863, ae 47.

Children:
1857. Chloe Ann 9, b about 1842; d Nov 15, 1854, ae 12 (tombstone, Hartland, VT)
1858. Miranda 9, b about 1845; d Mar 19, 1847, ae 2 (tombstone, Hartland, VT)
1859. Rozina 9, b about 1846; d July 7, 1847, ae 2 (tombstone, Hartland, VT)
1860. Dwight 9, b Sept 25, 1847; d June 23, 1904 (VT R)
1861. Cornelius 9, b June 8, 1848 (VT R); d June 4, 1912 (tombstone, Lebanon, NH, but Lebanon R give b 1846)

1120. Emeline Bagley 8, Jonathan 7, Thomas 6, Henry 5, Henry 4, Orlando 3, Orlando 2, Orlando 1 , b Dec 5, 1819; d July 6, 1862 of consumption; m Henry Huntley, b Windsor, VT, 1829, son Amos (VT R).

Children:
1862.   Sarah 9, b Oct 7, 1856; d Nov 1, 1857 (Hartland VT R)
1863.   Kate 9, b W Windsor, VT, Aug 15, 1858; m Mar 20, 1909,
Owen W. Waldo (Descendants of Aaron Huntley of MA)

1121.   Lucy Ann Bagley 8, Jonathan 7, Thomas 6, Henry 5, Henry
4, Orlando 3, Orlando 2, Orlando 1 , b July 16, 1820; m Sept
21, 1840, Sumner B. Small (Hartland VT R), b about 1820.

Children: (Census of 1860)
1864.   Alice A. 9, b about 1845
1865.   Herbert 9, b about 1846
1866.   Clement 9, b about 1848
1867.   Walter 9, b about 1851
1868.   George 9, b about 1853
1869.   Lucy 9, b Hartland, VT, Feb 28, 1855; m June 20, 1876,
Horson R. Perry, son Achad, b Hancock, VT, Jan 22, 1842 (VT R)
1870.   Edwin 9, b about 1859

1122.   Alonzo Bagley 8, Jonathan 7, Thomas 6, Henry 5, Henry
4, Orlando 3, Orlando 2, Orlando 1 , b Dec 26, 1823.

1123.   Simeon Bagley 8, Jonathan 7, Thomas 6, Henry 5, Henry
4, Orlando 3 Orlando 2, Orlando 1 , b Aug 14, 1829; d Sept 30,
1856.

1124.   Lucia Bagley 8, Jonathan 7, Thomas 6, Henry 5, Henry 4,
Orlando 3, Orlando 2, Orlando 1 , b Mar 4, 1827; d 1898; m Apr
23, 1848, Robert E. French (Hartland VT R), b 1824, d 1899
(tombstone, Hartland, VT)

Children: (tombstones, Hartland, VT except as noted)
1871.   Wallace A. 9, b 1854; d ~~1860~~ 1857
1872.   Dora A. 9, b 1861; d 1865
1873.   John M. 9, b 1864; d 1870
1874.   Clara A. 9, m ____ Dole of Brownsville, VT (Family R)
1875.   Ella A. 9, m _____ Martin of Hartland, VT (Family R) she b 1850 d 192
1876.   Robert E., Jr. 9, (Family R) d 1919   he b 1842 d 1916
1877.   Richard S. 9 (Family R) d 1898

1125.   Laura Bagley 8, Jonathan 7, Thomas 6, Henry 5, Henry 4,
Orlando 3, Orlando 2, Orlando 1 , b Mar 14, 1827; d Jan 6,
1904; m "Old" Charles French, Feb 5, 1849 (Hartland VT R), b
Apr 21, 1821, d Mar 13, 1897 (tombstone, Hartland, VT).

Children: (Census of 1860)
1878.   Carlos 9, b about 1850
1879.   Eva 9, b about 1853
1880.   Charles 9, b about 1855
1881.   George 9, b about 1857
1882.   Minnie 9, b about 1859
1883.   Female infant 9, b about 1860

1126.   Charlotte Bagley 8, Jonathan 7, Thomas 6, Henry 5,
Henry 4, Orlando 3, Orlando 2, Orlando 1 , b Nov 14, 1833; d

Mar 22, 1897, ae 64; m (1) Lucian Cabot, Jan 27, 1850, b May 22, 1827 (Hartland VT R); m (2) Charles O. Alexander, d Mar 18, 1912, ae 74. He was a Civil War soldier, Co H, 16th VT Vols (tombstone, Hartland, VT).

Children:
1884. Willie Cabot 9, b Feb 10, 1854
1885. Clarence Cabot 9, b Oct 28, 1855
1886. Aris Cabot 9, b Oct 28, 1855; d Dec 6, 1863 (tombstone, Hartland, VT)
1887. John Alexander 9 (Census of 1870 gives ae 14)
1888. Clarence L. Alexander 9 (Census of 1870 gives ae 4; tombstone says he d Oct 28, 1892, ae 28)
1889. Arthur A. Alexander 9 (Census of 1870 gives ae 2)

1127. Ellen Bagley 8, Jonathan 7, Thomas 6, Henry 5, Henry 4, Orlando 3, Orlando 2, Orlando 1 , b May 4, 1836; d Jan 9, 1918, ae 82; m Charles W. Whitaker, Mar 10, 1863 (Hartland VT R), b 1841; d Sept 16, 1880, ae 39 (tombstone, Hartland, VT).

Children:
1890. Fred 9; m Sarah; no children
1891. Harry 9, b 1867; d 1929; m Ellen Cullinan, b 1864; d 1932. 4 children: (1) Harry, d y; (2) Charles, b 1888; d 1942; m Anastasia, d 1926; 6 children; (a) Arthur, b 1909; m Emma; no children, (b) Warren, b 1911; m (1) Arthelia; m (2) Margaret; m (3) Irene; no children; (c) Francis, b 1912; m Gladys Ferrier; (d) Thomas, b 1916; m Lucy; (e) Charles, b 1918; d 1944; m Norma Best; (f) James, b 1921; m Margaret. (2) Walter E. b 1895; d 1946; m Aileen Hayes & had Aileen, b 1920, m Thomas Williams, b 1916, & had six girls: (a) Eileen Williams, b 1945; m Gary St Hill & had Scott St Hill, b 1969 & Kathryn St Hill, b 1972; (b) Eleanor Williams, b 1948; (c) Barbara Williams, b 1950; (d) Linda Williams, b 1953; m Ernest Shepard, Jr., & had Ernest Shepard III, 1972; (e) Joanne Williams, b 1955; & (f) Nancy Williams, b 1959. (3) Harold, b 1898; d 1959; m Louise Fahy, b 1899, & had 3 children; Francis, Mary Louise & Harold, who m Dorothy.
1891A. Otto 9, b 1871; d 1947; had a son William; & and a dau Grace, b 1875, who m Daniel O'Connell.

1128. Sanford Boutwell Bagley 8, Jonathan 7, Thomas 6, Henry 5, Henry 4, Orlando 3, Orlando 2, Orlando 1 , b Apr 11, 1841; d July 20, 1923, Brookfield, VT; m Emily A. Furber, Sept 28, 1868 (Hartland VT R), dau B. & Lois, b 1848, d 1919 (tombstone, Hartland, VT). Emily Furber wrote a long poem called "A Story by Father Bagley's Old Clock" which describes the family of Jonathan & Lydia Bagley. The old clock was in the possession of Otto Whitaker, son Charles & Ellen (Bagley) until 1934, when it was sold during the depression and not recovered by the family.

Child:
1892. Mabel Emily 9, b July 18, 1869 (Hartland VT R); d 1944 (tombstone, Hartland, VT)

1129. Julia Bagley 8, Jonathan 7, Thomas 6, Henry 5, Henry 4, Orlando 3, Orlando 2, Orlando 1 , b Apr 25, 1831; d Feb 15, 1853, ae 22, Hyde Park, VT; m Jasper Strong, b 1829, son Allen & Mary (Hart).

Child:
1893. Julia A. 9, b 1853, N Hartland, VT

1130. Nancy Ann Bagley 8, Thomas 7, Thomas 6, Henry 5, Henry 4, Orlando 3, Orlando 2, Orlando 1 , b Hartland, VT, Feb 24, 1818; d June 15, 1903, ae 85, Pasadena, CA; m Dec 3, 1841, James Madison Bridge, b Oct 31, 1816, Woodstock, VT, d Scranton, IA, Feb 20, 1879, only child of farm parents. Moved to IL in 1856; lived there until 1868 when they went to village of Sycamore and later to western Iowa (John Bridge Family in America by Rev Wm Bridge).

Children:
1894. Edward 9, b June 30, 1843; d Jan 10, 1864, Larkinsville, AL; sargeant in Co B, 55th Regt, IL Vols; wounded in his first battle at Shiloh; was in subsequent battles unharmed and died of sickness, b Windsor, VT
1895. Norman 9, b Dec 30, 1844; d Los Angeles, CA
1896. Susan Marcia 9, b Oct 15, 1851, Windsor, VT

1131. Emily Sophia Bagley 8, Thomas 7, Thomas 6, Henry 5, Henry 4, Orlando 3, Orlando 2, Orlando 1 , b Hartland, VT, July 10, 1819; d Oct 2, 1854; m Mar 10, 1842, Bezeleel Bridge (his second wife), b Mar 31, 1809, W Windsor, VT, d Nov 5, 1863, son Bezeleel & Hannah (Proctor) (John Bridge Family in Amnerica) .

Children:
1897. George Colimer 9, b W Windsor, VT Mar 17, 1843; d there Mar 7, 1906
1898. Henry Clay 9, b May 20, 1844; d July 31, 1847
1899. Susan Mansfield 9, b Sept 17, 1846; d July 22, 1847
1900. Charlotte Abi 9, b Sept 17, 1846, W Windsor, VT
1901. Frank Bezeleel 9, b Nov 29, 1850; d Jan 24, 1851
1902. Edwin Bagley 9, b June 6, 1852; d Oct 5, 1878

1132. Charlotte Bagley 8, Thomas 7, Thomas 6, Henry 5, Henry 4, Orlando 3, Orlando 2, Orlando 1 , b Feb 1, 1821; d 1854; m Alvin Spaulding in 1844.

1133. Lois Maria Bagley 8, Thomas 7, Thomas 6, Henry 5, Henry 4, orlando 3, Orlando 2, Orlando 1 , b Hartland, VT, Mar 7, 1823; d Oct 15, 1863; m Sept 13, 1842, Woodstock, VT, Sylvester Barnard Bridge, b Mar 1, 1815, d Dec 5, 1854, son Bezeleel & Hannah (Proctor), his second wife (John Bridge Family in America).

Children:
1903. Emeroy Maria 9, b W Windsor, VT, Aug 8, 1844; d there, Feb 19, 1871
1904. Ada Louise 9, b W Windsor, VT, Mar 9, 1847

1905. Ella Marcia 9, b W Windsor, VT, July 6, 1849
1906. Frank Parker 9, b Sycamore, IL, June 5, 1854; d Apr 22, 1875 Chicago

1134. Mary Bagley 8, Thomas 7, Thomas 6, Henry 5, Henry 4, Orlando 3, Orlando 2, Orlando 1, b Oct 9, 1824; d 1897; m Henry A. Billings, 1847.

1137. Marcia Bagley 8, Thomas 7, Thomas 6, Henry 5, Henry 4, Orlando 3, Orlando 2, Orlando 1, b Oct 16, 1828; d Mar 29, 1911; m Dracut, MA, where she worked in a mill, Feb 27, 1851, William Mansfield, b Dec 23, 1827, Lynn, MA, son William & Catherine. Moved to WS; settled Johnson's Creek. She fell and broke her hip and died from the injury. Her husband went to live with their dau, Marcia Mansfield Walters in Casselton, ND, until his death. Above sent to George Dwight Bagley of S Woodstock, VT, by Dallas Mansfield Walters in 1940; most of it taken from New England R in Los Angeles, CA.

Children:
1907. Frank Edwin 9, b Dec 30, 1851, Dracut, MA; d Apr 20, 1940, Havare, Mont.; m Mary Jane McDonald, Feb 21, 1876
1908. William Ernest 9, b May 9, 1853, Franklin, NH; d Minot, ND, Feb 2, 1922; m Mary E. Voight, Feb 29, 1883, Jefferson, WS
1909. Otto Adelbert 9, b Nov 21, 1854, Dracut, MA; d Jan 1, 1855
1910. Emily Edna 9, b Feb 3, 1859, Dracut, MA; d Aug 2, 1860
1911. Marcia Jeanette 9, b Aug 22, 1863, Johnson's Creek, WS; m Hugo H. Walters, Feb 8, 1882, Casselton, ND

1138. John Parker Bagley 8, Thomas 7, Thomas 6, Henry 5, Henry 4, Orlando 3, Orlando 2, Orlando 1, b Feb 24, 1836; d Apr 16, 1862, Pittsburgh Landing in Civil War; m Mary Ann Furber, Jan 1, 1858 (Hartland VT R), dau James & B. She m (2) Henry Jefferson Bagley, son Jefferson & Fidelia (Gallup), Mar 20, 1864, b Sept 13, 1837, d June 3, 1887 (tombstone, Hartland, VT).

1139. Edwin E. Bagley 8, Thomas 7, Thomas 6, Henry 5, Henry 4, Orlando 3, Orlando 2, Orlando 1, b Feb 25, 1831; d Mar 25, 1907; m Lucinda Colston, dau Charles & Lucy (Brown), Jan 31, 1859 (Hartland VT R), b Apr 10, 1832, d Nov 22, 1894 (Hartland VT R). At the time of m lived in Etna, IL. Returned to Hartland, VT, about 1861 as second child was b there. Commander of militia company before Civil War. Census of 1870 gives him as of Tinmouth, VT, ae 39; Lucinda, ae 38; son Edwin E., ae 8.

Children:
1912. Thomas 9, b Oct 9, 1859, Etna, IL; d Oct 25, 1864 (tombstone, Hartland, VT)
1913. Edwin E. 9, b Nov 24, 1861 (VT R); d 1925 (tombstone, Hartland, VT)
1914. John P. 9, b Hartland, VT, Apr 23, 1871 (VT R)

1140. Mary Bagley 8, Daniel 7, Thomas 6, Henry 5, Henry 4,

Orlando 3, Orlando 2, Orlando 1 , b 1824, Warren, VT; d Jan 28, 1887, ae 63, Lincoln, VT (VT R); m Benjamin Hanks, son Calvin, b Randolph, VT, May 5, 1802, d Lincoln, VT, Oct 7, 1867 (VT R).

1141. George Bagley 8, Daniel 7, Thomas 6, Henry 5, Henry 4, Orlando 3, Orlando 2, Orlando 1 , b about 1831; d Lincoln, VT, Jan 24, 1896, ae 65; m Betsey (given on death certificate of children), probably dau Jacob & Betsey Gifford. However, her death certificate gives her as Betsey Hanks, d Nov 11, 1876, Lincoln, VT, m, b Randolph, VT, dau Jacob & Betsey Gifford. The wife of George is supposed to have m Simon Gould of Lincoln, VT, Mar 12, 1898 (VT R). George was a lumberman.

Children:
1915. Fred S. 9, b Oct 9, 1858; d Hudson, NH, Aug 27, 1923 (NH R)
1916. Almer 9, b May 24, 1870, Lincoln, VT; d there Mar 21, 1949 (VT R)
1917. Augusta Sophia 9, b Dec 18, 1855, Lincoln, VT; d there Oct 28, 1929 (VT R)
1918. Parker W. 9, d Lincoln, VT, May 15, 1892, ae 28, a musician (VT R)
1919. Minnie Carrie 9, b Apr 13, 1875, Lincoln, VT; d there Nov 1, 1894 (VT R)

1142. Silas W. Bagley 8, Daniel 7, Thomas 6, Henry 5, Henry 4, Orlando 3, Orlando 2, Orlando 1 , b about 1837, Dummerstown, VT; d Lincoln, VT, June 9, 1899 (VT R); m Laura Pendall or Randall, Northfield, VT, Mar 13, 1861; lumberman.

1143. Walter A. Bagley 8, Daniel 7, Thomas 6, Henry 5, Henry 4, Orlando 3, Orlando 2, Orlando 1 , b Hartland, VT; d Warren, VT, Apr 10, 1905, ae 85 (tombstone, Warren, VT); m (1) Louise E. Young, dau Achael & Priscilla (Hetson), Warren, Aug 27, 1843, who is supposed to have died in child birth, May 7, 1870, ae 43; m (2) Emily Richardson of Warren, VT, July 8, 1874, b Sept 13, 1834, d Nov 3, 1909 (tombstone, Warren, VT & VT R). Another record says Louisa Emily Young, d Nov 3, 1903, ae 69, but this does not seem right. Manuf of clapboards.

Children:
1920. Sarah Louise 9, b Warren, VT, 1844; d Mar 25, 1915 (VT R)
1921. Walter, Jr., 9, d Mar 9, 1851, ae 4, (Warren, VT tombstone)
1922. Milford E. 9, b Apr 14, 1853, Warren, VT; d Nov 5, 1935 (VT R)
1923. Elizabeth 9, b about 1856 (Census of 1870 gives as 14)
1924. Ada 9, b Sept 3, 1858 (VT R)
1925. Louisa 9, b Mar, 1862
1926. Myra J. 9, b July 5, 1863
1927. Clara 9, b Sept 26, 1867 (VT R)
1928. Enoch 9, b about 1869 (Census of 1870 gives ae 11 mos)
1929. Male stillborn 9, b May 7, 1870 (VT R)

1147.   Roderick Bagley 8, Perkins 7, Thomas 6, Henry 5, Henry
4, Orlando 3, Orlando 2, Orlando 1 , b about 1831; d Saginaw,
MI, Nov 14, 1890; m Aug 21, 1854, Cavendish, VT, Frances
Shields, d Haverhill, MA, July 9, 1907, ae 71, dau John &
Lucinda (Davis). Veteran of Co F, 3rd VT Inf during Civil
War. Captured at Charlottesville; wounded at Fredericksburg;
deserted Mar 22, 1864 (Pension Rolls).

Children:
1930.   Lucian H. 9, b Hartland, VT, 1856; d Haverhill, MA, May
16, 1939, ae 83 (MA R)
1931   Willie C. 9, b Aug 11, 1859; d Oct 29, 1864 (Hartland VT
R)
1932.   Florence S. 9, b Dec 23, 1861; d Sept 15, 1865 (Family
R)
1933.   Walter 9, b May 4, 1865
1934.   Lulu 9, b May 4, 1865; d Sept 4, 1865
1935.   William 9, b 1866; d Jan 12, 1899, ae 53 (Haverhill MA
R)

1150.   Olive Bagley 8, Perkins 7, Thomas 6, Henry 5, Henry 4,
Orlando 3, Orlando 2, Orlando 1 , b about 1836; d Aug 19,
1856; m Andrew Jackson Walker, son Asa; Civil War veteran, Co
A, 1st VT Cavalry. He d July 14, 1877, ae 45.

Child:
1936.   Diana S. 9, b 1856; d Aug 27, 1857 (Family R)

1151.   William Washington Bagley 8, Perkins 7, Thomas 6, Henry
5, Henry 4, Orlando 3, Orlando 2, Orlando 1 , b Aug 3, 1838; d
Mar 11, 1926 (Claremont NH R); m Aug 31, 1862, Caroline Walker
(VT R), dau Asa & Chloe (Bartlett), and sister to Zina and
Andrew Walker, b Dec 2, 1842, d Sept 14, 1891, ae 49 (Hartland
VT R). Civil War veteran, Co B, 12th VT Vols and served nine
months. Lived Fieldsville, VT. Pension papers, dated July
18, 1898 , depose that he had no children,was not married, and
was not previously married.

Child:
1937.   Male 9, b Nov 30, 1870; d ae 10 (Hartland VT R)

1153.   Cyrus Ransom Bagley 8, Perkins 7, Thomas 6, Henry 5,
Henry 4, Orlando 3, Orlando 2, Orlando 1 , b Dec 20, 1847; d
Feb 20, 1911; m Corinth, VT, Aug 17, 1864, Jennie Olive
Sleeper when he was 17 and she was 15 (Hartland VT R), dau
Dudley, b Northfield, VT, 1848, d 1932 (VT R). Rev Flower of
Hartland, VT, told Dr Bagley, July, 1958, that Arnold, Cyrus
and William all went to a Civil War rally. Arnold and William
enlisted, and Cyrus said he was going to enlist. "By God, you
won't," said William; "By God, I will," said Cyrus, and he
did. Served Co B, 12 regt VT Vols.
     Following is a letter to a friend Joseph written while
in camp during Civil War (from The Vermonter):
     "Friend Joseph:
     I now take my pen in hand to let you know that I am well
weak yet as I have been in the hospital for a fortnight sick

with bilious fever. We are encamped near Washington and the truth is we are going to stall all winter but I don't care much if we do. It is cold nights down here as it is up in Vermont. I wisht I might go into the old butery now and then but I can't. I do not complain. We are having good times out here. The boys are all in good spirits singing and dancing all the time. Benj Dan. and Will are well. Williams says he should like to be there one day to go over onto the east hill ahunting and Ben would like to do the same and so should I. Do write and tell me about hunting as soon as you get this. Tell all about the cropes and all about the folks. Give my love to all the folks. Charley and Wallace are sick in the hospital and Ben says that Charley will never get any better but he may for all that you know.

> Write often will you
> Yours in heart
> Cyrus R. Bagley

Direct your letter this way — Mr Cyrus R. Bagley, Washington, D. C., Co B, 12 Regt VT Vols in care of Captain Ora Paul"

Children: (Hartland VT R except as noted)
1938.   George C. 9, b Oct 31, 1869
1939.   Charles 9, b Nov 20, 1871; d Sept 30, 1872
1940.   William P. 9, b 1674; d Oct 19, 1881 (tombstone, Hartland, VT)
1941.   Lulu M. 9, b Nov 30, 1875; d Sept 28, 1881
1942.   Alice 9, b Jan 3, 1877
1943.   Frank 9, b Mar 1, 1880, Woodstock, VT; d Oct 27, 1881 (VT R)
1944.   Dix Gerald 9, b Dec 2, 1880, Woodstock, VT; d Jan 13, 1938 (tombstone and NH R)

1161.   Henry Jefferson Bagley 8, Jefferson 7, Thomas 6, Henry 5, Henry 4, Orlando 3, Orlando 2, Orlando 1 , b Sept 13, 1837; m Mary Ann Thurber, dau James & B., Mar 20, 1864 (Hartland VT R). Supposed to have had five children and gone to Montville, ME.

1168.   John Judson Bagley 8, John 7, John 6, Jonathan 5, Henry 4, Orlando 3, Orlando 2, Orlando 1 , b July 24, 1832, Medina, Orleans Co, NY; d San Francisco, CA, July 27, 1881; m 1855, Frances Eliza Newbury, b Mar 4, 1832, Rutland, OH, d Dec 27, 1871, San Francisco, CA, dau Rev Samuel & Mary Ann (Sargent). He was the 16th governor of Michigan, 1873-1877.

Children:
1945.   Florence 9, b 1856, Detroit, MI
1946.   John Newbury 9, b Sept 8, 1860, Detroit, MI; d Jan 10, 1929
1947.   Katherine 9, b 1862; d 1871
1948.   Frances 9, b 1863
1949.   Margaret 9, b May 13, 1865
1950.   Olive 9, b Apr 13, 1868; d June 19, 1909, Concord, MA (MA R)
1951.   Helen 9, b 1867, Detroit, MI

1952.   Paul Frederick 9, b Oct 13, 1869

1188.   Marcus Elmore (Mercedes) Bagley 8, Thomas 7, Cutting 6, Jonathan 5, Henry 4, Orlando 3, Orlando 2, Orlando 1 , b Aug 18, 1828; mentioned as son of Thomas Bagley of Durham, NY, and executor of his will in 1875, resident Jerseyville, Jersey Co, IL (NY R); wrote to a nephew as late as July 12, 1912; d soon after; buried with wife and three children in Oak Grove Cemetery, Jerseyville, IL. On Feb 23, 1877, recorded Apr 4, 1878, he and his wife, Hattie M. of Jersey Co, IL, quit-claimed to Harry Bagley of East Durham, NY, all interest in the estate of his father, Thomas Bagley (NY R).

1189.   Harry Bagley 8, Thomas 7, Cutting 6, Jonathan 5, Henry 4, Orlando 3, Orlando 2, Orlando 1 , b about 1839; d July 29, 1912, Freehold, NY; m Emily Baldwin, b about 1839, d May 26, 1897 (History of Greene Co, NY). This book says that Cutting Bagley's highly respected grandson was Harry Bagley of Freehold, NY. Children are as listed in his will. He and his wife buried Durham, NY. Adm of the estate of Andrew Freese in 1884, and co-executor of estate of Margaret Bennett of Greeneville, NY in 1878. In both instances he is given as of Greenesville (Greene Co NY R). In May, 1883, he and his wife Emily, given as of Greeneville, sold land there (Greene Co NY Deeds). Census of 1870 for Durham, NY, gives Harry, ae 35, farmer, b NY; Emily, ae 36; Frank, ae 4; Edward Dailey, ae 23, farmer. Harry's mother's maiden name was Dailey.

      Harry & Emily, and Gilbert Merritt and Mary, his wife, sold land as part of estate of Seneca Merritt, deceased; probably Emily was an heir-at-law. This record says she d July 6, 1897. Harry was executor of her estate as she d intestate.

Children:
1953.   Frank B. (Harry) 9, b about 1866 (Census of 1870. Mr Roger Bagley of Manchester, CO, says his grandfather had two sons, Harry and Frederick. Unless we have missed a birth and Frank d young, Frank appears to have been called Harry.
1954.   Hattie 9, b 1864; d 1869 (tombstone, Durham, NY)
1955.   Frederick 9, b East Durham, NY, Oct 25, 1879; d there Aug 8, 1933

1193.   George H. Bagley 8, Henry 7, Cutting 6, Jonathan 5, Henry 4, Orlando 3, Orlando 2, Orlando 1 , b Aug 8, 1818; d Feb 21, 1871, Nunda, NY; m Margaret Howell, b Dec 28, 1826, d Sept 5, 1881; buried Howell lot in Nunda, NY. No children buried on lot.

1199.   Barnard Bagley 8, Barnard 7, Cuting 6, Jonathan 5, Henry 4, Orlando 3, Orlando 2, Orlando 1 , d prior to death of father and probably before 1850 (Watertown, NY Daily Times, of June 27, 1878).

1200.   George Augustus Bagley 8, Barnard 7, Cutting 6, Jonathan 5, Henry 4, Orlando 3, Orlando 2, Orlando 1 , b July 22, 1826; d May 12, 1915, Watertown, NY; m Sabine Clark in

170

1858, b about 1839, d Dec 24, 1916, dau Col William Ambrose
Clark; received academic training and studied law; admitted to
bar in 1847 and began practice in Watertown, NY; retired from
law and engaged in manufacturing of iron in 1853; president of
village of Watertown in 1866; supervisor of the town in 1865;
elected as a Republican to the 44th and 45th congresses of the
USA (Mar 4, 1875-Nov 13, 1879); resumed manufacturing of iron;
buried Brookside Cemetery, Watertown, NY; supposed to have
married twice.

Children:
1956.   Jessie 9, b Aug 4, 1860; d Watertown, NY, June 13, 1955
1957.   Ambrose Clark 9, b about 1862, Watertown, NY; d Boston,
MA, Feb 26, 1936, ae 72 (MA R)
1958.   Magdaline 9, b 1866; d before 1870 as not on Census of
1870; however, there was a Magdaline alive in 1960, Watertown,
NY, supposed to be a sister of Carrie -- letter to compiler of
this book
1959.   Carrie Sherman 9, b 1864; d 1960

1201.   Leverett Bagley 8, Augustus 7, Cutting 6, Jonathan 5,
Henry 4, Orlando 3, Orlando 2, Orlando 1, b Jan 23, 1832; d
Oct 1, 1905; m Ann Eliza Hallock, b 1838, d 1917 (East Haven
CO R).

Child:
1960.   Mary A. 9

1204.   Ambrose Bagley 8, Hall 7, Jonathan 5, Henry 4, Orlando
3, Orlando 2, Orlando 1, b Charleston, ME, Aug 2, 1837; d
there Apr 15, 1916 (ME R); m Harriet Ross, b Detroit, ME, May
11, 1847, d Apr 17, 1920, dau Hugh & Susan (Chase (ME R).

Children:
1961.   George William 9, b May 9, 1874, Corinth, ME; d W
Corinth, ME, June 1, 1943 (ME R)
1962.   Wallace Erwin 9, b Corinth of Charleston, ME, about
1875 (Census of 1880 gives ae 5); d 1958 (Corinth, ME
tombstone)
1963.   Hall 9, b Charleston, ME, Apr 17, 1880; d there, May
10, 1933 (ME R)

1205.   George Bagley 8, Hall 7, Jonathan 6, Jonathan 5, Henry
4, Orlando 3, Orlando 2, Orlando 1, d Dec 1, 1869, ae 40-1-2
(Corinth, ME tombstone).

1206.   Elethier Bagley 8, Hall 7, Jonathan 6, Jonathan 5,
Henry 4, Orlando 3, Orlando 2, Orlando 1, m Sewell Farrer
(Mrs Clark of Corinth, ME).

1207.   Charles H. Bagley 8, John 7, Jonathan 6, Jonathan 5,
Henry 4, Orlando 3, Orlando 2, Orlando 1, b about 1848; d Mar
3, 1889, ae 41-7-17 (Corinth, ME tombstone); m Ellen E., d May
23, 1890, ae 38 (tombstone, Corinth, ME).

Child:

1964.   Charles H. 9, d Feb 13, 1907 (tombstone, Corinth, ME)

1208.   William Chase Bagley 8, Currier 7, William 6, Jonathan
5, Henry 4, Orlando 3, Orlando 2, Orlando 1 , b Aug 19, 1833;
d 1911; m Ruth Walker, 1853, b 1838.

Children:
1965.   Ruth Gertrude 9
1966.   William Chandler 9, b Detroit, MI, Mar 15, 1874; d 1916
(Who's Who in America)

1209.   Francis H. Bagley 8, Currier 7, William 6, Jonathan 5,
Henry 4, Orlando 3, Orlando 2, Orlando 1 , b Jan 16, 1840; d
1878.

1210.   Sidney Currier Bagley 8, Currier 7, William 6, Jonathan
5, Henry 4, Orlando 3, Orlando 2, Orlando 1 , b Aug 18, 1842;
d 1919.

1213.   Clinton Bagley 8, Thomas 7, Nathan 6, Jonathan 5, Henry
4, Orlando 3, Orlando 2, Orlando 1 , b Dec 16, 1838; d Feb 18,
1901 (Walpole MA R), ae 64; m May 31, 1857, at Dedham, MA,
Mary Gibbs, b Methuen, MA, dau Tyler & Mary (Johnson),   d Mar
4, 1904, ae 64 (Walpole MA R). Civil War soldier, enl Aug 7,
1862, Co I, 35 MA Regt Inf; disch June 9, 1865 (Pension R
which is witnessed by Ethel Bagley and J. B. Hanscom); wounded
at South Mountain, Sept 14, 1862.   No children listed as
living on pension R.

Children:
1967.   Franklin J. 9, b Dec 16, 1858; d Nov 27, 1903, ae 44, b
Dedham, d Walpole, MA (Pension R)
1968.   Ida E. 9, b 1879; d Jan 15, 1892, ae 23 (Walpole MA R)

1214.   Sumner Bagley 8, Thomas 7, Nathan 6, Jonathan 5, Henry
4, Orlando 3, Orlando 2, Orlando 1 , b Walpole, MA, about
1840; d Apr 8, 1911; m Ella M. Polly, dau Edmund & Maria
(Shackley), d Norwood, MA, Mar 30, 1933, ae 91 (MA R).

Children:
1969.   Fannie M. 9, b about 1867; d Nov 25, 1903, ae 36
(Norwood MA R)
1970.   Walter S. 9, b about 1877, Norwood, MA; d July 8, 1952,
ae 75 (Brockton MA R)

1215.   Lewis Bagley 8, Thomas 7, Nathan 6, Jonathan 5, Henry
4, Orlando 3, Orlando 2, Orlando 1 , b about 1847; d Jan 15,
1879, ae 31 (Walpole MA R); m Emma Robey, b Charlestown, MA
(MA R).

Child:
1971.   Lewis C. 9, b Boston, MA; d Nov 20, 1905, ae 33
(Cambridge MA R)

1216.   George H. Bagley 8, Henry 7, Nathan 6, Jonathan 5,
Henry 4, Orlando 3, Orlando 2, Orlando 1 , b about 1845,

either Meredith Bridge, NH or Lowell, MA.

1217. Frank P. Bagley 8, Henry 7, Nathan 6, Jonathan 5, Henry
4, Orlando 3, Orlando 2, Orlando 1 b about 1849, probably
Lowell, MA.

BAGLEY INDEX, VOLUME 1

Bagley Index, Volume 1

Each Bagley, male or female has one number, beginning with the
first Orlando who is #1. Male Bagleys for whom we have
additional information are then carried over to a separate
place where that information is given. If the male lived long
enough to have children, even though we do not know them, and
he is not given as unmarried, he is carried over, but in each
case retains the same number which he was given under a list
of his parents' children. Female Bagleys are carried over
when we know they married, but likewise retain the same number
as they were given in the list of their parents' children.

Aahut, 852
Aaron, 182, 417, 582, 1117
Abbie, 1276, 1509
Abbott, 1252
Abby, 1481, 1676
Abel, 78
Abigail, 490, 493, 528, 587, 739, 1003, 1275, 1310, 1326, 1338
Abijah, 1325
Abner, 403, 894, 996, 1715
Achsah, 1519
Ada, 1924
Addie, 1547
Addison, 1607
Adelaide, 1106
Adoniram, 1403
Albert, 1064, 1066, 1443, 1450
Alexander, 480, 1019
Alice, 1069, 1448, 1531, 1942
Alfred, 1752
Almer, 1916
Almond, 977
Alonzo, 1122, 1337
Alphes, 737
Alphonse, 1451
Alton, 1739
Alvaretta, 1632
Alvira, 1270
Amanda, 1517, 1740
Ambrose, 1204, 1957
Amos, 365, 463, 466, 970
Amy, 1101, 1504, 1559
Andrew, 988, 1505, 1600
Ann, 100, 701, 948, 1110, 1468, 1678
Anna, 49, 125, 220, 284, 456, 459, 1479
Anne, 14, 202, 272, 457
Annugine, 1731
Aratus, 1420
Arnold, 1146
Arthur, 1534, 1556, 1620, 1738, 1788
Arvilla, 1494
Asa, 1007, 1589
Asabel, 536
Augusta, 889, 1218, 1290, 1917

Augustus, 565, 668, 849, 890, 1198, 1339

Barnard, 256, 268, 563, 585, 1199
Belinda, 1537
Benedict, 561
Benjamin, 13, 77, 243, 915, 1524, 1716
Bertha, 1558
Betsey, 409, 458, 516, 517, 557, 568, 583, 586, 623, 675, 940, 1233
Betty, 458, 497, 882, 1272

Candace, 1243
Carlos, 1608
Caroline, 1061, 1224, 1407, 1417, 1657
Carrie, 1619, 1959
Cassius, 1794
Celia, 1618
Charles, 425, 426, 434, 525, 608, 669, 725, 851, 853, 1006, 1035, 1047, 1207, 1256, 1267, 1269, 1291, 1340, 1343, 1429, 1475, 1496, 1498, 1555, 1561, 1564, 1638, 1658, 1672, 1685, 1727, 1741, 1763, 1777, 1890, 1939, 1964
Charlotte, 660, 682, 1126, 1132, 1266, 1404
Christiana, 266, 1329
Chloe, 1857
Clara, 1730, 1927
Clarenda, 1644
Clarissa, 1116
Clark, 1107
Clinton, 1213
Cordelia, 1324
Cornelius, 1861
Currier, 571
Curtis, 1759
Cutting, 255
Cynthia, 1089, 1540, 1541
Cyrenes, 1855
Cyrus, 1153

Daisy, 1383
Danforth, 1631
Daniel, 178, 405, 407, 533, 732, 937, 1068, 1261, 1581, 1641, 1789
David, 31, 121, 126, 130, 143, 270, 275, 288, 320, 328, 348, 454, 588, 603, 632, 683, 820, 956, 1223, 1233, 1245, 1321, 1333, 1384, 1418, 1426, 1585, 1588, 1624, 1640, 1666
Delia, 1166, 1195
Dennis, 845
Dix, 1944
Dolly, 252, 271, 283, 326, 464, 719, 1239, 1465
Dora, 1825
Dorcas or Dorcus, 226, 411, 522
Dorothea, 253
Dorothy, 34, 108, 120, 131, 139, 163, 244, 336, 347, 511, 524, 886, 941, 976, 998
Dwight, 1507, 1860

Ebenezer, 267
Edmund, 1542
Edward, 728, 857, 1072, 1135, 1478, 1515
Edwin, 1119, 1139, 1596, 1913
Elbridge, 850
Eleanor, 881, 893, 1005
Elethier, 1206
Elias, 225
Elijah, 134, 277, 602, 616
Eliza, 293, 495, 607, 658, 992, 1049, 1059, 1083, 1194, 1613, 1653
Elizabeth, 58, 132, 173, 262, 315, 332, 356, 435, 488, 568, 580, 703, 892, 895, 973, 1045, 1104, 1602, 1617, 1677, 1923
Elkins, 613, 1277
Ella, 1368, 1433, 1482, 1513, 1597, 1651
Ellen, 1046, 1111, 1127, 1136, 1228, 1579, 1594
Elmira, 1323
Elno, 1616
Elon, 1593
Emeline, 925, 984, 1120, 1375, 1686
Emily, 647, 741, 742, 1131, 1402, 1612, 1786
Emma, 1258, 1367, 1444, 1445, 1635, 1787
Enoch, 161, 199, 330, 360, 381, 447, 604, 777, 825, 1257, 1590, 1928
Ephraim, 420, 896
Esther, 634, 1292, 1327
Eunice, 461, 702
Eva, 1435, 1503, 1708
Evidall, 1749
Ezra, 1603

Fannie, 1969
Filone, 1734
Flora, 1511, 1791
Florence, 1932, 1945
Frances, 1577, 1654, 1948
Francis, 855, 975, 983, 1209, 1229
Frank, 1044, 1217, 1263, 1379, 1489, 1491, 1514, 1943, 1953
Franklin, 481, 1021, 1683, 1954, 1967
Franz, 1539
Fred, 1553, 1728, 1915
Frederick, 479, 954, 1115, 1148, 1260, 1567, 1754, 1850, 1955

George, 589, 667, 697, 776, 824, 944, 1108, 1118, 1141, 1193, 1200, 1205, 1216, 1221, 1236, 1264, 1283, 1430, 1523, 1535, 1552, 1583, 1599, 1652, 1674, 1684, 1735, 1938, 1961
Gideon, 885
Gilman, 686, 699, 1062, 1246, 1251
Grace, 1202, 1790
Greenleaf, 476, 1016
Gustave, 1676

Hall, 569, 1963
Hannah, 15, 52, 62, 124, 185, 292, 319, 331, 350, 357, 408, 418, 432, 444, 467, 559, 627, 673, 731, 750, 782, 812, 994, 1038, 1086, 1336, 1399, 1464, 1477, 1718

Harlow, 1736
Harold, 1274, 1710
Harriet, 663, 681, 727, 876, 982, 983, 1071, 1212, 1222, 1234,
1238, 1342, 1823, 1467, 1474, 1510, 1580
Harrison, 916
Harry, 274, 1189, 1369
Hattie, 1385, 1623, 1954
Helen, 1144, 1149, 1951
Hellen, 856, 614
Henri, 1856
Henry, 30, 117, 249, 257, 291, 540, 562, 573, 579, 590, 648,
661, 858, 909, 1067, 1161, 1278, 1427, 1548, 1565, 1598, 1692
Herbert, 1731
Herman, 1568
Hester, 768
Hiram, 665, 1461
Hollis, 1611
Horace, 1073, 1240, 1792
Hulda, 273, 529

Ida, 545, 1968
Ignatius, 947
Ina, 1712
Ira, 1057, 1424
Irene, 993
Isaac, 192, 819
Isabelle, 1470
Isadore, 785
Isaiah, 991
Isette, 697
Israel, 157, 383

J. C. Freemont, 1534
Jackson, 1252
Jacob, Note 7, 10, 61, 63, 123, 179, 279, 295, 453, 611, 649,
943, 946, 1023, 1365, 1372, 1378, 1656
James, 286, 421, 612, 626, 672, 784, 1042, 1080, 1085, 1227,
1289, 1320, 1506, 1512, 1518
Jane, 818, 997, 1158, 1253
Jason, 1479
Jefferson, 539, 575
Jemima, 267
Jennie, 694
Jeremiah, 452, 783
Jerusha, 59, 60, 201
Jesse, 519, 1076
Jessie, 1956
Joanne, 1853
Joel, 542, 1423
John, 2, note 7, 9, 50, 99, 102, 110, 135, 175, 251, 335, 404,
413, 416, 428, 433, 439, 448, 449, 462, 492, 547, 570, 606,
614, 680, 700, 722, 811, 871, 875, 877, 883, 979, 989, 1001,
1031, 1040, 1079, 1138, 1168, 1244, 1262, 1265, 1288, 1440,
1469, 1501, 1522, 1526, 1560, 1584, 1691, 1758, 1793, 1914,
1946
Jonathan, 33, 119, 137, 141, 258, 314, 351, 530, 570, 752,

911, 1017, 1400
Joseph, 12, 76, 176, 227, 366, 380, 424, 670, 775, 938, 955, 1500
Joshua, 133, 265, 321
Judith, 11, 35, 128, 177, 327, 438
Julia, 980, 987, 1082, 1129, 1629
Julie, 1088

Kate , 1761
Kathrine, 1947

Labina, 1630
Lafayette, 1284
Laura, 16, 1125, 1162, 1442
Lavinia, 1282
Lawrence, 1755
Leah, 1578
Leila, 1377
Leon, 1750, 1760
Leverett, 1196, 1201
Levi, 290, 628, 816, 950, 951, 1341, 1527, 1668
Levira, 778
Lewis, 1215, 1586, 1971
Lila, 854
Lilla, 1537
Lillie, 1386
Lizzie, 1036, 1381
Lois, 538, 632, 1133
Loren, 1070, 1605
Lorenda, 1643
Louis, 844
Louisa, 970, 1434, 1925
Lowell, 441
Lucia, 1124, 1439
Lucian, 1145, 1930
Lucius, 1533
Luella, 1551
Lucretia, 651, 1380
Lucy, 429, 451, 484, 583, 1018, 1078, 1105, 11521
Lulu, 1934, 1941
Luther, 842, 1528
Lydia, 73, 75, 81, 282, 325, 478, 631, 981, 1626, 1642, 1733, 1822, 1852

Mabel, 1892
Magdaline, 1958
Mahala, 749
Malinda, 1273
Marcia, 1137
Marcy, 678
Maretta, 1592
Margaret, 1670, 1949
Maria, 913, 1065, 1081, 1587, 1625
Marion, 1081, 1854
Martha, 1280, 1319, 1502, 1667, 1732
Martin, 1279

Martine, 1293
Mary, 5, 80, 105, 107, 127, 289, 322, 349, 352, 355, 406, 445,
455, 487, 489, 514, 555, 566, 578, 617, 624, 646, 666, 738,
779, 813, 872, 880, 887, 898, 924, 949, 974, 1000, 1034, 1074,
1112, 1134, 1140, 1191, 1247, 1248, 1281, 1330, 1406, 1476,
1532, 1582, 1639, 1650, 1651, 1659, 1671, 1675, 1729, 1743,
1762, 1783, 1820, 1960
Mattie, 1536
Maude, 1621
Medwin, 1538
Mehitable, 281
Melissa, 1037
Melvin, 1452
Melvina, 1520
Merah, 32, 105
Merriam, 56, 174, 203, 820, 848, 952
Michael, 874
Mildred, 1747
Milford, 1922
Minnie, 1919
Miranda, 1858
Miriam, 221, 1084
Molly, 240, 246, 260, 278, 318, 323, 334, 349, 431, 455
Morris, 1033
Moses, 51, 180, 263, 385, 414, 415, 513, 671, 829, 897, 1004,
1593
Myra, 1926

Nabby, 450
Nancy, 294, 410, 423, 427, 459, 556, 662, 705, 720, 1066,
1130, 1190, 1192, 1197, 1328, 1401, 1466
Nathan, 261, 313, 677
Nathaniel, 912
Nellie, 1615, 1742
Newell, 815, 1255, 1525
Nina, 1795

Olive, 532, 572, 1150, 1167, 1950
Oliver, 482, 1020
Orlando, 1, 3, 7, 28, 101, 140, 157, 247, 740, 748, 774, 1102,
1428, 1495
Orasmus, 1250
Orzilla, 781

Parker, 1918
Paul, 1952
Paulina, 733
Pauline, 843
Pearl, 1508
Perkins, 534
Peter, 191, 458
Phebe, 1591
Philip, 159, 183, 316, 422, 679
Philema, 1333
Philmore, 830
Phineas, 104, 241

Polly, 334, 362, 436, 535, 555, 615, 813
Preston, 1695
Priscilla, 1634

Rachel, 687
Ralph, 817
Randall, 945
Rebecca, 515, 942, 1058, 1271, 1563
Reuben, 386, 823
Rhoda, 54, 287, 361, 615, 635, 676, 726
Richard, 442, 630, 657, 927, 1211, 1322, 1601
Robert, 707, 1606
Roderick, 1147
Rosetta, 1633
Royal, 1609
Roxiena, 1090
Rozina, 1839
Russell, 879, 1594A
Ruth, 162, 285, 324, 364, 382, 440, 1965

Sabrina, 1630
Sally, 242, 333, 338, 387, 496, 527, 543, 545, 558, 577, 584, 605, 659, 685, 914, 1043, 1239, 1259, 1449
Sallyann, 1405
Samuel, 64, 122, 280, 591, 629, 653, 826, 884, 1226, 1382, 1422, 1717, 1753
Sanford, 1128, 1241
Sarah, 4, 6, 8, 29, 55, 74, 79, 109, 129, 142, 144, 160, 181, 184, 223, 264, 276, 317, 333, 353, 387, 430, 437, 477, 486, 618, 723, 751, 828, 846, 859, 873, 910, 926, 939, 978, 990, 1024, 1041, 1087, 1103, 1109, 1225, 1284, 1331, 1421, 1425, 1431, 1447, 1463, 1521, 1530, 1566, 1709, 1821, 1920
Sargent, 245, 512, 541
Seth, 103, 106
Sewell, 827, 1714
Shephard, 1334
Sidney, 1210
Silas, 1142
Simeon (Simon), 1002, 1123
Sophia, 609
Sophronia, 625, 1332
Stephen, 224, 520, 999, 1366
Submit, 564
Sukey, 363
Sumner, 1214
Susan, 664, 708, 780, 814, 1048, 1529, 1649, 1655, 1673
Susanna, 164
Susannah, 358, 1063, 1242
Susy, 446
Sylvestania or Sylvestin, 1356
Sylvia, 847

Thomas, 36, 158, 248, 359, 384, 412, 494, 518, 521, 523, 531, 560, 576, 633, 778, 1039, 1152, 1154, 1237, 1432, 1497, 1824, 1912
Timothy, 53, 190, 1462

INDEX TO NAMES OTHER THAN BAGLEY

Index to Names other than Bagley

Numbers refer to number of Bagley entry; children of Bagley girls are found under their consecutive number in Volume I or II.

Abbey, Alice, 1772
Abbey, Henry, 1772

Abbott, Polly, 612

Ace, William, 1813

Adams, Ann, 1073
Adams, Anna, 210
Adams, Archelus, 58, 205
Adams, Betsey, 513
Adams, Carver, 1031
Adams, Dorothy, 1010
Adams, Elizabeth, 208
Adams, Hannah, 206
Adams, Harrison, 1011
Adams, Jacob, 204
Adams, Jemima, 1009
Adams, John, 1015
Adams, Judith, 1012
Adams, Louisa, 1014
Adams, Lydia (Walton), 722
Adams, Mary, 209
Adams, Samuel, 58, 207
Adams, Sarah, 211
Adams, Theopilus, 478
Adams, Thomas, 1798
Adams, Walter, 1037

Alexander, Arthur, 1889
Alexander, Charles, 1126
Alexander, Clarence, 1887
Alexander, John, 1887
Alexander, Mary, 1019

Allen, Ann, 76
Allen, David, 462
Allen, Elizabeth, 462
Allen, Francis, 462
Allen, Mary, 76, 462

Ambrose, Dorothy, 10

Andrews, Sophia, 275

Annis, Charles, 3
Annis, Sarah, 3

Appleman, George, 1841

Appleton, Celestia, 912

Babcock, Albert, 1079
Babcock, Rebecca, 1079

Bailey, Betty, 452
Bailey, Daniel, 994
Bailey, Elizabeth, 676
Bailey, Hannah, 883
Bailey, Jerome, 316
Bailey, Molly, 941
Bailey, Moses, 883
Bailey, Phineas, 317
Bailey, Rebecca, 845
Bailey, Sarah, 442
Bailey, William, 30

Baker, Annie, 1804
Baker, Elisha, 1076
Baker, Eliza, 1076
Baker, Hiram, 1083
Baker, Hopi, 1802
Baker, Ira, 1801
Baker, Miriam, 1798
Baker, Nancy, 1799
Baker, Orlando, 1800
Baker, Phoebe, 1805
Baker, Rosie, 1806
Baker, Ruel, 1803
Baker, Samuel, 1807

Baldwin, Emily, 1149

Banfield, Betsey, 420
Banfield, George, 420

Barker, Christiana, 255

Barnard, Dorothy, 174
Barnard, Hannah, 182
Barnard, Mary, 727
Barnard, Merriam, 244

Barnes, Elmira, 1072
Barnes, Lydia, 92
Barnes, Sarah, 7

Barnett, Persis, 420
Barnett, Robert, 420

Bartlett, Chloe, 1151
Bartlett, Dorothy, 354
Bartlett, John, 253
Bartlett, Mehitable, 192
Bartlett, Nathan, 142
Bartlett, Stephen, 192, 253

Batchelder, Ebenezer, 49

Bayley, Abigail, 732
Bayley, Benjamin, 229
Bayley, Deborah, 230
Bayley, Jonathan, 79, 228
Bayley, Joshua, 130
Bayley, Rachel, 232
Bayley, Sarah, 231
Bayley, Thomas, 233
Bayley, William, 732

Bennett, Jeremiah, 262
Bennett, Ruth, 581

Best, Norma, 1691

Bigelow, Sarah, 183

Bickford, Eliza, 722
Bickford, Paul, 722

Billings, Henry, 1134

Blake, _____, 1252
Blake, Abigail, 248

Blaisdell, Ann, 1648
Blaisdell, Anna, 452
Blaisdell, Betsey, 533
Blaisdell, Daniel, 613
Blaisdell, David, 138
Blaisdell, Dorothy, 400, 454
Blaisdell, Emily, 1179
Blaisdell, Franklin, 1178
Blaisdell, Hannah, 142
Blaisdell, John , 941
Blaisdell, Jonathan, 10, 49
Blaisdell, Joseph, 398, 399
Blaisdell, Judith, 401
Blaisdell, Levi, 396
Blaisdell, Mary, 1180, 1646
Blaisdell, Merriam, 397
Blaisdell, Oliver, 2, 174, 454
Blaisdell, Randall, 1647
Blaisdell, Ruth, 402
Blaisdell, Samuel, 179
Blaisdell, Silas, 533
Blaisdell, Tillotson, 558
Blaisdell, William, 1645

Blatt, James, 1409

Blethen, Louisa, 775
Blethen, Philip, 779

Blumly, Elizabeth, 918

Boardman, Daniel, 722
Boardman, Elizabeth, 732, 952
Boardman, George, 1772
Boardman, Rachel, 953
Boardman, Sophia, 787
Boardman, William, 732, 953

Bowan, Jennings, 1772
Bowen, Phebe, 1772

Bowker, Calvin, 1767

Boyden, Estelle, 1584

Bradley, Emeline, 565
Bradley, Mercy, 876

Brewster, Charles, 1073
Brewster, Ephraim, 1059, 1769
Brewster, Erastus, 1073
Brewster, Sarah, 386
Brewster, Submit, 1073
Brewster, William, 1849

Bridge, Ada, 109
Bridge, Bezeleel, 1131
Bridge, Charlotte, 1900
Bridge, Edward, 1799, 1894
Bridge, Edwin, 1902
Bridge, Ella, 1905
Bridge, Emeroy, 1903
Bridge, Frank, 1901, 1906
Bridge, George, 1897
Bridge, Henry, 1898
Bridge, James, 1130
Bridge, Norman, 1895
Bridge, Susan, 1896, 1899
Bridge, Sylvester, 1133

Bridges, Edward, 631
Bridges, George, 1350
Bridges, Lois, 1349
Bridges, Lydia, 1347
Bridges, Rhoda, 1348
Bridges, Samuel, 1346
Bridges, Susa, 1345
Bridges, Vestula, 1344

Bronson, Hannah, 121
Bronson, Sarah, 121

Brown, Abigail, 30, 290
Brown, Abram, 146

Brown, Alexander, 482
Brown, Amos, 802
Brown, Andrew, 1018
Brown, Arthur, 1748
Brown, Asa, 1016, 1018
Brown, Comfort, 589
Brown, D., 1745
Brown, David, 407, 537
Brown, Dorothy, 147, 163
Brown, Eli, 1744
Brown, Elizabeth, 145
Brown, Eunice, 988
Brown, Guy B., 272
Brown, Harriet, 1017
Brown, Henrietta, 1016
Brown, Jacob II, 363
Brown, Jeremiah, 956, 986
Brown, John, 805
Brown, Jonathan, 808
Brown, Joseph, 801
Brown, Josiah, 537
Brown, Judith, 149
Brown, Lucinda, 1156
Brown, Lucy, 1139
Brown, Lucy M. 272
Brown, Lucy J. 272
Brown, Margaret, 588
Brown, Martha, 11
Brown, Moses, 81, 807
Brown, Nancy, 804, 956
Brown, Nathaniel, 34, 150, 163
Brown, Orlando, 151
Brown, Parker, 474
Brown, Polly, 803
Brown, Robert, 272
Brown, Sally, 234, 537
Brown, Samuel, 589
Brown, Sarah, 148, 956
Brown, Stephen, 363, 806
Brown, Susan, 809
Brown, Susie, 1746
Brown, William, 81

Bullard, Ebenezer, 603
Bullard, Lois, 603

Bullock, Willis, 1816

Bunker, Mary, 1019
Bunker, Robert, 1019

Burbank, Abigail, 34

Burkhart, Polly, 279

Burnham, Frances, 28

Burnham, John, 407
Burnham, Thankful, 407

Burroughs, Amy, 419
Burroughs, Sally, 419
Burroughs, Thomas, 419

Bush, Fannie, 1069

Button, Amherst, 1848A
Button, Elhanon, 1848A

Cabot, Aris, 1886
Cabot, Clarence, 1885
Cabot, Lucian, 1126
Cabot, Willie, 1884

Caldon, Amanda, 1295
Caldon, Byley, 1298
Caldon, Betton, 1297
Caldon, Edith, 1301
Caldon, Ella, 1300
Caldon, Marilla, 1294
Caldon, Nancy, 1299
Caldon, Robert, 618
Caldon, Sophia, 1296
Caldon, Thomas, 618

Campbell, John, 386
Campbell, Mary, 1032
Campbell, Rebecca, 386
Campbell, Sarah, 386

Carney, John, 719

Carney, Bertha, 1845
Carney, Ella, 1844
Carney, Lewis, 1089

Carr, Charles, 1394
Carr, Charlotte, 1398
Carr, Daniel, 675, 676, 1391
Carr, Elizabeth, 50
Carr, Esther, 678
Carr, Francis, 1393
Carr, Frederick, 675
Carr, George, 1395
Carr, Harriet, 1397
Carr, Helen, 1393
Carr, Jackson, 1396
Carr, John, 1393
Carr, Nathan, 1392
Carr, Sarah, 720

Carson,, Amanda, 1298

189

Colby, Anthony, 1
Colby, Beatrice (Felton), 1
Colby, Elizabeth, 8, 13
Colby, Hannah, 130, 188
Colby, Jacob, 52
Colby, John, 52, 186
Colby, Kezia, 10, 57, 62
Colby, Molly, 189
Colby, Samuel, 10
Colby, Sarah, 1, 330
Colby, Thomas, 1187
Colby, William, 5

Colley, Ann, 339, 453

Collins, Joseph, 129, 310
Collins, Mary, 312
Collins, Moses, 309
Collins, Sarah, 311

Colston, Albert, 1157
Colston, Charles, 1139
Colston, John, 1160
Colston, Lucinda, 1139, 1158
Colston, Sarah, 537
Colston, Theodore, 1159
Colston, William, 537

Conley, Ellen, 544

Coombs, Abigail, 816

Cope, Alice, 92

Corliss, Abigail, 604

Cowgill, Susan, 92

Cox, Antoinette, 1359
Cox, Charles, 1360
Cox, Elmina, 1358
Cox, Ezra, 635
Cox, Levi, 1360

Crabtree, Eliza, 878
Crabtree, William, 407

Craig, Louisa, 383
Craig, Peter, 383
Craig, Susanna, 383

Crandall, Polly, 1113

Cressey, Barnard, 1231
Cressey, Betsey Ann, 1232

Cressey, Laura, 1230
Cressey, Robert, 587

Crofts, Augusta, 1059

Crosby, Lucinda, 1076

Cullinan, Ellen, 1891

Culver, Andrew, 417
Culver, Sarah, 417

Cummings, Enoch, 877
Cummings, Mary, 877

Currier, Aaron, 263
Currier, Ann, 172
Currier, Barnard, 141
Currier, Benjamin, 30, 334
Currier, Daniel, 138, 149
Currier, David, 10, 57, 62, 218
Currier, Dorothy, 131
Currier, Ebenezer, 131
Currier, Edwin, 893
Currier, Eleanor, 455
Currier, Electa, 138
Currier, Eliphalet, 49, 171
Currier, Elizabeth, 219, 482
Currier, Hannah, 166, 167, 216, 339
Currier, Jacashel, 582
Currier, Jacob, 213, 749
Currier, James, 482
Currier, Jeremiah, 49, 168
Currier, Jerusha, 212
Currier, John, 49, 165
Currier, Judith, 169, 263, 350
Currier, Leonard, 131
Currier, Mary, 30, 180, 706
Currier, Moses, 170
Currier, Rachel, 31
Currier, Rebecca, 131
Currier, Richard, 62, 214, 217
Currier, Ruth, 192
Currier, Sarah, 138, 141, 215, 254, 482
Currier, Sere, 582
Currier, Thomas, 131
Currier, Timothy, 10, 33, 339

Cushing, Dorothy, 342
Cushing, Edward, 345
Cushing, Elizabeth, 241
Cushing, John, 139, 343
Cushing, Jonathan, 344
Cushing, Sarah, 346

Cutler, Mary, 17

Daley, Charles, 1113
Daley, Edward, 560
Daley, Grace, 1113
Daley, Mary, 560
Daley, William, 1113

Dane, Timothy, 794

Danforth, Lizzie, 1232

Daniels, Eliza, 1724

Davenport, Annie, 1042

Davidson, Lydia, 434
Davidson, Nathaniel, 434

Davis, Abigail, 640
Davis, Alice, 52
Davis, Amanda, 637
Davis, Amos, 1232
Davis, Charles, 1232
Davis, Cyrus, 638
Davis, Ebenezer, 705
Davis, Elias, 287
Davis, Eunice, 644
Davis, Harriet, 1641
Davis, Jane, 643
Davis, John, 52
Davis, Jonathan, 1268
Davis, Lucinda, 1147
Davis, Lydia, 887
Davis, Sabra, 636
Davis, Samuel, 642
Davis, Stephen, 607
Davis, Thomas, 645
Davis, Warren, 639

Day, Edgar, 1165
Day, Henry, 1164
Day, Ira, 546, 1163
Day, Mary, 936
Day, Orrin, 566

Dearborn, Charles, 1291
Dearborn, Esther, 1292
Dearborn, Hannah, 946
Dearborn, John, 617
Dearborn, Martine, 1293
Dearborn, Thomas, 431

Dela, Lewis, 877

Dennis, Samuel, 649

Dennis, Sophia, 649

Dodge, Sophronia, 678

Doke, Susanna, 244

Dort, Elseba, 1042
Dort, Esther, 1042
Dort, James, 1042
Dort, Thomas, 1042

Dow, Hannah, 9
Dow, Joseph, 556, 1177
Dow, Josiah, 78
Dow, Moses, 556
Dow, Sarah, 78

Downing, Mary, 416, 883

Downs, Huldah, 1033

Doyle, _____, 623
Dudley, Gilman, 254
Dudley, Maria, 254
Dudley, Moses, 580

Duncan, O., 264

Dupee, Isaac, 1573

Dustin, Samuel, 516

Dwyer, Mary, 760
Dwyer. O. Israel, 759
Dwyer, Reuben, 356, 761

Eastman, Dorothy, 608
Eastman, Sarah, 465

Eaton, Ann, 1008
Eaton, Bryant, 477
Eaton, Clemmie, 1032
Eaton, Kate, 1394
Eaton, Lydia, 434
Eaton, Samuel, 1032
Eaton, William, 1036

Eddy, Hannah, 897

Edmunds, Edward, 259, 260
Edmunds, John, 639, 1387
Edmunds, Polly, 259

Elliott, Harriet, 555
Elliott, John, 31
Elliott, Thomas, 31

Elliott, Timothy, 31

Ellis, Hannah, 585
Ellis, Thomas, 1219

Emerson, Phebe, 556

Emery, Mary, 141

Evans, Amelia, 1811
Evans, Benjamin, 1459
Evans, Clara, 1818
Evans, Clementine, 1874
Evans, Dudley, 720, 1458
Evans, Emma, 1813
Evans, Estelle, 1810
Evans, Ezekiel, 720, 1457
Evans, Harriet, 1816
Evans, John, 1456
Evans, Julia, 1812
Evans, Miranda, 1815
Evans, Sarah, 1460, 1796, 1808
Evans, Spencer, 1081, 1064
Evans, Thomas, 1796, 1809
Evans, William, 1817

Everett, Timothy, 1570

Hay, Louise, 1891

Fairbanks, _____, 384

Fales, Martha, 918

Farnsworth, Betsey, 542

Farrer, Sewell, 1206

Farrier, Gladys, 1891

Fasset, Francis, 1572

Favour, Aaron, 308
Favour, Anne, 119, 433
Favour, Cutting, 128
Favour, Dorothy, 305
Favour, Elizabeth, 304
Favour, Hannah, 306
Favour, Isaac, 302
Favour, Jacob, 301
Favour, John, 299
Favour, Judith, 303
Favour, Mary, 300
Favour, Moses, 307
Favour, Sarah, 298, 332

Felker, Elias, 1827

Felton, Beatrice, 1

Ferrin, Alonzo, 984
Ferrin, Hannah, 130
Ferrin, Jonathan, 130

Fernald, Jonathan, 818

Fesler, Asenath, 92

Fields, Frances, 1147
Fields, John, 1147
Fields, Sarah, 877

Fifield, Dolly, 757
Fifield, Edward, 355
Fifield, Elizabeth, 755
Fifield, John, 754
Fifield, Mary, 758
Fifield, Winthrop, 756
Fifield, O. Israel, 753

Fish, Anthony, 1068
Fish, Sally, 1068

Fisk, Elizabeth, 462

Fitts, Anna, 278
Fitts, Mary, 259
Fitts, Nathaniel, 101
Fitts, Rebecca, 101

Flanders, James, 315
Flanders, Zipporah, 253

Fletcher, Sylvia, 825

Foard, Betsey, 313, 606
Foard, William, 313

Folsom, Anne, 424
Folsom, Nathaniel, 424

Foot, James, 442

Foss, Eliza, 1287
Foss, Langdon, 1615
Foss, Serena, 1616

Foster, Arvilla, 748
Foster, Mary Ann, 1394

Fowler, Abigail, 491
Fowler, Abram, 491

Fowler, Betsey, 965
Fowler, Effie, 1033
Fowler, Elizabeth, 491, 947
Fowler, Eunice, 243
Fowler, Hannah, 9, 134
Fowler, Jacob, 947
Fowler, Robert, 964, 1033
Fowler, Sally, 365
Fowler, Samuel, 243
Fowler, Susan, 947
Fowler, Thomas, 9
Fowler, William, 9

Frame, Mary, 52
Frame, Sarah, 54

French, Belinda, 904
French, Carlos, 1878
French, Charles, 899, 1880
French, Clara, 1874
French, Dora, 1872
French, Eliphalet, 101
French, Ella, 1875
French, Eva, 1879
French, George, 1881
French, Hannah, 110, 295
French, John, 908, 1873
French, Jonathan, 100, 235, 239
French, Joseph, 902
French, Levinor, 903
French, Lizzie, 855
French, Louise, 906
French, Maryanne, 905
French, Minnie, 1882
French, Moley, 236
French, Moses, 295
French, Nancy, 237
French, Nicholas, 430, 904
French, Rebecca (Fitts), 101
French, Reuben, 1073
French, Richard, 1877
French, Robert, 1124, 1876
French, Sally, 901
French, Samuel, 238
French, True, 900
French, Wallace, 1871

Frost, Charlotte, 1722
Frost, Dolly, 378, 1026
Frost, Eliot, 160, 371
Frost, Elizabeth, 373
Frost, Emily, 1025
Frost, Enoch, 376
Frost, James, 377
Frost, Jane, 1027
Frost, Levi, 375

Frost, Love, 379
Frost, Nelson, 1030
Frost, Newell, 483, 1028
Frost, Polly, 1029
Frost, Ruth, 367, 369
Frost, Sarah, 370
Frost, Thomas, 368, 372
Frost, William, 374

Furber, B., 1128, 1138
Furber, Emily, 1128
Furber, James, 1138
Furber, Lois, 1128
Furber, Mary, 1138

Gage, Alice, 1054
Gage, Anna, 496
Gage, Anne, 1050
Gage, Caroline, 877
Gage, Charles, 1056, 1125
Gage, Clara, 1055
Gage, Isaac, 496
Gage, Rosetta, 1053
Gage, Sarah, 1051
Gage, Seth, 496, 1052

Gale, Jacob, 28

Gallup, Arch, 1772
Gallup, Esther, 1772
Gallup, Fidelia, 539, 1139
Gallup, Hazel, 1172
Gallup, Joseph, 539
Gallup, Wesley, 1772

Garland, Nellie, 1017

Gates, Jacob, 563
Gates, Zurviah, 563

Gavett, James, 1109
Gavett, Judson, 1847
Gavett, Libbeus, 1109
Gavett, Lydia, 1753
Gavett, Minnie, 1848

Gay, Henrick, 1827

George, Putnam, 1010

Gerrish, Azuba, 383
Gerrish, George, 359
Gerrish, Sumner, 812
Gerrish, Susannah, 359

Getchell, Emerson, 1300

Haddon, Susanna, 1

Hadsell, Emma, 1832
Hadsell, Emily, 1833
Hadsell, Fannie, 1835
Hadsell, George, 1834
Hadsell, Hannah, 1830
Hadsell, John, 1836
Hadsell, Lois, 1831
Hadsell, Thomas, 1087

Hale, Sophia, 679

Hadley, Capt., 533

Hall, _____, 1095
Hall, Adelia, 896
Hall, Benjamin, 896
Hall, Cyrena, 650
Hall, Elizabeth, 258
Hall, Eunice, 569
Hall, Lucy, 811

Hallock, Ann Eliza, 1161, 1201

Hamilton, Mildred, 92

Hancock, Lucy, 879

Hanks, Benjamin, 1140
Hanks, Betsey, 1141
Hanks, Calvin, 1140

Harmon, Daniel, 358
Harmon, Francis, 358
Harmon, O. Israel, 773

Harper, Margaret, 871
Harper, William, 871

Harriman, Mayo, 1203
Harriman, Samuel, 568

Harrington, Mary, 1893

Harris, Zurviah, 563

Hart, John, 683
Hart, Mary, 683, 1129
Hart, Susan, 683

Harvey, Emily T., 272
Harvey, John, 7

Hasey, Harrison, 856
Hasey, Harry, 1557

Hawkins, Lucy, 269

Hayes, Aileen, 1891

Heases, Abigail, 101

Heald, Sarah, 824

Hetson, Priscilla, 1143

Hewes, Lydia, 855

Hickok, Agnes, 121
Hickok, Annis, 272

Hildreth, Josiah, 136
Hildreth, Rebecca, 136

Hill, Cynthia, 1057
Hill, Thomas, 1057

Hilliard, Alvira, 608

Hills, Helen, 1774

Hobbs, Mary, 104

Hodgdon, Moses, 1724

Hodge, Michael, 403
Hodge, Sarah, 403

Hoit, Clara, 1455
Hoit, Daniel, 333
Hoit, Hannah, 333, 717
Hoit, Elijah, 715
Hoit, James, 708
Hoit, John, 708
Hoit, Lucina, 718
Hoit, Reuben, 333
Hoit, Roxanna, 1454
Hoit, Sarah, 716
Hoit, Susan, 1453

Hollis, Moses, 814

Hollister, Amos, 1814

Hooker, E. E., 429
Hooker, Sarah, 251

Hopkins, Ira, 1770
Hopkins, James, 406
Hopkins, Mary, 406

Huzlet, Elisa, 874
Huslet, Hazlett, 874
Huslet, Margaret, 874

Hussey, Arlene, 1557

Hyland, Adeline, 1032
Hyland, James, 1032

Jackman, Dorothy, 918
Jackman, Hannah, 823

Jackson, Burr, 1846
Jackson, Godfrey, 650
Jackson, Joshua, 1101
Jackson, Sylvinia, 650

Jagger, Charles, 1815
Jagger, Silas, 1811

Jameson, Hannah, 10
Jameson, John, 10

Jewell, Fanny, 604
Jewell, John, 52
Jewell, Ruth, 52
Jewell, Solomon, 604
Jewell, Thomas, 52

Jewett, Luther, 513
Jewett, Rebecca, 513

Johnson, Cynthia, 947
Johnson, Edward, 1219
Johnson, Mary, 1213
Johnson, William, 29

Jones, Abel, 733
Jones, Ann, 131
Jones, Ansel, 1773
Jones, Daniel, 1484
Jones, Hannah, 1485, 1486
Jones, Lois, 1483
Jones, Stephen, 431
Jones, William, 1487, 1488

Jordan, James, 1414

Judson, Olive, 251
Judson, Timothy, 251

Keeble, James, 1295

Kellam, Elisha, 1069
Kellam, Everett, 1780

Kellam, Hellen, 1779
Kellam, Luther, 1782
Kellam, Samuel, 1069
Kellam, William, 1781

Kelley or Kelly, Betsey, 512
Kelley, David, 626, 633
Kelley, Dorcus, 626
Kelley, Edmund, 528
Kelley, Marin B., 633
Kelley, Rachel, 626
Kelley, Salvin, 1114
Kelley, Stephen, 512

Kendrick, Hannah, 1663
Kendrick, James, 949
Kendrick, John, 28, 1664
Kendrick, Lydia, 12
Kendrick, Maria, 1662
Kendrick, Mary, 28
Kendrick, William, 1665

Keniston, Angelina, 1473
Keniston, Ellen, 1472
Keniston, George, 723
Keniston, John, 723
Keniston, Nancy, 723
Keniston, Paul, 1471

Kent, George, 1094
Kent, Judith, 14, 15

Kezer, Susan, 842

Kidder, Andrew, 699
Kidder, Elizabeth, 699
Kidder, Hannah, 699
Kidder, Jane, 1293

Kilmer, Jonas, 268

King, Abby B., 732
King, Margaret, 479
King, Nathan, 1799

Kinter, Edith, 800
Kinter, Ida, 1801

Knapp, John, 148

Knowles, Belinda, 158
Knowles, Mary, 815

Kyle, Sarah, 843

Lake, Harry, 1902

Lancaster, Anne, 47
Lancaster, Bagley, 48
Lancaster, David, 43
Lancaster, Dorothy, 46
Lancaster, Elizabeth, 41
Lancaster, Elisha, 45
Lancaster, Hannah, 840
Lancaster, Henry, 8, 44
Lancaster, Joseph, 8
Lancaster, Judith, 37
Lancaster, Mary, 38
Lancaster, Orlando, 42
Lancaster, Sarah, 39

Landry, Mary, 534

Lane, Abiah, 523, 1096
Lane, Gershom, 523
Lane, Thomas, 443, 444

Lanphear, Judith, 979

Lawrence, Amy, 525
Lawrence, Charles, 827
Lawrence, Phebe, 525
Lawrence, William, 525

Lee, Adeline, 1364
Lee, Emily, 1636
Lee, Emma, 1826
Lee, Frances, 639, 649
Lee, Nathan, 646
Lee, Pasahase, 1362
Lee, Rebecca, 1361
Lee, Ruth, 1113
Lee, Stephen, 639, 649

Leeman, Adam, 1306
Leeman, Anne, 1309
Leeman, Catherine, 1303
Leeman, Elijah, 1307
Leeman, Henry, 1305
Leeman, Jacob, 1304
Leeman, James, 1308
Leeman, Mary, 1302

Libby, Hartley, 1000

Lindsay, Betsey, 1753

Little, Sarah, 543

Lord, Taphena, 1070

Lovejoy, _____, 994

Lovejoy, N. Grace, 1713

Loveless, Felvia, 1807

Lowe, Marion, 280, 1028

Lowell, Abner, 175
Lowell, Mary, 175

Lyman, Eliza, 1085
Lyman, Emma Saunders, 1085
Lyman, Landers, 1085

Lyons, Annie, 1039
Lyons, Susan, 665

McDonald, Mary, 1907

Mack, Corrie 6., 272
Mack, Deborah, 27
Mack, Ebenezer, 23
Mack, Elisha, 1070
Mack, Elizabeth, 18
Mack, Johanna, 26
Mack, John, 6. 16
Mack, Jonathan, 22
Mack, Josiah, 20
Mack, Lydia, 19
Mack, Mary, 24, 1070
Mack, Orlando, 21
Mack, Rebecca, 15
Mack, Sarah, 17

Magoon, Charlotte, 608
Magoon, Jonathan, 608

Malone, Dorcus, 858

Mann, Ann, 1661
Mann, George, 1660
Mann, Jemima, 603
Mann, Joseph, 948

Manning, Phebe, 1085

Mansfield, Catherine, 1137
Mansfield, Emily, 1910
Mansfield, Frank, 1907
Mansfield, Marcia, 1911
Mansfield, Martha, 722
Mansfield, Otto, 1909
Mansfield, William, 1137, 1908

March, Sarah, 58

Marcy, Mary, 536

Marcy, William, 536

Marden, Eliza, 655
Marden, Hiram, 656
Marden, John, 289

Marsh, John, 531
Marsh, Nancy, 531

Marshall, Cummings, 586
Marshall, Richard, 586

Martin, _____, 1875
Martin, Esther, 10
Martin, Jonathan, 221
Martin, Mary, 1829
Martin, Sarah, 191

Martyn, Elizabeth, 139

Mason, Hannah, 317

Mead, Elno, 92
Mead, Ezra, 92
Mead, Harlan, 92
Mead, William, 92

Merrick, Edward, 1704
Merrick, Ellen, 1703
Merrick, Henry, 1707
Merrick, Joseph, 1705
Merrick, Stephen, 985
Merrick, William, 1706

Merrill, Abel, 14, 87, 94
Merrill, Anne, 84
Merrill, Benjamin, 465
Merrill, Christopher, 88
Merrill, Elvira, 999
Merrill, Hannah, 95, 98
Merrill, Isaac, 325, 326, 690
Merrill, Joseph, 999
Merrill, Joshua, 691, 693
Merrill, Judith, 12
Merrill, Lang, 606
Merrill, Lydia, 93, 326, 692
Merrill, Mary, 85, 87
Merrill, Nathan, 91
Merrill, Nathaniel, 29
Merrill, Orlando, 90
Merrill, Polly, 29, 694
Merrill, Roger, 29
Merrill, Ruth, 96
Merrill, Samuel, 999
Merrill, Sarah, 15, 82, 97, 465
Merrill, Thomas, 14, 15, 82, 96

Meserve, James, 419
Meserve, Lydia, 419
Meserve, Ruth, 419
Meserve, Sarah, 419

Metivier, John, 988
Metivier, Mary, 988

Milligan, Jennie, 1803

Mills, Hannah, 602
Mills, Sarah, 630

Minard, Elijah, 605
Minard, Hazen, 609
Minard, Thomas, 609

Mitchell, Mary, 359

Mittson, _____, 698

Moar, Eliza, 291

Monk, Caroline, 1080

Moody, Sabrina, 895

Moor, Betsey, 288
Moor, Leonard, 288

Moore, Polly, 1117

Morgan, Abigail, 1384D
Morgan, Charles, 1384I
Morgan, David, 1384F
Morgan, Henry, 1384G
Morgan, Jeremiah, 1384A
Morgan, Jonathan, 1384B
Morgan, Orlando, 1384H
Morgan, Rachel, 687, 1384C
Morgan, Sarah, 1384E
Morgan, Smith, 687

Morrill, Benjamin, 964
Morrill, Betsey, 954
Morrill, Charlotte, 395
Morrill, Clarissa, 944, 957
Morrill, Daniel, 278, 963, 965
Morrill, David, 464
Morrill, Mrs Deborah, 102
Morrill, Dolly, 156
Morrill, Dorothy, 389, 438
Morrill, Ephraim, 141, 610, 727
Morrill, Henry, 455, 958, 727
Morrill, Isaac, 1001

Nutt, Almira, 1524A
Nutt, Henry, 1091
Nutt, Illustrious, 813
Nutt, Mary, 817
Nutt, Valentine, 1524B

Nuttenberg, Mary, 1840

Nutter, Alonzo, 918
Nutter, Alvira, 919
Nutter, Charles, 1917
Nutter, John, 921
Nutter, Mary Ann, 920
Nutter, Nathan, 440, 922
Nutter, Ruth, 923

O'Connell, Daniel, 1891A

Odney, Iva, 988

Ordway, Elizabeth, 732
Ordway, George, 1299

Orne, Margaret, 1220

Osgood, Anna, 335, 441
Osgood, David, 36
Osgood, Lydia, 1011
Osgood, Philip, 919
Osgood, Sally, 441
Osgood, Samuel, 441
Osgood, Stephen, 395

Otis, Rebecca, 890

Overlock, Abigail, 1310
Overlock, Ansel, 1316
Overlock, Bickford, 1315
Overlock, Catherine, 628
Overlock, James, 1311
Overlock, John, 628
Overlock, Lydia, 1312
Overlock, Marguerite, 128
Overlock, Mary, 1313
Overlock, Michael, 625
Overlock, Nancy, 1314
Overlock, Rhoda, 1318
Overlock, Rufus, 1317

Page, Caleb, 571
Page, Jonathan, 603
Page, Joshua, 364
Page, Louisa, 571
Page, Submit, 571
Page, Thomas, 810

Page, Voda, 603

Pattee, Abigail, 778

Patten, Mary, 245

Patterson, Henry, 780, 781
Patterson, William, 792

Peabody, Chloe, 1118

Pearson, Hannah, 140

Peaslee, Hannah, 684
Peaslee, Isdore, 684
Peaslee, Polly, 684
Peaslee, Samuel, 684

Pendall, Laura, 1142

Percival, David, 1293

Perkins, Elizabeth, 3
Perkins, Jonathan, 248
Perkins, Olive, 248

Perry, Achad, 1774
Perry, Horson, 1774

Person, Kezia, 180
Person, Thomas, 180

Phelps, Diantha, 890
Phelps, Nathan, 890

Philbrick, Elizabeth, 973

Pickett, Mary, 485

Pike, _____, 536
Pike, Dorothy, 224

Pillsbury, Benjamin, 516
Pillsbury, Bridgett, 576
Pillsbury, Charles, 1627
Pillsbury, Ella, 1628
Pillsbury, Jane, 576
Pillsbury, Levi, 914
Pillsbury, Susanna, 467

Polly, Ella, 1214
Polly, Edmund, 1214

Poole, Abijah, 179

Pope, Mary, 1001

211

Potter, _____, 981
Potter, Eva, 1702
Potter, Harriet, 1701
Potter, John, 1699
Potter, Lydia, 1700
Potter, Mary, 1698

Powers, James, 823
Powers, Sarah, 823

Pressey, Hannah, 10

Prevost, Adelaide, 1837
Prevots, Fred, 1840
Prevost, George, 1842
Prevost, John, 1838
Prevost, Lewis, 1839
Prevost, Minnie, 1843
Prevost, Sarah, 1841
Prevost, Thepholis, 1081

Primrose, Edwin, 1039
Primrose, Hannah, 1039
Primrose, Maria, 1039

Proctor, Amos, 789, 791
Proctor, Hannah, 1131
Proctor, James, 786
Proctor, John, 787, 792
Proctor, Jonathan, 791
Proctor, Rhoda, 790, 794
Proctor, Sally, 793
Proctor, Sylvia, 795
Proctor, Thomas, 788, 796
Proctor, William, 361, 785

Purrington, Lydia, 175

Quimby, Joseph, 189
Quimby, Mary, 200

Rand, Cynthia, 784

Randall, Anne, 453
Randall, Isaac 453
Randall, Mary, 539

Read, Susanna, 543

Reed, Abram, 380
Reed, Betsey, 382
Reed, Eunice, 380
Reed, Lydia, 877
Reed, Marion, 777
Reed, Rachel, 381

Remick, Eliza, 494
Remick, Hannah, 494
Remick, William, 494

Rice, Elisha, 532

Rich, William, 647

Richards, Catherine, 357
Richards, Lydia, 791

Richardson, Emily, 1143
Richardson, John, 479
Richardson, Mary, 479
Richardson, Roxanna, 884

Rider, Susan, 1393

Ring, Anna, 1073
Ring, Mary, 348

Roach, Maria, 571
Roach, Margaret, 249
Roach, William, 471

Robey, Emma, 1215

Robinson, Eliza, 1117
Robinson, Luther, 1117

Rogers, Adeline, 1118
Rogers, Charles, 1408
Rogers, Cynthia, 383
Rogers, Mary, 534
Rogers, Rebecca, 247
Rogers, Sarah, 699
Rogers, William, 534, 1118

Rosengrant, Charles, 1804

Ross, Harriet, 1204
Ross, Hugh, 1204

Rowe, James, 1829
Rowe, John, 1086
Rowe, Mary Eliza, 1827
Rowe, Shelbourne, 634
Rowe, Sylvester, 583
Rowe, Thomas, 1828
Rowe, William, 1826

Rowland, Jerusha, 603

Runnells, Ebenezer, 80

Rutan, Lemuel, 1806

St. Hill, Gary, 1891
St. Hill, Kathryn, 1891
St. Hill, Scott, 1891

Sampson, Hannah, 92
Sampson, William, 92

Sanborn, _____, 349
Sanborn, Anna, 420
Sanborn, Dolly, 800
Sanborn, Dorothy, 745
Sanborn, Hannah, 134
Sanborn, James, 1294
Sanborn, John, 362
Sanborn, Josiah, 362
Sanborn, Orlando, 744, 799
Sanborn, Polly, 746
Sanborn, Sally, 743
Sanborn, Sarah, 798
Sanborn, Theodate, 134
Sanborn, Worcester, 134

Sargent, Abigail, 930
Sargent, Amos, 933
Sargent, Ann, 419, 704
Sargent, Christopher, 115
Sargent, David, 332
Sargent, Dorcus, 247
Sargent, Dorothy, 114
Sargent, Elijah, 709
Sargent, Elizabeth, 712
Sargent, Enoch, 543
Sargent, Harriet, 714
Sargent, John, 332, 457, 711, 929
Sargent, Jonathan, 706
Sargent, Joseph, 50
Sargent, Judith, 50
Sargent, Louisa, 512
Sargent, Lucy, 935
Sargent, Mary, 112, 713, 932, 1168
Sargent, Moses, 29, 114
Sargent, Nancy, 705
Sargent, Orlando, 111
Sargent, Sarah, 55, 113, 710, 931
Sargent, Susan, 934
Sargent, Susannah, 1
Sargent, Thomas, 29, 247
Sargent, William, 3

Saunders, Aaron, 1113
Saunders, Benjamin, 525, 1085, 1098
Saunders, Catherine, 1095
Saunders, Charles, 1099
Saunders, Eliza, 1085, 1097

Saunders, Emeline, 1095, 1096
Saunders, Henrietta, 1094
Saunders, John, 519
Saunders, Joshua, 519, 520, 525
Saunders, Lorena, 1113
Saunders, Lydia, 1091
Saunders, Lyman, 517
Saunders, Mary, 520, 1093
Saunders, Perry, 1100
Saunders, Polly, 519
Saunders, Ruth, 1092

Sawyer, _____, 624
Sawyer, Eunice, 200
Sawyer, Enoch, 543
Sawyer, Hannah, 616
Sawyer, Nathaniel, 543
Sawyer, Samuel, 543

Seagraves, John, 1080

Selley, Dolly, 348

Shackley, Maria, 1214

Sheppe, George, 1093

Shepard, Ernest, Jr., 1891
Shepard, Scott, 1891

Shields, Frances, 1147
Shields, John, 1147

Shoemaker, Savanna, 1847

Shorey, Abel, 1059
Shorey, Isabell, 1768
Shorey, Leonard, 1058
Shorey, Malvina, 1767
Shorey, Mary, 1764
Shorey, Moses, 1766
Shorey, Russell, 1765

Shortbridge, Elizabeth, 81

Shute, Hannah, 783
Shute, Sarah, 783

Siegfred, John, 1837

Sigley, _____, 1831

Sillowey, Rhoda, 725

Simpson, Charlotte, 603
Simpson, Ivory, 1411

Simpson, John, 603
Simpson, Ploomy, 603

Sinkler, Abigail, 778
Sinkler, Joshua, 778

Skidmore, Joseph, 1067
Skidmore, Mary, 1067

Slater, _____, 1830, 1832

Sleeper, Dudley, 1153
Sleeper, Jennie, 1153

Small, Alice, 1864
Small, Clement, 1866
Small, Edwin, 1870
Small, George, 1868
Small, Herbert, 1865
Small, Lucy, 1869
Small, Lydia, 530
Small, Sumner, 1121
Small, Walter, 1867

Smiley, Lovey, 1017
Smiley, Lydia, 1021

Smith, Aaron, 1057
Smith, Ardelia, 869
Smith, Charles, 387, 865
Smith, Cyrus, 1623
Smith, David, 860
Smith, Edith, 539
Smith, Elizabeth, 863
Smith, Ezekia, 351
Smith, Ezekiel, 351
Smith, Francis, 867
Smith, Graham, 868
Smith, Hester Ann, 866
Smith, Ida, 1623
Smith, Jennie E., 1623
Smith, Joseph 6
Smith, Lucy, 862
Smith, Luseba, 885
Smith, Lyman, 856
Smith, Marion, 861
Smith, Mary, 547, 870
Smith, Matthew, 17
Smith, Nancy, 778
Smith, Sarah, 351, 864
Smith, Timothy, 351

Snow, Kimball, 514
Snow, Lydia, 280
Snow, Mary, 157

Spaulding, Alvin, 1132

Speed, Christina , 630
Speed, David, 630

Spencer, Charlotte, 385
Spencer, Silas, 1079

Spinney, Annie, 937
Spinney, Eleanor, 937
Spinney, Stephen, 937

Spooner, Lavinia, 752

Spring, Fannie, 1623

Squier, Edwin, 1752
Squier, Lloyd, 1848
Squier, Mary, 1109
Squier, Sylvenius, 1752

Stanton, Lucy, 527

Stanwood, Hannah, 10
Stanwood, John, 10
Stanwood, Samuel, 10

Stark, George, 1079

Stavers, Jane, 442
Stavers, John, 442

Stetson, Meridan, 121

Stevens, Elizabeth, 34
Stevens, Ellen, 989, 1682
Stevens, Hannah, 29, 1681
Stevens, Judith, 49
Stevens, Mary, 29, 1680
Stevens, Samuel, 974

Stewart, Dorothy, 1623
Stewart, George, 1623
Stewart, Simon, 858
Stewart, Sarah, 178
Stewart, Theresa, 858

Stickney, Abigail, 407

Stiles, Deborah, 629

Stinson, _____, 632
Stinson, Ann, 996
Stinson, Lydia, 1016, 1018

Stockman, Ruth, 498

Stone, Alzoria, 1549
Stone, Judith, 979
Stone, Nathaniel, 1979
Stone, Rufus, 843

Streeter, Mary, 414

Strong, Allen, 1129
Strong, Jasper, 1129
Strong, Julia, 1893
Strong, Richard, 1751

Stuart, Ann, 1094

Sumner, Harriet, 576

Swasey, Betsey, 442

Swett, Abigail, 249
Swett, Ann, 1688
Swett, Enoch, 721
Swett, Hannah, 721
Swett, John, 249
Swett, Joseph, 1689
Swett, Lucy, 1687
Swett, Merriam, 721
Swett, Sarah, 777, 1690
Swett, Samuel, 978

Symes, Erastus, 1116

Tallman, Peleg, 1575

Taylor, Dorcas, 247
Taylor, Mary, 517, 519, 520, 523

Tenney, Ann, 704
Tenney, John, 704

Tewksbury, Isaac, 1092
Tewksbury, Ephraim, 1097

Thomas, Lydia, 523

Thompson, Francis, 1806
Thompson, Hannah, 53
Thompson, Mary, 53
Thompson, Peter, 53
Thompson, Sarah, 225

Thornton, Denae, 1170
Thornton, Cynthia, 1173
Thornton, Freeman, 1172
Thornton, George, 1175
Thornton, Hannah, 553

Voight, May, 1908

Wade, Polly, 268

Wadleigh, Benjamin, 123
Wadleigh, Mary, 78

Waitt, Albert, 722
Waitt, Levi, 722

Wakefield, Christopher, 1806
Wakefield, Danford, 1818
Wakefield, Philander, 1805

Waldo, Owen, 1863

Walker, Andrew, 1150, 1151
Walker, Asa, 1150, 1151
Walker, Caroline, 1151
Walker, Diana, 1936
Walker, Ruth, 1208
Walker, Zina, 1151

Walter, Elsie, 784

Walters, Della Mansfield, 11
Walters, Hugo, 1191

Walton, Jonathan, 1105
Walton, Lydia, 722

Ward, Edward, 1000
Ward, Joseph, 764
Ward, Nathan, 775
Ward, Simeon, 260

Weare, Joseph, 803
Weare, Lucy, 808
Weare, Mary Anne, 801

Webber, Martha, 977

Webster, David, 32, 594
Webster, Elizabeth, 584
Webster, Harriet, 988
Webster, Harvey, 596
Webster, Heman, 272, 599
Webster, Israel, 36, 37
Webster, Jeremiah, 595
Webster, Jeremy, 49
Webster, Linnus, 592
Webster, Mary, 199
Webster, Maude, 272
Webster, Melvin, 272
Webster, Merritt, 598
Webster, Noah, 600

Voight, May, 1908

Wade, Polly, 268

Wadleigh, Benjamin, 123
Wadleigh, Mary, 78

Waitt, Albert, 722
Waitt, Levi, 722

Wakefield, Christopher, 1806
Wakefield, Danford, 1818
Wakefield, Philander, 1805

Waldo, Owen, 1863

Walker, Andrew, 1150, 1151
Walker, Asa, 1150, 1151
Walker, Caroline, 1151
Walker, Diana, 1936
Walker, Ruth, 1208
Walker, Zina, 1151

Walter, Elsie, 784

Walters, Della Mansfield, 1137
Walters, Hugo, 1191

Walton, Jonathan, 1105
Walton, Lydia, 722

Ward, Edward, 1000
Ward, Joseph, 764
Ward, Nathan, 775
Ward, Simeon, 260

Weare, Joseph, 803
Weare, Lucy, 808
Weare, Mary Anne, 801

Webber, Martha, 977

Webster, David, 32, 594
Webster, Elizabeth, 584
Webster, Harriet, 988
Webster, Harvey, 596
Webster, Heman, 272, 599
Webster, Israel, 36, 37
Webster, Jeremiah, 595
Webster, Jeremy, 49
Webster, Linnus, 592
Webster, Mary, 199
Webster, Maude, 272
Webster, Melvin, 272
Webster, Merritt, 598
Webster, Noah, 600

Webster, Roswell, 272, 601
Webster, Roxanna, 597
Webster, Ruth, 36
Webster, Susannah, 57
Webster, Truman, 593

Weed, Abigail, 117
Weed, Anna, 47, 737
Weed, Bagley, 48
Weed, David, 43
Weed, Dorothy, 46
Weed, Elijah, 347, 735
Weed, Elisha, 8, 45
Weed, Elizabeth, 41
Weed, Ephraim, 8, 162
Weed, Hannah, 182, 734, 736
Weed, Henry, 44
Weed, Isaac, 347, 348
Weed, Lydia, 117
Weed, Orlando, 42
Weed, Sally, 348

Weir, Molly, 158

Wells, Betsey, 729
Wells, Dorothea, 33
Wells, Emily, 531
Weels, John, 33
Wells, Judith, 77
Wells, Mary, 128
Wells, Rachel (Currier), 31
Wells, Sarah, 130
Wells, Thomas, 33

Wentworth, Elizabeth, 34

Weston, Ann, 1076
Weston, Samuel, 1076

Whitaker, Aileen, 1891
Whitaker, Arthur, 1891
Whitaker, Charles, 1127, 1891
Whitaker, Francis, 1891
Whitaker, Fred, 1890
Whitaker, Grace, 1891
Whitaker, Harold, 1891
Whitaker, Harry, 1891
Whitaker, James, 1891
Whitaker, Mary, 1891
Whitaker, Otto, 1891A
Whitaker, Walter, 1891
Whitaker, Warren, 1891
Whitaker, William, 1891

White, Charles, 1344

Whited, Effie, 1817

Whitehouse, Lucy, 817

Whitney, Betsey, 842

Whitridge, Sarah, 1
Whitridge, William, 1

Whittemore, Hannah, 1623

Whitten or Whiten, David, 730
Whitten, Mary, 730
Whitten, Silas, 874

Whittier, Adelia, 1637
Whittier, James, 925
Whittier, Wendall, 1636

Wilcox, Lucy, 1113

Wildey, James, 564

Willey, Marion, 280

Williams, Amos, 1110
Williams, Barbara, 1891
Williams, Eileen, 1891
Williams, Eleanor, 1891
Williams, Henry, 1113
Williams, Joanne, 1891
Williams, Linda, 1891
Williams, Luke, 527
Williams, Lydia, 526
Williams, Latham, 527
Williams, Mary, 526
Williams, Nancy, 1891
Williams, Sarah, 1113
Williams, Stephen, 526
Williams, Thomas, 1891

Willis, Susannah, 516

Wing, Margaret, 479

Winthrop, Anne, 30

Wood, Amy, 1772
Wood, John, 435

Woodman, Dolly, 966
Woodman, Hannah, 200
Woodman, Harriet, 969
Woodman, John, 459
Woodman, Joshua, 200
Woodman, Stephen, 969

Young, Sally, 708
Young, Sharon, 272

York, Sarah, 358